The Spirit at the Cross:
Exploring a Cruciform Pneumatology

Australian College of Theology Monograph Series

SERIES EDITOR GRAEME R. CHATFIELD

The ACT Monograph Series, generously supported by the Board of Directors of the Australian College of Theology, provides a forum for publishing quality research theses and studies by its graduates and affiliated college staff in the broad fields of Biblical Studies, Christian Thought and History, and Practical Theology with Wipf and Stock Publishers of Eugene, Oregon. The ACT selects the best of its doctoral and research masters theses as well as monographs that offer the academic community, scholars, church leaders and the wider community uniquely Australian and New Zealand perspectives on significant research topics and topics of current debate. The ACT also provides opportunity for contributors beyond its graduates and affiliated college staff to publish monographs which support the mission and values of the ACT.

Rev Dr Graeme Chatfield
Series Editor and Associate Dean

The Spirit at the Cross:
Exploring a Cruciform Pneumatology

An Investigation into the Holy Spirit's
Role at the Cross

CAROLYN E. L. TAN

WIPF & STOCK · Eugene, Oregon

THE SPIRIT AT THE CROSS: EXPLORING
A CRUCIFORM PNEUMATOLOGY
An Investigation into the Holy Spirit's Role
at the Cross

Australian College of Theology Monograph Series

Copyright © 2019 Carolyn E. L. Tan. All rights reserved. Except for brief quotations in critical publications or reviews, no part of this book may be reproduced in any manner without prior written permission from the publisher. Write: Permissions, Wipf and Stock Publishers, 199 W. 8th Ave., Suite 3, Eugene, OR 97401.

Wipf & Stock
An Imprint of Wipf and Stock Publishers
199 W. 8th Ave., Suite 3
Eugene, OR 97401

www.wipfandstock.com

PAPERBACK ISBN: 978-1-5326-9569-8
HARDCOVER ISBN: 978-1-5326-9570-4
EBOOK ISBN: 978-1-5326-9571-1

Appendix 2: 𝔓46 (Hebrews 9)

Digital image reproduced with the permission of the Papyrology Collection, Graduate Library, University of Michigan; inventory number P. Mich. Inv. 6238; http://www.lib.umich.edu/papyrus-collection.

Appendix 3a–3b: Codices Sinaiticus, Vaticanus and Alexandrinus (Hebrews 9)

Digital images obtained under license from BibleWorks 10.0.

Appendix 3d: Codex Claromontanus (Hebrews 9:14)

Digital images reproduced with permission from Bibliothèque nationale de France (utilization reference number RDV-1904-001601). http://gallica.bnf.fr/ark:/12148/btv1b8468311.

Appendix 4: Desiderius Erasmus, *Novum Instrumentum*
(first edition, 1516; Hebrews 9).

Digital image reproduced with permission from The Center for the Study of New Testament Manuscripts (www.csntm.org), who digitized the book, and from the Lutheran School of Theology, Chicago, USA, who own the copyright to the book.

Manufactured in the U.S.A.   08/23/19

Contents

Acknowledgements | vii
Abbreviations | viii

1 Introduction | 1
2 Pneumatology beyond Christology? | 7
    2.1 The Spirit and the Son in History | 7
    2.2 "Spirit of Jesus/Christ/Son" in the New Testament | 16
    2.3 Summary | 28
3 Spirit as "Bond of Love"—John Vernon Taylor | 30
    3.1 Taylor's Biographical Context | 31
    3.2 Taylor's Theological Context | 33
    3.3 Taylor's Pneumatology | 39
    3.4 Taylor's *Pneumatologia Crucis* | 43
    3.5 Summary | 56
4 Spirit as "Coworker"—Jürgen Moltmann | 58
    4.1 Moltmann's Biographical Context | 58
    4.2 Moltmann's Theological Context | 61
    4.3 Moltmann's Pneumatology | 68
    4.4 Moltmann's *Pneumatologia Crucis* | 80
    4.5 Summary | 100
5 Spirit as "Unifier"—John Zizioulas | 102
    5.1 Zizioulas's Biographical Context | 102
    5.2 Zizioulas's Theological Context | 104

	5.3 Zizioulas's Pneumatology	119
	5.4 Zizioulas's *Pneumatologia Crucis*	128
	5.5 Summary	144

6 A Pneumatology of the Cross—The Biblical Basis | 146
    6.1 Pneumatology of *Hebrews* | 146
    6.2 "Through Eternal S/spirit" in Hebrews 9:14 | 161
    6.3 Pneumatic Sacrificial Metaphors in the New Testament | 187
    6.4 The Spirit in Covenantal Christology | 192
    6.5 Summary | 214

7 A Pneumatology of the Cross—The Theological Basis | 217
    7.1 Incorporating Barthian Pneumatological Perspectives | 216
    7.2 Towards a Multifaceted *Pneumatologia Crucis* | 249
    7.3 The Cross as "Crucible": A New Proposal for a *Pneumatologia Crucis* | 255
    7.4 A Crucible *Pneumatologia Crucis* and Atonement Theology | 269
    7.5 A Crucible *Pneumatologia Crucis* and Pneumatology | 274
    7.6 Summary | 281

8 Conclusion | 284

Appendices | 287
Bibliography | 299

Acknowledgements

THIS BOOK IS BASED on my dissertation for the Doctorate of Theology which was awarded by the Australian College of Theology in October 2017. It was only made possible by God's help, and the love and assistance of many people. I wish to thank my supervisor, Dr. Michael O' Neil for his patience, guidance, challenge, and encouragement throughout what has been a long and difficult journey in my attempt to answer the question: "What was the Spirit doing at the cross as Jesus was dying?" This was a question that I sincerely believe God put before me, and through the many times I considered giving up, the Holy Spirit lifted me up and pushed me along. I thank Professor Jürgen Moltmann for his gracious answers to my queries, and for his willingness to engage with my summation and observations on his own reflections concerning the Spirit's role at the cross. I thank my teachers, Dr. Michael Parsons, Dr. Richard Moore, Dr. John Olley, Dr. Evelyn Ashley and Dr. David Cohen, who helped me lay the theological, language, and biblical foundations needed for this venture. I thank Dr. Brian Harris and the Vose Seminary staff and students who have encouraged me to keep going. I thank the many who have upheld me in prayer throughout my journey, especially Mrs. Hilary Zulch, Dr. Richard Moore, and Mrs. Kath Moore. I thank the Australian College of Theology for their generosity in awarding me a grant for this publication. Last but not least, I thank my family and my church fellowship for their patience and understanding for the many occasions when I was unable to attend meetings, functions, and gatherings.

Abbreviations

ANF	*The Ante-Nicene Fathers: Translations of the Writings of the Fathers Down to A. D. 325*
BDAG	*A Greek-English Lexicon of the New Testament and Other Early Church Literature*
BDB	*The Brown-Driver-Briggs Hebrew and English Lexicon*
CD	*Church Dogmatics*
HALOT	*The Hebrew and Aramaic Lexicon of the Old Testament.*
LXX	*Septuagint*
NA²⁸	*Novum Testamentum Graece*, 28th rev. ed.
NIDOTT	*New International Dictionary of Old Testament Theology and Exegesis*, vol. 2, ed. Willem A. Van Gemeren (Grand Rapids: Zondervan, 1997)
NPNF	*A Select Library of the Nicene and Post-Nicene Fathers of the Christian Church*
PG	Jacques Paul Migne, *Patrologia Graeca* (1862)
PL	Jacques Paul Migne, *Patrologia Latina* (1891)
TDNT	*Theological Dictionary of the New Testament*

Bible Translations

CEB	*Common English Bible* (2011)
ESV	*English Standard Version* (2001)
KJV	*King James Version* (1769)

ABBREVIATIONS

NAB   *New American Bible* (2010)
NAU   *New American Standard Bible* (1995)
NIV   *New International Version* (2011)
NJB   *New Jerusalem Bible* (1985)
NKJV *New King James Version* (1982)
NRSV *New Revised Standard Version* (1989)
TNIV *Today's New International Version* (2001)
TNK   *TANAKH (Jewish Publication Society*, 1985)

1

Introduction

WHAT WAS THE HOLY Spirit doing at the cross of Jesus Christ? This odd question was raised, in a rather roundabout fashion, by my consideration of Amos Yong's "foundational" pneumatology which he put forward as a Christian theological approach to religious diversity and multiculturalism, and as a helpful concept towards meaningful interreligious interaction.[1] Such an interaction is inevitable in view of the growing multiplicity of cultural and religious paradigms in many societies resulting from migration as well as increasing interconnectedness and globalization. Indeed, the Second Vatican Council (1962–1965) seeks to reorientate Catholic theology towards greater openness and recognition of other faiths.[2]

The central idea in Yong's foundational pneumatology is his understanding of the Spirit as "symbolic of divine presence and agency in the world."[3] One of his key biblical texts is Acts 2:17 in which Peter tells the crowd gathered at Pentecost that through the risen and exalted Jesus, God has poured out his Spirit "upon all flesh." Yong understands the phrase "all flesh" to refer to all people, not just to believers in Jesus Christ, and that the pneumatic event carries a significance far beyond ecclesial boundaries.[4] He asserts that this Spirit is the one and the same Spirit who is involved in creation, re-creation, and final re-creation, so that creation, salvation, and eschatology are united by pneumatology.[5] Yong's foundational pneumatology is framed by three axioms: first, that God is universally active and

---

1. Yong, *Beyond the Impasse*, 35–74.
2. See Flannery, "*Nostra Aetate*," 738–42.
3. Yong, *Beyond the Impasse*, 68.
4. Yong, *Beyond the Impasse*, 41.
5. Yong, *Beyond the Impasse*, 36–40.

present in the Spirit; second, that the Spirit is God's life breath of the *imago Dei* in every human and the presupposition of all human relationships; and third, that everything that exists, including all of the development of every religious tradition, is "providentially sustained by the Spirit of God for divine purposes."[6]

For Christians, the first axiom and part of the second axiom are uncontroversial because the universal presence of the Spirit and the sharing of God's image by all humanity are biblical concepts (Gen 1:27; Ps 139:1–7), although the idea that all human relationships are pneumatically mediated has to be carefully nuanced. While those who are united with Christ share his Spirit and are thus one in the Holy Spirit (Eph 2:18; 4:4–5), this sharing of the Holy Spirit seems to exclude those not joined to Christ (John 14:17; Heb 6:4–6). Yong's third axiom, one which is critical for his foundational pneumatology, builds upon his assumption that the Spirit is universally present in every arena of human life and activity, including religion.[7] Thus he attributes to the Spirit not only humanity's religious impulse but also the variety of existential expressions of that impulse. Strongly in support of this view, Veli-Matti Kärkkäinen writes:

> The acknowledgement of the gifts of God in other religions by virtue of the presence of the Spirit—as well as the critical discernment of these gifts by the power of the same Spirit—means a real Trinitarian basis to Christianity's openness toward other religions.[8]

Both Yong and Kärkkäinen envisage the Spirit's involvement throughout creation, beyond the church, and it seems, beyond the christological horizon. Yet the "Spirit" who is the subject of Yong's foundational pneumatology is not some ambiguous animating spiritual force, but quite clearly and specifically, the Holy Spirit of the New Testament writers, the Spirit of Christ, as his key text demonstrates. After all, it is this Spirit, received by the risen and exalted Jesus from God the Father, who has been poured out on "all flesh," a phrase which Yong interprets widely and inclusively. For Yong and Kärkkäinen, there seems to be no distinction between the scope of the Spirit's work in creation and redemption, between *Spiritus vivificans* and *Spiritus salvificans*. According to the early disciples, however, the Spirit of Christ is given only to those who put their trust in Jesus, and whose indwelling presence is *sine qua non* for authentic relationship to Christ. In

---

6. Yong, *Beyond the Impasse*, 44–46.

7. Yong, *Beyond the Impasse*, 46.

8. Kärkkäinen, *Trinity*, 179; "How to Speak," 66. See also Kärkkäinen, *Theology of Religions*, 221–23; and Yong, "As the Spirit Gives Utterance," 299–314.

what way, then, can the Holy Spirit, the Spirit of Christ, be present among those who are outside this relationship? The issue Yong and Kärkkäinen's premise raises for systematic pneumatology is an important one, that is, how a ubiquitous understanding of the creative Spirit of the Old Testament coheres with the New Testament assertion that to have the indwelling Holy Spirit means to belong to Jesus Christ, and thus to God.

The early Christians experienced an unprecedented outpouring of the Spirit, which they interpreted as the dawn of the prophetically promised eschatological age. By their consistent referencing of the Hebrew Scriptures to explain the phenomenon, it is clear that these Jewish believers of Jesus recognized the outpoured Holy Spirit, τὸ πνεῦμα ἅγιον, as none other than the Spirit of the God of Abraham, Isaac, and Jacob. They boldly identified the Spirit of God with the Spirit of Jesus Christ (Acts 16:7; Rom 8:9; Gal 4:6; Phil 1:19; 1 Pet 1:11). Quite simply, to belong to Christ is to have the Spirit, and not to have the Spirit is not to belong to Christ (Acts 19:1–7; Rom 8:9). They were convinced that prior to Jesus's death "there was no Spirit [οὔπω γὰρ ἦν πνεῦμα], because Jesus was not yet glorified," (John 7:39)[9] indicating a distinct difference between their experience of the divine Spirit before and after Jesus's death and resurrection. More precisely, their pneumatic experiences began *after* Jesus's death and resurrection, and these experiences were christological in foundation and in content (John 14:16–17, 25–26; 15:26; 16:7–11; 1 John 4:2–3).

James Dunn makes an important observation that while an eschatological outpouring of God's Spirit was anticipated by Israel's prophets, "there was no expectation of a messianic figure bestowing the Spirit in pre-Christian Judaism."[10] On the other hand, the early Christians claimed that as Messiah, Jesus not only ushered in the eschatological age, but also received and poured out the promised Spirit after his exaltation (Acts 2:33; John 20:22).[11] Thus Dunn posits that the early Christians used the term "Spirit of Jesus/Christ/Son" to closely associate the outpoured Spirit of God with the risen crucified Jesus, and to emphasize that Jesus was *both the bearer and dispenser* of the Spirit.[12] He suggests that the cross, and indeed the entire Christ

---

9. Biblical quotations are taken from the *NRSV* unless otherwise stated. The *NIV* and *ESV* have "the Spirit had not been given," following an alternate text in Codex Vaticanus and a few Latin and Syriac versions (*NA28*, 320).

10. Dunn, "Towards the Spirit," 7.

11. This teaching about a Spirit-bestowing Messiah was attributed to John the Baptist by all four Evangelists (Mark 1:8; Matt 3:11; Luke 3:16; John 1:33). Dunn insightfully argues that if John had *God* in mind as the Spirit-bestower, he would not have spoken about untying the coming one's *sandals*; "Towards the Spirit," 9.

12. Dunn, "Towards the Spirit," 25.

event, changed human perception of the divine Spirit, from the impersonal Spirit of YHWH, (רוּחַ־יְהוָה), to the Spirit who bears the personality of Jesus Christ, τὸ πνεῦμα Ἰησοῦ Χριστοῦ,[13] and that Jesus's death and resurrection were together a watershed event with respect to the relationship between Jesus and the Spirit.[14] Concurring, Michael Green writes, "Jesus transposes the Spirit into a fully personal key."[15] If the cross-resurrection event was indeed the watershed event that demarcated Jesus as the *bearer* of the Spirit from his role as the *dispenser* of the Spirit,[16] what was the Spirit's role in this event? How did the Spirit of God come to be known as the Spirit of Christ? The Spirit's participation in Jesus's resurrection is explicitly affirmed (Rom 8:11), but the Spirit's activity at the cross is unclear.

Despite the current renaissance in pneumatology, the question "What was the Holy Spirit's role at the cross of Christ?," although often asked, has not been comprehensively answered. This question has come in many forms:

1. "What was the Holy Spirit doing at Calvary?" (John V. Taylor, 1972)[17]

2. "What does Jesus's experience of God on the cross mean for the Spirit of God, if we assume that the divine Spirit went with him, and that it was in the Holy Spirit that he suffered and died?" (Jürgen Moltmann, 1973)[18]

3. "Why did the outpouring of the Spirit have to wait until Jesus died and was glorified? What was it about those events that made them a turning point in the history of redemption? How did the mission of Jesus trigger Pentecost?" (Clark H. Pinnock, 1996)[19]

4. "[W]hat is the relation between the Spirit and the Son in the core work of salvation, which is the justifying, substituting atonement of Christ Jesus on the Cross?" (Paul F. M. Zahl, 2001)[20]

5. "What then does that cry of death mean for the Spirit of Life?" (D. Lyle Dabney, 2001)[21]

---

13. "[T]he impersonal Spirit, like the impersonal Logos, is now identified with Jesus and bears his personality"; Dunn, *Christ and the Spirit*, vol. 2, 52.

14. Dunn, *Christ and the Spirit*, vol. 2, 334–41.

15. Green, *I Believe*, 42.

16. Dunn, *Christ and the Spirit*, 334–41; Green, *I Believe*, 39–43; Ferguson, *Holy Spirit*, 53–56.

17. Taylor, *Go-Between God*, 102.

18. Moltmann, *Crucified God*, 64.

19. Pinnock, *Flame of Love*, 93.

20. Zahl, "Spirit in the Blood," 493.

21. Dabney, "Naming the Spirit," 55.

6. "Why is it the Holy Spirit that raises Christ from the dead? Christ is God, so death could never have held him, so why is there this need for the Spirit?" (John D. Zizioulas, 2008)[22]

7. "How do we develop a *pneumatologia crucis?* Why is it essential that Jesus have the Spirit in death?" (Myk Habets, 2010).[23]

As each of these questions were raised within the context of a broader discussion on pneumatology or Christology, the answers elicited were often brief, and vary in perspective and emphasis. Thus, it seems appropriate to investigate this issue more thoroughly, to further elucidate the relationship between the work of the Spirit and work of the Son at the cross in order to present a more comprehensive *pneumatologia crucis*.

The methodological approach employed here is primarily dialogical, seeking to engage with significant theologians, regardless of their denominational traditions, who have written substantially on the role of the Spirit at the cross within the last five decades during which a renaissance of pneumatology has been taking place. This survey of theological insights is used to draw up discrete categories of perspectives, in order to facilitate discussion. In each category, one theologian has been chosen as its major representative on the basis of their depth of interaction with the subject. In order to understand the perspectives of these key theologians more comprehensively, a brief description of their biographical and theological contexts precede the evaluation of their pneumatology and their insights concerning the role of the Spirit at the cross. This is done for a deeper and more comprehensive interaction with their pneumatological reflections. The strengths and limitations of their positions concerning the Spirit's role at the cross are then examined in the light of biblical warrant and doctrinal coherence, with scholarly interaction from other theological voices. These pneumatological perspectives are subsequently integrated with a textual, exegetical, and theological analysis of Hebrews 9:14, within the wider context of the pneumatology of the Epistle to the Hebrews, to provide the foundation for a new multifaceted approach to *pneumatologia crucis*.

A survey of relevant scholarship over the past five decades revealed three main approaches to the pneumatology of the cross.[24] These approaches are not mutually exclusive but overlap, and together contribute to a fuller vision of the role of the Spirit at the cross. They include: a mediatory role

22. Zizioulas, *Lectures*, 107.

23. Habets, *Anointed Son*, 165. Italics are original. (From here on, unless indicated, italics are original.)

24. This survey was limited to publications made available in English, although non-English originals were consulted in most cases.

(the Spirit being the "bond of love" between the Father and the Son in their moment of greatest separation), a participatory role (the Spirit is coworker with the Son at the cross), and an incorporative role (the Spirit unites humanity with the Son at the cross). An overview of each of these approaches is presented, followed by in-depth discussion of the arguments of their proponents. This study is limited to the activity of the Spirit at the cross, but the importance of the Spirit's work in illumination, conversion, and sanctification is not thereby denied or diminished. It is simply that these other aspects of the Spirit's work are not the primary focus of this investigation.[25] Representing the mediatory role of the Spirit at the cross is John Vernon Taylor, representing the participatory role is Jürgen Moltmann,[26] and representing the incorporative role is John D. Zizioulas. Other important theological voices in this study are John Owen, Karl Barth, Lyle D. Dabney, Bruce McCormack, Thomas F. Torrance, Frank D. Macchia, Clark H. Pinnock, Yves Congar, and Michael J. Gorman. In particular, Barth's vision of Jesus Christ as the Elect One in whom all others are brought into union, his pneumatic incarnational analogy for the formation of the body of Christ, and his insistence that the Word and the Spirit belong together and work together, supports the idea that Christ died and rose as the corporate Christ, through the power of the Spirit.

---

25. Studebaker suggests that the concept of an objective-subjective dichotomy between of the work of Christ and the Spirit has resulted in an Achiever-Applier paradigm in Protestant soteriology, a paradigm which he rightly questions; Studebaker, "Pentecostal Soteriology," 257.

26. Moltmann's *pneumatologia crucis* evolves over his long writing career, and he had three models; nonetheless, the participatory role of the Spirit at the cross characterizes his mature pneumatology; see chapter 4, §4.4.

2

Pneumatology Beyond Christology?

As this study is primarily concerned with the relationship of the Spirit and the Son at the cross, this chapter presents a brief summary of the development of pneumatology vis-à-vis Christology, and examines the theological significance of the terms "Spirit of Jesus/Christ/Jesus Christ" and "Spirit of his Son" within their exegetical contexts, as a preamble to the discussion of the Spirit's role at the cross.

2.1 The Spirit and the Son in History

In early Christianity the development of a formal doctrine of the Holy Spirit occurred secondarily to the doctrinal development of Christology. At the first ecumenical council in Nicaea in 325 CE, reference to the Spirit was limited to a brief faith statement with no attempt at any elucidation of the role of the Spirit within the Godhead.[1] This is not surprising because the theological issue at stake at that time was the divinity of Christ, and the Nicene Creed was formulated in a defensive response against Arian Christology. The effectiveness of this defense was, however, short-lived, because the use of the Nicene term ὁμοούσιος to describe the relationship between the Son and the Father, while affirming the divinity of the Son, rendered the doctrine of the Trinity open to modalism. Not surprisingly, Arian counter-theology persisted in reaction to this perceived danger.[2] Athanasius of Alexandria and the Cappadocian Fathers (Basil of Caesarea, Gregory

---

1. [Πιστεύομεν] . . . καὶ εἰς τὸ πνεῦμα ἅγιον ("we believe in the Holy Spirit"); Elowsky, *We Believe*, 1; Hunsinger, "Karl Barth's Doctrine," 177.

2. See González, *Story of Christianity*, 158–88; Olson, *Story of Christian Theology*, 141–96.

of Nyssa, and Gregory of Nazianzus) soon had to grapple with semi-Arian Pneumatomachian theologies that viewed the Spirit as a created being or an angel, based on heterodox biblical hermeneutics.[3] These fourth-century scholars undertook a difficult struggle to affirm the full divinity and Trinitarian status of the Spirit. Although the divinity and consubstantiality of the Holy Spirit was asserted at a synod in 362 CE over which Athanasius presided,[4] neither Athanasius nor Basil lived to see the modification of the Nicene Creed to include these axioms at the ratification of the creed at the Council of Constantinople in 381 CE.[5] Notably, the controversial term ὁμοούσιος was not used for the Spirit (as it was for the Son) in the Niceno-Constantinopolitan formula, an omission which some suggest may be related to the endeavor to garner support from semi-Arian bishops at the council.[6] Instead, biblical language was used in preference to philosophical terminology to describe the Spirit's divinity, resulting in the declaration that the Spirit is "co-worshipped and co-glorified with the Father and the Son."[7] The failure to assert that the Spirit was ὁμοούσιος with the Father and the Son left the creed vulnerable to the subordination of the Spirit to the other members of the Trinity. Perhaps unsurprisingly, a stronger statement regarding the divine οὐσία of the Spirit was subsequently declared in the Tome of Damasus at the Council of Rome, 382 CE.[8]

Despite the great effort they took to secure the Holy Spirit's place within the Godhead, it would appear, however, that Athanasius and the Cappadocian Fathers were motivated to do so because they closely associated the Spirit with the Son,[9] and they deduced that if the Spirit was seen

3. For example, Athanasius undertook to refute the Pneumatomachians (or "Spirit-fighters"; they were also called Tropici because they dismissed contrary Scripture as "tropes" or metaphors) who used "I am he who . . . creates the wind (ἐγώ . . . κτίζων πνεῦμα, LXX)" in Amos 4:13 as evidence that God created the Spirit; "To Bishop Serapion," I.3, 65. See Burgess, *Holy Spirit*, 94–95, 116–20.

4. Burgess, *Holy Spirit*, 95.

5. Shults and Hollingsworth, *Holy Spirit*, 24–29.

6. Elowsky, *We Believe*, 22. Among those who categorically used the term ὁμοούσιος for the Spirit in their writings were Athanasius ("To Bishop Serapion," I.27, 133), Epiphanus of Salamis ("Ancoratus," 6.6), Didymus ("On the Holy Spirit," 17), Gregory of Nazianzius ("On the Holy Spirit," 10–11), Augustine ("On the Trinity," 6.5.7), and Cyril of Alexandria ("Gospel of John," 10.2; Letter 55.40); from Elowsky, *We Believe*, 219–20, 230–32, 240–42, and Bettenson, *Later Christian Fathers*, 114.

7. σὺν πατρὶ καὶ υἱῷ συμπροσκούμενον καὶ συμδοχαζόμενον. Tanner, *Ecumenical Councils*, 24.

8. "If anyone denies that the Holy Spirit is truly and properly from the Father, and, like the Son, is of the divine substance and is true God, he is a heretic." Elowsky, *We Believe*, 241.

9. "But when we are made to drink of the Spirit, we drink of Christ"; "The Spirit

as a creature, the Son would inevitably be regarded as one too.[10] Ironically therefore, it would seem that their interest in the divinity of the Holy Spirit had more to do with their defense of Christology against Arianism than with pneumatological questions. Soon after the affirmation of the Spirit's divinity at Constantinople, the church's subsequent doctrinal focus returned, unsurprisingly, to christological issues, particularly the theological controversy concerning the relationship between the divinity and humanity of Jesus Christ. While the Chalcedonian Definition of 451 CE is prefaced by an affirmation of the Niceno-Constantinopolitan Creed,[11] the focus is once again Christology. In its description of the God-human hypostatic union in Christ, the Definition makes no mention of the Holy Spirit. Instead, it speaks of "one and the same only begotten Son, God, *Word*, Lord Jesus Christ," narrowing its perspective of Christology to the *Logos*.[12] Although the bishops sought to eliminate Nestorianism and Eutychianism by insisting on "both the unity of the person and separateness of the two natures," they did not elucidate the precise relationship between the two natures,[13] and the Chalcedonian Definition is silent regarding the Spirit's role in Jesus's birth, baptism, and ministry.[14]

Myk Habets notes that prior to the Nicene deliberations, traces of Spirit Christology can be discerned in the writings of Ignatius, Clement of Alexandria, Tertullian, Hippolytus, and Cyprian, although their strict adherence to the Father's *monarchia* led them towards adoptionist or docetic tendencies.[15] Significantly, while Irenaeus affirmed *Logos* Christology, he nuanced this perspective by portraying the Son and the Holy Spirit as the two hands of God,[16] and by highlighting the role of the Spirit at the

---

is said to be, and is, the image of the Son." Athanasius, "To Bishop Serapion," I:19, 24; 112, 127.

10. "For if the Spirit is a creature of the Son, it will be consistent for them to say that the Word is a creature of the Father." Athanasius, "To Bishop Serapion," I.21, 118–19.

11. Tanner, *Ecumenical Councils*, 83–84.

12. ἕνα καὶ τὸν αὐτὸν υἱὸν μονογενῆ θεὸν λόγον κύριον Ἰησοῦν Χριστόν. Tanner, *Ecumenical Councils*, 86.

13. Erickson, *Christian Theology*, 746.

14. For example, is the divinity of Jesus attributed only to the *Logos*, or also to the Spirit? Badcock may not be entirely accurate to suggest that "many of the distinctive themes of the doctrine of the Spirit in the New Testament appear to have *simply disappeared by the second century.*" Badcock, *Light of Truth*, 35, italics added. It must be borne in mind that Athanasius and the Cappadocian Fathers were fourth-century theologians.

15. Habets, *Anointed Son*, 57.

16. Irenaeus, "Against Heresies," ii.30.9, iv.20.4, v.6.1, 28.4 (*ANF* 1:406, 488, 531, 557); cited in Burgess, *Holy Spirit*, 58–59.

incarnation[17] and the Spirit-anointing of the Son by the Father.[18] Notwithstanding Irenaeus's balanced approach, *Logos* Christology subsequently predominated Spirit Christology. This is perhaps not unexpected given the internal threats of adoptionism and docetism, and the external forces of Greek philosophy, Gnosticism, and Jewish monotheism in the early centuries of Christian history.[19] Nevertheless, Habets rightly observes that one of the main deficiencies of the Chalcedonian Definition was "that it does not leave sufficient space for the equally important Spirit Christology of the Bible and the early church."[20]

In the centuries that followed, doctrinal development tended to append pneumatology to Christology, ecclesiology, and eschatology, particularly in the Western church. Augustine taught that the Holy Spirit is God, consubstantial and coeternal with the Father and the Son,[21] and conceived of the Spirit as *caritas* ("Love")[22] and *communio* ("Communion")[23] between the Father and the Son, and as *donum* ("Gift")[24] to humanity. Gary Badcock suggests that Augustine's motivation for presenting the Spirit as the

---

17. "The Word of the Father and the Spirit of God, having become united with the ancient substance of Adam's formation, rendered man living and perfect"; "Against Heresies," v.1.3 (*ANF* 1:527); cited in Burgess, *Holy Spirit*, 59. For Irenaeus, perfect humanity is conditioned both by the *Logos* and the *pneuma* of God; "Against Heresies," v.6.1, 28.4 (*ANF* 1:531, 557).

18. "And it is the Father who anoints, but the Son who is anointed by the Spirit, who is the unction"; "Against Heresies," iii.18.3 (*ANF* 1:446); cited in Burgess, *Holy Spirit*, 60.

19. Habets, *Anointed Son*, 55. Habets insightfully perceives that in using the philosophy and language of Greek culture to evangelize the educated, the apologists introduced foreign elements into Christian theology. His suggestion, however, that "[t]he Arian struggles were a direct consequence of a dominant Logos Christology" may be an overstatement, as the main concern of Arianism was the preservation of monotheism rather than a rejection of Logos Christology per se; see *Anointed Son*, 64.

20. Habets, *Anointed Son*, 79. Importantly he adds, "What is neglected is the constitutive role of the Holy Spirit, especially when it comes to the relation between the Spirit and the Christ"; *Anointed Son*, 80.

21. Augustine, "Gospel of St. John," tractate vi.5.7, xcv.1, xcix.1, lxxxiv.1 (*NPNF* 1/3:100, 7:369, 381, 333); cited in Burgess, *Holy Spirit*, 181–82; see also "On the Holy Trinity," iv.21, vi.5.7 (*NPNF* 1/3:85, 100).

22. Augustine, "On the Holy Trinity," xv.17.29, 31, 19.37 (*NPNF* 1/3:216, 219).

23. "Therefore the Holy Spirit is a certain unutterable communion of the Father and the Son" ("*Ergo spiritus sanctus ineffabilis quaedam patris filiique communion*"); Augustine, "On the Holy Trinity," v.11.12 (*NPNF* 1/3:93); Latin text obtained from http://www.thelatinlibrary.com/augustine/trin5.shtml.

24. Augustine, "On the Holy Trinity," v.11.12, 15:16 (*NPNF* 1/3:93, 95). Augustine also conceived of the "psychological" analogy of the Trinity in terms of memory, intellect, and will in the unity of one mind; "On the Holy Trinity," x.11.17–12.19 (*NPNF* 1/3:142–43).

communion of fellowship between the Father and the Son lay in his desire to define the Godhead (and thus all three Trinitarian members) in relational terms.[25] It must be said, however, that despite Augustine's desire to describe the Holy Spirit relationally, his pneumatological metaphors were functional rather than personal and this may have contributed negatively to his efforts to accord equal status to the Spirit within the Trinity. Nevertheless "Gift," "Love," and "Communion" have become enduring pneumatological metaphors into the twenty-first century, deeply influencing present day conceptualization of *pneumatologia crucis*. In his pneumatological deliberations Augustine went on further to suggest that the Spirit proceeded from both the Father and the Son since the Holy Spirit is Spirit of both:

> The Father and the Son are a Beginning of the Holy Spirit, not two Beginnings; but as the Father and Son are one God, and one Creator, and one Lord relatively to the creature, so are they one Beginning relatively to the Holy Spirit. But the Father, the Son, and the Holy Spirit is one Beginning in respect to the creature, as also one Creator and one God.[26]

Augustine's concept of the double procession of the Holy Spirit from the Father and the Son gained general acceptance in the Western church, and the *filioque* clause was later inserted into the Niceno-Constantinopolitan Creed at the Council of Toledo in 589 CE. The Eastern church, which had not been consulted, rejected this clause on the grounds that it implied two sources for the divine origin of the Holy Spirit, making the Spirit subordinate to the Son. This *filioque* controversy eventually led to the formal schism between the Western and Eastern churches in 1054 CE.[27]

Western medieval pneumatology was shaped by mysticism and scholasticism. Symeon the "New Theologian" (949–1022)[28] described his intense spiritual experiences in his writings and emphasized the importance of personal spiritual baptism. Although his pneumatology seemed autonomous to some extent with regard to the clerical hierarchy and sacraments, Congar notes that Symeon's pneumatology was entirely christological.[29] Bernard of Clairvaux (1090–1153) used the language of passion in his pneumatological

---

25. Badcock, *Light of Truth*, 72–73.

26. Augustine, "Gospel of St. John," tractate xiv.15 (*NPNF* 1/7:95); cited in Burgess, *Holy Spirit*, 181.

27. Burgess, *Holy Spirit*, 96. Shults and Hollingsworth also trace the origin of the *filioque* concept to Augustine; Shults and Hollingsworth, *Holy Spirit*, 32.

28. According to Congar, "the title 'New Theologian' refers to his having had and having communicated a (new) experience of God"; Congar, *Believe*, vol. 1, 93.

29. Congar, *Believe*, vol. 1, 95.

formulation, describing the Holy Spirit as the "kiss" between the Father and the Son, and given to the "Bride," the church, for her spiritual transformation.[30] Hildegard of Bingen (1098-1179) was a prophetic visionary who believed she was empowered by the Spirit to speak out against corruption in the political and religious spheres of her day, and exerted a strong influence over popes and princes.[31] Hugh of Saint-Victor suggested in 1137 that just as a man's spirit "descends" from his head to give life to his members, the Holy Spirit comes through Christ to Christians who are members of his body.[32] Joachim of Fiore (1135-1202) is best remembered for his division of human history into three successive and overlapping ages, the "ages" of the Father, the Son, and the Holy Spirit. He envisaged the third age as "the age of monks, contemplatives *viri spirituales*, all intimately penetrated by the Spirit," to be itself followed by God's eternal Sabbath.[33] Bonaventure (1217-1274) emphasized God's overflowing self-giving love and generosity in his gift of the Spirit at Pentecost.[34] These Christian visionaries presented different pneumatological perspectives but seemed to share a common understanding of the inseparability of Christ and the Spirit.

In the West the voice of medieval mysticism with its transformative experience of the Spirit was, however, overtaken by the rational scholasticism of the influential Thomas Aquinas (1224/25-1274).[35] In his appropriation of Aristotelian philosophy he asserted the unity and simplicity of God's essence. As the Unmoved Mover, God is, according to Thomas, the "pure act" who cannot be acted upon—the immutable and impassible God of classical theism.[36] He reaffirmed Augustine's pneumatological metaphors, particularly the concept of the Holy Spirit as "Love" and "Gift," and the idea that the Spirit is the bond that connects the Father to the Son (*duorum nexus*).[37] "Connection implies a unity of two things. For this reason it is attributed to the Holy Spirit, who is from the other two persons."[38] Not surprisingly, Thomas agreed with Augustine's *filioque*, and Thomas also asserted that the

---

30. Shults and Hollingsworth, *The Holy Spirit*, 39-40.
31. Shults and Hollingsworth, *The Holy Spirit*, 40; Congar, *Believe*, vol. 1, 121.
32. Congar cites Hugo's treatise *De sacramentis christianae fidei*; *Believe*, vol. 1, 116.
33. Congar, *Believe*, vol. 1, 126.
34. Kärkkäinen, *Pneumatology*, 53-54.
35. Shults and Hollingsworth, *Holy Spirit*, 41-44.
36. Olson, *Story of Christian Theology*, 340.
37. Aquinas, *Summa Theologiae*, Ia.39.8.1, in *Selections from Summa Theologiae*, 136.
38. Aquinas, *Selections from Summa Theologiae*, 135.

Father and Son are together one principle of the Holy Spirit.[39] Moreover, he perceived a logical ordering of the procession of the Word and the Spirit: the first procession or "generation" (of the Word) and the second procession or "spiration." By this he gave a logical priority of *Logos* over *pneuma*.[40] The growing religious and political hegemony of the institutional church favored the ordered dominance of the Word over the unpredictability of the Spirit. Spiritual "enthusiasts" were discouraged because they challenged institutional authority. Pneumatology became increasingly bound to ecclesiology, and in particular to the religious hierarchy.[41] There was "a tendency and even a temptation to give an absolute value to the Church as an institution by endowing its magisterium with an almost unconditional guarantee of guidance by the Holy Spirit."[42] Furthermore, since only the clergy were authorized to administer the sacraments that nourished the spiritual life of the church and of the individual, they wielded enormous "spiritual" power.[43] Before long, "spiritual" power morphed into ecclesial political power, and as church history tragically demonstrates, power corrupts.

In the sixteenth century Martin Luther and John Calvin essentially followed the Augustinian–Thomist formulations of the Holy Spirit.[44] Although Luther did not make pneumatology his focus in his polemic against Roman Catholicism, he nonetheless insisted that the Spirit played a vital part in drawing sinners into faith and union with Christ.[45] He emphasized the Christocentricity of the Spirit's work and also affirmed that the Spirit does not work apart from the Word.[46] Indeed, Luther intimately linked the work of the Spirit to Christ by stating that the Spirit "is called a witness, because he bears witness *only of Christ and none other*."[47] Calvin agreed with Luther on this point, but did more to advance pneumatological reflection and rightfully came to be called a "theologian of the Holy Spirit."[48] Calvin insisted that the Spirit's illumination is essential to understanding the Scriptures, declaring that "it [the Word of God] cannot penetrate into our minds

---

39. Shults and Hollingsworth, *Holy Spirit*, 44.
40. Shults and Hollingsworth, *Holy Spirit*, 42.
41. Heron, *Holy Spirit*, 95–97.
42. Congar, *Believe*, vol. 1, 152.
43. Heron, *Holy Spirit*, 97.
44. Shults and Hollingsworth, *Holy Spirit*, 45, 49.
45. Shults and Hollingsworth, *Holy Spirit*, 46.
46. "Therefore, the Holy Ghost only and alone is able to say: Jesus Christ is the Lord; the Holy Ghost teaches, preaches, and declares Christ . . . he works in the hearts of whom he will, and how he will, but never without the Word"; Luther, *Table Talk*, 119.
47. Luther, *Table Talk*, 121.
48. Shults and Hollingsworth, *Holy Spirit*, 49, 50, citing Benjamin B. Warfield.

unless the Spirit, as the inner teacher, through his illumination makes entry for it,"[49] and "[a]ccordingly, without the illumination of the Holy Spirit, the Word can do nothing."[50] Furthermore, he affirmed that it is the Spirit who alone produces faith and who breathes divine life into the believer.[51] It is through the Spirit by whom Christ unites himself to us, and we are united to Christ; eucharistic communion with Christ takes place only through the power of the Holy Spirit.[52] Indeed, "we cannot come to Christ unless we be drawn by the Spirit of God."[53] And while the Father gives us the Holy Spirit for his Son's sake, Calvin proposed that the Spirit was given to *Christ alone* for the express purpose of conferring this Spirit upon those who belong to him.[54] Calvin recognized that the Spirit's "general power" enlivens and nourishes humanity and the rest of creation, but for believers in particular, he is the sanctifying Spirit, "the root and seed of heavenly life in us."[55] Thus, it is clear that Luther and Calvin did not separate the Spirit's redemptive work from the Son's mission. More importantly, in his exposition of Hebrews 9:14, Calvin affirmed the Spirit's participation in Christ's soteriological work on the cross:

> He [the writer of *Hebrews*] now shows how clearly the death of Christ is to be regarded: not from its external act but from the power of the Spirit. Christ suffered as a man, but in order that his death might affect our salvation it came forth from the power of the Spirit. The sacrifice of eternal atonement was more than human work. He calls the Spirit eternal so that we know that the reconciliation which he effects is eternal.[56]

As a response to the Reformation insistence on salvation through Christ alone, the Council of Trent (1545–1563) affirmed the Holy Spirit's role in salvation and sanctification, without envisaging separate pneumatological and christological missions.[57] It is significant however, that by ap-

---

49. Calvin, *Institutes*, iii.2.34 (McNeill, 582).

50. Calvin, *Institutes*, iii.2.33 (McNeill, 580).

51. Calvin, *Institutes*, iii.1.1–4 (McNeill, 537–42). "But faith is the principal work of the Holy Spirit"; "faith itself has no other source than the Spirit"; "Consequently, he [the Spirit] may rightly be called the key that unlocks for us the treasures of the Kingdom of Heaven; and his illumination, the keenness of our insight"; iii.1.4 (McNeill, 541, 542).

52. Calvin, *Institutes*, vi.17.10, 12, 31–33 (McNeill, 1370, 1373, 1403–6).

53. Calvin, *Institutes*, iii.2.34 (McNeill, 582).

54. Calvin, *Institutes*, iii.1.2, 2.12 (McNeill, 538, 557).

55. Calvin, *Institutes*, iii.1.2 (McNeill, 538).

56. Calvin, *Epistle of Paul*, 121.

57. Shults and Hollingsworth, *Holy Spirit*, 52. Likewise Kärkkäinen, *Pneumatology*,

pealing to the constant activity of the Spirit within the church, the Council of Trent also asserted the trustworthiness and authority of ecclesial traditions in addition to canonical Scripture. Congar comments wryly that the conciliar statements "concealed a tendency and even a temptation to give absolute value to the Church as an institution by endowing its magisterium with an almost unconditional guarantee of guidance by the Holy Spirit."[58] Thus, while the Reformers emphasized the role of the Spirit in the divine inspiration of Scripture, the theologians of Trent emphasized the Spirit's enlightenment of the church leadership.

In the centuries that followed, the development of Western pneumatology seems to have followed two counter-trajectories.[59] On the one hand, movements like Quakerism, Pietism, the Holiness movement, Pentecostalism, and the charismatic movement emphasized the inward experience and encounter with the Holy Spirit as a person. On the other hand, Hegelian philosophy, Darwinianism, modern rationalism, and the emergence of the scientific paradigm led to negative or idealistic and abstract views of the Spirit. Friedrich Schleiermacher's concept of the Spirit as the common Spirit of the community of Christ depersonalized the Spirit, and unsurprisingly, he saw little relevance for the doctrine of the Trinity.[60] Liberal theology emphasized anthropology and ethics, disregarding "supernatural" phenomena, while fundamentalism was suspicious of spiritual "enthusiasm" and outward expressions of the more dramatic spiritual gifts. In reaction to Liberal Protestantism, Karl Barth's theology emphasized the transcendence of the triune God, humanity's natural incapacity for God, and Jesus Christ as the centerpiece of God's self-revelation. Although his *Church Dogmatics* was strongly Christocentric and the work of the Spirit closely associated with the work of the Son, Barth did not identify the Spirit with the Son. It is interesting to note that he acknowledged the work of the Holy Spirit in every volume, especially in the fourth.

As the charismatic movement of the 1950s and 1960s broadened across many Western denominations, theologians began afresh to grapple with and to reflect on pneumatological phenomena and practices. In the twentieth and twenty-first centuries, theologians from Reformed, Anglican, Baptist, Methodist, and Roman Catholic backgrounds, like Jürgen Moltmann, Clark Pinnock, John Taylor, Michael Green, Gary Badcock, Yves

---

82.

58. Congar, *Believe*, vol. 1, 152.

59. Evangelicalism as a whole moved along two streams—rationalism and pietism; Cross, "Proposal to Break the Ice," 50.

60. Schleiermacher, *Christian Faith*, §121, 560–65. His doctrine of the Trinity was placed at the end of his book, §171–72 (742–51).

Congar, Heribert Mühlen, Karl Rahner, Jacques Dupuis, and Lyle Dabney, among others, have highlighted the importance of pneumatology and ignited interest in the person and work of the Holy Spirit for theology as a whole. Thomas Smail, an evangelical who confessed to charismatic experiences, feels the urgency to define and articulate a more comprehensive pneumatology, yet he is particularly concerned that a schism between Spirit and Christ be avoided in the heat of spiritual experiences.[61] The tendency to emphasize spiritual empowerment to the detriment of Christ's sacrificial servanthood is a pastoral concern for him.[62] Pentecostal theologians like Michael Welker, Frank Macchia, Veli-Matti Kärkkäinen, Amos Yong, Terry Cross, among others, explore pneumatological issues against the backdrop of Christian theology and the concerns of the wider world. In Eastern Orthodoxy, where pneumatology has always been foundational for its theology and liturgy, scholars like John Zizioulas, Vladimir Lossky, and Kallistos (Timothy) Ware engage with both Protestant and Catholic thinking. In a sense, there appears to be an increasing ecumenical engagement on pneumatological issues across the kaleidoscope of ecclesiastic and theological traditions. Whether or not this pneumatocentric ecumenism may eventually embrace people of other faiths, and the world, is yet to be seen. It is timely, therefore, that Lyle Dabney has urged the study of Christian theology from the vantage point of the Holy Spirit.[63] The major theological voices chosen for this study, John Vernon Taylor, Jürgen Moltmann, and John D. Zizioulas, were selected chiefly on the basis of their ideas and not as ecclesiastical representatives. It is interesting to note, however, that they come from Church of England, Reformed, and Eastern Orthodox traditions, and that they all share a deep commitment to ecumenism, having all participated at one time or other in the World Council of Churches.

2.2 "Spirit of Jesus/Christ/Son"

Underpinning Yong's pneumatological formulation is his interpretation of Irenaeus's concept of the Son and the Spirit as the two hands of God, in which Yong envisages the "related yet *distinct economies* of the Spirit and the Son."[64] Do the Son and the Spirit have distinct economies, distinct missions? Is this what Irenaeus really meant to portray? Capturing a broader quotation from Irenaeus's *Against Heresies* is illuminating:

61. Smail, *Reflected Glory*, 12–20.
62. See Duggan, "Cross and the Holy Spirit," 135–46.
63. Dabney, "Starting with the Spirit," 3–4.
64. Yong, *Beyond the Impasse*, 103, 169, italics added.

Now God shall be glorified in His handiwork, fitting it so as to be conformable to, and modelled after, His own Son. For by the hands of the Father, that is, by the Son and the Holy Spirit, man, and not (merely) a part of man, was made in the likeness of God. Now the soul and the spirit are certainly a *part* of the man, but certainly not *the* man; for the perfect man consists in the commingling and the union of the soul receiving the spirit of the Father, and the admixture of that fleshly nature which was moulded after the image of God.[65]

Irenaeus's metaphor of "the hands of the Father" is preceded by his affirmation that humanity has been made to conform to *the Son*, and it is presented in the context of his insistence that humans are flesh–soul–spirit, aspects that cannot be separated. Indeed, for Irenaeus, for humans to be perfect and complete, their souls receive "the spirit of the Father," and their fleshly natures are molded after the Son ("the image of God"). In this passage, Irenaeus's emphasis is on the *unity* of the Father, Son and Spirit in the formation of the whole human. Yong seems to have taken Irenaeus's statement out of context. Although Eastern Orthodox Vladimir Lossky also refers to the "economy of the Son" and the "economy of the Spirit," by these terms he means the *one* (twofold) divine economy of the triune God in which both the Son and the Spirit work, and not two distinct and separate economies of the Son and the Spirit.[66]

In the New Testament, there is no sense that the Holy Spirit and the Son have separate missions. The first disciples of Jesus were Jews who believed that he was their divinely promised Messiah on the basis of his anointing with God's Spirit and resurrection from the dead. After Jesus's death and resurrection, the first Christians testified to divine empowerment, and to personal and unequivocal experience of the Holy Spirit; the indwelling of the Holy Spirit was seen as the hallmark of every believer of Jesus Christ, in every race, gender, and social strata.[67] They believed that the *eschaton* had begun, and that it began in Jesus through whom they too, received the Spirit. Their initially narrow vision for a renewed nation of Israel (Acts 1:6) exploded into a worldwide mission to carry the message of Jesus beyond geographical and racial boundaries to the ends of the earth (Matt 28:19; Luke 24:47; Acts 1:8). In the writings of these early Christians the terms "Spirit of Jesus" (τὸ πνεῦμα Ἰησοῦ), "Spirit of Christ" (τὸ πνεῦμα Χριστοῦ), "Spirit of Jesus Christ" (τὸ πνεῦμα Ἰησοῦ Χριστοῦ), and "Spirit of his Son"

---

65. Irenaeus, "Against Heresies," v. 6.1; *ANF* 1:531.
66. Lossky, *Mystical Theology*, 156.
67. Acts 19:1–7; Gal 3:1–2, 14; 3:28.

(τὸ πνεῦμα τοῦ υἱοῦ αὐτοῦ) emerged (Acts 16:7; Rom 8:9; Phil 1:19; Gal 4:6; 1 Pet 1:11). What did the New Testament writers mean by these terms? Perhaps an elucidation of these phrases may contribute to our understanding of *their* perception of the divine Spirit.

Acts 16:6–7

> They went through the region of Phrygia and Galatia, having been forbidden by the Holy Spirit to speak the word in Asia. When they had come opposite Mysia, they attempted to go into Bithynia, but the *Spirit of Jesus* [τὸ πνεῦμα Ἰησοῦ][68] did not allow them.

Among the New Testament narratives the Holy Spirit is given particular prominence in Luke-Acts.[69] In Acts, the Holy Spirit is portrayed as the agent of divine power promised by God and poured out by the exalted Jesus on his disciples, and as the director of the church's evangelistic mission.[70] The term "Spirit of Jesus" appears just once here in Luke-Acts and it appears at a critical point in Paul's evangelistic outreach.[71] He is prohibited from evangelizing in Asia and Bithynia, and is instead redirected westward to Macedonia (Acts 16:4–10).

The juxtaposition of the "Holy Spirit" in verse 6 with the "Spirit of Jesus" in verse 7 has been understood to indicate that both titles refer to the same Spirit, on the basis that the *divine* prohibition to Paul's initial plans was given not once but twice.[72] Hence, it is unlikely that Luke is indicating Jesus's human spirit or character here, although Bruce reasons that a prophetic utterance in Jesus's name may have occurred.[73] Against that view Marshall and Bock correctly point out that the actual manner of guidance is not detailed

---

68. κυρίου is substituted for Ἰησοῦ in Codex Ephraemi and a few Coptic versions, but the far greater weight of textual evidence is for Ἰησοῦ; see *NA28*, 435.

69. Sixteen times in Luke and 57 times in Acts, in contrast to 6 times in Mark, 12 times in Matthew, and about 12 times in John. The numbers are approximate for John because of the interpretative ambiguity of πνεῦμα and its cognates, e.g. John 6:63; 19:30.

70. Acts 1:8; 2:33; 8:29; 10:19–20; 13:2, 4; 16:6; 20:28.

71. Hur observes that the phrase "Spirit of Jesus" finds no comparable expression in the Jewish Bible or in intertestamental literature. He is convinced that the narrator means to emphasize that Jesus was not only God's Spirit-filled Messiah, but that he has also become the Spirit-dispenser; *Holy Spirit in Luke-Acts*, 141–42. This view is shared by Dunn, *Christ and the Spirit*, vol. 2, 339.

72. Bruce, *Book of Acts*, 306–7; Marshall, *Acts*, 262–63; Fitzmyer, *Acts of the Apostles*, 577–78; Bock, *Acts*, 527–28; Peterson, *Acts of the Apostles*, 454–55.

73. Bruce, *Book of Acts*, 307.

in the narrative. Instead they suggest that Luke means to emphasize that Jesus himself was guiding the progress of the gospel through the Spirit.[74] Bearing in mind that in Luke's narrative Jesus appears at key points of the mission—at the beginning of the entire mission (Luke 24:47–48; Acts 1:8), at Paul's commissioning as the apostle to the Gentiles (Acts 9:1–19), and here as the "Spirit of Jesus" at the start of the Aegean mission—Marshall's and Bock's interpretation seems reasonable. Interestingly, Fitzmyer notes a crescendo in Luke's description of this divine guidance in verses 6–10: "Holy Spirit," "Spirit of Jesus," and lastly, "God," emphasizing that this westward move of the gospel was clearly God's intention.[75] "Luke's change of expression here is not simply for stylistic variation but to recall an important theological perspective about the Spirit's relation to the ascended and enthroned Messiah."[76] Therefore the use of the term "Spirit of Jesus" here asserts the Christocentricity of the Holy Spirit.

Romans 8:9

> But you are not in the flesh [ἐν σαρκὶ]; you are in the Spirit [ἐν πνεύματι], since the Spirit of God [πνεῦμα θεοῦ] dwells in you. Anyone who does not have the *Spirit of Christ* [πνεῦμα Χριστοῦ][77] does not belong to him.

In this part of his letter to the Christians in Rome, Paul contrasts life controlled by the flesh to life controlled by the Spirit, as two mutually exclusive paradigms. Paul asserts that the indwelling of the Spirit is *the* criterion for life in relationship with God (Rom 8:6). Entry into the Spirit's domain is made possible by Christ's self-sacrifice (Rom 8:2–4). Being "in Spirit" (ἐν πνεύματι)[78] means that the "Spirit of God dwells in you" (πνεῦμα θεοῦ οἰκεῖ ἐν ὑμῖν). Thus, a mutual indwelling is indicated. Paul uses similar phrases to describe the union between Christ and his followers—"in Christ" (ἐν Χριστῷ Ἰησοῦ; Rom 8:1–2) and "Christ in you" (Χριστὸς ἐν ὑμῖν; Rom 8:10).[79] He

---

74. Marshall, *Acts*, 263; Bock, *Acts*, 527.

75. Fitzmyer, *Acts of the Apostles*, 577. "Luke makes it clear that the European mission is divinely prompted and works against human resistance"; Shepherd, *Narrative Function*, 221.

76. Peterson, *Acts of the Apostles*, 455.

77. There are no textual variants to the term πνεῦμα Χριστοῦ.

78. An anthropological understanding of ἐν πνεύματι in verse 9 (that is, referring to the human spirit) is considered less likely in view of the thrust of Paul's context with his focus on new life in the realm of God's Holy Spirit; Fitzmyer, *Romans*, 290.

79. ἐν Χριστῷ is of course an important theological phrase for Paul, and this term

insists that those without the "Spirit of Christ" (πνεῦμα Χριστοῦ) simply do not belong to Christ (Rom 8:9). Significantly, by the intentional juxtaposition of "Spirit of God" and "Spirit of Christ," Paul sees "the Spirit as integrally related to Christ as well as to the Father,"[80] and he also identifies the Spirit of God (πνεῦμα θεοῦ) with the Spirit of Christ (πνεῦμα Χριστοῦ)—both terms refer to the same Spirit.

Gordon Fee observes a chiasmic pattern in his structural analysis of Romans 8:8–11, from which he posits that the main point of Paul's argument in this section is found in verses 10 and 11, "which express the result of the reality of the indwelling Spirit."[81] According to Fee, since the Spirit of God is none other than the Spirit of Christ, the believer gains life as a result of Christ's work,[82] and since God raised Christ from the dead through the Spirit, believers are assured of bodily resurrection because the Spirit lives in them. Byrne concurs, adding that the ways that Paul refers to the Spirit, as "Spirit of God," "Spirit of Christ," and "Spirit of the One who raised Jesus from the dead" (Rom 8:9, 11), ties the eschatological Spirit to Jesus, so that anyone who does not have the Spirit of Christ is not destined to share in Christ's resurrection.[83] Dunn sums up simply and succinctly that "for Paul the Spirit is the Spirit of Christ."[84] Moo, however, rightly cautions that while Christ and the Spirit are "so closely related in communicating to believers the benefits of salvation that Paul can move from one to the other almost unconsciously," this does not mean "that Christ and the Spirit are equated or interchangeable."[85]

---

appears more frequently than Χριστὸς ἐν ὑμῖν.

80. Morris, *Epistle to the Romans*, 308.

81. Fee, *God's Empowering Presence*, 545.

82. In verse 10, Paul's switch from "Spirit of Christ" to "Christ" has been variously interpreted. Morris insists that there has been no change of subject, merely that the Spirit's indwelling is impossible without union with Christ; Morris, *Epistle to the Romans*, 309. Fee suggests that "Christ in you" is Pauline shorthand for "Spirit of Christ in you" or "Christ in you by his Spirit"; Fee, *God's Empowering Presence*, 548. Osborne sees a shift in focus from the Spirit onto Christ's atoning work as the basis for the indwelling of the Spirit; Osborne, *Romans*, 200–201. Importantly all three commentators agree that in Romans 8:9–11, the work of Christ and the work of the Spirit are tightly integrated.

83. Byrne, *Romans*, 240.

84. Dunn, *Romans 1–8*, 429.

85. Moo, *Epistle to the Romans*, 491.

Philippians 1:19

[F]or I know that through your prayers and the help of the *Spirit of Jesus Christ* [τοῦ πνεύματος Ἰησοῦ Χριστοῦ][86] this will turn out for my deliverance.

Paul writes from prison.[87] He had received a gift from the believers in Philippi by way of Epaphroditus and the latter was returning to Philippi after a serious illness. Paul took the opportunity to send the Philippians a personal letter of thanks and to update them on Epaphroditus's illness and his own situation. While he himself is facing an impending trial and possible martyrdom, Paul exhorts his beloved Philippians to reject false teaching, to keep united, and to remain true and loyal to Christ, sharing steadfastly with him the fellowship of Christ's sufferings.[88] Christ is the focus of this letter, particularly since Paul's imprisonment is the consequence of his evangelistic activity for Christ, and because Paul's life has become wholly defined by Christ (Phil 1:21). Even imprisonment is viewed not from the perspective of his own personal safety but from the standpoint of the spread of Christ's gospel—and from that latter perspective, imprisonment has had a positive and not a negative outcome (Phil 1:12–18). Hence, in the midst of his suffering, Paul positively rejoiced!

In verse 19, Paul describes his confidence that he will be delivered[89] through the prayers of the Philippians, and through the "help" of the "Spirit of Jesus Christ." Fee highlights that the noun ἐπιχορηγίας which is translated here as "help," literally means "supply or provision." The noncompounded word χορηγέω was used in Greco-Roman society as "a term for supplying choristers and dancers for festive occasions" or the provision of a husband for his wife.[90] This provision may indicate the help that the Spirit gives, or

---

86. There are no textual variants to this phrase.

87. The traditional location of this imprisonment is Rome (corresponding to Acts 28:30), although Caesarea and Ephesus have also been proposed; see the discussion in Martin, *Philippians*, 20–39.

88. Martin, *Philippians*, 46.

89. The word translated "deliverance" (σωτηρίαν) is interpreted variously as Paul's release from imprisonment or escape from death (Hawthorne), vindication (Fee, Martin), or eternal salvation (Hansen, Schreiner). The phrase τοῦτό μοι ἀποβήσεται εἰς σωτηρίαν is used by Job in his appeal before God (Job 13:16), and it strengthens the case that "deliverance" is in the context of eventual vindication rather than release from imprisonment or spiritual salvation. See Hawthorne, *Philippians*, 40; Fee, *God's Empowering Presence*, 737–38; Martin, *Philippians*, 82; Schreiner, *New Testament Theology*, 485; Hansen, *Letter*, 77–79.

90. Fee, *God's Empowering Presence*, 740–41. Its verbal root ἐπιχορηγέω is used in the Greco-Roman cultural background of marriage contracts and public service with

the provision of the Spirit himself.[91] Since Paul uses the participle form of that word in Galatians 3:5 to mean that God supplies *the Spirit*, the latter interpretation seems more likely here.[92] Furthermore, Fee notes that Paul links "prayer" and "supply of the Spirit" together in one prepositional phrase (διὰ τῆς ὑμῶν δεήσεως καὶ ἐπιχορηγίας τοῦ πνεύματος Ἰησοῦ Χριστοῦ), indicating that Paul requests prayer for a fresh anointing of the Spirit so that that he will be empowered to speak boldly, and that whatever the outcome of his imprisonment Christ will be exalted in him (Phil 1:20). "The Spirit" is itself qualified by the genitive "Jesus Christ" for which an anthropologic or ethical interpretation (that is, Jesus's human spirit or fortitude) would make little sense because the context is prayer for *God's* provision of spiritual assistance. The scholarly consensus is that τοῦ πνεύματος Ἰησοῦ Χριστοῦ refers to the Holy Spirit.[93]

However, could not the phrase "Spirit of God" or "Holy Spirit" have sufficed for Paul's prayer request?[94] Why specifically "the Spirit *of Jesus Christ*"? In this letter, Paul sees the humiliation and exaltation of Christ as central not only to the content of his gospel, but also as the paradigm for the new life in Christ. By belonging to Christ, Paul shares in the Spirit of the one who was imprisoned, tried, tortured, and killed, and who rose from the dead. The Spirit who enabled and empowered Jesus through his own suffering, is the very Spirit who now dwells in Paul. This "Spirit of Jesus Christ" will see Paul through his imprisonment, impending trial, and possible martyrdom, help him speak with all boldness and to imitate Jesus (just as Paul exhorts the Philippians to imitate him in Phil 3:17), guaranteeing Paul's eschatological resurrection and eternal destiny with Christ (Phil 3:14; 21). Hence Fee is right in stating that the phrase "Spirit of Jesus Christ":

---

the sense of "providing generous support"; *BDAG*, 386–87. See also 2 Pet 1:11 and Col 2:19.

91. ἐπιχορηγίας is a "verbal" noun, so that τοῦ πνεύματος may be interpreted as a subjective or objective genitive (see Hawthorne, *Philippians*, 40 and Hansen, *Letter*, 79, n. 156).

92. Thus, Fee and Hansen (Fee, *God's Empowering Presence*, 740–41; Hansen, *Letter*, 79). Hawthorne's argument for the subjective genitive seems weak. It is based on the "idea of the Spirit bringing assistance to Christians, especially as they bear witness to their faith when they are brought before judges," a concept which he draws from non-Pauline NT writings (Hawthorne, *Philippians*, 40–41).

93. For example, see Lightfoot, *Epistle to the Philippians*, 90–91; Schweizer, *Spirit of God*, 60; Dunn, *Jesus and the Spirit*, 318; Motyer, *Message of Philippians*, 85; Hawthorne, *Philippians*, 41; Ladd, *Theology*, 503; Fee, *God's Empowering Presence*, 735; Schreiner, *New Testament Theology*, 485; Hansen, *Letter*, 80.

94. Elsewhere in his letter Paul refers to the sharing (κοινωνία) in the Spirit by the believers (Phil 2:1), and when he describes "those who worship in the Spirit of God" (Phil 3:3).

is the key to Christ's being glorified in every way: by Paul's being "supplied" the Spirit of Jesus Christ, who will live powerfully through Paul as he stands trial.[95]

Galatians 4:6

And because you are children [υἱοί, "sons"], God has sent the *Spirit of his Son* [τὸ πνεῦμα τοῦ υἱοῦ αὐτοῦ][96] into our hearts, crying, "Abba! Father!"

Paul makes this statement in the context of his polemic against agitators who insisted that Torah observance was necessary for followers of Jesus to remain in right relationship with God, which made male circumcision and adherence to Sabbath and food laws mandatory for both Jew and Gentile Christians. At the heart of the argument is the fundamental question about how people become Abraham's true sons (Gal 3:6; "descendants" in *NRSV*).[97] Paul argues that the Abrahamic covenant predates the giving of the Torah by 430 years (Gal 3:17–18), that it is the Spirit that God promises (Gal 3:14), and that the true heir (τὸ σπέρμα, "the seed") of Abraham's promise is Christ, God's Son (Gal 3:16; 4:4). The Torah was given as a pedagogue to the people prior to the coming of Christ (Gal 3:19–23) and has now outlived its purpose (Gal 3:24–25). Hence it is only by belonging to Christ, Abraham's heir, through faith, that both Gentile and Jewish believers inherit God's promise, the Spirit (Gal 3:29). In Christ Jesus, they have been adopted as God's sons (Gal 3:26; 4:5; "children" in *NRSV*) with all the legal privileges that sonship brings, regardless of race, social status, and gender (Gal 3:28). Because[98] they are *sons* (ὅτι δέ ἐστε υἱοί) and no longer slaves, God sent forth the Spirit of his *Son* into their hearts, and like Jesus, they can address God by the family endearment "*Abba*" (Gal 4:6).[99] Since the Galatians have undoubtedly received the Holy Spirit (Gal 3:2–5), they are already validated as sons of Abraham, as God's sons. Therefore, subsequent

---

95. Fee, *God's Empowering Presence*, 743.

96. τοῦ υἱοῦ is omitted only in 𝔓[46] but is present in all other ancient manuscripts; NA28, 584.

97. Fee, *Galatians*, 7.

98. According to Bruce, this is the most natural reading of ὅτι; Bruce, *Commentary on Galatians*, 198. See also Longenecker, *Galatians*, 173; Hansen, *Galatians*, 120; Martyn, *Galatians*, 391.

99. For the discussion concerning the different ordering of the bestowal of sonship and reception of the Spirit in Romans 8:14–15 and Galatians 4:6, see Bruce, *Commentary on Galatians*, 198; Longenecker, *Galatians*, 173; Fee, *Galatians*, 152–53.

submission to the Torah is a renegade step, relinquishing the freedom of life as God's sons in the Spirit through Christ to return to "a yoke of slavery" under the Torah (Gal 5:2).[100]

The idea of "sonship" is key to Galatians 4:4–7. Inclusion into divine sonship, accompanied by the privilege of receiving the promised Spirit, is based on faith in Christ, the Son of God. Hence the identity of the Spirit of God as the "Spirit *of the Son*" is critical. Furthermore, Fee notes the parallelism between "God sent his Son" (ἐξαπέστειλεν ὁ θεὸς τὸν υἱὸν αὐτοῦ; Gal 4:4) with "God has sent *the Spirit* of his Son" (ἐξαπέστειλεν ὁ θεὸς τὸ πνεῦμα <u>τὸ πνεῦμα</u> τοῦ υἱοῦ αὐτοῦ; Gal 4:6), and observes that "Paul deliberately conjoins the work of the Son and the Spirit."[101] This intentional choice of terminology is also noted by Longenecker who suggests that by using the term τὸ πνεῦμα τοῦ υἱοῦ αὐτοῦ, Paul "highlight[s] the integral nature of sonship and the reception of the Spirit."[102]

1 Peter 1:10–11

> Concerning this salvation, the prophets who prophesied of the grace that was to be yours made careful search and inquiry, inquiring about the person or time that the *Spirit of Christ* [πνεῦμα Χριστοῦ][103] within them indicated when it testified in advance to the sufferings destined for Christ and the subsequent glory.

In addressing Christians who were living in a hostile society and facing persecution, Peter[104] encourages and exhorts them by drawing their attention to Jesus Christ who suffered, died, and was raised in glory. He persuades them that their salvation is not based upon trumped up unsubstantiated ideas but is grounded in the foreknowledge[105] of God the Father, in the Holy Spirit's sanctifying work and in the shedding of Jesus's blood for their sins (1 Peter 1:2, 10; 2:5, 24). The difficulties that the believers are facing are not surprising, given that they too, like the ancient Hebrews, are foreigners and sojourners in this hostile world, looking forward to their

---

100. This summary of Paul's argument follows Fee, *Galatians*, 147–51.

101. Fee, *God's Empowering Presence*, 405.

102. Longenecker, *Galatians*, 174.

103. The word Χριστοῦ is omitted only in Codex Vaticanus, but it is present in all other ancient manuscripts; *NA28*, 697.

104. While Petrine authorship of 1 Peter has been challenged (for example, see Jobes, *1 Peter*, 5–19), Petrine authorship will be assumed in this work because the question of authorship does not impact the issues discussed here.

105. κατὰ πρόγνωσιν.

heavenly home (1 Peter 2:11). Their heavenly citizenship requires them nonetheless to behave as God's holy priesthood and spiritual household, God's own people (1 Peter 2:5, 9). Their example and role model is none other than Jesus himself. Peter stresses that Jesus's suffering and sacrificial death were divinely planned, revealed to God's prophets beforehand and manifested at the right moment in history.

Peter explicitly identifies the Spirit who inspired the ancient prophets of Israel as the "Spirit of Christ." The dialogue between those prophets and the Spirit precludes the interpretation of "Spirit of Christ" as Jesus's *human* spirit because Jesus lived in human form centuries after them. Similarly, it is unlikely that by "Spirit of Jesus" Peter means an *attitude* characterized by Christ because an actual interaction between the prophets and the Spirit is portrayed. There is a wide consensus among commentators that by "Spirit of Christ" Peter means the Spirit of God.[106] This is "the Holy Spirit sent from heaven" (1 Peter 1:12)[107] who not only revealed the good news to the ancient prophets, but who empowers Peter and other evangelists to proclaim the gospel (1 Peter 1:12), who sanctifies Christ's followers (1 Peter 1:2), who builds them up into a spiritual house (οἶκος πνευματικὸς; 1 Peter 2:5) of which the cornerstone is Jesus Christ, and who is the Spirit[108] of glory (and of the glorified Christ) and of God that now rests upon Peter's persecuted hearers (1 Peter 4:13–14). Thus "Peter says, in effect, that the Spirit who inspired the prophets also inspired the evangelists and gave them true insight into the true meaning of the prophets."[109] In the context of Peter's message, the phrase "Spirit of Christ" becomes the lynchpin that holds Israel's prophetic traditions and the gospel together in one divine strategy of redemption for humanity.[110]

---

106. See Marshall, *1 Peter*, 47; Michaels, *1 Peter*, 44; McKnight, *1 Peter*, 70, 73; Jobes, *1 Peter*, 101, 103; Achtemeier, *1 Peter*, 105; Skaggs, *1 Peter, 2 Peter, Jude*, 21.

107. Possibly a reference to the Spirit's coming at Pentecost; see Marshall, *1 Peter*, 46, and Hillyer, *1 and 2 Peter, Jude*, 40.

108. In 1 Peter 4:14, the phrase ὅτι τὸ τῆς δόξης καὶ τὸ τοῦ θεοῦ πνεῦμα is interesting. The parallelism between τῆς δόξης and τοῦ θεοῦ as adjectival genitives of the same noun τὸ πνεῦμα, and the grammatical structure enclosing both adjectives between the repeated article τό and its noun πνεῦμα strongly suggest that the capitalized "Spirit" applies to both "Spirit of glory" and "Spirit of God"; thus *NIV, TNIV, NAU, NJB, NKJV*, and *ESV*, contra *NRSV* and *KJV*.

109. Marshall, *1 Peter*, 47. "In 1 Peter 1:11 the point seems to be that the Spirit who was the agent of revelation to the prophets of old is the same Spirit of Christ known to the first century church"; Jobes, *1 Peter*, 101. The discussion as to whether this passage supports the preexistence of Christ will not be entered into here.

110. "This phrase points therefore to the continuity between prophets and gospel: both have the same inspirer and ultimately the same content"; Achtemeier, *1 Peter*, 110. "Peter contends that this salvation, which the Asian Christians have enjoyed and

Comments

The New Testament writers were Jews or Gentiles familiar with Hebrew Scripture. In the gospel narratives and Acts, the evangelists undoubtedly had the Spirit of YHWH in view when they wrote about the Holy Spirit. For example, Luke understood that Jesus was the prophesized Spirit-anointed servant (Luke 4:1–19; cf. Isa 61:1–2), and the Spirit poured out at Pentecost was none other than God's prophetically promised Spirit (Acts 2:17–18; cf. Joel 2:28–29). While this in itself was a very bold claim by the early disciples of Jesus, far greater is the significance of the emergence in their writings of the terms "Spirit of Jesus" (τὸ πνεῦμα Ἰησοῦ), "Spirit of Christ" (τὸ πνεῦμα Χριστοῦ), "Spirit of Jesus Christ" (τὸ πνεῦμα Ἰησοῦ Χριστοῦ), and "Spirit of his Son" (τὸ πνεῦμα τοῦ υἱοῦ αὐτοῦ) since these titles were likely intended to denote the Spirit *of God*, as shown by the exegetical examination above. Such an identification of the Holy Spirit of YHWH with the Spirit of Jesus Christ is tantamount to the claim of divinity for Jesus of Nazareth—a teaching which would have represented blasphemy to devout first-century Jews.[111] Yet it is clear that these terms were not arbitrary but were carefully chosen for specific christological reasons—in Acts 16:7, to emphasize Jesus's leadership, through the Spirit, of the Western Gentile mission; in Romans 8:9, to anchor life in the Spirit's domain to the work of Christ; in Philippians 1:19, to show that Paul views his imprisonment, earthly life and eternal destiny completely through a christological lens, and that he participates in Christ's suffering and glory through his Spirit; in Galatians 4:6, to assure the Gentile believers that they are truly sons of Abraham and sons of God because they have already received their inheritance—the Spirit of God's Son; and in 1 Peter 1:11, to highlight that Christ is the centerpiece of the whole of God's redemption plan in which the Holy Spirit's work is integral.[112]

The contexts within which all these terms reside are christological, and yet also clearly pneumatological. In Acts 16:6–10, Luke affirms that the Holy Spirit, as the director of the apostolic mission, is the Spirit of Jesus. In Romans 8:1–17, Paul's discourse concerns the contrast between

---

for which they earnestly hope, is the very salvation that the ancient prophets (cf. Matt 13:17) were seeking in all its details but never found"; McKnight, *1 Peter*, 72–73. "The title for the Spirit in v. 11 (the Spirit of Christ) is unique in the New Testament and can be interpreted as the author's successful attempt to show the link between the past and the present: the Spirit is the means by which the readers are linked to the Old Testament and the sufferings of Christ"; Skaggs, *1 Peter, 2 Peter, Jude*, 21.

111. Dunn, *Christ and the Spirit*, vol. 2, 329–30.

112. Remarkably, the Johannine writings are absent from this lineup despite John's close association of Jesus with the Holy Spirit (John 14:16; 20:22), his high Christology, explicit pneumatology, and clear depiction of Jesus as the divine Son.

flesh-life (under the law) and Spirit-life (through Christ), the Spirit being both the Spirit of God and the Spirit of Christ. In Philippians 1:12–26, the imprisoned Paul is facing possible martyrdom for Christ and asks for prayer to be freshly anointed by the spirit of Jesus Christ. In Galatians 3:1—4:7, Paul identifies the indwelling of the Spirit of the Son as the criterion for being Abraham's descendants and God's sons. In 1 Peter 1:10–12, Peter affirms that Jesus Christ is indeed the one whom Israel's prophets foretold, and that it was none other than the Spirit of Christ who made these revelations to them. In all these passages, the Holy Spirit is in view rather than Jesus's human spirit, or an attitude that Jesus displayed. While the New Testament writers do not confuse the Holy Spirit with the person of Jesus Christ,[113] they clearly see continuity between the Spirit of God and the Spirit of Jesus Christ. This poses difficulties for the notion that the Son and the Spirit have "different economies."

Up until the latter half of the twentieth century, the Spirit's role in relation to the cross does not appear to have been the subject of much reflection. In his survey of the work of the Spirit in *De Spiritu Sancto*, Basil of Caesarea includes creation and the spiritual rebirth of Christians, and Christ's incarnation, miracles, exorcisms, and healings, and limits the Spirit's participation at the cross to the resurrection.[114] This is despite his assertion that "in every operation the Spirit is closely conjoined with, and inseparable from, the Father and the Son."[115] This tendency to exclude the Spirit from considerations concerning the cross has become, as it were, a deeply ingrained habit in Christian scholarship. Atonement theories, for example, typically fail to mention the Holy Spirit. The latter's role is viewed as beginning with the resurrection and not before. Whether Christ's atonement is interpreted through the metaphorical lenses of the law court (substitution, justification), commerce (redemption), war (victory over evil), cultic worship (sacrifice), personal relationship (restoration of honor, reconciliation) or ethics (moral example),[116] there are three main characters involved, namely the

---

113. Paul, however, seems to come close to identifying the Spirit with Christ in 2 Cor 3:17 and 1 Cor 15:45. Dunn is unconvinced that Paul viewed the Holy Spirit and Christ as one ontological entity, proposing instead a functional identity; Dunn, *Christ and the Spirit*, vol. 1, 115–25; also *Christ and the Spirit*, vol. 2, 78, and n. 31. Fee asserts, as does Dunn, that "the Lord" comes from Paul's citation of Exodus 34:34, so that Fee's translation reads, "Now 'the Lord' is the Spirit"; by the words "the Lord," "Paul does not intend either God or Christ; he intends the Spirit," in *God's Empowering Presence*, 309, 311–12, see also n. 91.

114. Basil, "On the Holy Spirit," xix.49 (*NPNF* 2/8:30–31).

115. Basil, "On the Holy Spirit," xvi.37 (*NPNF* 2/8:23).

116. Green and Baker, *Recovering the Scandal*, 23; I have slightly modified their categories.

Father, the Son, and humanity, and sometimes the devil as the fourth. If we accept the Augustinian principle *omnia opera trinitatis ad extra indivisa sunt* ("all external operations of the Trinity are indivisible") as theologically correct, would not the Holy Spirit have been involved in the most critical part of God's redemptive mission, at the cross? Or does his role cease on Good Friday and resume at Easter? How does the Spirit of God become the Spirit of Christ? The following chapters present a detailed examination on theological perspectives concerning this very issue.

2.3 Summary

Pneumatology has taken a slow and meandering course in the history of Christian doctrinal development, often in the wake of christological debates. For early Christian theologians, the "Who am I?" question generally concerned Jesus Christ rather than the Holy Spirit, except when dogmatic determination regarding the identity of the Spirit was inseparably intertwined with christological doctrine and thus unavoidable. For Athanasius and the Cappadocian Fathers, the defense of the full divinity and coequality of the Spirit with the Son and the Father within the Godhead became necessary in order to repudiate Arianism. If the Spirit is a creature, so possibly is the Son. Once the pneumatological Constantinopolitan extension to the Nicene Creed was established, christological issues once again took center stage. Augustine suggested pneumatological metaphors like "Love," "Gift," and "Communion," perhaps in an effort to depict the Spirit in relational terms to the Father and the Son. Such metaphors, however, have had the opposite effect of subordinating the Spirit to the other Trinitarian members, and encouraged perspectives of the Spirit in terms of the Spirit's functions rather than personhood. Augustine's assertion that the Spirit proceeds from the Father *and the Son* eventually led to the *filioque* controversy and major ecclesiastical schism. In the Western church, pneumatology has often been appended to Christology, ecclesiology, and eschatology, and although Calvin emphasized the work of the Spirit in drawing people to Christ, producing faith, opening their minds to Scripture, and uniting them to Christ, Christ remained center stage. The following centuries saw the development of pneumatology progress and diminish in two simultaneous counter-trajectories, with strong emphasis on the personal presence and work of the Holy Spirit on the one hand, and a rationalizing abstraction on the other.

However, in the past five decades, there has been a resurgence in pneumatological reflection. Societies have become increasingly diverse, while global interconnectedness and technological advancement proceed at an accelerating pace. Christian ecumenists have increasingly turned to pneumatology as the space for interaction, suggesting that the presence and gifting of the Spirit can be discerned in other religions. Associated with this idea is the notion that the Son and the Spirit have different, albeit overlapping, spheres of activity, and that the Spirit reaches beyond the christological horizon to those who do not belong to Christ. The contexts in which the New Testament terms "Spirit of Jesus/Christ/Jesus Christ" and "Spirit of his Son" appear reveal that the early disciples identified the Spirit of God with the Spirit of Christ. They asserted that the Holy Spirit's indwelling presence marked out those who belonged to Christ (and therefore to God as his true "sons") regardless of race, gender, and social status. Thus, it is unlikely that they would have disengaged the Holy Spirit from Jesus Christ, nor would they have understood the Holy Spirit to be other than the Spirit of Christ. The scandalous cross and humiliating execution of their Messiah became the very instrument of their redemption into God's eschatological kingdom of the Holy Spirit. Jesus's messiahship was credentialed by the Spirit's anointing and vindicated by his resurrection by the Spirit. If the Holy Spirit was evident at Jesus's birth, baptism, ministry, and resurrection, it is reasonable to think that the Spirit also participated in the focal point of his mission, his atoning death.

In the following chapters, therefore, some scholarly perspectives of the Holy Spirit's role at the cross, namely, as the "bond of love" between the Father and the Son (chapter 3), as the Son's coworker at the cross (chapter 4), and as the unifier between humanity and Christ (chapter 5) are examined, after which biblical (chapter 6) and theological arguments (chapter 7) are made for the Spirit's active participation at the cross of Christ, and a new constructive proposal for a *pneumatologia crucis* is offered.

3

Spirit as "Bond of Love" —John Vernon Taylor

> What was the Holy Spirit doing at Calvary? First, in a mystery that we cannot plumb, he must have been about his eternal employ between the Father and the Son, holding each in awareness of each other, in an agony and bliss of love that must forever lie infinitely beyond our understanding.[1]

THE IDEA THAT WITHIN the eternal immanent Godhead the Holy Spirit exists as the "bond of love" between the Father and the Son is deeply embedded within Western Christian traditions, and this idea has been attributed to Augustine.[2] As an extension of this concept is the view that the Spirit bridged the separation between God the Father and God the Son when Jesus died. A significant proponent of this position, and possibly the first, is John Vernon Taylor. In order to understand his stance on *pneumatologia crucis*, a brief biographical sketch will first be presented, followed by an overview of his theology and pneumatology.

---

1. Taylor, *Go-Between God*, 102.
2. "And the Holy Spirit, is neither of the Father alone, nor of the Son alone, but of both: and so intimates to us a mutual love, wherewith the Father and the Son reciprocally love one another"; Augustine, "On the Holy Trinity," xv.17.27 (*NPNF* 1/3:215). See also "On the Holy Trinity," vii.4.6 (*NPNF* 1/3:108).

3.1 Taylor's Biographical Context[3]

John Taylor was born in Cambridge in 1914. His father was a scholar and an educator who subsequently became a bishop of the Church of England. Growing up in the compound of a boys' boarding school in Ramsgate on the south coast of England where his father was headmaster, Taylor met Christians from India, China, and Africa who stimulated his interest in overseas mission. Taylor studied English Literature at Cambridge, and subsequently trained for the Anglican ministry at Wycliffe Hall in Oxford. He was ordained in 1938 and served as a curate in London (1938–1940) and in Lancashire (1940–1943), during which time he married Peggy Wright, a student of the London Royal School of Music. The Taylors subsequently lived as missionaries in Uganda where he administered and taught at the Bishop Tucker Theological College in Mukono. Expecting to assist the warden of the college, Taylor found himself bearing sole responsibility when the incumbent suddenly resigned. His tenure as warden began in crisis, in the midst of an indigenous revival movement in which numerous conversions occurred in scenes of spirited preaching, public confession, and emotion-charged singing. However, the revivalists regarded "everything traditional in African religion and culture as dangerously unredeemed," and the focus on individual repentance and conversion soon trended towards fundamentalism and an anti-European outlook.[4] Inheriting a legacy of hurt, resentment, suspicion, and division, Taylor brought a generous and patient spirit, courtesy and reverence for others, and healing.[5] In the midst of tension and sensitivities, he was able to develop creative ways of worship and sharing of the word through drama and music, incorporating African drums and spirituals. The Taylors had three children, a son and two daughters, the youngest being born in Africa. They remained there until 1954 when they had to return to England for the sake of their eldest child who was having serious difficulties adjusting to life in boarding school in Kenya. She had been sent there because the Ugandan educational facilities were inadequate at that time. For Taylor, this was a bitter disappointment. He had from childhood, naively upheld the life of a missionary as *the* Christian ideal.[6]

---

3. These biographical details were obtained from Wood, *Poet, Priest and Prophet*, 17–51; Wood, "Christian Mission," 427–33; Nemer, "Tribute"; Barrington-Ward, "John Taylor." This chapter was graciously read and critiqued by Reverend Dr. David Wood in 2011.

4. Wood, *Poet, Priest and Prophet*, 30.

5. Wood, *Poet, Priest and Prophet*, 26–30.

6. Wood, *Poet, Priest and Prophet*, 47.

This was a reversal of all we had planned and hoped. Of course it had real compensations, yet it was a very painful wrench and the disappointment grew worse when, after a year, I still had no other job. I felt absurdly angry with God, and took it out on my innocent family in a nasty, prolonged grouchiness. Slowly and painfully I was brought to see what was a childishly romantic image of myself as a lifelong Christian missionary. It was my spiritual self-importance that had to die.[7]

However, during the year of uncertainty and depression that followed, Taylor discovered a gift for writing. He also came upon the English translation of Dietrich Bonhoeffer's *Letters and Papers from Prison* which had been recently published. This book became an important milestone in Taylor's theological development. Through Bonhoeffer, he began to see God through the crucified Christ, suffering in the midst of creation in order to redeem it—the "Beyond in the midst."[8] Shortly after this event, Taylor was given the opportunity to return to Africa for short periods at a time over the next three years as a research worker in Uganda and Northern Rhodesia for the International Missionary Council. During this period, he lived for three months in a thatched hut in a Ugandan village and "was brought into a more complete and intimate experience of Africa than ever I met when wearing a missionary hat."[9] Back in England, Taylor subsequently served as Africa Secretary to the Church Missionary Society from 1959 until 1963. He published his research in 1963 in his book *The Primal Vision*, in which he gave "African spirituality a new place in Western understanding and show[ed] how we can all enter another's world with reverence and there discern the form the crucified Christ might take within it."[10] Taylor was then appointed General Secretary of the Church Missionary Society from 1963 until 1973, and in this position, he travelled extensively in Asia, Africa, and the Middle East, encouraging innovative approaches to mission, and playing a global role as conciliator in the World Council of Churches conferences. In 1975, Taylor was appointed Bishop of Winchester, a post he held until his retirement in 1985. Over this same period he served as Chairman of the Doctrine Commission of the Church of England.

---

7. Taylor, *Matter of Life*, 63–64.

8. Taylor, *Go-Between God*, 5; Taylor, *Christlike God*, 24–29. "Experiences of God are experiences of the ordinary seen in the context of an otherness which enfolds them all and lies within them all"; Taylor, *Christlike God*, 25.

9. Taylor, *Matter of Life*, 64.

10. Barrington-Ward, "John Taylor."

Within both the secular scene and the worlds of all faiths he sought to discern the action of the Spirit and the form of the wounded God in the midst. He gathered this experience into the rich anthology of *The Go-Between God* (1972).[11]

In his retirement, Taylor further explored his vision of the suffering God in his book *The Christlike God*, published in 1992. He died in Oxford on 31st January 2001, and while his chaotic timekeeping and administrative style seemed considerably unstructured,[12] he was warmly remembered as a gifted theologian and priest, for his love of poetry, drama, and art, for his gentle sensitivity to those around him, his creativity, humility, and magnetism, and for his great sense of humor.[13]

3.2 Taylor's Theological Context

John Taylor has been called one of the greatest evangelical missionary statesmen of the twentieth century.[14] His theology develops in a methodological paradigm which may be described as experiential, humanistic, relational, and communal, and crucicentric. With Bonhoeffer and Luther, Taylor believes "that the cross is the only true picture of God that the world has ever seen."[15]

Experiential

Taylor emphasizes that the Bible is a record of the theological reflection of human beings on their *experiences* of God's self-revelation, and for the New Testament writers, their experiences of God's self-revelation in Jesus of Nazareth.[16] His own theology is shaped by his experiences in Africa, and by his love of drama, music, art, and poetry. Taylor also places great

---

11. Barrington-Ward, "John Taylor."
12. Wood, *Poet, Priest and Prophet*, 150–51. "John Taylor is a deeply uninstitutional man at the heart of the religious establishment"; Wood, *Poet, Priest and Prophet*, 151.
13. Barrington-Ward, "John Taylor."
14. Wood, "Christian Mission," 428.
15. Wood, *Poet, Priest and Prophet*, 53.
16. Taylor, *Christlike God*, 7–21. In defense of allowing experience to contribute to the theological task, Terry Cross insightfully asserts that "if evangelical theology will thrive in the twenty-first century, it must come to terms with its pietistic stream and examine ways that experience can influence theological method"; "Proposal to Break the Ice," 51.

importance on a personal encounter with God,[17] which he terms the "experience of the numinous,"[18] a concept he borrowed from Rudolph Otto.[19] By this Taylor means the sudden and inward perception of God within the ordinary things of life—for example, in the light upon a landscape, the brilliance of flowers in the sunshine, or the particular harmonies of a song—which, for Taylor, are all indicators of God's immanent presence in the world.[20] Following Otto and Schleiermacher, Taylor sees in all humans the potential for an awareness of God's presence. Like Schleiermacher's portrayal of Jesus as someone with perfect God-consciousness, Taylor describes Jesus as "a man totally alive to God."[21] What sets Taylor apart from Otto and Schleiermacher is his firm belief that this awareness of God is initiated by the Holy Spirit.[22] Furthermore, where Schleiermacher calls the Holy Spirit the "common Spirit of the new corporate life founded by Christ"[23] and seems ambiguous about attributing personhood to the Holy Spirit,[24] Taylor is explicitly clear about the deity and personhood of the Holy Spirit.[25] Nevertheless, Taylor is convinced that experiences of God are not confined within religious or mystical contexts but may occur suddenly, surprisingly, and unexpectedly in the midst of ordinary experiences, to ordinary people. Hence, he describes God as the self-giving Creator who is the "Beyond in the midst."[26]

Humanistic

Following Bonhoeffer, Taylor highlights the humanity of Jesus. In a statement that encapsulates the humanistic emphasis in his theology, Taylor writes:

17. "For there is no substitute for personal encounter as the mainspring of spiritual conviction and action"; Taylor, *Christlike God*, 55.

18. Taylor, *Christlike God*, 33.

19. The English "the numinous" is translated from Rudolph Otto's German *das Numinose*, a term which he coined from the Latin *numen* meaning "divine power" or "divinity" to describe the holy presence of God which elicits a unique feeling of awe from humans; Otto, *Idea of the Holy*, 7–24.

20. Taylor, *Christlike God*, 32–35.

21. Schleiermacher, *Christian Faith*, §94, 395; Taylor, *Matter of Life*, 41.

22. Taylor, *Christlike God*, 83.

23. Schleiermacher, *Christian Faith*, §121, 560–65.

24. Schleiermacher is uncomfortable with the traditional doctrine of the Trinity which he believes has unsolved difficulties. *Christian Faith*, §171–72, 742–51.

25. Taylor, *Go-Between God*, 5–7.

26. Taylor, *Go-Between God*, 5; *Christlike God*, 24–29.

> Precisely by becoming nothing but man God disclosed the whole truth of himself, all we shall ever see; and, as a man, God did and does for humankind that which he alone can do.[27]

Taylor does not deny the divinity of Jesus, but by stressing that God revealed Godself in human form, Jesus, Taylor makes three assertions. First, he is adamant that the divinity and humanity of Jesus are inseparable. On the one hand, he maintains that the incarnation was not a temporary earthly guise for the Son of God, but that the humanity and earthly history of Jesus throws light upon "the ultimate mystery of God's inmost being,"[28] and that "God the Son has never put off the humanity that was his in Jesus Christ."[29] According to David Wood, his biographer and disciple,[30] Taylor maintains as his core belief that the incarnation is not a crossing of the gulf between human and divine because there is, in fact, no such gulf.[31] Taylor does not confuse the Creator with the creature, but nonetheless asserts that humanness is in some way a genuine expression of God's own nature. He uses the linguistic metaphor of *"translation"* for the incarnation, seeing Jesus as God's Word "translated" into "the inadequate language of human intercourse," a translation that nonetheless "gives us true equivalents of the Original."[32] On the other hand, Taylor also maintains that since Jesus suffered and died as God-man, God suffered in Christ. He considers the view of God as inaccessible, immutable, and impassable to be a philosophical imposition on the biblical portrait.[33] Interestingly, Taylor does not explore the theological implications and ramifications of his view that God experienced death in Jesus.

Second, Taylor argues against the separation between sacred and secular in daily living. Sharing Bonhoeffer's concern with the question of "what Christianity really is, or indeed who Christ really is, for us today,"[34] Taylor insists that Christianity must be relevant to contemporary day-to-day life because Jesus demonstrated that God comes to us as the "Beyond in the midst" of this very world. Long before it became fashionable, Taylor takes to

---

27. Taylor, *Christlike God*, 135.
28. Taylor, *The Christlike God*, 141.
29. Taylor, *The Christlike God*, 141.
30. "Disciple" is Wood's own term for his relationship with John Taylor (from an interview with Reverend Dr. David Wood on September 1, 2011 at Edith Cowan University, Mount Lawley, Western Australia).
31. Wood, *Poet, Priest and Prophet*, 124. See Taylor's *The Christlike God*, 126–28.
32. Taylor, *The Christlike God*, 141, 142.
33. Taylor, *The Christlike God*, 101–39.
34. Bonhoeffer, *Letters and Papers from Prison*, 279. This quotation comes from the English translation of Bonhoeffer's letter dated April 30, 1944 to his student and close friend, Eberhard Bethge.

task the obsessive impulse in industrialized societies to grow, to acquire, and to consume far beyond their actual needs, and that this is done to the detriment of poorer nations and the ecological environment.[35] He argues that this growth-at-all-costs mentality is a seductive form of idolatry against which the biblical "theology of enough" stands.[36] Instead, Taylor challenges Christians to demonstrate Christlikeness in their daily living and in daily choices, and to do so not in isolated communes, but as active participants in the larger society.

Third, it is clear that Taylor holds to a Spirit Christology.[37] In *The Go-Between God* he reiterates that Jesus was "one who lived totally and uniquely in the Spirit"[38] even hinting at one point that "the Creator Spirit at the heart of it all . . . emerged incarnate in the manhood of Jesus of Nazareth,"[39] although he soon clarifies that "it was not the Spirit but the Word which was made flesh and dwelt among us."[40] While acknowledging that he sails close to adoptionism, Taylor nevertheless denies that this is his position, stating that Spirit and Logos are "almost identical concepts"[41] and that the Spirit has always been pointing and bearing witness to the Logos.[42] Interestingly, in *The Christlike God* published twenty years later, the *crucified Christ* takes center stage, but still within a Trinitarian context.

Relational and Communal

Taylor was profoundly influenced by his encounter and engagement with tribal cultures in Africa. In his semi-autobiographical *The Primal Vision* he emphasizes the importance of the relational perspective on selfhood in the African community, as opposed to the European focus on the individual. In Africa it is a case of "I am because I participate."[43] According to Taylor, for the African, selfhood is defined relationally rather than as an individual center of rational consciousness, and the relationships which are deemed significant are not only horizontal but also vertical. One's

---

35. Taylor, *Enough is Enough*.
36. Taylor, *Enough is Enough*, 40–62.
37. Taylor, *Go-Between God*, 84–88.
38. Taylor, *Go-Between God*, 88.
39. Taylor, *Go-Between God*, 34.
40. Taylor, *Go-Between God*, 61.
41. Taylor, *Go-Between God*, 89. In this book, Taylor does not explore in-depth relationships within the immanent Trinity, but keeps his focus on the Spirit and Jesus.
42. Taylor, *Go-Between God*, 191.
43. Taylor, *Primal Vision*, 85.

ancestors, existing as *shades*, continue to influence and interact with the present.[44] Taylor's emphasis on relationships and community is closely linked with the importance he places on the genuine interpersonal encounter, that is, being truly "present" for others, being aware of them, and giving them our full attention. For Taylor, developing an attitude of attentive awareness and humble receptiveness is particularly crucial in the context of Christian mission among people of other faiths. It means the willingness to hear and reflect on what others are saying about their beliefs without dismissing those beliefs as inconsequential.[45] According to Taylor this relational principle operates throughout creation (even at a molecular level), and between creation and God.[46] Importantly, he sees *the Holy Spirit* as the one who brings about this awareness of "the other," hence his conceptualization of the Spirit as the "Go-between God."[47] In *The Christlike God*, Taylor stretches this idea of relationality beyond mere awareness of others to the concept of "co-inherence," meaning a reciprocal indwelling of one with another, an idea similar to *perichoresis*. Indeed, he suggests that co-inherence is inherently divine, "the mode of God's loving, the objective for which God desires an 'other.'"[48] Taylor sees the Spirit as the mediator of co-inherence and communion.[49]

This theme of co-inherent community not only informs Taylor's pneumatology, but also his Christology, ecclesiology, ethics, and missiology. In his Christology, Taylor sees Jesus not only as an individual, but also as a corporate being, particularly in his use of the title "Son of Man."[50] "And Jesus, as we have seen, certainly expected to incorporate others with himself

---

44. "The sense of the personal totality of all being, and of a humanity which embraces the living, the dead and the divinities, fills the background of the primal worldview"; Taylor, *Primal Vision*, 85.

45. The great significance that Taylor gives to this attentive awareness as a basic relational principle for missional outreach is indicative of the deep influence of his mentor and predecessor in the Church Missionary Society, Max Warren, who named it a "theology of attention"; Kings, "Theologies," 298–303.

46. Taylor, *Go-Between God*, 31.

47. Taylor, *Go-Between God*, 29.

48. Taylor, *Christlike God*, 212. He also states that "Christianity, like its parent Judaism, teaches that human life achieves its transcendent potential in the exchange and interflow between persons in community"; *Christlike God*, 238.

49. Taylor, *Go-Between God*, 43.

50. Taylor, *Christlike God*, 94, 96–97. "[T]he Son of Man was a plural image and by adopting it Jesus was implying that those who were ready to be incorporated with him into that role could share it, just as they could share in his knowledge of God as *Abba*"; *Christlike God*, 96–97.

in the obedience of the covenant, the cross and the kingdom."[51] While he does not systematically explore how this incorporation occurs or when it occurs, Taylor affirms that it is the Spirit who unites us with Christ so that in Christ we become a new humanity.[52] Taylor's approach to ecclesiology is inclusive and ecumenical, his ethics call for authentic Christlike living and active engagement with community and society, and his missiology is incarnational and "en-cultured." Wood observes that "Christian mission, as [Taylor] understands it, embraces the whole of life: all the facts, all the beauty and all the pain. Only God is catholic, while we remain sectarian."[53] Taylor himself is convinced that it is only the Spirit's mediation between humans that makes evangelism possible.[54]

Crucicentric

The cross is the fundamental key to Taylor's theology. With Luther, Barth, and Bonhoeffer, Taylor's view of God is shaped by the crucified and resurrected Jesus.[55] Through the cross, Taylor sees the servant God, the suffering God, the redeeming God, and the victorious God. In his later book, *The Christlike God*, he portrays the triune God as "the Self-Giver" (the Father), "the Given Self" (the Son), and "the In-Othering Self" (the Spirit).[56] "Self-giving" forms the key theme of Taylor's Trinitarian analogy, a theme which he sees revealed in the cross. Although he modestly presents his analogy as

---

51. Taylor, *Christlike God*, 176. This statement is pregnant with theological implications about the corporate character of Christology, but it is unfortunately not unpacked for his readers.

52. Taylor, *Go-Between God*, 134, 142, 143.

53. Wood, "Christian Mission," 428.

54. "For the ground of all our evangelism is the fact that the Holy Spirit, the Go-Between, not only stands between one believer and another, but between the Christian and every other being with whom he is given the communion of mutual awareness"; Taylor, *Go-Between God*, 151.

55. The crucicentricity of Taylor's theology distinguishes him from Schleiermacher although they share a similar concept in their respective descriptions of "God-consciousness" and "experience of the numinous." For Schleiermacher, Christ effects redemption through the communication of his sinless perfection to those who are united in fellowship with him rather than through his becoming a vicarious sacrifice on the cross. According to Schleiermacher, Christ suffered and died in supreme *sympathy* with human misery and sinful state, thereby becoming humanity's perfect "satisfying representative"; *Christian Faith*, §104.4, 458–61. Furthermore, in Schleiermacher's view, the resurrection and ascension are not relevant to redemption; *Christian Faith*, §99.1, 418–19.

56. Taylor, *Christlike God*, 123.

a mere reinterpretation of Augustine's well-known concept of the Trinity as "Lover," "Beloved," and "Love," Taylor's model is arguably stronger because the name "In-Othering Self" for the Holy Spirit is less impersonal than "Love." Taylor's Trinitarian model, however, tends towards modalism, as "the Self-Giver," "the Given Self," and "the In-Othering Self" may be viewed as three expressions of one divine Self.[57] Nevertheless, Taylor clearly distinguishes between the Father, the Son, and the Spirit.

For Taylor, the cross also answers the theodicy question because within it he sees God's annihilation of evil, "the deformed product of our higher nature, not the residual habit of some sub-human past."[58] According to Taylor, evil has profound ontological effects for humanity, and is more than a series of external misdeeds. Taylor envisages evil as an infection that has taken root in and corrupted humanity, but which Jesus, the incarnate Son has completely "absorbed" and destroyed, breaking the power of evil and freeing us from the slavery of sin.[59] Taylor further suggests that in the crucified Christ, God not only bears the burden of human sin, but shoulders responsibility for it. "The God who in Christ was reconciling the alienated uncomprehending world to himself is perhaps more ready than his defence counsel to admit responsibility and show that he is sharing the consequences."[60]

In summary, Taylor's theology is experiential, humanistic, relational, and communal, and crucicentric. For Taylor, the presence of the self-giving God, "the Beyond in the midst," is experienced through the Spirit in everyday reality, in relationships, in nature, and in life events. He emphasizes the genuine humanity of Jesus, the empowering role of the Spirit in Jesus's life and ministry, and the corporate character of Christology. Above all, Taylor's pneumatic Christ is the crucified, risen Christ, through whom the infection of sin and death has been overcome through his death and resurrection.

3.3 Taylor's Pneumatology

John Taylor's metaphors for the Holy Spirit, the "Go-Between" and "In-Othering" God, highlight the Spirit's role as the divine communicator. Following Augustine in describing the Holy Spirit as "Communion," Taylor

---

57. Just as Karl Barth's theological prism is "revelation," Taylor's theological prism is "gift." Interestingly, the Trinitarian analogies used by both theologians seem to border on modalism.
58. Taylor, *Christlike God*, 199.
59. Taylor, *Matter of Life*, 47.
60. Taylor, *Christlike God*, 204.

stresses that the Spirit acts anonymously and unnoticed.[61] His pneumatological imagery arises out of his experience of a particular moment during a train journey from Oxford to London. It was 1966; he was the General Secretary of the Church Missionary Society and was in the midst of preparing a series of addresses on the Holy Spirit. Suddenly, the passing landscape of cornfields that he had been looking at ceased merely to be an object but became a subject "imbued with power" that spoke to him. In that moment of charged intensity and awareness, he wondered about the source of that current of mutual communication.

> Who effects the introduction between me and that which is there, turning it into a presence towards which I surrender myself? As soon as the question took that form the answer fell into place. So *this* is what is meant by the Holy Spirit! This is the essential power of his nature. This is why he is the universal Spirit of God, leaving no individual and no culture without his witness and challenge. This is how God acts upon human beings, maybe upon all created things, working from within, making them more aware.[62]

Taylor subsequently draws upon this insight in the development of his pneumatology. He comes to characterize the activity of the Holy Spirit, not within the familiar categories of Christology, ecclesiology, mission, or eschatology, but using broad non-theological terms,[63] perhaps because he wishes through his writings to involve audiences beyond Christian academia and the church. According to Taylor, the Spirit primarily acts in three ways, namely, creating greater sensitivity and awareness, stimulating choice, and urging self-sacrifice.[64]

First, the Spirit is "the anonymous opener of our eyes," inspiring fresh discoveries and insights. The Spirit mediates mutual awareness at all levels—between believers, between humans, within creation, between creation and God.[65] Taylor emphasizes the role of the Spirit in creation,[66] describing the

---

61. Taylor, *Go-Between God*, 43.

62. Taylor, *Matter of Life*, 3.

63. In *Go-Between God*, Taylor articulates his pneumatology using dynamic categories, e.g. "conception," "labour," "birth," "breath," "growing," "meeting," "playing," etc.

64. Taylor, *Go-Between God*, 29–34, 47.

65. Taylor, *Go-Between God*, 31, 83, 151. See nn. 149 and 155.

66. Taylor, *Go-Between God*, 180–81. "[N]othing can emerge from chaos without that mediation between one and another which I have suggested is the action of the Holy Spirit" (*Go-Between God*, 30).

Holy Spirit as "totally primordial."[67] Not only does he attribute to the Spirit the mediation of recognition between beings, but he also sees the Spirit as the one who enables flashes of insight in all fields of creativity. According to Taylor, the Spirit's activity is not confined to the church or to some "sacred" dimension but is also detected, for example, in art, music, drama, science, and mathematics, and throughout nature.

Second, Taylor suggests that the Spirit compels choice. The spontaneous change in form or behavior and the subsequent organic selection that go on in nature are not, in his opinion, random processes, but demonstrative of the Spirit's continuing activity in creation. By presenting fresh insights to creatures, the Spirit sets up before them the necessity to choose between the actual and the potential.[68] Change entails risks, and may be for better or worse, but growth and development cannot take place without change. Taylor perceives that this principle of spontaneity and choice, operating even within the dimension of subatomic particles, holds true for humanity's relationship with God. He points to the history of God's dealings with Israel, and in particular Moses's challenge to the Israelites to choose between life and death, between prosperity and adversity, between loving and rejecting God (Deut 30:15–20). Building upon Taylor's insight, perhaps it can also be said that Jesus presented the same kind of challenge to first-century Israel to accept or reject him, providing no opportunity for middle of the road fence-sitting.

Third, beneath the red tooth and claw in rivalry and self-preservation that pervades the whole creation, Taylor identifies "the law of self-oblation," the deeper principle of sacrifice which has always been at work, but which has been supremely revealed to us through the living and dying of Jesus, the man-for-others.[69] Taylor asserts that this principle is an inherent feature of persuasive love, through which the Creator Spirit draws humans to greater sensitivity and true humanity. Thus, Jesus commands those united with him "to follow the law of the Lamb in the midst of the law of the wolves."[70] It is here that Taylor believes the Creator Spirit is revealed and recognized as the Spirit of Jesus, the Spirit of the cross, the Spirit of sacrificial "self-giving." In stark contrast, self-centered grasping for spiritual power is exposed as a deceptive counterfeit. It is the Spirit of the cross that indwells the new and

---

67. Taylor, *Go-Between God*, 45.
68. Taylor, *Go-Between God*, 32–33.
69. Taylor, *Go-Between God*, 33–36. Bonhoeffer's influence is evident here.
70. Taylor, *Go-Between God*, 36. He cites examples in nature in which animals have been observed to sacrifice their own well-being and lives to protect their young.

true humanity, just as it is only in Christ and through the Spirit of Christ that the new humanity exists.[71]

Taylor's unorthodox way of categorizing the Spirit's activities is congruent with his abolition of the sacred-secular and physical-spiritual divisions which are, in his view, artificial. With Bonhoeffer, he insists that spiritual truths, the gospel, and Jesus must relate realistically to a contemporary, multicultural, and multi-faith world. He refuses to accept that the Spirit is in any way confined to the church or even to Christianity. In this respect, Yong, Kärkkäinen and Taylor are in agreement. Furthermore, there is a panentheistic aspect to Taylor's pneumatology, as revealed in the following quotation:

> And it is essential for our doctrine of the Holy Spirit to recognize that so much can be said about him which is universal. Just as he works anonymously through all the processes of creation, so to all men of all beliefs at all times he gives the unexpected opening of the eyes, the deep awareness of that "other"—God or creature—the overwhelming gusts of power, the double vision of what is and what might be, the call to sacrifice, the gifts of prophecy and prayer and healing and ecstasy.[72]

Taylor insists that Christ transcends all religions. Having engaged with many people from different faiths, Taylor comes to the significant conclusion that religion is "a tradition of response"[73] to the call of God. He suggests that ambiguity and a mixture of truth and untruth can be found in all faiths because religion is used by humans not only to draw nearer to God, but also perhaps to escape from God.[74] Hence, Taylor affirms that many people in many cultures have had authentic experiences of God, and that their religious beliefs and practices are the result of their reflection on these experiences. He is convinced that the Spirit speaks to humans all over the world, and religious pluralism reflects the various ways humans have interpreted (or misinterpreted) God's self-disclosure. Taylor goes on to propose that the Spirit works continually to draw all people towards Christ, even from within their own religious framework. Indeed, Christ challenges all religious

---

71. "We are the new humanity, inasmuch as the Go-Between Spirit makes us one with Christ"; "[t]he church, then, because it is possessed by the Spirit of the New Man, Jesus Christ, lives the life of the new mankind in the midst of the old world"; Taylor, *Go-Between God*, 142, 112. "The gift of the Holy Spirit is the mutual indwelling of disciples and the Lord"; Taylor, *Christlike God*, 251.

72. Taylor, *Go-Between God*, 83.

73. Taylor, *Go-Between God*, 183.

74. Taylor, *Go-Between God*, 190.

traditions even as he challenged, transformed, and fulfilled Judaism. "[Jesus's] total abandonment to the Spirit sets him free, culturally, intellectually and morally, to stand back and judge the truth of each religious tradition with detachment."[75] Taylor suggests that the Spirit continually transforms all religions from within, even secularism, and he boldly anticipates the evolution of a Jesus-centered Hinduism and a Messiah-centered Islam.[76] In this way Taylor seeks to reconcile his panentheistic pneumatology with his Christocentricity[77] as he endeavors to respect the religions of others and to appreciate that which is godly in their traditions without diminishing the truth of Jesus Christ and the necessity for mission.

In short, Taylor's panentheistic yet Christocentric pneumatology is built upon his vision of the Holy Spirit as the "Go-between God," who is "Communion" itself, and who is the Spirit of the crucified Christ. For Taylor, the Spirit of Christ mediates our awareness of God and of others, opens new pathways, and promotes growth and development, calls Christians to self-sacrificial living, and calls the world to Christ.

3.4 Taylor's *Pneumatologia Crucis*

What was the Holy Spirit doing at Calvary?[78] First, in a mystery that we cannot plumb, he must have been about his eternal employ between the Father and the Son, holding each in awareness of each other, in an agony and bliss of love that must forever lie infinitely beyond our understanding. For Jesus this included both the forsakenness and the ultimate trust. This is a theme that stirred the imagination of many artists. But beyond the inwardness of the Trinity, the Spirit of communion spilled out into other awarenesses: his concern for others, surpassing the pain, and their deepening perception of him. The thief's and the centurion's recognition of him, whatever that means, was the start of

---

75. Taylor, *Go-Between God*, 191.

76. Taylor, *Go-Between God*, 192.

77. "Jesus Christ, who was conceived by the Holy Spirit and to whom the Holy Spirit has been directing men's attention ever since"; "The Spirit always points to Jesus"; "[t]he Spirit-filled life is the Christ-centred life"; Taylor, *Go-Between God*, 36, 61, 177.

78. Wood reveals that Taylor's question "What was the Holy Spirit doing at Calvary?" did not originate from Taylor himself, but that it was put to him by Max Warren. Wood comments that this question is one "which seems such an obvious question to ask once it is asked, although it seems not to have been asked much, if at all, in the history of Christian thinking"; Wood, *Poet, Priest and Prophet*, 116–17.

a turning of the eyes that has been going on ever since. Here in its ultimate intensity is the power of God and the wisdom of God.[79]

This passage from *The Go-Between God* encapsulates Taylor's perspective on the role of the Spirit at the cross. Using poetic imagery Taylor puts forward some intriguing insights concerning the event at Golgotha, namely its Trinitarian nature, its dialectic of forsakenness and trust, and its inclusion of humanity.

For Taylor, the event of the cross is thoroughly Trinitarian. There is a natural tendency to see Jesus on the cross as the abandoned and godforsaken Redeemer, completing his redemptive act of sacrifice alone, because his cry of dereliction drew no loving reply from his heavenly Father or manifested comfort from the Spirit. Taylor, however, does not interpret this silence as absence. He depicts the Father as the suffering parent who observes the ongoing pain and death of his only Son—an agony of full awareness that must watch silently and in apparent powerlessness. As for the Spirit, he is the eternal *communio* and the "In-Othering" God, through whom the Father experiences the Son's suffering, and the one who empathetically suffers with the Son and the Father. Taylor's Trinitarian perspective of the cross is illustrated by two pictures placed adjacent to the above quotation. One is a reproduction of a fifteenth-century Austrian painting of the iconic *Gnadenstuhl* ("seat of grace") in which God the Father holds the cross upon which the dying Son hangs, and the Spirit, represented as a dove, hovers on the Father's chest and touches the Son with its beak. The second picture is William Blake's sketch of the Trinity in which the Father embraces the dying Son while the Spirit hovers with outstretched wings embracing the pair. These images eloquently reinforce Taylor's point that the Father and the Spirit were intimately involved in the event at Golgotha. Indeed, according to Taylor, it is the Spirit who holds the Father and the Son in loving and empathetic awareness of each other at the time of their greatest separation and agony. This means that the moment of dark solitude and rejection at Golgotha does not signify love's end but instead God's full expression of love. Although Taylor does not himself use the term "bond of love" for the Spirit's role at Calvary, his portrayal of the Trinity at the cross captures the essence of this concept that has developed and taken root in contemporary Western dogma.

Taylor suggests that Jesus's voluntary submission to separate from his Father shows his complete trust in God to vindicate him. "For Jesus, this [the cross-event] included both the forsakenness and the ultimate trust."[80]

---

79. Taylor, *Go-Between God*, 102.
80. Hebrews 5:7.

Jesus's anguished prayer to his *Abba* before his capture (Mark 14:36) gives us a glimpse of the depth of that trust. He chooses to drink the bitter cup placed before him because it comes from his *Abba*'s hand. Jesus trusts God to bring him safely through death and defeat into new life and victory. Taylor sees Jesus as "one who lived totally and uniquely in the Spirit" and that "the immediacy of the *Abba*-relationship with God is the gift of the Holy Spirit."[81] Such childlike trust which Jesus demonstrates towards his heavenly Father is inseparable from the love they share, a love in which Taylor sees the Spirit intrinsically involved. Is Jesus's profound trust in God related to the Spirit's presence within him? Following the lines of Taylor's pneumatological reflections, the answer seems to be resoundingly in the affirmative.

Beyond seeing the cross as a Trinitarian event, Taylor suggests that humanity is also included through the Spirit's power. He points to Jesus's concern for those around him and the responses of the thief (Luke 23:42) and the centurion (Mark 15:39) to Jesus as indicators of the Holy Spirit's presence. At the cross, the Spirit of communion and intra-Trinitarian love creates mutual awareness and recognition between the Son and the people around him. According to Taylor, at the cross the Spirit draws humans towards Jesus. He sees this turning of human eyes towards Christ as the work of the Holy Spirit, demonstrating the power and wisdom of God.[82] However, although he touches on the unifying activity of the Spirit[83] and the corporateness of Christ,[84] it is the Spirit's noetic role that Taylor emphasizes when describing the inclusion of humanity at the cross.

Taylor leaves little doubt, however, about the Spirit's subsequent actions:

> I can find no better words to describe what happened next than the familiar opening: "And the earth was waste and void; and darkness was upon the face of the deep; and the Spirit of God was brooding upon the face of the waters. And God said, Let there be light; and there was light (Gen. 1:2–4)."[85]

> The risen Christ is not only a universal Messiah to inaugurate a new Israel drawn from the ends of the earth: he was that before his passion. Now he is the second Adam to pioneer a new kind of manhood. The Kingdom of God is a new creation brought

---

81. Taylor, *Go-Between God*, 88, 94.
82. Taylor, *Go-Between God*, 102.
83. Taylor, *Go-Between God*, 134, 142, 143.
84. Taylor, *Christlike God*, 94, 96–97.
85. Taylor, *Go-Between God*, 102.

into being out of nothingness through the working of the Creator Spirit.[86]

Taylor perceives that with the resurrection of Jesus Christ, nothing short of a new creative act took place through the power of the Holy Spirit, a creative act that was as primordial, explosive, and miraculous as was the first. With the risen Jesus, a new humanity was born, a community over whom God is Father, Christ is Lord, and the Spirit is its indwelling life and power. According to Taylor, as a consequence of the God-human reconciliation at the cross, humanity's experience of, and relationship with, the Holy Spirit changed forever:

> At the heart of this ferment of new life and new meaning was an unheard-of relationship with the Holy Spirit... The Spirit of the New Testament is essentially the spirit of Sonship—which is the spirit of Jesus himself... they are not speaking of moments of possession or exceptional endowment but of a permanent presence; not so much of a power as of a partner who lives in their life; not so much as an individual encounter as of a life in fellowship.[87]

Wood comments that Taylor's tantalizing answer to the question, "What was the Holy Spirit doing at Calvary?," was initially brief and superficial, and suggests that he engaged in a deeper exploration of this subject years later.[88] In two subsequent books both published in 1986, *A Matter of Life and Death* and *Weep Not For Me*, and again in 1992 in *The Christlike God*, Taylor reflects further on the cross and views the event as one in which God absorbed and defeated evil.

> So we do not see God averting evil to protect his human child; we see him absorbing evil, letting it come upon him in the person of his human child, and so turning the evil into overwhelming good. This is the essence of forgiveness...[89]

---

86. Taylor, *Go-Between God*, 103.
87. Taylor, *Go-Between God*, 84–85.
88. Wood, *Poet, Priest and Prophet*, 120–21.
89. Taylor, *Weep Not for Me*, 13, quoted in Wood, *Poet, Priest and Prophet*, 121. "The self-givenness of the Son in the self-surrender of Jesus broke the power of evil, entrenched as it was in the highest, human level of the creative process, and freed us from the slavery of sin"; *Christlike God*, 203. Taylor explains that this idea was drawn from Andrew Elphinstone's treatment of Gustav Aulen's atonement theology.

Although the Spirit is not named in this passage, Wood deduces that for Taylor, the Spirit must be involved in this divine victory over evil.[90] Such a conclusion seems reasonable in the light of Taylor's insistence that the Spirit is present with the Father and the Son at the cross. Indeed, further on in the same book, Taylor suggests that it is through the indwelling agency of the Spirit that Christ bears the consequence of human sin: "The atonement was the supreme substitution, God bearing the burden of his Other's self-destruction. The gift of the Holy Spirit is the mutual indwelling of disciples and Lord."[91]

As we piece together Taylor's various insights concerning the cross event into a coherent *pneumatologia crucis*, the formulation that emerges seems to be the following: the cross is the redemptive event in which evil and death are, through the Spirit, swallowed up in Christ and destroyed in his death; this agonizing experience wrenches from Jesus his wretched cry of desolation, a cry which hints at the Father's own heartbreaking loss of his beloved Son; the Spirit, indwelling the Father and the Son, simultaneously endures their separation and embraces them in divine love, flowing out to include some people in the vicinity of the cross. Although Taylor's view of the Spirit's role at the cross mainly focuses on his mediating role between Father and Son, his linkage of Christ's atoning work *at the cross* with the Spirit's mutual indwelling in Jesus and his disciples hints at the possibility of a much broader and more profound pneumatic unity of Christ and humanity at the cross, and provides a basis for fruitful theological development. Taylor's *pneumatologia crucis* is congruent with his Trinitarian analogy which has the Father as "the Self-giver," the Son as "the Given Self," and the Spirit as "the In-Othering Self." The analogy itself arises out of Taylor's overall relational and communal outlook and is modeled on the theme of divine self-giving at the cross. Taylor's empathetic "bond of love" vision of the Holy Spirit is not without precedent and its conceptual origin has been commonly attributed to Augustine,[92] although David Williams suggests that its roots may lie as far back as the second century, in the writings of Athenagoras and Epiphanus.[93]

---

90. Wood, *Poet, Priest and Prophet*, 121.
91. Taylor, *Christlike God*, 250–51.
92. Badcock, *Light of Truth*, 181.
93. Williams, *Vinculum Amoris*, 15.

The Spirit as the "Bond of Love" between the Father and the Son: A Critique

In his reflections on the Trinity, Augustine seems concerned to discover a relational role for the Holy Spirit within the Trinity, in the way the terms "Father" and "Son" denote relationship. Citing 1 John 4:8, 13, 16 and Romans 5:5, Augustine attempts to show that the Trinitarian member who is rightly named "Love" (as in "God is love") must be the Holy Spirit. First, from 1 John 4, Augustine juxtaposes verse 8 ("God is love") with verses 13 (believers abide in God because God has given them God's *Spirit*) and 16 (God is love, so those abiding in *love* abide in God) to conclude that, without denying, of course, that both Father and Son love, it is the Holy Spirit who particularly bears the name "Love."[94] He supports his methodology by pointing out that the third Trinitarian member is named "Holy Spirit" in the New Testament although it is clear that both the Father and the Son are also "spirit."[95] It seems, however, that Augustine has taken 1 John 4:8, 13 and 16 out of their authorial context, namely, a compelling affirmation and assurance that the Johannine believers are the ones abiding in God *because* they have God's Spirit (ὅτι in 4:13 is causal),[96] and since God is love, their lives must therefore reflect God's loving character. Instead, Augustine appears to use these verses to identify "Spirit" with "love." Second, in Romans 5:5 (through the Spirit which has been given to us, God's love is shed abroad in our hearts) Augustine perceives additional justification for his naming the Spirit "Love," and also "Gift."[97] In the main, Augustine uses this Pauline passage to assert that fallen humanity is neither able to love God nor to obey God's commandments without the indwelling presence of the Holy Spirit,[98] or to affirm that it is the Holy Spirit who ensures the horizontal unity of all believers into one community,[99] and their vertical union with God.[100] Interestingly, in his "Treatise on Faith and the Creed," Augustine alludes to unnamed "some,

---

94. Augustine, "On the Holy Trinity," xv.28–31 (*NPNF* 1/3:215–17).

95. Augustine, "On the Holy Trinity," v.11.12 (*NPNF* 1/3:93).

96. Marshall, *Epistles of John*, 218, 219; Smalley, *1, 2, 3 John*, 250; Kruse, *Letters of John*, 163; Lieu, *I, II, III John*, 184, 186.

97. Augustine, "On the Holy Trinity," xv.17.28, 18.32 (*NPNF* 1/3:216, 217).

98. E.g., Augustine, "Enchiridon," 117 (*NPNF* 1/3:225); "Treatise on the Merits," ii.27 (*NPNF* 1/5:56); "Treatise on the Spirit," 49, 59 (*NPNF* 1/5:104, 110); "Gospel According to St. John," tractate lxxiv.1 (*NPNF* 1/7:333); "Gospel of St. John," Sermon lxxviii.4, 5 (*NPNF* 1/6:492).

99. E.g., Augustine, "Gospel of St. John," tractate xxvii.6, tractate xxxix.5 (*NPNF* 1/7:175, 223).

100. Augustine, "Faith and the Creed," ix:19 (*NPNF* 1/3:329).

however, who have gone so far as to believe that the communion of the Father and the Son, and (so to speak) their Godhead (*deitatem*), which the Greeks designate θεότης, is the Holy Spirit."[101] While he does not identify himself among these "some," it is apparent that he agrees with this idea; one suspects that he may even be the source for this tentative idea. Thus, Augustine portrays the Holy Spirit as the mutual "Love"[102] and "Communion"[103] between the Father and the Son, although it appears that his scriptural evidence for this concept is weak. Romans 5:5 provides stronger support for the concept of the Spirit as God's indwelling presence in believers and hence to *the unity of believers to God*, than to the notion that the Spirit is the love that *unites the Father and the Son*. Nevertheless, Augustine does assert that this loving union is not limited to God, but reaches out to enfold humanity: "The Holy Spirit also, whether we are to call Him that absolute love which joins together Father and Son, and joins us also from beneath, that so that it is not unfitly said which is written, 'God is love.'"[104]

According to Badcock, the titles "Love" and "Communion" may themselves be derived from Augustine's view of the Spirit as "Gift."[105] Indeed, Augustine frequently juxtaposes "Love" and "Gift" in describing the Spirit.[106] However, Badcock's suggestion that Augustine portrays the Holy Spirit as the reciprocal gift *between the Father and the Son*,[107] in the same way as "Love" and "Communion" are reciprocated, has been recently rejected by Adam Kotsko. According to Kotsko, instead of seeing the Spirit as "the gift of the Father to the Son, nor even the gift of the Father and the Son to each other," he emphasizes that Augustine portrays the Holy Spirit as a gift to *humanity*, so that the Spirit who belongs to both the Father and the Son is the same Spirit who dwells in those who belong to Christ.[108] Kotsko goes further, and describes Augustine's "refusal to think of the Holy Spirit as a

---

101. Augustine, "Faith and the Creed," ix:19 (*NPNF* 1/3:329).

102. Augustine, "On the Holy Trinity," xv.17.29, 31, 19.37 (*NPNF* 1/3:216, 219); "Gospel of St. John," tractate ix.8 (*NPNF* 1/7:65).

103. Augustine, "On the Holy Trinity," v.11.12 (*NPNF* 1/3:93); "Faith and the Creed," 9:19 (*NPNF* 1/3:23).

104. Augustine, "On the Holy Trinity," vii.4.6 (*NPNF* 1/3:108). Note that Augustine seems less certain of the first part of his statement.

105. Badcock, *Light of Truth*, 73. See Augustine, "On the Holy Trinity," v.15.16 (*NPNF* 1/3:95).

106. Augustine, "On the Holy Trinity," vi.5.7, xv.17.27–29, 18.32, 19.37 (*NPNF* 1/3:100, 215–17, 219–20).

107. Badcock, *Light of Truth*, 73.

108. Augustine, "On the Holy Trinity," v.15.16, 16.17; xv.26.46, 17.29 (*NPNF* 1/3:95, 224).

reciprocal gift between Father and the Son (5.16)—a possibility . . . that he does not even consider."[109] Here, however, Badcock is right, since Augustine does explicitly link together the Son's birth and the Spirit's procession with the Father's giving of the Spirit to the Son:

> But the Father gave Him [the Son] this [the Spirit] too, not as to one already existing, and yet not having it; but whatever He gave to the only-begotten Word, He gave by begetting Him. Therefore He so begat Him as that the common Gift should proceed from Him also, and the Holy Spirit should be the Spirit of both.[110]

> (Sed hoc quoque illi pater dedit (non iam existenti et nondum habenti), sed quidquid unigento uerbo dedit gignendo dedit. Sic ergo cum genuit ut etiam de illio donum commune procederet et spiritus sanctus spiritus esset amborum).[111]

Interestingly, while the "bond of love" concept is clearly consistent with Augustine's vision of the Holy Spirit as the mutual *communio* and *caritas* (perhaps even *donum*) between the Father and the Son,[112] the commonly used term *vinculum caritatis*[113] does not appear to have been applied by Augustine himself to the Spirit as the union between the Father and the Son, despite scholarly references made to Augustine's *de Trinitate* as its source.[114] However, Augustine does use the term *vinculum caritatis* to refer to the Spirit in his commentary on John 6:41–50, where he writes of the unity of the body of Christ as enacted by the eucharistic sharing of bread, and the rootedness of that unity in the Spirit of Christ. Referring to the Holy Spirit, Augustine declares "O mystery of piety! O sign of unity! O bond of love! (*mysterium*

---

109. Kotsko, "Gift and *Communio*," 1–12; 6, 11.

110. Augustine, "On the Holy Trinity," xv.17.29 (*NPNF* 1/3:216).

111. Latin text from http://www.thelatinlibrary.com/august.html.

112. Augustine, "On the Holy Trinity," v.11.12, vi.5.7, xv.17.27–29 (*NPNF* 1/3:93, 100, 216).

113. Badcock, *Light of Truth*, 181; Karl Barth, *CD*, I/1, §12.2, 470; Bruce, *Gospel of John*, 304; Heron, "Filioque," 313. David Williams notes that some scholars use the term *vinculum amoris* rather tan *vinculum caritatis*; Williams, *Vinculum Amoris*, 15–18.

114. For example, "Augustine carried the present thought a stage further by combining the teaching of the Paraclete sections with that of their context. The Spirit, according to him, is the bond of love (*vinculum caritatis*) who binds the Father and the Son together and is the full expression of the love which flows between the Lover and the Beloved"; Bruce, *Gospel of John*, 304. "Thus the Spirit is the bond of love (*vinculum caritatis*) between the Father and the Son ("On the Holy Trinity," xv.17.29). This conviction gradually permeated the Western church, as one may see, for example, at the Council of Toledo in 589"; Heron, "Filioque," 313. Both Bruce and Heron cite Augustine's "On the Holy Trinity," but the term "*vinculum caritatis*" is not found in the passage they refer to.

pietatis, signum unitatis, vinculum caritatis)."[115] Note that here, the Spirit is the "bond of love" *between believers and Christ*, not between the Father and the Son. Significantly, John Calvin emphasizes that the Holy Spirit is the bond that unites believers to Christ; even when he highlights that the Holy Spirit "is called 'Spirit of Christ' not only because Christ, as eternal Word of God, is joined in the same Spirit with the Father," Calvin himself does not refer to the Spirit as the "bond of love" between the Father and the Son.[116] Nevertheless, this latter meaning has become popular, and its concept has become embedded in Western pneumatological reflection. Karl Barth, for whom the intra-Trinitarian "bond of love" idea anchors his commitment to the *filioque*, uses the term without attributing it directly to Augustine, but rather to "*the train of Augustine,*" meaning Augustine's disciples.[117]

> [T]he begetter and the begotten are together the origin of the Holy Spirit, and so the origin of their unity. The Holy Spirit has been called the *vinculum caritatis* . . . It is God's good will and resolve that His relationship to us should be comprehended in His being, in the begetting of the Son; that we may be called His children in Him, in the Son through the Holy Spirit, through the same *vinculum caritatis* which unites the Father and the Son.[118]

John Taylor extends the concept of the Spirit as the intra-Trinitarian "bond of love" to the Spirit's role at the cross, and this perspective of *pneumatologia crucis* is also initially held by Jürgen Moltmann, asserting the Spirit is "the link joining the bond between the Father and the Son, with their separation,"[119] and that "the Spirit is the binding force that locks the union and the separation of the Father and the Son together."[120] Although Moltmann later moves in a different conceptual direction, the "bond of love" view of *pneumatologia crucis* has stimulated the theological imagination of other scholars. For example, according to Keith Clements, "[i]n the cross, the Spirit endured the most extreme tension conceivable, between the holiness of the Father and the forsakenness of the Son made one with alienated, sinful flesh." [121] Alan E. Lewis writes, "Of course, that the Father and the Son hold to each

---

115. Augustine, "Gospel of St. John," tractate xxvi.13 (*NPNF* 1/7:172). This phrase has become part of the eucharistic liturgy in Catholic tradition, with the substitution of "*sacramentum*" for "*mysterium*."

116. Calvin, *Institutes*, iii.1.1, 2 (McNeill, 538, 539).

117. Barth, *CD*, I/1, §12.2, 470; italics added. See chapter 7, §7.1 in this book.

118. Barth, *Dogmatics in Outline*, 44–45.

119. Moltmann, *Trinity and the Kingdom*, 82.

120. Moltmann, "Trinitarian Story," 77–78; see chapter 4, §4.4 of this book.

121. Clements, "Atonement and the Holy Spirit," 170.

other in mutual love precisely where, for the sake of love, they are radically sundered by death, is the act of the Spirit, that bond or chain of love between the Father and the Son."[122] In more prosaic language, Gary Badcock comments that "[b]uilding on the traditional Western view, which understands the Holy Spirit's personal character in terms of the relation of love bonding the Father and the Son together, the theology of the cross is thus able to assume a pneumatological form."[123] Note that Taylor, Moltmann and Badcock, like many others, accept the Trinitarian concept of the Spirit as the "bond of love" between the Father and the Son as established biblical doctrine, and apply it unreservedly to the Spirit's role at the cross.

Lyle Dabney, one of Jürgen Moltmann's doctoral students, correctly and incisively perceives that the death and resurrection of Jesus Christ is nothing less than a Trinitarian God-event (*dreieinigen Gottesgechehen*) through which the Holy Spirit's identity is revealed.[124] "Thus the Spirit of God is revealed in the history of the Son; he is accordingly the *Spiritus Crucis*, the Spirit of the devotion [*Hingabe*] and resurrection of Jesus Christ. Only in this God-event is the Spirit of God located and this is the way he is identified."[125] Dabney emphatically asserts that the Spirit is present with the Son at the cross. Accepting the premise that the Spirit is the intra-Trinitarian *vinculum caritatis* between the Father and the Son, he modifies this "bond of love" idea for the Spirit's role at the cross.[126] He points out that Spirit-endowment and divine sonship are interconnected, stating that the Son of God is one "whose life and work in its entirety is defined by the Spirit of God"[127] and "the sonship of Jesus Christ is rooted in his relationship to the Spirit."[128] This divine sonship does not mean earthly exaltation or exclusion from suffering, but the exact opposite. Dabney reminds us that according to Mark's Gospel, it is *the Spirit* who drives out Jesus (ἐκβάλλει) into the wilderness to be tempted (Mark 1:12). According to Dabney, when Jesus addresses God as "*Abba*,

---

122. Lewis, *Between Cross and Resurrection*, 251.

123. Badcock, *Light of Truth*, 185. See also McIlroy, "Relational and Trinitarian Theology," 28.

124. Dabney, *Die Kenosis des Geistes*, 116.

125. "*Der Geist Gottes wird also in der Geschichte des Sohnes offenbar; er ist dementsprechend der Spiritus Crucis, der Geist der Hingabe und Auferstehung Jesu Christi. Allen in diesem Gottesgeschehen ist der Geist Gottes zu lokalisieren und auf diese Weise zu identifizieren.*"; Dabney, *Die Kenosis des Geistes*, 121.

126. Dabney, *Die Kenosis des Geistes*, 90, 116–57. Like many, Dabney also uses the term "*vinculum caritatis*" which he attributes to Augustine, but this actual term is not present in any of Augustine's writings which Dabney cites.

127. Dabney, "Naming the Spirit," 47.

128. Dabney, "Naming the Spirit," 56.

Father" in Gethsemane (Mark 14:36), such a relational address indicates the Spirit's activity *in Jesus*.[129] He comes to this view on the basis that Romans 8:15 and Galatians 4:6 show that the early church identified such an address as "the 'witness' of the Holy Spirit that one is a child of God."[130] In short, he conflates Mark 14:36 with Romans 8:15 and Galatians 4:6, concluding that the Spirit enables *Jesus* to address God as *Abba*, rather than that *believers* are enabled by the Spirit to do the same, simply because the Spirit is the Spirit of *the Son*. Notwithstanding the questionable logic of his conflation, Dabney certainly sees in Hebrews 9:14 strong support for the role of the Spirit at the cross.[131] Based on his premise that "[i]t is, then, as the Christ, the one defined by the Spirit of God, that Jesus freely takes up the suffering of the cross,"[132] Dabney suggests that Jesus's cry of desolation on the cross, in which he no longer addresses God as *Abba*, as evidence of the negation of divine sonship, and thus the "abnegation" or rejection of the Spirit's work.[133] "For at his death the cry of Jesus speaks not of intimate sonship but of loss, of estrangement and desolation . . . Jesus dies, therefore, not simply as '*the abandoned Son of God*,' but as '*the one who in his abandonment experienced the utter negation of himself as the Son of God*.'"[134] According to Dabney, it is not that the Spirit is absent at the cross, but rather that the Spirit represents "*the presence of God with the Son in the absence of the Father*"[135] and "*the living God in the death of the Father's Son*,"[136] so that the cross is a kenotic event for the Spirit[137] even as it is a kenotic event for the Son.[138] Dabney suggests that since the Son experi-

---

129. Dabney, *Die Kenosis des Geistes*, 143.

130. Dabney, "Naming the Spirit," 48.

131. "There we read of Jesus 'who through the eternal Spirit offered himself without blemish' to God on the cross (9:14). The Spirit of God is portrayed here "not as the 'property' of Jesus, but rather as the power that bears his office and sacrifice"; Dabney, "Naming the Spirit," 53.

132. Dabney, "Naming the Spirit," 51.

133. "The Spirit who plumbs 'everything, even the depths of God' (1 Cor. 2:10), has plumbed even the depths of death in God, and in that death all the life and work of God's Spirit comes to grief. On the cross, the *negation of the Son* means the *ab-negation of the Spirit*"; Dabney, "Naming the Spirit," 56; the latter sentence is the English translation of the German sentence "*Die Leugnung des Sohnes in seiner Verlassenheit am Kreuz also die Ableugnung des Geistes*" which appears in his published doctoral dissertation; Dabney, *Die Kenosis des Geistes*, 154.

134. Dabney, "Naming the Spirit," 55; *Die Kenosis des Geistes*, 153.

135. Dabney, "Naming the Spirit," 56; *Die Kenosis des Geistes*, 155.

136. "*Der lebendige Gott im Tod des Vaters Sohn*"; Dabney, *Die Kenosis des Geistes*, 156.

137. Dabney, "Naming the Spirit," 57.

138. Dabney, "Naming the Spirit," 53–55.

ences the negation of his sonship at the cross, and it is through the Spirit that he is the Father's Son, then the Son's "loss" of sonship must surely mean the "abnegation" and frustration of the Spirit's work despite his continuing presence with the Son throughout the event. Although Dabney maintains that the Spirit accompanies Christ into death itself, and that "[I]t is precisely the kenotic work of the Spirit of life to plunge himself into death, hell and the grave, to 'empty himself' into the abyss of death and raise the one who died on the cross to new life,"[139] the Spirit's activity at the cross seems at best, a "self-emptying," and at worst, an abnegation or utter rejection, until after Christ has died, whereupon the Spirit raises Christ from the dead.

Dabney's interpretation of the "bond of love" *pneumatologia crucis* is based upon his understanding that Jesus's cry of dereliction signifies the abnegation of the Spirit's "son-making" work. It appears that for Dabney, Jesus's divine sonship is fully constituted by the presence of the Holy Spirit in him. Therefore, when Jesus no longer addresses God as Father, but as "God," then, according to Dabney, Jesus's sense of filial intimacy disappears at the cross, leading to Dabney's conclusion that the Spirit's work is nullified. However, this view denies the presence of the eternal Logos, the second person of the Trinity, as the subject of Jesus Christ (John 1:1–3, 14).[140] While it is very likely that Jesus Christ experienced a human's close filial intimacy with God through the mediation of the Spirit, as all human "sons of God" do in Christ,[141] Jesus is at the same time the eternal Son, the Logos. Jesus Christ's sonship is *by nature*, while our sonship is *by adoption* through the indwelling presence and power of *the Spirit of the Son*. Thus, Jesus's cry of dereliction cannot be interpreted as an actual loss of his divine sonship, as that would imply that the Son has abandoned his human body. This docetic view does not square with the biblical assertion that it is God's own Son whom God gave up for humanity on the cross (John 3:16; Rom 8:3). Moreover, it is surely as God's obedient *Son* that Jesus dies on the cross. Dabney's proposal that the Spirit's work is abnegated at the cross on the basis that Jesus addresses God as "God" and not as *Abba*, seems tenuous. A stronger alternative is Barth's suggestion that Jesus's cry of dereliction represents *humanity's* separation from God, that "[Jesus Christ] cries with man in his need,"[142] and "It is at once the death-cry of the man who dies in Him and the birth-cry of the man

---

139. Dabney, "Naming the Spirit," 57.

140. Barth, *CD*, I/2, §15, 149–50.

141. The Spirit is God's "son-maker" with respect to humanity (πνεῦμα υἱοθεσίας; Rom 8:15) precisely because he is *the Spirit of the Son* (Gal 4:4–6). Without the indwelling Spirit, human beings cannot be "sons" (or children) of God.

142. Barth, *CD*, IV/1, §59, 215.

who comes to life in Him."[143] Similarly, Gérard Rossé states, "In the abandonment, Jesus attains human suffering and death—and, more generally, the existential situation of man—and makes them his own in the more painful and profound reality of the 'loss of God.'"[144] "Had God forsaken Him? (Mark 14:36)" Barth asks, to which he immediately replies:

> No, His God had not really forsaken Him. In that strange and scandalous reversal we have a necessary fulfilment of the divine purpose which the Son accepts in fear and trembling as the will of His Father, and which the participants in what is done to Jesus must serve *nolentes volentes*.[145]

Nevertheless, Dabney concurs with Barth in asserting that the Spirit journeys with the Son throughout his journey into the doom and depths of hell in order to resurrect him.[146] As he does so, is the Spirit a powerless shadow or helpless companion to the Son? Can the Spirit's work really be characterized as *kenotic*? While there is certainly explicit support for the kenosis of the Son (Phil 2:6–8), there is little biblical support for the notion of the kenosis *of the Spirit*. In both Old and New Testaments, the Spirit of God is never portrayed as powerless, degraded, or humiliated. He can be grieved (Isa 63:10; Eph 4:30), and he prays for and alongside humanity in wordless groans (Rom 8:26), but that is not the same as humiliation. On the contrary, John Zizioulas presents the opposite vision of the Holy Spirit as God's *power* at the cross, suggesting instead that the Holy Spirit empowers the Son throughout his suffering and death, and raises him up to life.[147]

The strengths of the vision of the Spirit as the "bond of love," mediating between the Father the Son at the cross of Jesus Christ, is the rootedness of the cross event in the embrace of divine love, and it relates the cross to the heart of intra-Trinitarian relations. Love is emphasized over retribution and wrath. The cross of Christ is placed at the theological center of Christian dogma, and rightly so. It is unsurprising, therefore, that the deeply ingrained Western "bond of love" concept has influenced contemporary understanding of the role of the Spirit at the cross. Unfortunately, a "bond of love" view of *pneumatologia crucis* relegates a mainly passive role to the Spirit, while the Father and the Son appear to be the main actors in that event. While there is ample biblical support for the Spirit's role in unifying believers to

---

143. Barth, *CD*, IV/3.2, §70, 413.
144. Rossé, *The Cry of Jesus*, 111–12.
145. Barth, *CD*, IV/1, §59, 239.
146. Barth, *CD*, IV/1, §59, 215.
147. See chapter 5, §5.4 in this book.

Christ and with each other,[148] and for the love between the Father and the Son,[149] there is no explicit scriptural support for the idea that the Spirit is that very love between the Father and the Son, or even that the Holy Spirit is the personification of "love," which Augustine himself admits.[150] Ironically, portraying the Spirit as personified love depersonalizes the Spirit.[151] It also subordinates the Spirit to the Father and the Son, despite Augustine's insistence on their equality within the Godhead.[152] Furthermore, can mediation between the Son and the Father be the limit of the Spirit's participation in the atoning death of the Christ? If Paul's assertion that sinful humans died with Christ (Rom 6:4–6) indicates spiritual reality and not simply an abstract idea, then Taylor's "bond of love" *pneumatologia crucis* inadequately explains how this takes place. In the "bond of love" perspective, the cross is construed as primarily an event within the Trinity, and humanity's participation is confined to the people standing in the vicinity of the cross (Taylor),[153] or not mentioned (Dabney). Notwithstanding its weaknesses, however, the "bond of love" idea has value in emphasizing God's enduring love for humanity demonstrated in the cross of Christ, and if the concept is applied to the Holy Spirit's ongoing work of *uniting humanity to Christ* and not to the so-called bond uniting the Father and the Son at the cross.

3.5 Summary

John Vernon Taylor's theology is molded by his experiences among African tribes and in ecumenical and interfaith encounters. He was deeply influenced by the theologies of Frederich Schleiermacher, Dietrich Bonhoeffer, Rudolph Otto and Max Warren, among others. As a person who loved art, drama, and poetry, his sensitivity and creativity played a part in his emphasis on relationships and community. Thus, his methodological paradigm is experiential, humanistic, relational, and communal, but it is also thoroughly Christocentric and crucicentric. Unsurprisingly, Taylor's pneumatology demonstrates these same characteristics. He himself describes the Spirit in

---

148. 1 Cor 12:12–13; Eph 2:18; 4:4–6; 1 John 3:24b.

149. Mark 1:11; John 3:35; 5:20; 14:31; 15:9, 10.

150. Augustine, "On the Holy Trinity," xv.17.27 (*NPNF* 1/3:215).

151. "We need to exercise caution here so that we do not de-personalise the Spirit by eliminating the Spirit's participation as person in the *koinonia* of Father and Son, relating to them in ways appropriate to the Spirit"; Macchia, *Justified in the Spirit*, 301–2.

152. Augustine, "On the Holy Trinity," i.4.7 (*NPNF* 1/3:20).

153. Taylor, *Go-Between God*, 102. Nevertheless, in his later writings, Taylor hints at a broader participation of humanity at the cross; *Christlike God*, 94, 96–97, 250–51.

unorthodox categories, as one who mediates awareness, compels choice, and urges self-sacrifice. His key theological theme is "self-givenness," and his Trinitarian analogy consists of "the Self-Giver" (the Father), "the Given Self" (the Son), and "the In-Othering Self" (the Holy Spirit). Drawing on Augustine's idea that the Spirit is the mutual love between the Father and the Son, Taylor portrays the Spirit as the "Go-between" God, and was probably the first to articulate a "bond of love" perspective of the Spirit's role at the cross, a view which has become popular in contemporary pneumatology. However, the biblical basis for an intra-Trinitarian "bond of love" role for the Spirit is tenuous at best, although the Holy Spirit's role in unifying humanity to Christ is biblically explicit. As such, the "bond of love" idea applied between the Holy Spirit and believers in Christ rather than between the Father and the Son, may offer a more positive contribution to the understanding of the Spirit's overall work at the cross.

4

Spirit as "Coworker"—Jürgen Moltmann

Jürgen Moltmann is a controversial theologian who has contributed greatly to the reshaping of pneumatology in the twentieth century. He challenges the tendency in Western church traditions to subordinate the Spirit to Christ, argues for a relational, passable, and mutable understanding of God, introduces the concept of an egalitarian "social" Trinity that is open to creation and creation's suffering, and envisages a deeper, broader, and more holistic pneumatology. He emphasizes that the *eschaton* is the ultimate goal of creation and salvation. In the history of Christian theology, Moltmann is recognized for his bold and timely proclamation of eschatological hope in the face of the hopelessness and protest atheism that arose from the ravages and brutality of the Second World War.[1]

4.1 Moltmann's Biographical Context

This brief review of significant milestones in Moltmann's life is not intended to be comprehensive, but seeks to highlight important events that shaped his theology, and which provided the impetus for his pneumatological imagination.

Operation Gomorrah and Imprisonment

Born in 1926 in Hamburg, he was conscripted into Hitler's army at the age of seventeen. On 24 July 1943, the British launched their devastating "Operation Gomorrah." A bomb exploded near him, and his friend beside him was

---

1. Grenz and Olson, *20th-Century Theology*, 170–72.

killed instantly. Moltmann survived. In that awful moment, he asked, "My God, where are you?" That night, he became a seeker after God.² Müller-Fahrenholz insightfully comments that the incident was paradigmatic for Moltmann for whom "theology arises out of a question."³

Moltmann was captured by the British on 15 February 1945.⁴ In the prisoner of war (POW) camp near Ostend, he experienced hopelessness and despair.⁵ Several months after the end of the war on 8 May 1945, he was sent to Camp 22 in Kilmarnock in Scotland. There he became an interpreter between the prisoners and their Scottish and Irish overseers who treated the prisoners kindly. Their forgiveness and hospitality toward their former enemies shamed him profoundly.⁶ In September 1945, the German prisoners were confronted with photographs of Belsen and Buchenwald concentration camps. As horror seeped in, he asked, "Was this what we had fought for?"⁷ An immutable and apathetic God, whom Moltmann termed the God of theism, no longer offered satisfactory answers to the destruction and genocide perpetrated by a "Christian" nation, and the failure of its national institutional church to protest.⁸ This feeling of guilt and shame left an enduring stamp on his theology. He read Psalm 39 and found in it the echo of his own tortured lament and turmoil. In Jesus's cry of godforsakenness on the cross (Mark 15:34), he encountered the Christ "who understands you completely, who is with you in your cry to God and has felt the same forsakenness you are living now."⁹ Moltmann was subsequently transferred to Norton Camp in Nottinghamshire, England, where "intellectually famished" ex-soldiers were nourished by a well-stocked library and an ecumenical cast of excellent teachers.¹⁰ This ecumenical experience shaped his outlook.¹¹

2. Moltmann, *Broad Place*, 17.
3. Müller-Farenholz, *Kingdom and the Power*, 19.
4. Moltmann, *Broad Place*, 26.
5. Moltmann, *Broad Place*, 27.
6. Moltmann, *Broad Place*, 28–29.
7. Moltmann, *Broad Place*, 29.
8. Moltmann, *Broad Place*, 156.
9. Moltmann, *Broad Place*, 30.
10. Among them were Anders Nygren from Holland, Franz Blanke and Karl Ludwig Schmidt from Switzerland, Matthew Black from Scotland, Birger Forell from Sweden, and leading ecumenists John Mott, Willem Visser't Hooft and Martin Niemöller. The camp was set up by the British YMCA and funded by John Barwick, an American businessman. The library was maintained by the YMCA and the International Student World Federation; Müller-Farenholz, *Kingdom and the Power*, 21; Moltmann, *Broad Place*, 31–32.
11. Müller-Farenholz's observation (*Kingdom and the Power*, 21–23) is confirmed by Moltmann's own reflection: "My origin is Reformed—my future is ecumenical!";

Theological Education in Göttingen (1948–1952)

Among Moltmann's mentors were Otto Weber, Gerhad von Rad, Ernst Wolf, and Hans-Joachim Iwand.[12] Iwand's teaching of Luther's *theologia crucis* touched Moltmann profoundly, and he drew deeply from this theological well for his 1972 *Der gekreuzigte Gott* (*The Crucified God*).[13] It was also through Iwand that Moltmann met his beloved wife, Elisabeth Wendel, a theologian in her own right, whose feminist views influenced his Trinitarian theology.[14] From Gerhad von Rad, Moltmann developed his theme of anticipatory promise with its roots in God's covenant history with Israel.[15] Ernst Wolf was a brilliant teacher of church and doctrinal history who, as the editor for major theological journals, helped publish the young theologian's writings. Otto Weber was Moltmann's doctoral supervisor whose blend of biblical studies and Reformed theology made him a compelling teacher and preacher. Weber introduced several Dutch theologians to his students, and one of them, Arnold van Ruler, put him on "the track of the forward hope in eschatology for the kingdom of God and his righteousness on earth."[16] After graduating, Moltmann pastored a small farming community in Wasserhorst, Bremen (1953–1958). Although his pastoral ministry was brief, he notes that "this congregation taught me 'the shared theology of all believers,' the theology of the people."[17]

Encounter with Das Prinzip Hoffnung (Principle of Hope)

In 1960, Moltmann came upon Ernst Bloch's *Das Prinzip Hoffnung* (*The Principle of Hope*). A Jewish-Marxist philosopher, Bloch pointed out the overarching paradigm of messianic hope within the promissory covenant history of Judaism and the resurrection history of Christianity, hope which the world seemed to have lost and which needed to be regained. The solution he advocated, however, was atheistic and Marxist. Moltmann was

---

Broad Place, 87.

12. Decades later Moltmann reflected that "Iwand aroused our theological passion, but for scholarly work we went to Ernst Wolf and Otto Weber"; Moltmann, *How I Have Changed*, 14.

13. Moltmann, *Broad Place*, 41–44. Meeks suggests that of all his Göttingen teachers, it was Iwand who contributed most to Moltmann's dialectical approach and eschatological insights; Meeks, *Origins of the Theology of Hope*, 30–41.

14. Moltmann, *Broad Place*, 327. Elisabeth sadly passed away in 2016.

15. Müller-Farenholz, *Kingdom and the Power*, 21.

16. Moltmann, *Broad Place*, 65.

17. Moltmann, *Broad Place*, 59.

deeply impacted by Bloch's messianic philosophy and asked, "Why has Christian theology let go of its most distinctive theme, hope?"[18] Moltmann became convinced that the solution to the prevailing hopelessness did not lie in atheism. He therefore "set out to search for a *theology* of hope."[19] After a series of essays, Moltmann's *Theologie der Hoffnung* (*Theology of Hope*) was published in 1964. In it, he repositioned Christian eschatology and lifted it up from its doctrinal status as an afterthought, often one of the "last things" to be discussed in systematic theology, to become paradigmatic for Christian theological thinking.

Conflict with Liberation Theologians

At a conference in Mexico City in 1977, Moltmann found himself being vehemently rejected by several Latin American liberation theologians who were unhappy with an open letter to José Miguez Bonino he had published, in which he had criticized the superficial Marxism and revolutionary rhetoric of liberation theologians.[20] During his flight home to Tübingen, Moltmann was despondent, and reflected that although he saw himself as being on the side of liberation theologians, since he was neither black, nor female, nor oppressed, he did not seem to belong among their number. This marked a turning point in two ways. First, he resolved to turn his attention from programmatic themes to more classical categories of theology, thereafter writing a six-volume series which he called "contributions to systematic theology."[21] Second, he realized that as a white male he still had a pertinent voice in liberation theology, and that was to address God's liberation of the oppressors,[22] or as Müller-Farenholz aptly termed it, "liberation theology for the First World."[23]

4.2 Moltmann's Theological Context

Over his long and prodigious publishing career, some distinctive features have remained consistent in Moltmann's theology. First, his theology appears

---

18. Moltmann, *How I Have Changed*, 15.
19. Moltmann, *Broad Place*, 79. Italics added.
20. Moltmann, *Broad Place*, 227–28.
21. Moltmann, *Trinity and the Kingdom*; *Doctrine of God*; *God in Creation*; *Way of Jesus Christ*; *Spirit of Life*; *Coming of God*.
22. Moltmann, *Broad Place*, 230–31.
23. Müller-Farenholz, *Kingdom*, 126.

to be structurally framed by the centrality of the crucified and resurrected Christ, and a simultaneous orientation towards and from the eschatological horizon. Second, a major thematic complex that threads through much of his work, and around which many subthemes gather, is his dialectic of "shared suffering and coming glory."[24] Third, Moltmann's theological method emphasizes solidarity, freedom, openness and praxis.

Moltmann's Theological Framework: Christological Center and Eschatological Horizon

Like John V. Taylor, Moltmann's theology is crucicentric.[25] Following Luther, he insists that "everything is decided by the cross (*crux probat omnia*)"[26] and that "there is no true *theology of hope* which is not first of all a *theology of the cross*."[27] For Moltmann, the Trinity is revealed at the cross,[28] and that it is the crucified and risen Christ who mediates the fatherhood of God and the power of the Spirit.[29] While Moltmann's theology centers on the crucified Jesus it simultaneously looks out towards the horizon of the eschatological future. Without the christological center, the eschatological horizon is empty, and without the *eschaton*, Christ's death is meaningless.[30] This dialectical format permeates Moltmann's theology.[31] He highlights the contradiction and continuity in the cross and resurrection, in that while death and life are complete opposites, yet it is the crucified Jesus in whom eschatological life has begun.[32] For Moltmann, Christ is not the One who

---

24. Even at the age of eighty-one, Moltmann continues to grapple with "God's creative justice which brings the victims justice and puts the perpetrators right"; Moltmann, "Final Judgement," 565.

25. Moltmann, *Crucified God*, 27. Bauckham notes that the crucified Christ is Moltmann's criterion for Christian theology; Bauckham, *Theology of Jürgen Moltmann*, 3.

26. Müller-Fahrenholz, *Kingdom*, 71.

27. Moltmann, *The Experiment Hope*, 72.

28. Moltmann, *Experiment Hope*, 80; Bauckham, *Theology of Jürgen Moltmann*, 4.

29. Moltmann, *Experiment Hope*, 78.

30. Moltmann, *Way of Jesus Christ*, 214.

31. Meeks traces the source of Moltmann's conceptual dialectics from Karl Barth and Ernst Bloch, with critical influence from Hans Joachin Iwand; Meeks, *Origins*, 16, 34–41.

32. Moltmann, *Crucified God*, 174–76. "Now the proclamation of the Easter witnesses that God has 'raised' this dead Jesus 'from the dead' amounts to nothing less than the claim that this future of the new world of the righteousness and presence of God has already dawned in this one person in the midst of the history of death"; Moltmann, *Crucified God*, 175.

will be but who is *coming*,[33] and that "the future is new, and not merely an extension of the past."[34] Moltmann suggests that God's eschatological orientation not only directs history towards the future, but also allows the future to expose the contradictions of our present reality.

Moltmann's Controlling Theme: Messianism: "Shared Suffering and Coming Glory"

Bauckham sums up the essence of Moltmann's thinking with the word "messianic."[35] Others have described Moltmann's theology using the words "hope," "promise," "history," and "love."[36] "Messianism" is perhaps the best word to capture the dynamism of Moltmann's theology, and in particular its christological center and eschatological orientation. It captures Moltmann's emphasis on the promissory and covenantal history of God with the people of Israel, and the cruciform, pneumatological, and eschatological history of Jesus of Nazareth, as the experiential and theological bases for Christian doctrinal development. The term "messianism" also highlights Israel's continued significance in God's history with the world, a personal conviction that Moltmann often emphasizes. However, perhaps the phrase "shared suffering—coming glory" may be added to the word "messianism" to emphasize Moltmann's preoccupation with suffering and theodicy.[37]

The concept of *suffering* echoes frequently throughout his writings. Indeed, Moltmann admits that for him, "the question of God is deeply bound up with the experience of suffering."[38] His theology grew in the shadow of the Holocaust.[39] Moltmann sees the cross event as a "universal theodicy

---

33. Moltmann, *Experiment Hope*, 53.

34. Grenz and Olson, *20th-Century Theology*, 176. Beck insightfully observes that "Advent" (appearance, arrival) and "Novum" (new) are fundamental categories in Moltmann's eschatology; Beck, *Renewal of All Things*, 233.

35. Bauckham, *Messianic Theology*, 1. Moltmann himself encapsulates his six-volume contributions to systematic theology under the term 'messianic theology'; McDougall, *Pilgrimage of Love*, xii.

36. "Hope"—e.g. Smith, "Hope, Theology of," 575–79; Grenz and Olson, *20th-Century Theology*, 171–72; "Promise"—e.g. Morse, *Logic of Promise*, 110; "History"—e.g. Müller-Farenholz, *Kingdom*, 230; "Love"—e.g. McDougall, *Pilgrimage of Love*, xiii, 154.

37. "It was characteristic of Moltmann's theology from the beginning to give prominence to the question of God's righteousness in the face of the suffering and evil of the world"; Bauckham, *Theology of Jürgen Moltmann*, 10.

38. Moltmann, *History and the Triune God*, 26.

39. "When I wrote the theology of the cross, I wanted to express something that had been stirring within me for a long time: How can one speak of God in Germany 'after Auschwitz'? I discovered my own answer in the question: How can Christians speak

trial" which culminates in Christ's death, but whose resurrection becomes the foretaste of God's eschatological answer.[40] According to Moltmann, God suffers in Christ for and with humanity, with the victims as well as the perpetrators of evil. Moreover, he envisages God's solidarity with the rest of suffering creation, through the immanent Spirit. Moltmann is deeply concerned with the current ecological crisis which he believes has been brought about by humanity's objectification and exploitation of nature.[41]

The theme of suffering, however, is only one side of Moltmann's dialectical theology. It is *liberation* from suffering and future participation in God's *"coming glory"* that occupies much of his theological reflection. He uses the Sabbath metaphor to portray God's goal for creation, a real future that forms the basis for hope. "The sabbath opens creation for its true future. On the sabbath the redemption of the world is celebrated in anticipation. The sabbath is itself the presence of eternity in time, and a foretaste of the world to come."[42]

For Moltmann, the messianic redemption is not to bring humanity *back* to a primal state of purity, but *forward* into God's eschatological feast of creation in which God indwells a liberated creation fully and gloriously, the kingdom of God. It is the ultimate Year of Jubilee towards which all earthly and temporal Jubilee Years and Sabbath days point.[43]

Moltmann's Methodological Paradigm: Solidarity, Freedom, Openness, Praxis

Moltmann's theology emerges from his pragmatic view of sin as evil and suffering.[44] He depicts an empathetic God whose eschatological future is a trustworthy reality, and he insists that Christians, as God's heralds, have a concrete political responsibility towards this suffering world.

---

about God after Golgotha?"; Moltmann penned these reflections in the foreword of McDougall's *Pilgrimage of Love*, xii.

40. Moltmann, *Way of Jesus Christ*, 211–12.

41. Moltmann, *God in Creation*, 23–32. Pointedly he writes, "The scientific objectification of nature leads to the technological exploitation of nature by human beings"; Moltmann, *God in Creation*, 27.

42. Moltmann, *God in Creation*, 276.

43. Moltmann, *God in Creation*, 287–90.

44. Bauckham, *Theology of Jürgen Moltmann*, 209; Moltmann, *Way of Jesus Christ*, 127. Moltmann himself explains how he came to see sin in this way: "When I searched for a 'theology after Auschwitz' in 1972, I followed the path of Christ's passion and his descent into hell into such depths of evil that the concepts of sin, guilt, and godlessness were struck out of my hands"; Moltmann, in McDougall, *Pilgrimage of Love*, xiv.

A. Solidarity

The power of Moltmann's theology lies not in his concept of a God who suffers, but in his conviction that God *shares* creation's suffering. God is neither masochistic nor sadistic. For Moltmann, the cross represents God's solidarity with his fallen and suffering creation.

> In the cross of Christ, God took absolute death upon himself in order to give his infinite life to man condemned to death. To recognize the new God-situation in the cross of Christ, however, also means to recognize that [in] the cross, our inescapable suffering, and our hopeless despair exist in God. A theology of the cross must in this way become part of a Trinitarian theology, or else it cannot take up the problem of suffering... God not only participates in our suffering but also makes our suffering into his own, and takes our death into his life.[45]

Moltmann's own solidarity with those who are disadvantaged and oppressed impels him to champion liberty and egalitarianism in religious, social, political, and economic spheres. On a critical note, however, Müller-Fahrenholz detects in Moltmann a "certain romantic socialist glorification of the 'poor people' which was widespread in the 1970s."[46]

B. Freedom

Moltmann's messianic theology is energized by a compelling drive towards freedom.[47] Müller-Fahrenholz suggests that if a catch phrase could be applied to Moltmann's programmatic writings, it should be "kingdom of freedom": "God's rule opens up freedom. Consequently, God's rule is effective in history as liberation."[48] God's "rule" does not, however, imply a dominating imposition of divine government. Indeed, Moltmann resolutely stands against any form of authoritarian domination, whether political, religious, social, economic or ecological, and perhaps this is in response to the National Socialism that had gripped Germany.[49] Moltmann's concept

---

45. Moltmann, *Experiment Hope*, 80.

46. Müller-Fahrenholz, *Kingdom*, 120.

47. "... it must be maintained that Christian faith is essentially messianic faith, and messianic faith is always liberating faith"; Moltmann, *Theology Today*, 22.

48. Müller-Fahrenholz, *Kingdom*, 111.

49. "... he [Arnold von Ruler] wanted to preserve the state in the kingdom of God, but not the church as God's emergency measure, whereas my negative experiences with the state made me turn rather to the reverse idea: in the kingdom of God I had no wish

of freedom is not simply the continuation of the old with certain limits removed, but infused with the sense of "newness" (*novum*). This "freedom" is eschatological, and speaks of radical and transformative change.

Perhaps it is this orientation towards freedom together with his strong sense of egalitarianism that leads Moltmann to formulate his "social Trinity" model of eternal mutual and perichoretic relationships of three divine Persons, united in love and purpose. He restricts the "monarchy of the Father" to the inner-Trinitarian constitution of God—the Father is the origin of the divine persons of the Son and the Spirit; God is not the Father of the cosmos. Moltmann categorically rejects the idea of a "world monarchy of a universal Father" as a model for human society.[50] "Here the three Persons are equal; they live and are manifested in one another and through one another."[51] It is for his Trinitarian model that Moltmann has attracted the justifiable criticism of tritheism.[52] Moltmann, however, takes pains to emphasize that he is not describing three Gods, but one (triune) God whose unity nonetheless "lies in the *union* of the Father, the Son and the Spirit, not in their numerical unity."[53]

c. Openness

Another characteristic of Moltmann's theology is his openness.[54] He engages with voices from various ecclesiastical and theological traditions, religions and philosophies, scientific disciplines, cultures and peoples. For Moltmann, theology is adventurous,[55] dialogical, and public.[56] His is not a systematized and monolithic theology, but one that evolves as he engages and responds to the world around him while remaining deeply christological and rooted in Scripture.[57] This openness is reflected in Moltmann's rejection of the concept of the triune God as a closed circle. "The union of the

---

to see 'any authority and power' any more, and knew that I had Paul on my side (1 Cor. 15:24)"; Moltmann, *Broad Place*, 65.

50. Moltmann, *Trinity and the Kingdom*, 162–66.
51. Moltmann, *Trinity and the Kingdom*, 176.
52. Hunsinger, "Crucified," 278.
53. Moltmann, *Trinity and the Kingdom*, 95.
54. Bauckham recognizes that Moltmann's theology is "*structurally* open—to dialogue with and enrichment from all theological traditions and other academic disciplines, and to the world in its suffering and hope"; *Messianic Theology*, 141.
55. Moltmann, *Coming of God*, xiii–xiv.
56. Beck, *Renewal of All Things*, 102.
57. Bauckham, *Messianic Theology*, 140.

divine Trinity is open for the uniting of the whole creation with itself and in itself."⁵⁸ The eschatological Sabbath "opens creation for its true future ... It is the Sabbath which manifests the world's identity as creation, sanctifies it and blesses it."⁵⁹ Moltmann's openness also expresses itself in a generous ecumenism that threads through his theology, perhaps a reflection of his ecumenical experiences as a prisoner of war.⁶⁰

Although Moltmann's openness gives strength and shape to his ecumenicity and relevance to contemporary issues, his commentators have observed that such openness also has had negative outcomes, namely, exegetical laxity, and speculative rhetoric.⁶¹ Beck comments, perhaps too harshly, that some of Moltmann's statements represent "rhetoric gone out of control."⁶² Müller-Farenholz, however, defends Moltmann's speculative tendency as "the development in thought of a truth grasped intuitively," and that theology is itself "a reflective development of experiences of faith" with a long and venerable tradition going back to early Christianity.⁶³ Moltmann is no stranger to controversy and criticism and seems to relish them. He insists that his way of thinking "is experimental—as adventure of ideas" and that his "style of communication is to suggest."⁶⁴

D. Praxis

Moltmann's theology had a practical thrust from the beginning, seeking to transform society in the light of the coming future of God.⁶⁵ He himself sums up his theology using the phrases "a biblical foundation," "an eschatological orientation," and "a political responsibility."⁶⁶ In his writings and speeches, Moltmann regularly engages with contemporary issues of ecclesiastical structure, liturgy, and ministry, issues of interreligious relationships, issues of social, economic, and religious oppression of people groups, and issues of nuclear, economic, and ecological threat in the world. He was actively involved in Christian-Jewish and Christian-Communist dialogues, and in

---

58. Moltmann, *Trinity and the Kingdom*, 96.
59. Moltmann, *God in Creation*, 276.
60. Müller-Fahrenholz, *Kingdom*, 22.
61. Bauckham, *Theology of Jürgen Moltmann*, 25–26. Despite this critical observation, Bauckham is one of Moltmann's most positive commentators.
62. Beck, *Renewal of All Things*, 118.
63. Müller-Fahrenholz, *Kingdom*, 236.
64. Moltmann, *Coming of God*, xiv.
65. Bauckham, *Theology of Jürgen Moltmann*, 6.
66. Moltmann, *History and the Triune God*, 182.

ecumenical working groups in the World Council of Churches.[67] In addition, he joined the committee of the German-Polish Society and became coeditor of the *Deutsch-polinische Hefte*, in order to "become involved in concrete terms" in postwar German-Polish reconciliation.[68] Moltmann refuses to see "salvation" restricted to personal reconciliation with God, but more comprehensively to include its pragmatic outworking in the struggle for justice, liberty, and equality for all humanity, transforming not only people and culture, but institutions, organisations, and systems.

In short, Moltmann's theological center is the risen crucified Christ, and his horizon is the coming *eschaton*. As such, his theology can be described as "messianic," encompassing Trinitarian empathy with those who suffer, and the anticipation of God's promised liberation and glory. Within his dialectical framework, Moltmann's methodological paradigm is characterized by his solidarity with the disadvantaged and oppressed, by his championing of freedom, by his willingness to be open to changing ideas, cultures, and people, and by his readiness to engage and get involved. These features are apparent in his social Trinitarian model, his religious ecumenism, his strong stance on gender equality, and in his concern for social justice, resource equity, and ecological health. Moltmann is unsurprisingly suspicious of the authoritarian power of hierarchies, preferring egalitarianism. His developing pneumatology shares the same characteristics that pervade his theology.

4.3 Moltmann's Pneumatology

Despite the eschatological thrust of Moltmann's theology, pneumatology was not a strong feature in his early writings. In his *Theology of Hope*, in which he asserts "[i]t is therefore right to emphasize that Christian eschatology is at heart *Christology* in an eschatological perspective,"[69] reference to the Spirit is infrequent and peripheral. Although the *Theology of Hope* seeks to champion an eschatological *orientation* for the whole of theology rather than to explicate the *content* of eschatology,[70] pneumatology is integral to eschatology and merits greater attention than is given in the book. In Moltmann's *Crucified God*, the Spirit seems an afterthought to his Christology. Even in *The Church in the Power of the Spirit*, ecclesiology

---

67. Moltmann, *Broad Place*, 119–30, 170–75, 266–82.
68. Moltmann, *Broad Place*, 82–83.
69. Moltmann, *Theology of Hope*, 179; italics added.
70. Bauckham, ed., *Eschatology*, xiii. Bauckham rightly highlights the christological center of Moltmann's eschatology.

is emphasized over pneumatology.[71] In his first review of Moltmann's theology, Bauckham is rightly critical of Moltmann's inadequate pneumatology.[72] Whether it was in response to Bauckham's criticism or due to his own evolving theological reflection, pneumatology grew in importance for Moltmann, and in the next series of books which he presented as "systematic contributions to theology,"[73] pneumatology came into its own. Intriguingly, Moltmann had planned to write a series of books on the doctrines of the Trinity, creation, Christology, eschatology, and theological method, intending to integrate pneumatology into each of them; but even as he completed *The Way of Jesus Christ*, he strongly felt that it was crucial to devote an entire book to the doctrine of the Holy Spirit. Thus, *The Spirit of Life* became his fourth and unplanned book in the series.[74] Moving from his earlier rather narrow christological perspective of eschatology, Moltmann affirms in *The Spirit of Life* that "it is *pneumatology* that brings Christology and eschatology together."[75] Bauckham later observes that "Moltmann's theology has become more and more strongly pneumatological."[76] Moltmann himself counts his later discovery of the Spirit as "giver of life" as one of the "high spots" in his life.[77]

> In my book [*The Crucified God*], however, I did not get further than seeing a binity of God the Father and Jesus the Son of God. Where is the Holy Spirit, who according to the Nicene Creed is to be worshipped and glorified together with the Father and the Son? What role does the Spirit play in the history of Jesus with God his Father and the history of this God with Jesus the Son?[78]

The features of Moltmann's mature pneumatology may perhaps be summarised as dynamic and holistic, empathetic and kenotic, and messianic and eschatological.

---

71. Beck, *Renewal of All Things*, 95.

72. "The second criticism, acknowledged by Moltmann (*Der Gekreuzigte Gott*, 184), finds his doctrine of the Holy Spirit in *The Crucified God* inadequate. The Spirit in *The Crucified God* is the divine love which overcomes the negative, resolves the dialectic, and opens the future"; Bauckham, *Messianic Theology*, 110.

73. Moltmann, *Trinity and the Kingdom*, xi.

74. Bauckham, *Theology of Jürgen Moltmann*, 4; Moltmann, *Broad Place*, 346.

75. Moltmann, *Spirit of Life*, 69. Italics added.

76. Bauckham, *Theology of Jürgen Moltmann*, 21.

77. Moltmann, *Broad Place*, 294.

78. Moltmann, *History and the Triune God*, 174.

Dynamic and Holistic Pneumatology

Moltmann bemoans the common tendency among Christians to think of the Holy Spirit as non-corporeal and otherworldly, a tendency which he attributes to the translation of the Hebrew word רוּחַ (*rûaḥ*) into "πνεῦμα," "*Geist*," "*spiritus*," or "ghost."[79] The words "spirit" and "ghost," in particular, promote an antithesis between the material and the non-material, and have led to the perceived distancing of the divine Spirit from embodied humans and material creation, and to the conceptual separation between spirit and body in humans themselves. Moltmann points out that the Old Testament usage of רוּחַ as a metaphor for Spirit of God emphasizes that for the Hebrews the divine Spirit can be sensed and experienced in this present world as "life," "vitality," "force," and "energy." Thus, Moltmann's controlling metaphor for pneumatology is "life," or more accurately, "life force" (*Lebenskraft*)[80] and it is unsurprising that he chose *Der Geist des Lebens* (or "Spirit of Life") for his book on pneumatology. By portraying the Spirit as life itself, he emphasizes the immanence of the Spirit in creation. "Through his Spirit, God himself is present in his creation. The whole creation is a fabric woven and shot through by the efficacies of the Spirit. Through his Spirit God is also present in the very structures of matter."[81] Moltmann eschews the pantheistic view which blurs the distinction between God and creation, but holds to a panentheistic view in which God *indwells* his creation without dissolving into it, remaining simultaneously transcendent over creation.[82] Moltmann maintains that God is "Wholly Other," and coins the paradoxical term "immanent transcendence" to describe the dialectical presence of God both in and over creation.[83]

> Finally, the Spirit of God himself represents believers and creation in their sighs for liberty through his "sighs too deep for words" (Rom. 8:26). The dumb sighs of nature and the uttered cry of human beings for liberty are gathered up by the Spirit

---

79. Moltmann, *Spirit of Life*, 40.

80. In the English translation *The Spirit of Life*, Moltmann's term *Lebenskraft* is translated variously as "energy," "power" and "force" (e.g. "energy of life": *The Spirit of Life*, 40, *Der Geist des Lebens*, 53; "power to live," "power of life": *The Spirit of Life*, 41, 42, *Der Geist des Lebens*, 54, 55; "life force": *The Spirit of Life*, 42 (in two places), *Der Geist des Lebens*, 55, 56).

81. Moltmann, *God in Creation*, 212.

82. "By the title 'God in Creation' I mean God the Holy Spirit. God is 'the lover of life' and his Spirit is *in* all created things . . . This doctrine of creation, that is to say, takes as its starting point the indwelling Spirit of creation"; Moltmann, *God in Creation*, xiv.

83. Moltmann, *Spirit of Life*, 34.

into his own sighing. In the bondage of creation, in the pains of the body and in the yearning of believers, the Spirit is co-imprisoned and co-suffering, and keeps the waiting and the hoping alive through his own wordless and inexpressible sighs. We can surely understand this as meaning that God the creator, who has entered into his creation through his Spirit, himself holds created being in life (Ps. 104:30), and therefore also suffers with its suffering.[84]

The idea of the Creator Spirit is important to Moltmann's pneumatology. He draws upon Genesis 1:2, and Psalms 33:6 and 104:29–30 to support his pneumatological view of creation, and his exegesis relies heavily on his interpretation of רוּחַ as the divine Spirit in these biblical passages.[85] Moltmann translates רוּחַ אֱלֹהִים (*rûaḥ ʾelōhîm*) in Genesis 1:2 as "Spirit of God" rather than "wind from God"[86] although both translations are contextually valid.[87]

While רוּחַ אֱלֹהִים in Genesis 1:2 has been commonly understood as "Spirit of God," the word רוּחַ in Psalms 33:6 and 104:30 is more naturally understood as "breath" than as "Spirit." In Psalm 33:6 which states "By the word of the LORD the heavens were made, and all the host by the רוּחַ ('breath') of your mouth," there is a parallelism between "word of the LORD" and "breath of your mouth." Replacing "breath" with "spirit" destroys this parallelism. Likewise, in Psalm 104:29–30, playing on the word רוּחַ, there is an antithesis between "when you take away their רוּחַ ('breath'), they die" and "when you send forth your רוּחַ ('breath'), they are created." Hence in this context, the term רוּחַ is better translated as "breath" than "spirit." Psalm 104 as a whole emphasizes the supremacy of God as Creator, and the utter dependence of creation on God's enduring care and provision for his creation. This psalm affirms the intimate relationship between God and his creation, but cannot proof text the idea that God *himself* indwells his creation. The Old Testament certainly does underscore the vital dependence of living things upon God with the concept that God's own "breath" is the source of life.[88] Genesis 6:3 directly links the presence of God's רוּחַ in hu-

---

84. Moltmann, *God in Creation*, 69.

85. Moltmann, *Spirit of Life*, 41–42, 45.

86. For example, in the *NRSV* the term רוּחַ אֱלֹהִים is translated "a wind from God," while in the *NIV* it is translated "Spirit of God."

87. Wenham argues for "wind of God" while Hamilton translates the phrase as "Spirit of God"; Wenham, *Genesis*, 16–17; Hamilton, *Genesis*, 111–14.

88. The phrase רוּחַ חַיִּים (*rûaḥ ḥayyim*, "breath of life") in Genesis 6:17 and 7:15, emphasizes the Old Testament linkage between breathing and living. In the story of the flood, God mitigates his intention of destroying "all flesh that has breath of life" by

mans with their staying alive, since the verb יָדוֹן (yādôn; LXX, καταμείνῃ) is probably better translated "remain" (NRSV) rather than "to contend" (NIV).[89] It must be stressed, however, that the terms "wind" and "breath" are metaphors, since God does not have lungs, and anaerobic organisms are also living creatures. The wind reminds us of God, and is created by God, but the wind is not God.

Does the description of God's רוּחַ in humans and animals literally mean that God himself "indwells" them? Moltmann seems to think so. By combining the apostolic teaching that τὸ πνεῦμα τὸ ἅγιον indwells Christ's disciples, with the life-giving presence of רוּחַ אֱלֹהִים in creation, he extends the Holy Spirit's indwelling to encompass all creation. For Moltmann, the Spirit's post-Pentecost presence and power penetrates beyond the circle of Christ-followers, and even beyond humanity into the wider "community of creation" and the cosmos.[90] In some sense he is right, because there is only one divine Spirit. However, while the first Christians, who were Jews, recognized a continuity between רוּחַ אֱלֹהִים and τὸ πνεῦμα τὸ ἅγιον, they also insisted that while the Spirit was "with" them in Jesus, it was only after his death and resurrection that the Spirit was "in" them; they even asserted that the unbelieving world *cannot* receive the Spirit of truth (John 14:17).

That is not to say that Moltmann makes no distinction at all between *Spiritus vivificans* and *Spiritus sanctificans*. It is the Christ event through which, according to Moltmann, *Spiritus vivificans* "becomes" *Spiritus sanctificans*. He points out, "The messianic era does not merely bring an *outpouring* of the gifts of the Spirit on men and women. It also *awakens* the Spirit itself in the whole enslaved creation."[91] While the verb "awakens" is an anthropomorphic term, by using it Moltmann indicates that the messianic era affects the Spirit in some way. He suggests that "'[t]he Holy Spirit' does not supersede the Spirit of creation but transforms it."[92] Thus, according to Moltmann, it is not that the divine Spirit is absent from the world prior to Pentecost, but that the Spirit's eschatological presence and efficacy become apparent (or to use

---

commanding Noah to bring into the ark specimens from "all flesh that has breath of life."

89. In the NRSV the verse is translated, "Then the LORD said, 'My spirit [רוּחִי] shall not abide [לֹא־יָדוֹן] in mortals forever, for they are flesh; their days shall be one hundred and twenty years.'" In the NIV, on the other hand, לֹא־יָדוֹן is translated "will not contend." Wenham links the phrase "my spirit" with Ezekiel 37:14, "I will put my spirit in you and you shall live . . ." and therefore understands the Spirit of God as the "spirit of life"; Wenham, *Genesis*, 141.

90. Moltmann, *Spirit of Life*, 8–10.

91. Moltmann, *God in Creation*, 69.

92. Moltmann, *God in Creation*, 263.

his terminology, the Spirit "awakens") consequent to the death and resurrection of Jesus Christ. This is an extraordinary idea and may be Moltmann's creative attempt to reconcile the differences between the Old Testament and New Testament perspectives of the Spirit. While his claim that the Holy Spirit "indwells" creation (and therefore all humanity) does not align with Scripture, Moltmann's postulation that the Christ event effected a real change in the Spirit's engagement with creation, is a useful one.

Like Taylor, Moltmann rejects as artificial the separation of "body" from "spirit." The tendency to denigrate the physical and elevate the "spiritual" is according to Moltmann, a Platonizing influence which he regards as unfortunate. Spirituality has taken "the form of a kind of hostility to the body, a kind of remoteness from the world, and a preference for the inner experiences of the soul rather than the sensory experiences of sociality and nature."[93] This has led to the dissociation between sacral and secular dimensions of life, and the result of its effect on pneumatology has been an overly restrictive view of the Spirit. For the individual, "spiritual" experiences are confined to religious settings, so that day-to-day work and entertainment are not seen as areas that the Spirit influences nor is interested in. Moltmann sees the consequence of this mind-set in the apathy among many Christians over political and ecological issues. They are not interested in these issues because they believe that God is not interested in these issues either. Dangerously, such a perspective allows and promotes the domination and exploitation of nature on the individual and corporate level.[94] In alignment with the testimony of the Gospels and Pauline teaching (1 Cor 15:12–19, 35–54), Moltmann emphasizes that Jesus was resurrected in *body* and soul, and the *eschaton* involves the renewal of the whole cosmos, physical and spiritual.[95] Moltmann rightly points out that the coming eschatological reality in which "God will be all in all" (1 Cor 15:28)[96] demands that Christians should be actively concerned with the health and well-being of the whole of God's creation, not just with humanity's survival.

---

93. Moltmann, *Spirit of Life*, 8.
94. Moltmann, *God in Creation*, 20–32.
95. Moltmann, *Coming God*, 70.
96. 1 Corinthians 15:28 is a key biblical text for Moltmann's eschatology, which he interprets from a pneumatological perspective.

Empathetic and Kenotic Pneumatology

Moltmann's concept of the indwelling God who participates in the struggles of humanity and creation takes specific form in his imagery of the Spirit as the divine Shekinah. He cites Franz Rosenzwig:

> The Shekinah, the descent of God to man and his dwelling among them, is thought of as a divorce which takes place in God himself. God himself cuts himself off from himself, he gives himself away to his people, he suffers with their sufferings, he goes with them into the misery of the foreign land, he wanders with their wanderings.[97]

For Moltmann, the medieval Jewish mystical doctrine of the Shekinah provides a way of understanding God that makes divine pathos the starting point. The Shekinah represents a kenotic "self-differentiation" and "dichotomy" within God which allows God to simultaneously reign in heaven and dwell with the humble and weak.[98] This divine Shekinah kenosis is, according to Moltmann, God's renunciation of God's impassibility, becoming able to suffer with those who suffer, because of his willingness to love.[99] Moltmann defines the Shekinah as God's "special, willed and promised presence in the world" or "God himself, present at a particular place and at a particular time."[100]

The concept of Shekinah developed from cultic language, the belief that God dwells (or "tabernacles") with God's people in the ark of the covenant and later in the Jerusalem temple. The Shekinah manifests God's loving covenant partnership with God's people. Moltmann extends this metaphor for God's indwelling presence among a particular people, to the concept of God's immanence in creation. In other words, Moltmann adopts a specific metaphor for God's presence among God's people and universalizes it to the idea of the indwelling of God in all creation. According to Moltmann, the sinful choices of humanity have condemned God's good creation to distortion, deception, and death. Nevertheless, "[t]he God who in the Spirit dwells in his creation is present to every one of his creatures and remains bound to each of them, in joy and sorrow."[101] Moltmann suggests that God's faithfulness to his creation results in an estrangement within himself, because the

---

97. Rosenzwig, *Der Stern der Erlösung*, 192, quoted in Moltmann, *Trinity and the Kingdom*, 29, 227, n. 22.
98. Moltmann, *Trinity and the Kingdom*, 27.
99. Moltmann, *Spirit of Life*, 51.
100. Moltmann, *Spirit of Life*, 48.
101. Moltmann, *God in Creation*, 15.

Shekinah does not abandon corrupted creation but remains with it despite the Shekinah's own great yearning and homesickness to be reunited with God. "His Shekinah indwells every one of his creatures; but this Shekinah is now alienated from God himself."[102] According to Moltmann, the Shekinah suffers with suffering creation, in anticipation of the eschatological fulfillment of God's glory, when "God will be all in all." Moltmann suggests that whenever God's creatures relinquish their self-seeking and surrender themselves to the will of God, living entirely in the prayer, "Thy will be done," the Shekinah in them "is united with God himself."[103]

Although the idea of the Shekinah is an attempt to envisage the empathetic participation of God in the history and experiences of his people, there are some inherent difficulties with this concept, and with the way Moltmann applies it to pneumatology. First, the idea that "God cuts himself off from himself" implies a dichotomy within God. Perhaps this notion arises from the perceived need to "isolate" God's interaction with unholy sinners, or to preserve God's transcendence while affirming his empathetic immanence in creation. This view of God may derive from an anthropological perspective of material beings who cannot occupy more than one space at a time. Spatial limitation is unlikely to apply to an omnipresent God whose transcendence and immanence are not mutually exclusive. In Scripture, there is no contradiction between God's simultaneous presence among God's people and God's cosmic rule, nor is there the concept that God is somehow partitioned.

Second, the Shekinah model of the Spirit promotes the idea of estrangement within God. The idea of *estrangement* between the Spirit and other persons of the Trinity is not supported by the biblical testimony. It is speculative and leads to theological difficulties with understanding Trinitarian relationships. The notion also clashes with Moltmann's own social Trinitarian model in which eternal *unity* in love is fundamental. Nonetheless, Paul's allusion to the "wordless groaning" of the Spirit who helps and intercedes on behalf of believers who have the firstfruits of the Spirit, suggests that the Spirit empathizes with those he indwells, sensing their suffering and tension as they and all creation await the *eschaton* (Rom 8:22–26). There might be the possibility that the Spirit's empathy signals a reciprocal tension within the Spirit himself, but it does not indicate that the Spirit is in any way estranged from the Father or the Son. Beck rightly comments, "There are obvious Trinitarian difficulties in explaining how the Holy Spirit

---

102. Moltmann, *Spirit of Life*, 50.
103. Moltmann, *Trinity and the Kingdom*, 28–30; *Spirit of Life*, 47–51.

can be alienated from the Father and the Son in the way that Moltmann describes, without his position falling into tritheism."[104]

Third, the concept of the eschatological reunion of the estranged Shekinah with God is reminiscent of the Neoplatonic "return to the One,"[105] and to the Gnostic concept of the eventual recapture of divine "light particles" entombed in humans.[106] According to New Testament teaching, the Holy Spirit indwells those who believe in Christ, uniting them to God in Christ, and to all other believers. While this unity will be fulfilled and manifested in all its glory at the *eschaton*, there is no indication that the indwelling Spirit within believers is somehow alienated *from God* prior to the *eschaton*. On the other hand, believers can alienate *themselves* from the Holy Spirit, causing him to grieve, through their sinful disobedience (Eph 4:30).

Fourth, does empathy signify kenosis? The Greek verb κενόω, means "to empty" and is applied to Jesus who, though divine, "emptied himself" (ἑαυτόν ἐκένωσεν) of his divine power and privilege to become human (Phil 2:7) and to die on the cross (Phil 2:8). Paul is referring to Jesus's self-humiliation and exaltation by God, contrasting it with the human attitude of "empty conceit," κενοδοξίαν (Phil 2:3); he is not addressing the issue of divine impassibility. The idea of "emptying oneself" is not used of God anywhere else in Scripture. Moltmann, however, understands divine kenosis as God's renunciation of impassibility through the Shekinah.[107] This seems to be a contradiction in terms. If God is able to suffer with those who suffer, then this has always been a divine possibility. If so, then God has always been passible. Impassibility is a negative attribute, whereas passibility implies at least the possibility of suffering. If there is no possibility of suffering, one cannot "renounce" or "empty out" something that is not there in the first place. Moltmann nonetheless rightly links God's loving nature to God's willingness, and therefore ability, to suffer with God's creatures. It is my contention that it is unnecessary to refer to God's empathy as kenosis, if empathy is characteristic of true love, since God loves because God is love itself (1 John 4:8). In loving God's creatures, God is simply being God. In order to love creatures empathetically, God does not need to partition Godself.

---

104. Beck, *Renewal of All Things*, 158.
105. Ferguson, "Neoplatonism," 821–22.
106. Borchert, "Gnosticism," 485–88.
107. Moltmann, *Spirit of Life*, 51.

Messianic and Eschatological Pneumatology

In keeping with his overall theology, Moltmann's pneumatology has Christ as its center and the *eschaton* as its horizon. He points out that the English term "Christ" or Greek "Χπιστός," is derived from the Hebrew מָשַׁח (*māšah*, "to anoint"), referring to the ritual and spiritual anointment of Israel's kings. Christ, or Messiah, is therefore God's *anointed* one, who is anointed with the fullness of the divine Spirit. Unlike previous Israelite kings, only Jesus fully succeeds in embodying God's rule, justice, peace, and compassion. In his first book on Christology, *Der gekreuzigte Gott* (*The Crucified God*), Moltmann rejects the two christological approaches current at that time, namely "Christology from above," or a Christology which begins with a metaphysical doctrine of God, and "Christology from below," a Christology from an anthropological perspective, because he percieves that both approaches ignore the messianic history of Jesus.[108] In their place, he proposes a messianic and eschatological Christology.[109]

The life, ministry, death, and resurrection of Jesus of Nazareth form the basis and presupposition for Moltmann's Trinitarian doctrine of God and Christology. Encapsulated in his provocative title, *The Crucified God*, Moltmann asserts that in Jesus "[God] humbles himself and takes upon himself the eternal death of the godless and the godforsaken, so that all the godless and the godforsaken can experience communion with him."[110] Moltmann perceives that in Jesus the triune God experiences and overcomes death at the cross. Despite insisting that only a Trinitarian perspective of the cross avoids patripassianism in Christ's incarnational death, Moltmann initially devotes his attention to the Father and the Son, with little examination of the Spirit's role in the history of Jesus. He addresses this deficiency in *Der Weg Jesu Christi* (*The Way of Jesus Christ*), published nineteen years after *The Crucified God*. In this later book, Moltmann promotes a Spirit Christology since "[t]here was no time and no period of his life when Jesus was not filled with the Holy Spirit."[111] He asserts that "Jesus' relationship to God as Son, like the sonship and daughterhood of later believers, is defined entirely and wholly pneumatologically (cf. Rom. 8:14, 16)."[112] Moltmann applies the idea of a pneumatologically constituted sonship to intra-Trinitarian relations in

---

108. Moltmann, *Crucified God*, 85–97.

109. Moltmann, *Crucified God*, 97.

110. Moltmann, *Crucified God*, 286. "God experiences the cross, but this also means that he has absorbed this death into eternal life, that he suffers it in order to give the forsaken world his life"; *Power of the Spirit*, 63.

111. Moltmann, *Way of Jesus Christ*, 81.

112. Moltmann, *Way of Jesus Christ*, 142.

eternity, and comes to the unorthodox conclusion that the Holy Spirit is the divine "mother" of God's messianic Son.[113] Moltmann states that "[the Son] comes into the world from the Father and from the Spirit,"[114] leading to the rather strange notion that the Son has two sources, the Father and the Spirit. This idea differs significantly from his earlier conception of the Trinity in *The Trinity and the Kingdom* in which the *Father* is the eternal source of the Son and the Spirit.[115] Notwithstanding the apparent inconsistency in his Trinitarian formulations, a subject which goes beyond the scope of this book, Moltmann remains constant in his view that the Son is, from eternity, never without the Spirit. On this point he is supported by Augustine who posits that the Father's eternal gift of the Spirit to the Son coincides with his eternal begetting of the Son.[116]

Moltmann applies his Shekinah concept of the Spirit to Jesus. The Shekinah (Holy Spirit) indwells Jesus as the messianic Son,[117] finding its "abiding dwelling-place."[118] The Shekinah "participates in his weakness, his suffering, and his death on the cross."[119] "Through the Shekinah, the Spirit binds itself to Jesus' fate, though without becoming identical with him. In this way *the Spirit of God* becomes definitively *the Spirit of Christ*, so that from that point onwards it can be called by and invoked in Christ's name." [120] Since Moltmann identifies the Shekinah with the Holy Spirit and asserts that the Spirit is the determining agent in the divine sonship of Christ, his claim that the Shekinah also indwells all living beings is then confusing because not all living things are sons of God. Beck observes that Moltmann conceptualizes the kenosis of the Spirit at several levels—in creation, in Israel, in Jesus, in the church, in

---

113. Moltmann, *Way of Jesus Christ*, 82–87. "If the Messiah is called the Son of God, then to be consistent we have to talk about the Spirit as his divine 'mother'"; Moltmann, *Way of Jesus Christ*, 86.

114. Moltmann, *Way of Jesus Christ*, 86.

115. "But the inner coherence immediately becomes perceptible when we understand the Son as *the Word* (Logos). The Father utters his eternal Word in the eternal breathing out of his Spirit. There is in God no Word without the Spirit, and no Spirit without the Word. In this respect the uttering of the Word and the issuing of the Spirit belong indissolubly together"; Moltmann, *Trinity and the Kingdom*, 169–70.

116. "But the Father gave Him [the Son] this [the Spirit] too, not as to one already existing, and not yet having it; but whatever He gave to the only-begotten Word, He gave by begetting Him. Therefore He so begat Him as that the common Gift should proceed from Him also, and the Holy Spirit should be the Spirit of both"; Augustine, "On the Holy Trinity," xv.17.29 (NPNF 1/3:216).

117. Moltmann, *Way of Jesus Christ*, 85–86.

118. Moltmann, *Way of Jesus Christ*, 90.

119. Moltmann, *Way of Jesus Christ*, 93.

120. Moltmann, *Spirit of Life*, 62.

believers.[121] Moltmann's universalization of the concept of "kenosis" seems to overextend a concept based on particularity.

Less controversially, Moltmann asserts that the Holy Spirit constitutes not only the Messiah but also the messianic people of God by his indwelling presence. Prior to his exaltation, Jesus is the bearer of the Spirit; after his resurrection, Jesus becomes the Spirit-giver, the one through whom the Father pours out the eschatological Spirit. "Here it cannot be forgotten that in the whole of the New Testament the Spirit is understood eschatologically."[122] The Spirit unites Christ's followers to God through Christ, and "the whole people will itself be made a bearer of the Spirit."[123] Thus the unifying Holy Spirit creates, in the messianic people, the true "temple" of God, which is the body of Christ. The Spirit of God is the Spirit of Christ, and the messianic people are, by definition, a pneumatic people. The Spirit glorifies the Son, and the Father through the Son, and this glorification is the "consummation of creation."[124] In this present age, the existence of God's messianic people heralds to the rest of the world God's coming kingdom and the eschatological destiny of the cosmos.[125] Since it is through the Spirit that Christ comes, and through Christ that the Spirit is poured out, the Spirit's eschatological history cannot be understood apart from Christ or from the cross. As Moltmann writes:

> The true perception that the messianic history of Christ from his incarnation to his exaltation is the work of the eschatological Spirit must not pass by Christ's death on the cross, through which the Father, in the Spirit of self-giving, has become the Father of forsaken men and women. The transfiguration of Christ in the Spirit of glory must not be allowed to cast so dazzling a light that our eyes are blinded to his death in abandonment by God. Pneumatic Christology is only realistic when it is developed into the Trinitarian theology of the cross.[126]

To sum up, Moltmann's pneumatological vision develops over time. Shaped by his Christocentric focus and eschatological orientation, and by his methodological paradigm of solidarity, freedom, openness, and praxis, Moltmann's mature pneumatology is characterized by its emphasis on the

---

121. Beck, *Renewal of All Things*, 159–60. Despite his discomfort with Moltmann's idea of estrangement between the Shekinah and God, Beck accepts Moltmann's premise that the Spirit only indwells through the process of kenosis.

122. Moltmann, *Trinity and the Kingdom*, 89.

123. Moltmann, *Spirit of Life*, 55.

124. Moltmann, *Trinity and the Kingdom*, 126.

125. Moltmann, *Spirit of Life*, 55–57.

126. Moltmann, *Power of the Spirit*, 37.

dynamic vitality and holistic inclusiveness of the Spirit, the Spirit's empathetic and kenotic participation in the struggles and suffering of humanity and creation, the Spirit's messianic indwelling and empowerment of Christ and his followers, and the Spirit's role as the agent of the *eschaton*. Moltmann uses the Jewish kabbalistic doctrine of the Shekinah as a metaphor for the Holy Spirit, extending its original application, perhaps ill-advisedly, from God's particular presence among his people, to a universal vision of the Spirit's habitation in all creation. By this, he attempts to reconcile the Old Testament portrayal of God's רוּחַ with the New Testament description of τὸ πνεῦμα τὸ ἅγιον. Moltmann's focus on the crucified and risen Christ, and growing pneumatological emphasis, led him, unsurprisingly, to an enduring interest in the role of the Spirit at the cross.

4.4 Moltmann's Pneumatologia Crucis

In the same way that Moltmann's pneumatology evolves, likewise his *pneumatologia crucis*. His initial thought in *The Crucified God* (*Der Gekreuzigte Gott*, 1972) is that the Spirit "proceeds" from the event at the cross between the Father and the Son. Shortly after, he champions the idea of the Spirit as "the bond of love" uniting the Father and the Son at the cross, an idea he held onto for over a decade (1974–1989).[127] Subsequently, in *The Spirit of Life* (*Der Geist des Lebens*, 1991) and thereafter, he argues for the Spirit's role as the Son's coworker at the cross. It is intriguing that Hebrews 9:14, which becomes the key biblical text in Moltmann's development of a *pneumatologia crucis* particularly after 1974, has been the same basis for his different perspectives. This section will examine in turn each of Moltmann's three pneumatological formulations.

The Spirit Proceeds from the Cross

In *The Crucified God*, Moltmann makes these extraordinary statements:

> In the cross, Father and Son are most deeply separated in forsakenness and at the same time are most inwardly one in their surrender. What *proceeds from* this event between Father and Son is the Spirit which justifies the godless, fills the forsaken with love and even brings the dead alive, since even the fact that

---

127. Moltmann, "The Crucified God"; *Power of the Spirit* (1975); *Experiment Hope* (1975); *Trinity and the Kingdom* (1980); *Humanity in God* (1983); and *Way of Jesus Christ* (1989). The year of publication of Moltmann's books refer to the year the German originals were published.

they are dead cannot exclude them from this event of the cross; the death in God also includes them.[128]

The Son suffers in his love being forsaken by the Father as he dies. The Father suffers in his love the grief of the death of the Son. In that case, whatever *proceeds from* the event between the Father and the Son must be understood as the spirit of the surrender of the Father and the Son, as the spirit which creates love for forsaken men, as the spirit which brings the dead alive.[129] It is the unconditioned and therefore boundless love which proceeds from the grief of the Father and the dying of the Son and reaches forsaken men in order to create in them the possibility and the force of new life.[130]

Because this death took place in the history between the Father and the Son on the cross on Golgotha, there *proceeds from* it the spirit of life, love and election to salvation.[131]

Anyone who speaks of God in Christian terms must tell of the history of Jesus as a history between the Son and the Father. In that case, "God" is not another nature or a heavenly person or a moral authority, but in fact an "event." However, it is not the event of co-humanity, but the event of Golgotha, the event of the love of the Son and the grief of the Father from which the Spirit who opens up the future and creates life in fact *derives*.[132][EXT]

What leads Moltmann to make these assertions? His main concern in *The Crucified God* is to develop a theology of the crucified Christ as a theological response to the spiritual crisis in Christianity in the aftermath of the Holocaust. For the survivors of World War II, "[a] theology which did not speak of God in the sight of the one who was abandoned and crucified would have nothing to say to us then."[133] For Moltmann, God revealed his love and Trinitarian identity in the crucified Christ.[134] Dissatisfied with the view that portrays God as a remote and wrathful judge, Moltmann comes

---

128. Moltmann, *Crucified God*, 252; italics added.

129. In German, all nouns are capitalized, thus it is the English translator who has rendered *Geist* here as "spirit" rather than "Spirit." It is likely that Moltmann has the Holy Spirit in view, since it is the Spirit who "creates love" and "brings the dead alive."

130. Moltmann, *Crucified God*, 253; italics added.

131. Moltmann, *Crucified God*, 255; italics added.

132. Moltmann, *Crucified God*, 255; italics added.

133. Moltmann, *Crucified God*, xvii.

134. Moltmann, *Crucified God*, 254.

to the conclusion that only a Trinitarian theology of the cross encompasses the New Testament affirmation that "God is love" and that God reconciled the world to himself in the godforsaken crucified Christ. Moltmann's contention is that God did "die" at the cross—not the triune God but God the Son, the Second Person of the Trinity. Thus "God is dead and yet is not dead."[135] This concept underpins Moltmann's vision of God's empathy with the godforsaken and the godless, an empathy which signifies incarnational participation, not just sympathy. For Moltmann, God himself, in Christ, bears the world's evil and overcomes it.

If the Son died, then what of the Father? Here Moltmann sees the divine Father, grief-stricken and bearing the loss of his divine Son. God the Father "gave up" (παρέδωκεν) his Son to redeem sinful humanity, as his freely willed and loving sacrifice (Rom 8:31).[136] It is clear that Moltmann's preoccupation is with the Father and the Son at the cross. A *Trinitarian* theology of the cross, however, necessarily involves the Spirit. It is at this point that Moltmann seems to take an unexpected turn. Having cited Bernhard Steffen's assertion that the strongest biblical basis for a belief in the Trinity is "the divine act of the cross, in which the Father allows the Son to sacrifice himself through the Spirit,"[137] a reference to Hebrews 9:14, Moltmann apparently overlooks Steffen's words "through the Spirit" (*durch den Geist*) and proposes instead that the Spirit "proceeds from" (*aus . . . hervogeht*) the "event between Father and Son" (*Geschehen zwischen Vater und Sohn*). Yet what Moltmann envisages is significant because he perceives that the Spirit includes (*einschließt*) godless and godforsaken humanity into the cross event, indeed, into the "death in God" (*Tod in Gott*).[138]

There are three observations that can be drawn from Moltmann's earliest formulation of a *pneumatologia crucis*. First, the Spirit "proceeds from" (*aus . . . hervogeht*) and "derives from" (*aus . . . entspringt*) the love of the Son and the grief of the Father at the cross. Second, the Spirit proceeds from an "event" (*Geschehen*) between the Father and the Son, the "event of Golgotha" (*Golgathageschehen*), rather than from divine persons. Third, the Spirit's own actions are not toward the Father and the Son, but rather toward humanity, new life, and the future.

First, Moltmann uses an interesting phrase "*aus . . . hervogeht*" (translated as "proceeds from") to describe the relationship of the Spirit to the

---

135. Moltmann, *Crucified God*, 253.

136. Moltmann, *Crucified God*, 249–52.

137. Moltmann quotes from Bernhard Steffen's 1920 *Das Dogma vom Kreuz. Beitrag zu einer staurozentrishen Theologie* in *Crucified God*, 249.

138. Cross-referenced with *Der Gekreuzgite Gott*, 231–34.

cross event. It is a phrase that appears in German translations of John 5:29, of which the Greek term is ἐκπορεύονται, referring to the emergence of the dead from their graves at the call of the Son of Man on the day of judgment. A similar word "*ausgeht*" appears in John 15:26 which states that the Spirit "proceeds from" (ἐπορεύται, same root verb as in John 5:29) the Father. That Moltmann seems to be linking the "procession" of the Spirit from the cross event with John 15:26 is suggested by his use of the same phrase in his references to John 15:26 later in his discussion on the *filioque*.[139] With his repeated and emphatic use of the word *hervogeht* Moltmann almost seems to imply that the *source* of the Spirit is the cross event. Indeed, further on in the same chapter he states that the Spirit "derives from" (*aus . . . entspringt*) the cross event.[140] Nevertheless, Moltmann has clarified that he did not intend to imply that the cross event is constitutive for the Spirit. Rather, he meant to emphasize that the cross event "gives the Spirit a form."[141] Indeed, his theological construction of the social Trinitarian model demands the full divinity, eternity, subjectivity, and personhood of the Spirit, and in his discussion on the *filioque*, he argues that the Spirit proceeds from "the Father of the Son."[142] Importantly, for Moltmann, the cross event is profoundly significant for the Spirit, so that we can no longer understand the identity, the history, and the relationships of the Spirit (or to use Moltmann's terminology, the Spirit's *gestalt*) without the cross of Christ. In other words, the Spirit is the cruciform Spirit.

Second, Moltmann suggests that the Spirit proceeds, not from divine persons, but from an "event" (*Geschehen*, "happening" or "occurrence"). He uses the concept of "event" to emphasize the reality and concreteness of its occurrence—that it actually happened, both as a historical and an eschatological event.[143] For Moltmann, what occurred at Golgotha was an event which, on the one hand, united the Father and the Son in the conformity of their will for humanity's redemption, and on the other hand, was an event which separated them through the action and the experience of ultimate godforsakenness. This godforsakenness is the consequence of sin. It is the "absolute death, the infinite curse of damnation and sinking into nothingness" that was swallowed up into the "bifurcation" (*Entzweigung*, "break" or "division") in God and destroyed, in order that humanity was set free for

---

139. Moltmann, *Trinity and the Kingdom*, 182 (*Trinität und Reich Gottes*, 198).

140. Moltmann, *Crucified God*, 255 (*Der Gekreuzgite Gott*, 234).

141. Moltmann, letter dated 11 July 2015, in response to my summary of his *pneumatologia crucis* which he graciously read.

142. Moltmann, *Trinity and the Kingdom*, 182–85.

143. Moltmann, *Crucified Christ*, 252, 257.

community with God, for "eternal salvation, infinite joy, indestructible election, and divine life."[144] What happened on the cross was divine unconditional love for the enemy. In this way, Moltmann presents the cross event as an event within God, an intra-Trinitarian event, a joint effort by members of the Trinity.[145] "[T]he death of the Son is not the 'death of God,' but the beginning of that God event in which the life-giving [S]pirit of love emerges from the death of the Son and the grief of the Father."[146]

Third, according to Moltmann, the Spirit's actions at the cross are directed outwards to include humanity into the "death in God," in order to regenerate new life in them, and to bring about God's eschatological future. "[T]hen the Trinity is no self-contained group in heaven, but an eschatological process open for men on earth, which stems from the cross of Christ."[147] It is noteworthy that at this juncture Moltmann does not describe any direct action that the Spirit undertakes towards the Father and the Son, although this aspect of his pneumatological thinking later changes. Here in *The Crucified God* Moltmann attributes to the Spirit the drawing in of sinners into the place of divine judgment, surrender, and love at the cross, to bring to life the dead, to make "sons" out of sinners, and to pour God's love into human hearts. Thus, the event at the cross is not only a Trinitarian event, but according to Moltmann, one in which humanity participates through the Spirit. This is an important concept not only for the formulation of a *pneumatologia crucis* but also because it gives the Spirit a soteriological role, and it places humanity at the cross with Christ. This raises questions for a rigid objective-subjective dichotomy between the work of the Son and the work of the Spirit.

The Spirit Unites the Father and the Son at the Cross

Both Moltmann and Taylor regard Jesus's cry of dereliction in Mark 15:34 as an important key to understanding the cross event, and interpret the moment to be one of the Son's godforsakenness, and the Father's loss of the Son. The vision of the Holy Spirit as the "bond of love" between the Father and the Son at the cross remained with Moltmann for a considerable time, and

---

144. Moltmann, *Crucified Christ*, 254.

145. Moltmann, *Crucified Christ*, 253.

146. Moltmann, *Crucified Christ*, 261. In keeping with Moltmann's pneumatological idea of the "procession" of the Spirit from the cross event, the word "*Geist*" is better translated "Spirit" rather than "spirit."

147. Moltmann, *Crucified Christ*, 257–58.

he repeated this theme in numerous publications, beginning with his article in the April 1974 edition of *Theology Today*:

> The event at the cross is an event within God. It is an event between the sacrificing Father and the abandoned Son in a power of sacrifice that deserves to be named the Spirit. In the cross, Jesus and the Father are in the deepest sense separated in abandonment, yet are at the same time most inwardly united through the Spirit of the sacrifice. From the event between Jesus and his Father at the cross, the Spirit goes forth which upholds the abandoned, justifies the despised, and will bring the dead to life.[148]

While in this article Moltmann has introduced the concept that the Spirit unites the Father and the Son at the cross, there remains within his *pneumatologia crucis* his vision of the Spirit *going forth* to uphold, justify, and bring new life to humanity.

From 1975 to 1989, the "bond of love" theme appears frequently in Moltmann's writings.

In *The Church in the Power of the Spirit* (1975):

> As the Gethsemane story aims to show, Christ's giving of himself to death on the cross unites the Son and the Father at the very point where the separation and mutual abandonment is at its deepest. The Son offers himself through the Spirit (Heb. 9:14). The power that leads him into abandonment by the Father is the power that at the same time unites him with the Father.[149]

In *The Trinity and the Kingdom* (1980):

> The surrender through the Father and the offering of the Son take place "through the eternal Spirit." The Holy Spirit is therefore the link in the separation. He is the link joining the bond between the Father and the Son, with their separation.[150]

In *Humanity in God* (1983):

> The passion of Jesus signifies, at first, an inner conformity of will between the Son, who was delivered up, and the Father, who delivered him up. This profound conformity of will is also the content of the Gethsemane event, and it is established precisely at the point of the widest separation between Father and Son. At

---

148. Moltmann, "The Crucified God," 16. Moltmann reproduces this passage in *The Experiment Hope* (on page 81), published the following year.
149. Moltmann, *Power of the Spirit*, 95.
150. Moltmann, *Trinity and the Kingdom*, 82.

the foot of the cross, the Son and the Father are united in a single act of submission. The letter to the Hebrews expresses this, saying that Christ offered himself as a sacrifice to God "through the eternal Spirit." The Spirit is the binding force that locks the union and the separation of the Father and the Son together.[151]

In *The Way of Jesus Christ* (1989):

> The Epistle to the Hebrews expresses this by saying that Christ sacrificed himself to God "through the eternal Spirit" (διὰ πνεύματος αἰωνίου; 9:14). The surrender of the Father and the Son is made "through the Spirit." The Holy Spirit is the bond in the division, forging the link between the originally lived unity, and the division between the Father and the Son experienced on the cross. It was the Holy Spirit through whom Jesus proclaimed with authority, and performed signs and wonders; but the Spirit who was Jesus' active power now becomes his suffering power. The One who sent him in power to the poor, to bring them the kingdom of God, made himself poor, in order that through his suffering the poor might be made rich (2 Cor. 8:9). The sufferings of Christ are also the sufferings of the Spirit, for the surrender of Christ also manifested the self-emptying of the Spirit. The Spirit is the divine subject of Jesus' life-history; and the Spirit is the divine subject of Jesus' passion history. This means we must even add that Jesus suffered death in "the power of indestructible life" (Heb. 7:16), and through this power "of the eternal Spirit" (Heb. 9:14) in his death destroyed death. Consequently, through the slain Christ, indestructible life is opened up to all the dying.[152]

These four passages all share in common Moltmann's affirmation of the Holy Spirit as the one through whom Jesus offers himself as a sacrifice to God, and as the one who unites the forsaking Father and the godforsaken Son. Having largely ignored Hebrews 9:14 in his first pneumatological formulation in *The Crucified God*, this text now becomes central to Moltmann's pneumatology of the cross. He interprets "through the eternal Spirit" as a reference to the Spirit's unifying activity between the Father and the Son on the cross, for which he uses the related nouns *Verbindung* ("link") and *Verbindende* ("bond" or "bandage"). Indeed, after 1975 Moltmann confines the Spirit's unifying activity to the Godhead and no longer emphasizes the Spirit's *procession* from the cross event towards humanity.

---

151. Moltmann, "Trinitarian Story," 77–78. Interestingly, on page 79 there is a reproduction of a painting, entitled "*Gnadenstuhl*, the Seat of Grace," similar to the fifteenth century painting of the Trinity in Taylor's book *Go-Between God*.

152. Moltmann, *Way of Jesus Christ*, 174.

In *The Way of Jesus Christ*, Moltmann makes two changes in his *pneumatologia crucis*. First, Moltmann limits the "bond of love" concept to one sentence, while he describes in far greater depth the Spirit's empowerment of Jesus for ministry and submission to suffering and death. Importantly, the phrase "through the Spirit" of Hebrews 9:14 now not only refers to the Spirit's function as the link between the Father and the Son at the cross but is extended to include Jesus's pneumatic empowerment. The Spirit enables Jesus to die the death that destroys death. Second, it is through "the slain Christ" that "indestructible life is opened up to all the dying." "Indestructible life," however, is Moltmann's cipher for the Spirit. Perhaps this hints at Moltmann's return to his earlier concept of the Spirit's inclusion of humanity at the cross. Nonetheless it is now through the person of Christ and not through the cross event that the Spirit flows out towards humanity. It seems that with *The Way of Jesus Christ* Moltmann begins to move away from a simplistic "bond of love" model of *pneumatologia crucis*.

How does Moltmann's "bond of love" pneumatological model compare with Taylor's? At first glance, there seems little difference between the two formulations. Both adopt the Augustinian image of the Spirit as *communio* between the Father and the Son to envisage the Spirit's role at the cross. Both suggest that the Spirit flows out to involve humanity in the cross event, although Moltmann is less consistent in maintaining this point. They differ in one, albeit small, detail. Taylor suggests that it is through the Spirit that the Father and the Son remain in loving empathetic *awareness* of each other even while they are separated. Taylor does not himself use the term "bond of love" for the Spirit at the cross. Moltmann concretizes the role of the Spirit from engendering "awareness" to becoming a "link" or "bond" uniting the Father and the Son. Myk Habets, however, rightly considers that Jesus's cry of dereliction is not an indication of "an actual separation of the Son from the Father in the ontological realm of the Godhead (immanent Trinity)."[153]

Oddly enough, in *The Trinity and the Kingdom* Moltmann makes contradictory statements regarding the concept of the Holy Spirit as the "bond of love" (*Band der Liebe*) linking (*verbindet*) the Father and the Son. While he himself utilizes this concept for the Spirit's activity at the cross, using the same terminology, he rightly criticizes Barth for applying this very pneumatological model to *eternal* intra-Trinitarian relationships.

> The Spirit is [for Barth] merely the common bond of love linking the Father with the Son. He is "the power that joins the Father and the Son." But this bond is already given with the relationship of the Father to his beloved Son and vice versa. The Father

---

153. Habets, *Anointed Son*, 166, n. 189.

and the Son are already one in their relationship to one another, the relationship of eternal generation and eternal self-giving. In order to think of their mutual relationship as love, there is no need for a third Person in the Trinity. If the Spirit is only termed the unity of what is separated, then he loses every centre of activity. He is then an energy but not a person. He is then a relationship, but not a subject.[154]

Moltmann correctly observes that if the Holy Spirit is understood to be nothing more than the mutual love between the Father and the Son in eternity, then the personhood of the Spirit is in doubt. Furthermore, the Father shares a reciprocal and direct relationship with the Son, needing no intermediaries. Indeed, Moltmann criticizes Augustine himself for proposing this very idea because it essentially reduces the Trinity to a duality, writing, "Ever since Augustine, whenever the Spirit is merely termed the *vinculum amoris* between the Father and the Son, it is enough to assume a "duality" in God. The third "mode of being" [Revealedness] does not add anything special and individual to the Revealer and his Revelation."[155] Moltmann made this statement in the context of his critique of Barth's supposed modalistic Trinitarianism, and they indicate Moltmann's clear objection to the notion that within the framework of eternal intra-Trinitarian relationships the Spirit should be viewed as nothing more than the mutual love between the Father and the Son. Surprisingly, he sees no contradiction in applying this very same concept for the Spirit's role at the cross. Since for Moltmann the immanent Trinity must be understood from the economic Trinity, he undermines the consistency of his own Trinitarian thinking by his commitment to a limited "bond of love" *pneumatologia crucis*. It is perhaps not surprising therefore, that Moltmann eventually develops a broader pneumatological model in *The Spirit of Life*.

The Spirit Partners Christ at the Cross

Moltmann's pneumatological thought evolves over almost two decades, and the role of the Spirit at the cross of Christ continues to interest him. In his *opus magnum* on pneumatology, *The Spirit of Life*, Moltmann asks again, "Where is the Spirit in the death of Christ? How did the 'Spirit of God' become the 'Spirit of Christ'?"[156] He postulates that "the Spirit himself was involved in Jesus' suffering because he rested on the Son and accompanied

---

154. Moltmann, *Trinity and the Kingdom*, 142.
155. Moltmann, *Trinity and the Kingdom*, 143.
156. Moltmann, *Spirit of Life*, 60.

him into his passion."[157] Hebrews 9:14 continues to be the foundation text for Moltmann's *pneumatologia crucis*, as it "stresses the operation of the Spirit in Jesus' passion and death"[158] and "[i]n the 'theology of surrender,' Christ is made the determining subject of his suffering and death *through the Spirit of God*."[159] What has changed, however, is his theological interpretation of that passage. Moltmann moves away from the idea that the Spirit "proceeds" from the cross, and the idea that the Spirit "binds" the Father and the Son together at the cross, to the idea that the Spirit partners the Son during his passion and death.

> But if we remember Israel's concept of the Shekinah, we can say that if the Spirit "leads" Jesus, then the Spirit accompanies him as well. And if the Spirit accompanies him, then it is drawn into his sufferings, and becomes his *companion* in suffering. The path the Son takes in his passion is then at the same time the path taken by the Spirit, whose strength will be proved in Jesus' weakness. The Spirit is the transcendent side of Jesus' immanent way of suffering. So the *"condescendence"* of the Spirit leads to the progressive *"kenosis"* of the Spirit, together with Jesus. Although the Spirit fills Jesus with the divine, living energies through which the sick are healed, it does not turn him into a superman. It participates in his human suffering to the point of his death on the cross... Through the Shekinah, the Spirit binds itself to Jesus' fate, though without becoming identical with him. In this way the *Spirit of God* becomes definitively the *Spirit of Christ*, so that from this point onwards it can be called by and invoked in Christ's name.[160]

In his new vision of the Spirit as the Son's companion at the cross, Moltmann makes four points. First, the Spirit accompanies the Son throughout his passion and death, empowering the Son for his self-surrender. Second, the Spirit kenotically indwells the Son and suffers with the Son. Third, the Spirit experiences the Son's death but does not himself die. Fourth, the Spirit who accompanies and suffers with the Son is the same Spirit who raises him to life.

---

157. Moltmann, *Spirit of Life*, 67.
158. Moltmann, *Spirit of Life*, 62.
159. Moltmann, *Spirit of Life*, 63, italics added.
160. Moltmann, *Spirit of Life*, 62.

A. The Spirit Accompanies and Empowers the Son

Moltmann maintains that as Messiah, Jesus is the Spirit-filled Son from start to finish. The Spirit not only empowers Jesus to proclaim the kingdom of God and to perform miracles but is the very divine power of suffering that sees him through betrayal, trial, torture, and crucifixion. Envisaging what lay before him, Jesus could have, if he chose, escaped. Instead, he chose obedience. According to Moltmann, it is *the Spirit* that enables Jesus to resolutely walk this path of obedience to his Father's will.

> [The Spirit] is the power that makes him ready to surrender his life, and which sustains this surrender . . . It is not the Romans who are the controlling agents in Christ's passion and death, and not even death itself. It is Christ himself who is the truly active one, through the operation of the divine Spirit who acts in him. In the "theology of surrender," Christ is made the determining subject of his suffering and death through the Spirit of God.[161]

Conflating the Markan account of Jesus's prayer in Gethsemane, in which he addresses God as *Abba* (Mark 14:36), with Paul's teaching that it is the Spirit who enables mortal humanity to cry Ἀββὰ ὁ πατήρ (Rom 8:15; Gal 4:6), Moltmann is convinced that the Spirit must have been present with Jesus during his passion. Indeed, he identifies the Spirit as the one who reveals the Father's will to Jesus at Gethsemane, and who empowers the latter to obey. Moltmann's position is based upon the understanding that the filial relationship to God of the "new" humanity is defined by the indwelling of the Spirit, so that Jesus, as the first "new" human, could not have addressed God in such terms without the indwelling of the Spirit. Moltmann assumes that Jesus's awareness and experience of the fatherhood of God is *entirely* pneumatically mediated, an assumption which he derives from the association of the Spirit with the declaration of divine sonship in the biblical accounts of Jesus's baptism.[162] While his assumption can be challenged on the basis that Jesus's awareness of his divine sonship may be determined as much by the Logos as by the Spirit, the fundamental significance of the Spirit for Jesus's messiahship does support the notion that the Spirit remains with him throughout his passion. To put it another way, it does not seem logical that the Spirit would leave the Messiah, whose very messiahship is

---

161. Moltmann, *Spirit of Life*, 63.

162. Moltmann, *Spirit of Life*, 60–61. "In the Spirit [Jesus] knows himself to be the beloved Son. So, the Spirit is the real determining subject of this special relationship of Jesus to God, and of God to Jesus"; Moltmann, *Spirit of Life*, 61.

pneumatically determined, at the time of his chief task for which he was anointed. If the Spirit departs from Jesus prior to his suffering and death, then he is no longer the Messiah or Christ at Golgotha, neither for Israel nor for the world. If he is no longer the Messiah at that point, then his suffering and death cannot be redemptive for humanity, or vicarious. David Lauber misreads Moltmann when he asserts that Moltmann interprets Jesus's plea to his Father at Gethsemane "as Jesus' forced acquiescence to the Father's will in contradiction to his own. Jesus is overpowered by the will of the Father and reluctantly accepts the ineluctability of the events to come."[163] While Moltmann uses evocative language in his portrayal of Jesus's agony of decision, he does not hold the view that Jesus was *forced* to surrender his will. On the contrary, according to Moltmann, Jesus *freely chooses* to obey his Father, and the Holy Spirit enables him to do so.

B. The Spirit Kenotically Indwells the Son

If we accept, however, that the Spirit indwells Jesus throughout his messianic life, ministry, passion, and death, then as Moltmann rightly asks, "what, conversely, does this way of suffering which Jesus takes mean for the divine Spirit itself?"[164] Here Moltmann draws upon his kenotic and empathetic pneumatological framework of the Shekinah. The Spirit is not the Son; he stands over against the Son. Yet at the same time, according to Moltmann, the Spirit is not unaffected by the Son's life and experiences. As the Son's companion throughout the Son's messianic endeavor, the indwelling Shekinah Spirit suffers with the Son, and the history of the Son is also the history of the Spirit. Moltmann uses the term "*Einfühlung*" to describe the Spirit's profound "one-feeling" empathy with Jesus.[165] Nevertheless, Moltmann insists that "the Spirit does not suffer in the same way, for he is Jesus' strength in suffering, and is even the 'indestructible life' in whose power Jesus can give himself vicariously 'for many.'"[166]

Moltmann describes three aspects of the Spirit's indwelling: first, the Spirit suffers with the Son, second, the Spirit undergoes kenosis, and

---

163. Lauber, *Descent into Hell*, 117, also 119. In his book, Lauber focuses on Karl Barth's and Hans Urs von Balthasar's understanding of Christ's death, and he uses Moltmann's views as contrast. Unfortunately, in so doing, Lauber has caricatured Moltmann's perspectives.

164. Moltmann, *Spirit of Life*, 62.

165. Moltmann, *Spirit of Life*, 61; *Der Geist des Lebens*, 74. It is also through the Spirit that the Father experiences the suffering and death of his Son. This aspect will not be discussed in this study.

166. Moltmann, *Spirit of Life*, 64.

third, the Spirit's suffering differs in character from that of the Son. With regard to the first aspect, does Moltmann have sufficient biblical warrant for the idea that the Spirit suffers with the Son, or is the concept based purely upon the Jewish kabbalistic doctrine of the Shekinah? Moltmann refers to the New Testament witness that the Holy Spirit can be "quenched" (1 Thess 5:19) and "grieved" (Eph 4:30).[167] The possibility that one is able to "quench," "extinguish" or "snuff out" (σβέννυμι) the Spirit refers to the attitude of resistant disobedience that alienates the divine Spirit from oneself. It is difficult to infer directly from 1 Thessalonians 5:19 that the Spirit "suffers" as a result of this human resistance. On the other hand, the idea that the indwelling Spirit can be "grieved," "saddened," "pained," or "offended" (λυπέω) by the malicious thoughts and actions of those he indwells (Eph 4:30) is, if not an anthropomorphism, an implication that the Spirit can feel sorrow. Interestingly in Isaiah 63:10, we read that the rebellion of the Israelites "provoked" or "grieved" (עָצַב, *āṣav*; παρώξυναν, LXX) God's holy s/Spirit. Both Ephesians 4:30 and Isaiah 63:10 suggest that the Spirit is saddened by and alienated from humans by their sinful behavior, but these passages by themselves do not indicate that the Spirit suffers with those who suffer. Moltmann also refers to the "inexpressible groaning" (στεναγμός ἀλάλητος) of the Spirit as he intercedes for God's people (Rom 8:26).[168] He sees the Spirit groaning empathetically with the collective groaning (συστενάζει) of decaying creation (Rom 8:22) and the groaning (στενάζω) of each Spirit-indwelt earthly child of God who waits in anticipation for his or her full redemption (Rom 8:23), although the direct linkage of the Spirit's "groaning" with that of creation and the believer is not made explicitly in Romans. Nevertheless, it seems reasonable that Paul does indeed imply such a linkage because he applies the same verb στενάζω to the Spirit, to creation, and to the believer, juxtaposing all three ideas. If so, this gives significant support to the view that the Spirit can and does suffer empathetically with humanity, and by extension, to the idea that the Spirit who indwells and empowers Jesus also suffers with him.

Second, Moltmann extends the notion of the possibility of the Spirit even further with his assertion that the transcendent Spirit indwells Jesus *kenotically*.

> The phraseology about the "descent" of the Spirit on Jesus, as its "resting" on him, suggests that the Spirit should be interpreted as *God's Shekinah*. What is meant is the *self-restriction* [*Selbsteinschränkung*] and *self-humiliation* [*Selbsterniedrigung*] of the

---

167. Moltmann, *Spirit of Life*, 51.
168. Moltmann, *Spirit of Life*, 64.

eternal Spirit, and his feeling identification [*Einfühlung*] with Jesus' person and the history of his life and suffering—just as, according to the rabbinic idea, God's Spirit has committed itself to the history of Israel's life and suffering.[169]

There is no unequivocal and direct evidence from Scripture that pneumatic indwelling necessarily involves kenosis, and it appears that Moltmann bases his idea of the Spirit's kenotic indwelling in Jesus entirely on the Shekinah doctrine. The kenosis of the Son is, on the other hand, clearly portrayed in Philippians 2:6–8. Does the kenosis of the Son automatically signify the kenosis of the indwelling Spirit? If, as Moltmann himself suggests, the Spirit is the *transcendent* side of the Son's *immanent* suffering,[170] would that not militate against a kenosis of the Spirit? Moltmann's references to the "descent" of the Spirit in the baptism accounts of Jesus and God's giving of the Spirit "without measure" in John 3:34 are insufficient grounds to conclude that the Spirit underwent "self-restriction" and "self-humiliation," and that the Spirit "surrenders itself *wholly* to the person of Jesus."[171] Empathy is not equivalent to kenosis, which Moltmann seems to assume. Clark Pinnock is probably more accurate in his nuanced statements regarding the Spirit and kenosis:

> In becoming dependent, the Son surrendered the independent use of his divine attributes in incarnation. The Word became flesh and exercised power through the Spirit, not on its own. The Son's self-emptying meant that Jesus was compelled to rely on the Spirit . . . Spirit is important for understanding the kenosis [of the Son]. Spirit enabled Jesus to live within the limits of human nature during his life.[172]

For Pinnock, the Spirit's indwelling enables the preexistent *Son* to undergo the kenosis of the incarnation, a life and ministry dependent on the Spirit, and a Spirit-empowered submission to crucifixion and the second death. Thus, the Spirit himself does not undergo kenosis but he enables the Son to do just that.

Third, Moltmann suggests that the Spirit's suffering differs in character from that of the Son. Here again, the idea is not based on Scripture, but upon Spirit Christology. Since, according to the tenets of Spirit Christology, it is the Holy Spirit who empowers Jesus rather than the Logos, then

---

169. Moltmann, *Spirit of Life*, 61.
170. Moltmann, *Spirit of Life*, 62.
171. Moltmann, *Way of Jesus Christ*, 94, italics added. Moltmann suggests that in Jesus "the Shekinah found its abiding dwelling place"; Moltmann, *Way of Jesus Christ*, 90; see also *Spirit of Life*, 61.
172. Pinnock, *Flame of Love*, 88.

it stands to reason that the Spirit's "self-restriction" and "self-humiliation" cannot signify powerlessness. Indeed, Moltmann states that the Spirit is Jesus's *strength* in his suffering and Jesus's *power* of self-surrender. Since it is also by the power of the Spirit that God raises Jesus from death to life, the so-called "kenosis" of the Spirit cannot signify any surrender of the Spirit's divine power. The obvious question then arises, "How can the Spirit's indwelling in Jesus be kenotic if the indwelling leads to Jesus's empowerment and strengthening?" The Spirit's empowering role contradicts a self-kenotic state. Looking from a different perspective, perhaps it is the *response* to the suffering that differentiates the Son from the Spirit, not the *experience* of suffering—the Son responds to his suffering in submission, the Spirit responds to the shared suffering in power.

c. The Spirit Experiences the Son's Death

Moltmann maintains that the Spirit "experiences" the Son's death. There are two aspects to this idea. First, that the Son dies, and second, that the Spirit remains with the Son as the latter dies, without dying himself. To begin with, did the Son of God die on the cross? In the New Testament, it is usually "Jesus" or "Christ" who dies on Golgotha. Nevertheless, in Romans 5:10, it is the *Son of God* who dies. Elsewhere, Paul testifies that God sent his own Son in the likeness of sinful flesh (Rom 8:3), that God gave up his Son for all of us (Rom 8:32), and that "the Son of God . . . gave himself for me" (Gal 2:20). The writer of the Epistle to the Hebrews maintains that Jesus went to the cross as God's Son (Heb 6:6), and that it is his very divine sonship that ensures us of divine sonship through the new covenant in his blood. The writer of the Fourth Gospel identifies the crucified Jesus as God's only Son, the preexistent λόγος (John 1:1; 3:16). The Johannine letters affirm that it is "the blood of Jesus his Son" that "cleanses us from all sin" (1 John 1:7), and that "God sent his Son to be the atoning sacrifice for our sins" (1 John 4:10)—God's Son, Jesus Christ, who is himself "true God and eternal life" (1 John 5:20).

But did the Son of God, *as God*, die on that cross? A comprehensive exploration of this seemingly simple question deserves another book in its own right. Suffice it to say that for Moltmann, the answer has been consistently "yes," and by that he means that Christ's death was equally a human and a God event. It was a God event because, according to Moltmann, atonement is only possible for God.[173] God himself suffers in Christ, and endures

---

173. Moltmann, *Spirit of Life*, 134.

death *vicariously* for all sinners.[174] Moltmann asserts that Jesus died as Son of God, the Second Person of the Trinity, and his death is empathetically experienced by the Father through the indwelling Spirit, so that the cross event is a thoroughly Trinitarian event.

> In that case one would have to put the formula in a paradoxical way: God died the death of the godless on the cross and yet did not die. God is dead and yet is not dead ... The Son suffers in his love being forsaken by the Father as he dies. The Father suffers in his love the grief of the death of the Son.[175]

> ... Jesus died the death of God's Son in godforsakenness.[176]

> On Golgotha the Spirit suffers the suffering and death of the Son, without dying with him.[177]

> The Spirit participates in the dying of the Son in order to give him new "life from the Dead."[178]

What then does *the Spirit* experience as Christ the Son dies? According to Moltmann, the Spirit not only "suffers" the death of the Son, without dying with him, but "participates" (*nimmt ... teil*, "takes part") in the Son's death in order to raise him from the dead. By this Moltmann indicates that there is both continuity and discontinuity in the reciprocal relationship between the Son and the Spirit; continuity in that the Spirit maintains his solidarity with the Son through his death, and discontinuity in that the Spirit himself does not die because the Spirit is life itself. This is the reason that Moltmann rightly emphasizes that the death and resurrection of Jesus must be seen as two sides of one event, and cannot be separated. Moltmann reasons that when Jesus died he did not only share the suffering of others who have been similarly executed, but by virtue of his redemptive task, he must have also died the second death of ultimate godforsakenness which is unredeemed humanity's fate. In short, Moltmann asserts that Jesus

---

174. Moltmann, *Spirit of Life*, 135. McCormack and Habets disagree with Moltmann, insisting that Jesus's death was a human death and not a death *of God*, but a death *experienced* by God; McCormack, "Loud Cries and Tears," 55; Habets, *Anointed Son*, 163, n. 189, and 168, n. 193.

175. Moltmann, *Crucified God*, 253.

176. Moltmann, *Way of Jesus Christ*, 167.

177. Moltmann, *Spirit of Life*, 64.

178. Moltmann, *Spirit of Life*, 68. The original German reads, "*Der Geist nimmt am Sterben des Sohnes teil, um ihm das neue »Leben aus den Toten« zu geben*"; *Der Geist des Lebens*, 81.

suffered hell itself.[179] If the Spirit "participates" in the Son's death, does the Spirit also experience hell with the Son? Moltmann's answer is both "yes" and "no." "Yes" in that it was through the strength of the indwelling and empathetic Spirit that Jesus endures the ultimate godforsakenness on behalf of the godforsaken world. "No" in that the Spirit does not die with the Son but interceded for the Son as he died.[180] Rather confusingly, Moltmann also tentatively suggests that, within the limits of metaphorical terminology, the Spirit may have been "yielded up" by the Son as he drew his last breath (Mark 15:37; John 19:30).[181] Moltmann does not elaborate further on this "yielding up," nor does he press the point, and seems not to notice the conflict that he has introduced into his thinking regarding the nature of the Spirit's "participation" in the Son's death. If the Spirit was actually "yielded up," then how did the Spirit's companionship with the Son remain unbroken throughout his passion, death, and resurrection? Where was the Spirit on Holy Saturday if not with the Son?

Pentecostal theologian Frank D. Macchia, for whom "embrace" is a key theme, emphasizes the Spirit's role at the cross.[182] He sees the Christ event as "an event of the Spirit," and the cross "as the place where the Spirit's presence is most profoundly at work as a source of grace in the midst of the worst of blasphemy, sin and death."[183] Macchia's Logos-responsible Spirit Christology is built around Jesus as the Spirit-indwelt Messiah and the one through whom God pours out the Spirit. For Macchia, justification is brought about by the Son *and the Spirit*.[184] In agreement with Taylor, Moltmann, and Dabney, Macchia insists that the Spirit is with and in Christ throughout his suffering and death at the cross, and raises him to life.[185] Indeed, at times, the Spirit almost seems to take center-stage at the cross for Macchia, although it may be argued that he is considering the cross from the vantage point of the Spirit.

> The Spirit who descended with Christ into suffering and alienation at the cross brought to fulfilment the Spirit's longstanding

---

179. Moltmann, *Spirit of Life*, 136.
180. Moltmann, *Spirit of Life*, 64–65.
181. Moltmann, *Spirit of Life*, 64.
182. Macchia, *Justified in the Spirit*, 8, 74, 145, 155–56, 161–62, 166, 176–85.
183. Macchia, *Justified in the Spirit*, 156.
184. In his Trinitarian theology of justification, Macchia uses the term "pneumatological soteriology" pointedly, asserting, "All soteriological categories must be defined within the realm of the indwelling Spirit"; *Justified in the Spirit*, 186.
185. "The striking point is that Jesus as the holy dwelling place of the Spirit descends to the place of the godforsaken in order to open up the sacred to the profane"; Macchia, *Justified in the Spirit*, 178.

intercession for creation in the midst of its groaning for liberty. In the cross, the Spirit now wilfully opens up to be assailed by the dark forces that keep creation in bondage in order to remain true to this intercession.[186]

D. The Spirit Raises the Son to Life

Where [Jesus's] own person is concerned, the Spirit of God is not only the one who leads Jesus to his self-surrender to death on the cross. He is very much more the one who brings Jesus up out of death.[187]

Moltmann criticizes Protestantism for its one-sided tendency to restrict Christ's redemptive work to his death, and its rare inclusion of his resurrection, his living lordship, and his *parousia*.[188] He rightly stresses that the significance of Jesus's resurrection extends beyond God's vindication of his righteous Son, or God's revelation of Jesus's true divine identity.[189] According to Moltmann, Jesus's resurrection must first of all be understood eschatologically. Jesus's rising from the dead signals the beginning of God's new aeon, the first fruits of Ezekiel's prophetic vision, in which God breathes his Spirit of new life into the dead.[190] This is not the general resurrection of the dead for *judgment*, but the resurrection into God's *glory*, in which God is all in all through the indwelling Spirit. Moltmann rightly asserts that Jesus's resurrection signifies the death of death and its power. Although Jesus's resurrection occurred, as it were, in the midst of history and time, it is essentially an eschatological event. Believers who continue to live in present history have a foretaste of the *eschaton* through the indwelling of the Spirit (Rom 8:11).[191] New life through the Spirit's power is life in the power of the resurrection.[192] "Understood as an event that discloses the future and opens history, the resurrection of Christ is the foundation and promise of life in the midst of the history of death."[193]

186. Macchia, *Justified in the Spirit*, 179–80.
187. Moltmann, *Spirit of Life*, 65.
188. Moltmann, *Spirit of Life*, 81.
189. Moltmann, *Way of Jesus Christ*, 231.
190. Ezekiel 37.
191. Moltmann, *Way of Jesus Christ*, 241. "Believers are possessed by the Spirit of the resurrection, and through it are born again to a well-founded hope for eternal life"; Moltmann, *Spirit of Life*, 153.
192. Moltmann, *Way of Jesus Christ*, 263.
193. Moltmann, *Way of Jesus Christ*, 241.

Second, according to Moltmann, Jesus's resurrection "completes" his incarnation. "Christ was born in Bethlehem and born again from the dead ... His incarnation is consequently completed by his resurrection, not in his death on the cross."[194] Although the cross of Christ is central to Moltmann's theology, he sees the goal of soteriology (and Christology) as the *eschaton*. And for Moltmann, it is pneumatology that underpins and unites Christology and eschatology. Jesus's birth, life, ministry, death, and resurrection were thoroughly pneumatic events.

> No other Christ takes the place of Jesus. The one exalted is the one same as the one humiliated, the one raised the same as the one crucified. Where do we find the continuity in this discontinuity between death and life, end and beginning? I believe that this continuity in discontinuity can be seen in the presence of the Holy Spirit in Christ's life, death, and resurrection. In Gethsemane and on Golgotha the Son *feels* forsaken by the Father but is sustained by the Holy Spirit.[195]

Third, Jesus's resurrection signifies not only the renewal of humanity, but also the renewal of all creation, and his resurrection is *cosmic* in its inclusiveness.

> So we may add that Jesus' death on the cross was solitary, and exclusively his death, but his raising from the dead is inclusive, open to the world, and embraces the universe, an event not merely human and historical but cosmic too: the beginning of the new creation of all things.[196]

Since Moltmann understands Genesis 1:2 pneumatologically, it is not surprising that he envisages a cosmic role for the Spirit, both in creation and re-creation. Indeed, as the Spirit grows in theological importance for Moltmann, pneumatology becomes the key theme that threads through and holds together his doctrines of creation and God, Christology, soteriology, and eschatology. In particular, Moltmann rejects the traditional dichotomy between Christ's so-called "objective" accomplishment of salvation on the cross, and the Holy Spirit's so-called "subjective" conferral of that salvation on believers.[197] He insists that both pneumatology and Christology

---

194. Moltmann, *Way of Jesus Christ*, 249.

195. Moltmann, "Hope and Reality," 82–83. Italics added. In this 1999 publication, Moltmann maintains that the Spirit remains with Jesus throughout his life, death, and resurrection, and does not abandon him.

196. Moltmann, *Sun of Righteousness*, 55.

197. Moltmann, *Spirit of Life*, 81, 103.

are fundamental for soteriology. It is therefore all the more curious that in his statement above, published in 2010, that he describes Jesus's death as a "solitary" event. By this Moltmann does not deny the participation of the Spirit nor the vicarious nature of Jesus's death, nor the fact that Jesus dies "in solidarity with the whole sighing creation, human and non-human—the creation that 'sighs' because it is subject to transience,"[198] but it appears that for Moltmann, Jesus dies in solidarity for, not in union with, a creation that is subject to death and transience. In contrast, he perceives the beginning of the rebirth of the cosmos in Christ's resurrection.

At first glance, there appears an incongruity in Moltmann's thoughts here. How can creation be reborn without first dying? Furthermore, if Christology is understood cosmically (Col 1:15–20), and "through [Christ Jesus] God was pleased to reconcile to himself all things, whether on earth or in heaven, by making peace through the blood of the cross" (Col 1:20), then surely salvation itself must be cosmic in its reach. Even the Isaianic prophecy of "a new heaven and a new earth" (Isa 65:17), affirmed in Revelation 21:1, presumes the passing away of the old. Perhaps it is the "now-and-not-yet" tension of an inaugurated eschatology that underlies Moltmann's statement. The old is still in the process of passing away, but the new has already come in the presence of Jesus of Nazareth whose suffering and death, according to Moltmann, represent the apocalyptic end-time suffering and death.[199] Nevertheless, even in the context of an inaugurated eschatology, by indicating that Jesus's death is "solitary," Moltmann seems to underplay Paul's teaching that believing sinners (though not the cosmos) are *united* with Christ in his death, burial, and resurrection, as the very basis of their freedom from the power of sin and their eschatological life in the Spirit of the Son (Rom 6:3–11, 8:9–11). For Paul, the concept of believers being "in Christ" is a key category in his theology of salvation. Although Moltmann accepts that Christ died vicariously for sinners, and that in his death, "death" itself was destroyed,[200] he stops short of articulating the idea that all who belong to Christ have died and risen with him. For Moltmann, Christ's representation appears to be external rather than inclusive. Perhaps this is because Moltmann desires to emphasize his futuristic view of eschatology. In contrast to John V. Taylor and John D. Zizioulas (whose views will be the focus of the following chapter), Moltmann sees Christ's vicarious death as a death, through the work of the Spirit, *in solidarity* with godless and

---

198. Moltmann, *Spirit of Life*, 169.

199. "His death is then the anticipation of the death that is universal and absolute ... In 'the sufferings of Christ,' the end-time sufferings of the whole world are anticipated and vicariously experienced"; Moltmann, *Way of Jesus Christ*, 155.

200. Moltmann, *Way of Jesus Christ*, 169.

godforsaken humanity, and with the suffering and dying creation, but not an *inclusive* death. On the other hand, Moltmann views Christ's resurrection as a globally and cosmically inclusive event.

4.5 Summary

Jürgen Moltmann's theology, arising from the bitter trauma of his war experiences, was molded by his ecumenical theological training, by his interaction with Jewish and Marxist philosophers and liberation theologians, and by his wife Elisabeth. He became convinced that the crucified and risen Christ reveals the God who suffers empathetically with his creatures. His messianic theology, with shared suffering and coming glory as its controlling theme, is structurally framed by a christological center and an eschatological horizon. Moltmann's methodological paradigm emphasizes solidarity, openness, and inclusiveness, freedom and praxis. These characteristics are reflected in his egalitarian social model of the Trinity, his religious ecumenism, his readiness to explore ideas, his championing of gender equality, his defense of the poor, oppressed, and disadvantaged, his concern for equitable sharing of global resources and ecological health, and his suspicion of authoritarian power.

Moltmann's pneumatology, growing in importance in his writings over the decades, reflects these same features. With "Life" as his central metaphor for the Spirit, Moltmann emphasizes the Spirit's dynamic "livingness," holistic inclusiveness, and universal empathy with the suffering of humanity and creation. He correctly highlights the Spirit's indwelling and empowerment of the Messiah and the messianic community, and asserts that pneumatology unites Christology and eschatology. Moltmann employs the Jewish kabbalistic Shekinah doctrine extensively in his pneumatology but widens its application from a metaphor for God's particular presence in time and space with his people, to describe the Spirit's empathetic indwelling in all creation.

Given Moltmann's focus on the crucified and risen Christ, and his increasing pneumatological emphasis, it is not surprising that he developed an enduring interest in the role of the Spirit at the cross. His *pneumatologia crucis* evolved over several years and appeared in three different forms. First, he suggests that the Spirit "proceeds" from the cross event to include humanity. In this model he seems to imply that the cross event is in some way constitutive for the Spirit. He held onto this model for a relatively short time before moving onto his second model in which he portrays the Spirit as the "bond of love" between the Father and the Son. Here, in agreement with John V. Taylor, he developed the Augustinian idea of the Spirit as *communio* to envisage the Spirit's mediation at the cross between the forsaking Father and the godforsaken Son. Although Moltmann championed this idea for over a decade, as he engaged more fully with pneumatology, he developed a wider role for the Spirit in the cross event. In his third model, he portrays the Spirit as the Son's companion and coworker through the latter's life, ministry, and death, and as the power of the Son's resurrection. This model appears to have more biblical support than Moltmann's first two models, but his overdependence on the Shekinah doctrine for much of his creative pneumatological formulation undermines the systematic soundness of his *pneumatologia crucis*. Curiously, despite his strong emphasis on the Spirit's indwelling, and his conviction that Christ died vicariously for sinners, Moltmann perceives that Christ died a solitary death, in "solidarity" with those who suffer and die, but not it seems, in "union" with sinners.

5

Spirit as "Unifier"—John D. Zizioulas

THE INCLUSION OF AN Eastern Orthodox theologian as one of the major voices in this study of *pneumatologia crucis* offers an alternative paradigm to the predominantly Western theological perspective presented thus far. Among the growing number of contemporary Orthodox scholars, John D. Zizioulas has gained acclaim for his analysis and articulation of the Eastern perspective in conversation with Western tradition. Indeed, he has been called "one of the best known theologians of the contemporary Orthodox church, a central figure in the ecumenical scene and one of the most cited theologians at work today."[1] His inclusion in this study, however, is not motivated by his acclaimed scholarship and importance, but for his intriguing concept that Christ died on the cross as the pneumatologically constituted corporate Christ.

5.1 Zizioulas's Biographical Context[2]

Unlike John V. Taylor and Jürgen Moltmann, Zizioulas rarely offers autobiographical details in his writings, nor has a formal biography been published thus far. He was born in 1931 in Katafygio, Kozani, in the northern region of Greece, but little is known about his childhood and formative years. Zizioulas's theological education began in the University of Thessaloniki in 1950 and continued at the University of Athens. He spent a graduate semester at the Ecumenical Institute of the World Council of Churches at Bossey near Geneva, where he encountered Western Christian traditions

---

1. Knight, *Theology of John Zizioulas*, 1.
2. Zizioulas's biographical details were obtained from Fox, *God as Communion*, and from Kalaitzidis, "Academic Laudatio."

for the first time. This led to his lifelong engagement with an issue that has shaped his theological thinking, namely, ecumenism.[3] Zizioulas graduated from the University of Athens with a Bachelor of Theology in 1955 at the age of twenty-four. He subsequently received a scholarship from the World Council of Churches to pursue postgraduate research on the Christology of Maximus the Confessor at Harvard Divinity School in the United States. Among his teachers were Georges Florovsky in patristics and Paul Tillich in philosophy. These were significantly formative years for Zizioulas.[4] Having received his Masters in 1956, he returned to Greece for his obligatory two-year military service, after which he undertook his doctoral research in Harvard on the unity of the church in the bishop and the Eucharist during the first three Christian centuries, under the direction of A. G. Williams, professor of church history. Zizioulas returned to Athens in 1964, and successfully defended his thesis at the University of Athens in 1965. From 1966 to 1967, he worked as research assistant to Gerasimos Konidaris, professor of church history at the University of Athens. Subsequently, from 1967 to 1970, he was the Secretary of the "Faith and Order" Commission of the World Council of Churches in Geneva. Not only was he active in organising theological programs and conferences on various ecumenical issues, Zizioulas also became a leading voice in inter-Christian dialogue, and he lectured on Orthodox ecclesiology and Orthodox sacramental theology at the Graduate School of Ecumenical Studies at Bossey. He soon gained an international reputation, and in 1970, Zizioulas was appointed as assistant professor in patristic theology at the University of Edinburgh where he remained for three years. In 1973, he moved to the University of Glasgow to take up the chair of systematic theology and he remained there for fourteen years. Thereafter, Zizioulas was invited to become professor of dogmatic and creedal theology at the University of Thessaloniki where he remained until his retirement in 1998. In addition, Zizioulas held visiting professorships teaching systematic theology at the Universities of London and Geneva, and the Gregorian in Rome.

Patricia Fox notes that Florovsky was a strong influence on Zizioulas particularly in the area of patristic theology and ecumenism, and both men "were committed to working toward a neo-patristic synthesis that could provide the basis for a union between West and East."[5] Florovsky, a Russian émigré, was a prominent Orthodox theologian who was passionate about patristic theology and ecumenism, and played an important role in securing

---

3. Fox, *God as Communion*, 4.
4. Kalaitzidis, "Academic Laudatio," 1.
5. Fox, *God as Communion*, 4.

Orthodox participation in the World Council of Churches in 1950. Zizioulas himself was for many years heavily involved in the "Faith and Order" Commission of the World Council of Churches, where he was a member of work groups on "Eucharist" and on "Development of Conciliar Structures." "Such was the quality and originality of his work that he was soon after co-opted onto the permanent membership of the Commission in Geneva."[6] In Geneva, Zizioulas was in constant contact with Protestants, Roman Catholics, and pre-Chalcedonian Eastern Churches, and he in turn became a spokesman for his own Orthodox tradition. In 1975 Zizioulas was appointed the delegate of the Ecumenical Patriarchate of Constantinople on the central committee of the World Council of Churches, and he represented the Patriarchate at numerous General Assemblies (Uppsala 1968, Nairobi 1975, Vancouver 1983, Canberra 1992). He is a founding member of the International Joint Commission for Theological Dialogue with the Roman Catholic Church and leads in international Anglican-Orthodox dialogue. He is, at the time of writing, the theological advisor to the Ecumenical Patriarchate. Having published frequently in journals and various periodicals, it was in 1985 that his best-known work in English, *Being as Communion*, appeared. In June the following year, Zizioulas was bestowed the very unusual and great honor of being ordained as Metropolitan of Pergamon although he was a lay person, for his significant contributions to Orthodox ecclesial theology and his ecumenical endeavors.[7] As the twentieth century drew to a close, Zizioulas turned his attention to global ecological concerns, in keeping with his awareness of and active engagement with existential issues.[8]

5.2 Zizioulas's Theological Context

Methodological Paradigm

Zizioulas's theological preoccupation is with ontology.[9] His thinking is shaped by his ecumenicity and openness to new perspectives, by his emphasis on freedom in community, by his eschatological orientation, and by

---

6. Fox, *God as Communion*, 5.
7. Kalaitzidis, "Academic Laudatio," 4.
8. Fox, *God as Communion*, 6.
9. For example, with regards to ecclesiology, he states, "the revelation of Christ ceases to be a system of ideas as the Tübingen school conceived it, and becomes a truth *ontological in character*"; Zizioulas, *Eucharist, Bishop, Church*, 15. Zizioulas understands the fall not only in terms of moral corruption, but also more importantly, the human rejection of true personhood as *Imago Dei*, a rejection of freedom, communion, and union with God; Zizioulas, "Human Capacity," 422–26.

his focus on the Eucharist upon which he models his theology. Intriguingly, these are features he shares with John V. Taylor and Jürgen Moltmann, except that Taylor and Moltmann focus on the cross while Zizioulas emphasizes the Eucharist. Nonetheless, the death and resurrection of Christ are integral to the Eucharist.

A. Ecumenicity and Openness

A notable feature of Zizioulas's methodological paradigm, unusual perhaps for an Orthodox theologian, is his relative openness to innovative thinking.[10] Having lived, worked, and taught for many years in Glasgow, Edinburgh, and Geneva, Zizioulas's lifelong goal is to find common ground between Eastern and Western Christian traditions in order to recover ecumenical unity.[11] It might even be said that this is the goal that drives his theology. To achieve this, Zizioulas adopts Georges Florovsky's neo-patristic synthesis, and returns to the church's patristic roots, not to absolutize the past, but to reflect on time-honored ideas from a new perspective so that they might speak to existential issues. Kalaitzidis credits Zizioulas for the tentative steps recently being taken in Orthodox theology to overcome "introversion, theological provincialism and isolationism," and for inspiring many Orthodox theologians to move "from a cultural hermeneutic to a properly theological hermeneutic, and from a vague 'pneumatocracy' to a christocentric and sacramentally-grounded perspective."[12] Zizioulas himself asserts that "Orthodox theology in our time must operate in an ecumenical context and so in dialogue with other Christian traditions. And it cannot take place in a cultural vacuum that ignores current philosophical trends, and it cannot simply repeat the traditions of the past."[13] Nonetheless, certain aspects of Zizioulas's neo-patristic and philosophical thought, particularly his concept of "communion"

---

10. Zizioulas's innovative thinking does not, however, mitigate his acceptance of the Eastern Orthodox teaching that the gendering of humankind and sexual reproduction are part of fallen human nature and do not reflect God's original design; e.g. *Communion and Otherness*, 56–58, 260; see also Lossky, *Mystical Theology*, 108–9. This doctrine has patristic roots, particularly in the writings of Gregory of Nyssa and Maximus the Confessor, and is based on a literal reading of Gal 3:28: ". . . there is no longer male and female; for all of you are one in Christ Jesus"; Gregory of Nyssa, *On the Making of Man*, xvi, xvii (*NPNF* 2/5:402–5); Maximus, "Difficulty 41": 1304D–1305C, 1308D–1309B (Louth, 156–7, 159).

11. "As the late Fr. Georges Florovsky liked to repeat, the authentic catholicity of the Church must include both the West and the East"; Zizioulas, *Being as Communion*, 26.

12. Kalaitzidis, "Academic Laudatio," 12.

13. Zizioulas, *Lectures*, ix.

as an ontological category fundamental to the "being" of God,[14] have met with skepticism in some quarters of the Orthodox tradition.[15] John Behr, for example, is uncomfortable with what he considers is Zizioulas's "social" or "communitarian" understanding of the triune God, because of its perceived tendency towards tritheism.[16] An importance difference between Zizioulas's concept of the Trinity and the "social Trinity," it must be stressed, is that while proponents of the latter typically attribute equal status to the three divine Persons, Zizioulas is insistent on the monarchy of the Father.[17] Indeed, as will be detailed later, the doctrine of the monarchy of the Father is a key pillar in Zizioulas's Trinitarian theology.

B. Freedom in Community

Douglas Knight suggests that "Zizioulas' central concern is human freedom and the relation of freedom and otherness."[18] It may, however, be more accurate to say that his concern is first for *divine* freedom, and then for human freedom. Indeed, for Zizioulas, to *be* God is to be by definition, free, and that true "being" is freedom.[19] Human freedom subsequently derives its existence, character, and form from divine freedom, because God is the ontological source of all "being." By "freedom," however, Zizioulas rejects the popular understanding in which "self" is the reference point, for this leads to individualism and isolation. Instead, he asserts that true "freedom" can only be understood and realized in relationship with others, that is, in community, and that true human personhood can only exist in communion with God. Indeed, Zizioulas perceives individualism to be a corruption of true personhood, and a consequence of humanity's fall.[20] Knight rightly perceives that Zizioulas has contributed a fundamental and significant insight to contemporary theology, namely "that communion

---

14. Zizioulas, *Being as Communion*, 84, 134.

15. Brown insists that such skepticism is based on a misunderstanding of Zizioulas's precepts (particularly his ontology of personhood), and it derives from a specifically Anglican post-liberal form of Orthodoxy; Brown "Anglophone Orthodox Theology," 35–50.

16. Behr, *The Nicene Faith, Part 2*, 310, n. 110, 414–15.

17. Zizioulas insists on the monarchy of the Father, and specifically that the Father is the origin and cause of the divine being of God; Zizioulas, *Communion and Otherness*, 113–54.

18. Knight, *Theology of John Zizioulas*, 1.

19. Zizioulas, *Being as Communion*, 18.

20. Zizioulas, *Being as Communion*, 101–3.

and freedom are not opposed."[21] To the concept of "freedom" Zizioulas adds the idea of "uniqueness," particularly in the context of *personhood*. According to Zizioulas, a person exists as "a free, unique and unrepeatable entity."[22] He credits the Cappadocian Fathers, especially Basil, with the development of the important concept that the very "being" of God is personal. Based on his interpretation of Basil's writings, Zizioulas asserts that God is not an amorphous divine "substance" from which three persons emerge; the one God *is* three persons.[23]

Moreover, according to Zizioulas, how God *is*, or God's way of being, defines freedom and personhood for all created beings. Human personhood and freedom derive from and are based upon the personhood and freedom of God, and not the other way around. It is unsurprising therefore, that Zizioulas rejects Boethius's approach to personhood in terms of rational individuality,[24] defining personhood instead in relational terms of freedom, uniqueness, and community.[25] This notion of "freedom in community" underpins his Trinitarian and sacramental theology, Christology, pneumatology, and ecclesiology, and leads to his dogged emphasis on the motif of "*the one and the many*," which has become his catch phrase and title for one of his recent books.[26] This motif, which he is convinced is rooted in biblical and patristic thinking, pervades Zizioulas's own reflections, and it has become a framework upon which he constructs his whole theology.[27] By "one," he does not mean "alone," and his view of "oneness" is more in relational terms of unity rather than in arithmetic terms of singularity. Hence, "the one" for Zizioulas also signifies "the many."

Zizioulas's motif of "the one and the many" is paradigmatic for his dialectical theology. For example, as mentioned above, he asserts that

21. Knight, *Theology of John Zizioulas*, 1.

22. Zizioulas, "Human Capacity," 408; Zizioulas, *Being as Communion*, 33, 46–47, 49.

23. Zizioulas, *Being as Communion*, 40.

24. "*Persona est naturae rationalis individua substantia*" (a person is an individual substance of a rational nature); Boethius, "De persona et duabus naturis," iii.D (Migne, PL 64).

25. Zizioulas, "Human Capacity," 405–6, 409–10; *Being as Communion*, 46–47. Zizioulas probably goes too far in his personalist ontology when he suggests that personhood *only* exists in relationship with others: "There cannot be a person without relationship to other persons, so if all the relationships which constitute a person disappear, so does that person"; Zizioulas, *Lectures*, 57.

26. Zizioulas, *One and the Many*.

27. Zizioulas, *Being as Communion*, 145–49. Zizioulas states, "Personhood and nature are two aspects of existence which correspond to the two basic ontological principles of particularity and totality, the 'many' and the 'one.' This is a key idea in patristic thought"; Zizioulas, *Communion and Otherness*, 56.

"freedom" and "communion" belong together, and together they signify liberty for relationships, not isolated selfhood. "Personhood" means freedom and uniqueness, yet within community. The bishop is "the one" who in the Eucharist unites "the many," meaning the eucharistic assembly.[28] In the Eucharist, the local church united with her bishop represents the whole catholic body of Christ.[29] God is both "one" and "many" (three),[30] and significantly, Zizioulas envisages Christ as "one" and "many" through the work of the Holy Spirit.[31] He states:

> Another important contribution of the Holy Spirit to the Christ event is that, because of the involvement of the Holy Spirit in the economy, Christ is not just an individual, not "one" but "many." This "corporate personality" of Christ is impossible to conceive without Pneumatology.[32]

c. Eschatological Orientation

Like Jürgen Moltmann, Zizioulas sees history from the vantage point of the future. He asserts: "The truth of history lies in the future, and this is to be understood in an ontological sense: history is true, despite change and decay, not just because it is a movement *towards* an end, but mainly because it is a movement *from* the end, since it is the end that gives it meaning."[33] Zizioulas is emphatic that the church is the forerunner of God's eschatological kingdom, and that she is rooted in the future. As the community of the new humanity in Christ through the Spirit, the church represents the *telos* of God's creation.[34] Zizioulas observes that in the liturgy of John Chrysostom, the eucharistic assembly remembers not only the death, resurrection, and ascension of Christ, but also "the coming again a second time in glory."[35]

---

28. Zizioulas, *Eucharist, Bishop, Church*, 66–68, 105–6, 160; *Being as Communion*, 136–37.

29. Zizioulas, *Being as Communion*, 133–36; *Eucharist, Bishop, Church*, 107–28, 161.

30. "The faith in 'one' God who is at the same time 'three', i.e. 'many', implies that unity and diversity coincide in God's very being"; Zizioulas, *One and the Many*, 336.

31. Zizioulas, "Human Capacity," 435–45; *Eucharist, Bishop, Church*, 14–18; *Being as Communion*, 107–14; *Communion and Otherness*, 289–96; *Lectures*, 108; Zizioulas, *Eucharistic Communion*, 12–14.

32. Zizioulas, *Being as Communion*, 130.

33. Zizioulas, *Being as Communion*, 96.

34. Zizioulas, *Communion and Otherness*, 67.

35. Zizioulas, *Lectures*, 154; see also *Eucharistic Communion*, 58–60.

By "remembering the future," the body of Christ acknowledges that her true origin is from the future, God's eschatological future.

> At the Eucharist, consequently, we place the events and persons of the past and the present within the context of the Kingdom which will come, and that not simply psychologically (through a movement of our imagination towards the future) but *ontologically*, i.e. with the purpose of giving these events and persons substance, so that they are not destroyed (by time and death) and live eternally.[36]

According to Zizioulas, it is the involvement of the Spirit that ensures the eschatological ontology of Christ and his church. The Spirit acts to draw history towards the *eschaton*, and to bring a foretaste of the *eschaton* into history. The Spirit "makes of Christ an eschatological being, the 'last Adam.'"[37] Baptism represents birth in the Spirit into the eschatological community, the body of Christ, and "a radical conversion from individualism to personhood,"[38] and "[i]nasmuch as the Last Supper is not an event of familial life but an event for 'the friends of the Lamb,' the Supper marks an eschatological 'inbreaking' in the natural course of historical life."[39]

D. Eucharistic Focus

Zizioulas understands the Eucharist as an "icon of the Kingdom."[40] As such, the Eucharist is the central metaphor in his theology.[41] For Zizioulas, it is through the Eucharist that God the Father, Son and Holy Spirit, the church and the coming kingdom of God, can be best perceived, understood, and experienced. He insists that the Eucharist is much more than the mere remembrance of Christ's death. It is also the "presentation and offering of the body of Christ to the Father,"[42] and through the *epiclesis*, the Spirit "gives life to the Body (John 6:63)." This life is nothing less than the resurrection life of Christ, and it is life in ecclesial community.[43] According to Zizioulas, it is in celebrating the Eucharist that redeemed humanity experiences and

---

36. Zizioulas, *Eucharistic* Communion, 61.
37. Zizioulas, *Being as Communion*, 130.
38. Zizioulas, *Being as Communion*, 113.
39. Zizioulas, *Eucharistic Communion*, 4.
40. Zizioulas, *Eucharistic Communion*, 60.
41. Zizioulas, *Eucharist, Bishop, Church*, 14–18; *Being as Communion*, 114–22.
42. Zizioulas, *Lectures*, 117.
43. Zizioulas, *One and the Many*, 81.

expresses communion with God in Christ through the Holy Spirit; it is within the eucharistic moment that Christology, pneumatology, ecclesiology, and eschatology converge. Furthermore, because the ontological unity of *all* believers in Christ through the Spirit is celebrated in the Eucharist, Zizioulas suggests that the Eucharist may provide a platform upon which to work towards ecumenical unity, where ideological agreement may be difficult to achieve. "The view of the Divine Eucharist as the supreme sensible incorporation of the Church in space and time into Christ does indeed form an essential presupposition for any research on the unity of the Church."[44]

Zizioulas's Personalist Ontology

It is important to appreciate that Zizioulas's Trinitarian theology, Christology, and pneumatology are based upon and are inseparable from his understanding of "person" as "being-in-relation." Not only does he describe personhood in ontological terms ("a free, unique and unrepeatable entity") but also in relational terms. In other words, by asserting that "being" is primarily relational, *ontology* itself is for Zizioulas relational through and through. He insists that there can be no "being" without relationship with an "other" to relate to. Zizioulas not only stresses that relationships constitute personhood, but also that the very basis of ontology *is* personhood. He insists that just as there is no impersonal "human essence" which exists unattached to human persons, there is also no impersonal "divine essence" or "substance" which exists apart from the persons of the Father, Son and Holy Spirit. He cites Basil's statement that ἐν τῇ κοινωνίᾳ τῆς θεότητος ἐστίν ἡ ἕνωσις ("in the communion of the Godhead/divinity is the unity"),[45] as the basis of his understanding of "communion" (κοινωνία) as a fundamental ontological category:

> One of the striking peculiarities of St. Basil's teaching on God, compared with that of Athanasius and certainly with that of the Western Fathers, is that he seems to be rather unhappy with the notion of substance as an ontological category and tends to replace it . . . with κοινωνία. Instead of speaking of the unity of God in terms of his one nature, he prefers to speak of it in terms of the *communion of persons*: communion is for Basil an ontological category. The *nature* of God is communion.[46]

---

44. Zizioulas, *Eucharist, Bishop, Church*, 17.

45. Basil, "On the Holy Spirit," 18.45, in *St. Basil the Great*, 80–81; Greek text from "De Spiritu Sancto" (Migne, *PG* 33:149D).

46. Zizioulas, *Being as Communion*, 134.

John Behr, however, disagrees with Zizioulas's interpretation of Basil's statements and remarks, "It is extremely unlikely that Basil here means that the 'divinity' itself, the divine nature, is to be identified with 'communion,' for it is as partaking of *the same divinity* that the Father and the Son are in unity."[47] A detailed examination of their hermeneutical positions lies beyond the scope of this book, suffice to say that Behr understands Basil's use of the term κοινωνία in terms of "commonality" or "sameness," whereas Zizioulas interprets it in terms of "community" or "relationship." Interestingly, a similar tension exists between "oneness" and "threeness" in our limited comprehension of the Trinity. However, *both* aspects of "commonality" and "community" presuppose that distinct entities participate in this κοινωνία. A single entity cannot have things in "common" by itself; one can only have things in "common" with another. It is only when there is "otherness" that one can possibly conceive of "commonality" and "community." It is important to note that for Zizioulas, divine "otherness" does not equate to the individuality that we experience in our fallen state, an individuality that is an alienated and fragmented parody of true personhood in communion with God.[48] He is correct in saying that "[t]he task of working out an understanding of communion linked organically with an understanding of otherness appears to be imperative in theology today."[49] Yet despite their differences in interpreting Basil's use of the word κοινωνία, Zizioulas and Behr fully agree that the divine persons are distinct without being disunited.

Lucian Turcescu challenges Zizioulas's assertion that the conceptual roots for a personalist ontology can be traced to the Cappadocian Fathers, suggesting instead that these views arise from existential philosophy.[50] He maintains that Zizioulas has misread Gregory of Nyssa. In responding to Turcescu's critique, Zizioulas points out that while modern existential philosophers derive their understanding of ontology from human personhood, he derives his own ontological perspective from divine personhood, or more specifically, from the Cappadocian view of the Trinity.[51] Moreover, as Aristotle Papanikolaou correctly highlights, Zizioulas's personalist ontology is drawn mainly from the theology of Gregory of Nazianzus rather than that of Gregory of Nyssa.[52] Alexis Torrance provides a conciliatory position in this debate, in which argument about terminology seems to

47. Behr, *The Nicene Faith, part 2*, 310, italics added.
48. Zizioulas, *Being as Communion*, 102–3.
49. Zizioulas, *Communion and Otherness*, 14.
50. Turcescu, "'Person' Versus 'Individual,'" 97–104.
51. Zizioulas, *Communion and Otherness*, 171–77.
52. Papanikolaou, "Existentialist in Disguise?," 602.

predominate, by stressing that terminological precision or imprecision aside, he accepts that there is an *ideological* continuity between the patristic period and Zizioulas's thinking.[53]

Catherine Mowry LaCugna, a Roman Catholic theologian, generally agrees with Zizioulas's relational view of ontology, and with his theology of personhood. Although she comes from a Western ecclesial tradition, she, too, draws upon the Cappodician view of intra-Trinitarian relations to inform her own understanding of personhood.[54] Nonetheless, she questions Zizioulas's claim that personhood has absolutely no ontological content apart from relationship with another. She makes the reasonable suggestion that in the definition of personhood, heteronomy needs to be balanced with autonomy.[55] It appears, however, that LaCugna applies the terms "autonomy" and "heteronomy" with regard to horizontal relations between people, whereas Zizioulas identifies creaturely autonomy as that which separates the creature from *both* God and community, resulting in an individualism that is a product of the fall, corrupting both vertical and horizontal relations.[56] LaCugna's statements, on the other hand, are limited to human relationships in the context of gender stereotypes of male autonomy and female heteronomy, and she makes the valid point that authentic personhood is not necessarily dependent on relationships with other humans. Instead, she asserts that Jesus Christ exemplifies a higher *theonomy*, with a rootedness not in self or another human but in God. Jesus, as *the* theonomous person, integrates "the tensions of autonomy and heteronomy into genuine freedom and community."[57] In her concept of theonomous personhood as truly authentic personhood, LaCugna accepts that no genuine personhood exists apart from right relationship with God, even if horizontal relationships may be lacking. Thus, in that sense, there is less of a distance between LaCugna and Zizioulas as the former suggests.

---

53. Torrance, "Personhood and Patristics," 700.
54. LaCugna, *God for Us*, 243–49, 260–62.
55. LaCugna, *God for Us*, 266, 310, n. 77.
56. Zizioulas, *Communion and Otherness*, 204.

57. LaCugna, *God for Us*, 293. "His [Jesus's] personal authority (*exousia*) was always referred back to and rooted in God. For Christians, Jesus is the paradigm of what it means to *live in the name of God*: Jesus's whole reality was identified with God's through serving and caring for others, even to the point of giving up his own life"; LaCugna, *God for Us*, 294.

Zizioulas's Trinitarian Theology

Where Taylor and Moltmann are Christocentric in their theology, Zizioulas is intentionally and explicitly Trinitarian. The Father, the Son, and the Holy Spirit are often mentioned together in his discussions. Rarely does he focus exclusively on one person of the Godhead to the exclusion of the other persons. The two key features of Zizioulas's Trinitarian theology are first, his personalist ontological approach to the Trinity, and second, his grounding of the Trinity in the monarchia of the Father.

Zizioulas contends that the Trinity is primordial, and that there is no "being" (οὐσία) as an ontological category which is prior to the persons or hypostases (ὑποστάσεις) of the Trinity.[58] In other words, there is no "being" to which "person" is subsequently added. Both "being" and "person" are inseparable and co-fundamental. Zizioulas insists that in our understanding of the Trinity, both οὐσία and ὑπόστασις must be given their full ontological content in order to prevent the tendency towards Sabellianism. In addition, he points out that because the Cappadocians understood God's "being" to refer to both τί ἐστιν (*what* he is), which is οὐσία, and ὅπως ἐστιν (*how* he is), which is ὑπόστασις, both οὐσία and ὑπόστασις are integrated ontologically.[59] Zizioulas adheres to Eastern Orthodox apophaticism in his insistence that *what* God is (his οὐσία) remains utterly unknowable and unapproachable since God has only revealed *how* he is (his ὑποστάσεις).[60] Contrary to the interpretation, or misinterpretation, of some of his more vociferous detractors,[61] Zizioulas does not denigrate the importance of οὐσία for God's being, although he is reluctant to apply the term ὁμοουσίας to the relationship between the Father and the Son, because of the perceived danger of modalism.[62] For Zizioulas, there is *one* God who is irreducibly Father, Son and Spirit, one οὐσία in three ὑποστάσεις; he rejects tritheism absolutely and unambiguously. While Jürgen Moltmann may be accused of leaning towards tritheism, Zizioulas is not in any sense a tritheist, although

---

58. Zizioulas, *Being as Communion*, 39. "Given the fact that, according to these Fathers, there is no *ousia* in the nude, that is, without hypostasis, to refer to God's substance without referring simultaneously to his personhood, or to reserve the notion of being only to the substance, would amount to making a false ontological statement." Zizioulas, *Being as Communion*, 125.

59. "In both cases, the verb is *to be* (ἐστίν or εἶναι), that is, *being*"; Zizioulas, *Communion and Otherness*, 125.

60. Zizioulas, *Lectures*, 56–57.

61. See for example, Loudovikos, "Person Instead of Grace," *The Heythrop Journal* 52 (2011), 686.

62. Zizioulas, *Communion and Otherness*, 120.

his personalist ontological understanding of the Trinity requires a unifying factor if tritheism is not to be its logical conclusion.

It is the doctrine of the monarchia of the Father that becomes the unifying factor for Zizioulas's personalist Trinitarian ontology.[63] While he steadfastly agrees with the concept of "one οὐσία in three ὑποστάσεις" (upon which he has framed his catch phrase "the one and the many"), he holds that the unity of the three persons who exist in κοινωνία is grounded, not in their common οὐσία, but in the monarchy of the Father. Thus Zizioulas insists that the Trinity is united, not by an impersonal divine "substance" or "essence," but in the *person* of the Father, because "the substance never exists in a 'naked' state, that is, without hypostasis, without 'a mode of existence.'"[64] Papanikolaou rightly discerns that the concept of the monarchia of the Father is crucial to Zizioulas's personalist ontology, not an addendum, because if it is true that the origin of our triune God is the Father and not an amorphous divine "substance," then the very "being" of God is personal. And since God is the source of all ontology, personhood (defined by Zizioulas in terms of uniqueness, freedom, and community) is thus foundational to ontological existence, not an added characteristic.

> The real issue, then, is not whether [Zizioulas] has been influenced by modern personalism, but whether a Trinitarian theology that affirms the monarchy of the Father is the only way to ground a personal ontology, and whether such an ontology does correct and justify the various modern, philosophical understandings of personhood. If the core of Christian faith is communion with God the Father, in the person of Christ, by the power of the Holy Spirit, it is difficult to think how such a communion does not imply an ontology that is relational and personal.[65]

Does Zizioulas hold firmly to the doctrine of the monarchy of the Father simply because it supports his personalist ontology? Is it his own personalist perspective that influences his interpretation of the Cappadocian writings, to see within them convincing evidence for this doctrine, thus in some sense a circular argument? Whether or not that is the case, Zizoulas's personalist ontological approach to the Trinity is important for his Christology and pneumatology, and thereby, his *pneumatologia crucis*.

---

63. Zizioulas, *Communion and Otherness*, 118. Zizioulas traces the origins of the doctrine of the monarchy of the Father to Gregory of Nazianzus. However, Gregory himself does not seem to have completely excluded a substantial understanding of the Trinity, using the term ὁμοουσία to refer to the Father, Son and Holy Spirit; Gregory of Nazianzus, "On the Holy Spirit," 10 (*NPNF* 2/7: 321; *PG* 36:144A).

64. Zizioulas, *Being as Communion*, 41; see also *Communion and Otherness*, 113–54.

65. Papanikolaou, "Existentialist in Disguise?," 606.

Zizioulas's Christology

Zizioulas's Christology is underpinned by his ontological understanding of creation, the fall, and salvation. In keeping with Athanasian theology (and Eastern Orthodox theology in general), Zizioulas maintains that humanity was created for communion with God, and that the goal of creation is *theosis*, that is, union with God.[66] When the first humans disobeyed God, that communion was interrupted. Since created beings are made from nothing, without life-giving communion with the uncreated God, they return to nothing; death becomes their destiny. According to Zizioulas, the fall, therefore, is not only a moral problem of sin but also an ontological problem, signifying a return to the state of eventual nothingness.[67] This concept can be traced to Athanasius, who taught that createdness itself carries within it the threat of transience which can only be overcome by union with the uncreated God.[68] Death is understood less as judicial punishment, and more as the inevitable ontological result of disrupted human-divine communion. Furthermore, according to Athanasius, since it was through the Word whom God made all things, and the Word through whom humanity is united to God, and since salvation signifies the restoration of human-divine communion, it is unsurprising that it was the Word himself who should play a key role in effecting salvation.[69] This is the reason, Athanasius explains, why the Word took on human form: "For it will appear not inconsonant for the Father to have wrought its salvation in Him by Whose means He made it."[70]

Affirming Athanasius's ontological understanding of the fall, Zizioulas perceives sin as primarily a fatal *ontological* change in humanity, which subsequently expresses itself in sinful acts, and which leads to death. In other words, sin is not only what we *do*, it is what we have actually *become*, and death represents more than judgment for sin, but its inevitable existential consequence resulting from the break in life-sustaining communion with

---

66. "The only way that something created can transcend death and deterioration is to remain in constant communion with the eternal God. God and the world have to be in communion, and the means chosen for this communion is mankind. Communion with God is the purpose of man's creation." Zizioulas, *Lectures*, 89.

67. Zizioulas, *Lectures*, 89. See also Lossky, *Mystical Theology*, 97–99, 126–28, 133; Ware, *The Orthodox Way*, 52.

68. "For transgression of the commandment was turning them back to their natural state, so that just as they have had their being out of nothing, so also, as might be expected, they might look for corruption into nothing in the course of time." Athanasius, "On the Incarnation," iv.4 (*NPNF* 2/4:38).

69. Athanasius, "On the Incarnation," i.3–5 (*NPNF* 2/4:37–39).

70. Athanasius, "On the Incarnation," i.4 (*NPNF* 2/4:36).

God.[71] By rebelling against God and rejecting his purpose for humanity, Zizoulas maintains that humans have lost their vital communion with God, a communion for which humanity was created in the first place, and without which humanity becomes "non-being" and "non-person."

> The ultimate meaning of the Fall was, therefore, in the fact that by perverting personhood (which is *the only* way of communion with God) man turned the difference between uncreated and created natures into a *division* between the two, and thus ruined God's purpose in creating man: communion.[72]

> Idolatry, i.e. turning created existence into an ultimate point of reference, is the form that the Fall takes, but what lies behind it is the fact that man refuses to refer created being to communion with God.[73]

> Death intervenes not as a punishment for an act of disobedience but as a result of this individualisation of nature to which the whole cosmos is subjected.[74]

But why should the *whole* cosmos be subjected to the same ontological consequence of *human* disobedience? Following Maximus the Confessor,[75] Zizioulas explains:

> Man was created at the end of all creation so that he would bring all that is created to the uncreated God and unite them in permanent relationship . . . but man refused to accept that this was his purpose. He decided not to follow this plan, but to make another world in which he would become God himself.[76]

Zizioulas asserts that humanity's role to unite all creation to God arises on the basis that humans not only share materiality with the rest of creation, but also as the *imago Dei*, freedom. Since the life-giving relationship with God has to be freely willed, and humans are the only creatures

---

71. Zizioulas, "Human Capacity," 424.
72. Zizioulas, "Human Capacity," 434.
73. Zizioulas, *Being as Communion*, 102.
74. Zizioulas, *Being as Communion*, 105. "Whatever is created lives under the permanent threat of non-existence. When it severs its bond with the uncreated, turns towards itself and seeks to draw its powers of survival from its own self, it is deceived and its dissolution begins"; Zizioulas, *Lectures*, 93.
75. Maximus the Confessor, "Difficulty 41":1305B–1312B (Louth, 157–60).
76. Zizioulas, *Lectures*, 90. See also Lossky, *Mystical Theology*, 109–10, 165; Ware, *The Orthodox Way*, 49–50, 54 for similar insights.

endowed with the capacity of free will, Zizioulas asserts that it is humanity's responsibility to unite creation to God. Thus, creation's destiny is inseparably entwined with human history, and "'all creation groans and suffers' (Rom. 8:22) as it looks forward to man's reconciliation with the uncreated."[77] This uniquely Eastern Orthodox perspective of humanity's role in creation may have been based upon a particular understanding of Colossians 1:19 (cf. Eph 1:10) which declares that in Christ, God reconciles all things to himself. However, Christ's telic role in this cosmic reconciliation appears to have been read back into God's purpose for creating humanity. Such a connection seems speculative.

Nonetheless, it is precisely this ontological perspective of the fall and its consequences that for Zizioulas, in keeping with patristic and Eastern Orthodox theological tradition, Christ and the salvation he brings *must* deal comprehensively with ontological corruption, and not merely address the moral issue. It is the radical re-creation of humanity that God achieves through the work of the Son and the Spirit. As Athanasius pithily summed up, "For He was made man that we might be made God" (αὐτὸς γὰρ ἐνηνθρώπησεν, ἵνα ἡμεῖς θεοποιηθῶμεν).[78]

> The eternal survival of the person as a unique, unrepeatable and free "hypostasis," as loving and being loved, constitutes the quintessence of salvation, the bringing of the Gospel to man. In the language of the Fathers this is called "divinisation" (*theosis*), which means participation not in the nature or substance of God, but in his personal existence.[79]

In keeping with Athanasius's insights on the key significance of the incarnation not only for humanity's salvation but also the eschatological renewal of and consummation of creation, the *corporate* nature of Christology is vitally important for Zizioulas's theology. "The one and the many" is exemplified in Jesus Christ who is both the one man Jesus of Nazareth, and also the corporate Christ.[80] For Zizioulas, Christ's sacrificial death was not so much *in place of* humanity, but *with* humanity *in himself*. Indeed, Zizioulas asserts that "Christ does not simply stand vis-à-vis each man, but

---

77. Zizioulas, *Lectures*, 94.

78. Athanasius, "On the Incarnation," liv.3 (*NPNF* 2/4:65); Greek text from *Athanasius: De Incarnatione*, 85.

79. Zizioulas, *Being as Communion*, 49–50.

80. "Through such an understanding of the hypostatic union we can thus throw light on another aspect of the christological mystery: Christ as the 'catholic' man or as the 'one' who is at the same time 'many'"; Zizioulas, "Human Capacity," 438.

constitutes the ontological ground of every man."[81] A purely substitutionary atonement "would not affect man's being ontologically. For such a Christology may answer man's needs for forgiveness but not his problem of death (unless death is deprived of its ontological content and becomes a penalty imposed and removed according to the wish of the Judge)."[82] Using the terminology of Wolfhart Pannenberg, Christ is not humanity's *exclusive* representative, but humanity's *inclusive* representative.[83] Based on Paul's insight that "one has died for all: therefore all have died" (2 Cor 5:14), Pannenberg suggests that Christ's death on the cross extends beyond vicarious expiation (exclusive representation), and *includes* all humans who commit themselves to Christ in baptism.[84]

> The thought here of inclusive representation makes Jesus the representative of all humanity. This is in keeping with Paul's description of Christ as the second Adam. There takes place in him paradigmatically that which is to be repeated in all the members of the humanity that he represents. At any rate, in Paul, Christ's death includes ours in such a way as to change its character. By linking our death to Christ's in the act of baptism, our death takes on a new sense that it does not have of itself. It is a death in hope.[85]

Zizioulas's christological formulation goes beyond Cyril of Alexandria's "God in flesh" (ἐν σαρκός) concept.[86] He insists that it is not so much the *human (flesh) principle* that Jesus Christ incorporates within himself, but *every human being*. For Zizioulas, union with Christ is an *ontological* union of multiple individual human hypostases with the hypostasis of the Second Person of the Trinity. "This adoption of man by God, the identification of his

81. Zizioulas, "Human Capacity," 441.

82. Zizioulas, "Human Capacity," 441.

83. Pannenberg, *Systematic Theology*, 429–37. Pannenberg suggests that the basic idea of inclusive representation may have originated from Hegel, although the latter's misunderstanding of the Chalcedonian distinction between the human and divine natures of Christ led to his notion that God died on the cross.

84. Pannenberg, *Systematic Theology*, 429. Pannenberg explicitly distinguishes himself from Barth's more universalist position, in which Christ's death incorporates *all* humanity, by insisting that Christ's inclusive representation does not take away the responsibility of each human to either accept or reject union with Christ.

85. Pannenberg, *Systematic Theology*, 429–30.

86. Cyril of Alexandria wrote, "It follows, therefore, that He Who Is, The One Who Exists, is necessarily born of the flesh, taking *all that is ours* into himself so that all that is born of the flesh, that is us corruptible and perishing beings, might rest in him"; *On the Unity of Christ*, 59, italics added. Note that for Zizioulas, Christ takes into himself not only "all that is ours," i.e., sinful flesh, but indeed *our very selves* into himself.

hypostasis with the hypostasis of the Son of God, is the essence of baptism."[87] Hence, those who commit themselves to Jesus Christ are not merely aligned to his teaching and ideology, but become in a very real way, part of him (1 Cor 12:12–13). According to Zizioulas, by becoming part of Christ, a believer's "hypostasis of biological existence" which is constituted by physical birth, is transformed into a "hypostasis of ecclesial existence" which is constituted in Christ *by the Spirit*.[88] Having built upon the insights of Paul, Athanasius and Cyril, Zizioulas consistently attributes the ontological union of human hypostases with Christ to the agency of the Holy Spirit.

To sum up, Zizioulas views the theological landscape through the lens of ontology, and his motif "the one and the many" shapes his Christology, pneumatology, and ecclesiology. The fundamentally relational character of Zizioulas's ontological understanding is evident in the development of his personalist ontology, his Trinitarian theology and his corporate Christology. Zizioulas views creation, sin, and salvation through his relational ontological lens. Accordingly, the goal of creation is *theosis*, and sin is regarded as a rupture in the God-human relationship, due to humanity's deliberate disobedience. Death results from this break in communion with the life-giving God. Thus, for Zizioulas, the fall does not only involve moral failure but more importantly, ontological corruption. Through the death and resurrection of the corporate Christ, who as "the one and the many" is the second Adam and humanity's inclusive representative, humankind, and indeed all creation, are reunited with God. The incorporation of humanity into Christ takes place through the power of the Holy Spirit.

5.3 Zizioulas's Pneumatology

It bears repetition that in Zizioulas's view, Christology and pneumatology should not be considered as disparate dimensions. Christ is not Christ without the Spirit, and the Spirit is the Spirit of Christ.[89] "Christology is pneumatologically conditioned in its very roots."[90] He observes that patristic theology did not divide the economy between Christology and pneumatology, and states categorically that "it is extremely dangerous for the unity of

---

87. Zizioulas, *Being as Communion*, 56.
88. Zizioulas, *Being as Communion*, 49–59.
89. "The Holy Spirit always acts *through* Christ, because Christ is the point where all mankind and all creation are gathered up and brought into living communion with God on whom there are no confines"; Zizioulas, *Lectures*, 108.
90. Zizioulas, "Human Capacity," 441–42.

the Economy to speak of a special 'Economy of the Spirit.'"[91] Similarly, the church of Christ cannot exist without the Spirit, because the church as the body of Christ is from its very inception, according to Zizioulas, constituted *both* christologically and pneumatologically, and not constituted in Christ and subsequently indwelt by the Spirit.[92] Moreover, Zizioulas insists that the Holy Spirit is no mere *assistant* to the individual reaching Christ, "but the very '*in*,' in which he is participant in Christ. Baptism was from the beginning '*in* the Spirit' and '*into* Christ.'"[93]

Zizioulas passionately believes that through the balanced synthesis of Christology and pneumatology an ecumenical solution to the ancient rift between the Western and Eastern ecclesial trajectories can be found. This conviction is one that he holds in common with Taylor and Moltmann. Zizioulas does not, however, share their view of the Spirit's role as the "bond of love" between the Father and the Son. He generally ignores this popular Western idea, except to assert that while "love" is an *attribute* of the Spirit, "[t]he Greek Fathers did not believe that we can describe the persons by assigning an attribute to each of them that way,"[94] and to point out that the biblical texts used to support the notion that the Spirit is the gift from the Father to the Son refer to the divine economy and not to the immanent Trinity.[95] Vladimir Lossky traces the rootedness of this idea to substantialist ontological thinking, and expresses even more strongly the Eastern Orthodox rejection of the idea:

> Indeed, according to the western conception the Father and the Son cause the Holy Spirit to proceed, inasmuch as they represent the one nature: while the Holy Spirit, who, for western theologians, becomes "the bond between the Father and the Son," stands for a natural unity between the first two persons. The hypostatic characteristics (paternity, generation, procession), find themselves more or less swallowed up in the nature or essence which, differentiated by relationships—to the Son as Father, to the Holy Spirit as Father and Son—becomes the principle of unity within the Trinity. The relationships, instead of being characteristics of the hypostases, are identified with them.[96]

---

91. Zizioulas, *One and the Many*, 77.
92. Zizioulas, *One and the Many*, 75–90.
93. Zizioulas, "Human Capacity," 442; Zizioulas, *Being as Communion*, 110–11.
94. Zizioulas, *Lectures*, 66.
95. Zizioulas, *One and the Many*, 44.
96. Lossky, *Mystical Theology*, 57.

Dismissing the intra-Trinitarian "bond of love" notion, Zizioulas offers other perspectives on the Spirit's work, centered upon his core emphasis that the Holy Spirit is both the Spirit of communion and also of freedom, and the Spirit of the *eschaton*. Hence, the work of the Spirit not only unites but also differentiates, not only brings together but also ensures freedom—the true freedom of the *eschaton*.[97] While the sphere of the Spirit's activity encompasses all creation, Zizioulas focuses on his work with regard to Jesus Christ, humans, and the church. He sees the Holy Spirit's agency as foundational and critical for the very existence of true personhood, Christology, and ecclesiology. Hence, it is not surprising that in Zizioulas's mind, these are overlapping and integrated categories.

Spirit of Communion

In keeping with the theological consensus, Zizioulas affirms that the Holy Spirit is the Spirit of κοινωνία, uniting believers with the Son and with each other.[98] Zizioulas may reject the "bond of love" role for the Holy Spirit with regard to intra-Trinitarian relationships, but he strongly and repeatedly affirms the Spirit's role in uniting Christ with those who believe in him, and creating fellowship among all members of his body:

> The Father initiates the whole economy of God for man and brings the Church into existence. Jesus Christ, the Son of God, provides the body that is the literal embodiment of the communion and love of God, while the Holy Spirit enables the communion of the created with the uncreated so this body can enable the communion of every being with every other.[99]

Zizioulas, it must be stressed, places greater emphasis than many Western theologians on the *corporate* existence of Christ:

> *Koinonia* is decisive also in our understanding of the Person of Christ. Here the right synthesis between Christology and Pneumatology becomes extremely important. What does it mean that Christ is a "Pneumatic" being, a Person "born by the Spirit," anointed with the Spirit, etc., if not that He is in His very being a relational being? The Spirit is a Spirit of *koinonia*. If we cannot have Christology without Pneumatology, this means that

---

97. This bi-directional reciprocity is encapsulated in the title of Zizioulas's book, *Communion and Otherness*.

98. "It is the Spirit that gathers us all in Christ"; Zizioulas, *Lectures*, 150.

99. Zizioulas, *Lectures*, 139.

> we must stop thinking of Christ in individualistic terms and understand Him as a "corporate person," and inclusive being. The "head" without the "body" is inconceivable. The Church is the Body of Christ because Christ is a Pneumatological being, born and existing in the *koinonia* of the Spirit.[100]

> Only when pneumatology is allowed to be as foundational as Christology [for the formation of the Church], can we see that Christ embraces all of us within him and that Christ is the community of which we are members.[101]

Perhaps Zizioulas can be criticized for his almost exclusive focus on the corporateness of Christ so that the singular humanity of Jesus in time and place may be forgotten, and that Christology and ecclesiology are almost merged into one. It must be borne in mind, however, that for Zizioulas, Christ is a true *Person*, meaning that he is by Zizioulas's definition fundamentally a being-in-community with other beings, and a being who is also really and truly free because of the full indwelling of the Spirit. In Zizioulas's mind, Christ is only Christ when he exists in community with all who are united with him through the Holy Spirit, someone who is *par excellence* "the one" and also "the many." Importantly, for Zizioulas, it is *the Holy Spirit* who unites humanity with Christ.

Indeed, Zizioulas makes the rather intriguing statement in a passage on the importance of the *epiclesis* in the liturgy of the Eucharist: "The Eucharist portrays the mastery of the Church par excellence precisely because of this synthesis [of Christology and pneumatology]: without Christ there is no community, but unless there is a community to invoke the Spirit, *Calvary is no longer Calvary*."[102] Instead of stating that without Christ, Spirit, and ecclesial community the Eucharist is no longer the Eucharist, Zizioulas seems to suggest that without Christ, Spirit, and ecclesial community the event at Calvary—that is, *the cross event*—would lose its redemptive and transformative significance. This idea will be explored further in the following section on Zizioulas's *pneumatologia crucis*.

Since theosis as creation's goal informs his theology, it is unsurprising that Zizioulas's vision of a pneumatic Christology flows beyond ecclesial boundaries. While he applies the term "Body of Christ" correctly to the *church* united with Christ through the Spirit, Zizioulas also envisages *all creation* united to God in Christ because that is God's eschatological goal

---

100. Zizioulas, *One and the Many*, 51.
101. Zizioulas, *Lectures*, 151.
102. Zizioulas, *One and the Many*, 81; italics added.

of which the church is the foretaste.¹⁰³ Furthermore, Zizioulas provides another intriguing pneumatological insight:

> The salvation of creation will take place in the Son, and then be presented to the Father by the Son. The Holy Spirit has his own contribution to this plan. *He makes the incorporation of creation in the Son possible by enabling creation to open to its incorporation in the Son.* Its natural limitations mean that, left to itself, creation cannot sustain any relationship with God, while the Fall puts a further barrier to creation's openness. However, through intervention of the Spirit this openness becomes possible and thus the incorporation of creation in the Son can be accomplished as the work of all three persons of the Trinity, Father, Son and Holy Spirit.¹⁰⁴

Here Zizioulas reiterates that while salvation takes place in the Son, it is not the Son who incorporates the created into himself, but *the Holy Spirit* who carries out the incorporation. Having made that assertion, he then goes on to postulate that this union occurs through the Spirit's work on *creation* rather than on the Son, so that it is not so much that the Son is empowered by the Spirit to incorporate believers into himself, but that the Spirit renders creation *open* to union with the Son. This is an interesting concept. Zizioulas does not himself cite biblical texts to support it, but perhaps Paul's teaching that no one is able to proclaim Jesus as Lord without the inner working of the Holy Spirit (1 Cor 12:3), and the Johannine vision of the Holy Spirit as *paraclete* (John 16:7–14) may provide some scriptural basis to this idea.

Spirit of Freedom

Zizioulas balances the concept of the Spirit as κοινωνία with the concept of the Spirit as the Spirit of freedom. Drawing upon 2 Corinthians 3:17, Zizioulas sees the Spirit bringing freedom to all he indwells. By "freedom" Zizioulas is not referring to the Pauline idea of freedom from the Mosaic law, or the freedom enjoyed by God's adopted heirs, or even the freedom to choose between good and evil; on the contrary Zizioulas does not regard this as true freedom because he perceives that God, who is absolutely free, is above good and evil, above affirmation and negation.¹⁰⁵ Instead, Zizioulas regards

103. Zizioulas, *Lectures*, 135–36.
104. Zizioulas, *Lectures*, 132. Italics added.
105. Zizioulas, *Being as Communion*, 90–91, 120–21. He follows Maximus the Confessor's insights here, and calls this "a new concept of freedom" which is "determined not by choice but by the movement of a constant affirmation, a continual 'Amen'";

"freedom" as an *ontological* characteristic of true personhood, a freedom that ensures the distinctiveness and uniqueness of beings-in-community. This freedom prevents the collapsing of many hypostases into one amalgamated hypostasis, but maintains the uniqueness of each hypostasis within the united whole—yet again, "the one and the many" paradigm.[106] This is not the pseudo-freedom of individualism or of moral independence, but is the true freedom that exists only in affirmative communion.[107]

Zizioulas examines the Spirit's liberating work with reference to Christ, the church, and Mary. With regards to Christ, Zizioulas suggests the following. The hypostatic particularity of the Son lies in his becoming history. While the Father and the Spirit become *involved* in history, only the Son *becomes* history. The Christ event is a historical event which occurred in a specific place and time. Through the action of the Spirit, however, this Trinitarian event transcends history. According to Zizioulas, the Spirit liberates the Son from history.

> Now if *becoming* history is the particularity of the Son in the economy, what is the contribution of the Spirit? Well, precisely the opposite: it is to liberate the Son and the economy from the bondage of history. If the Son dies on the cross, thus succumbing to the bondage of historical existence, it is the Spirit that raises him from the dead. The Spirit is *beyond* history, and when he acts in history, he does so in order to bring into history the last days, the *eschaton*.[108]

> The Holy Spirit frees Christ from the confines of history and is with Christ at every critical juncture.[109]

This is an important pneumatological insight. Jesus of Nazareth is not only a great moral teacher who lived over two thousand years ago in Palestine, but also the pneumatic Christ who through the Spirit is free from the restrictions of time and space, so that he is present everywhere and in every time. Even more importantly, his work on the cross transcends the limitations of space and time, impacting those who live before and after the first century, throughout the world. This, according to Zizioulas, is the work of the eschatological Spirit.

Zizioulas, *Being as Communion*, 121.

106. This understanding of the Holy Spirit's work is shared by Vladimir Lossky; see *Mystical Theology*, 165–70, 184–85.

107. "Man is only free in communion"; Zizioulas, *Being as Communion*, 122.

108. Zizioulas, *Being as Communion*, 130.

109. Zizioulas, *Lectures*, 107.

In regard to the church, Zizioulas proposes that it is the Spirit who ensures the freedom and integrity of all human hypostases united to the hypostasis of the Son:

> By being the body of Christ, the Church exists as the hypostasisation of all particular beings in the unique *hypostasis* of Christ, which guarantees the ontological truth, the eternal survival, the ἀεὶ εἶναι, of these beings thanks to his resurrection. This hypostasisation takes place *in the Holy Spirit* which means freedom (2 Cor. 13:13) and as foretaste of the eschatological state of existence (Acts 2:18). The Spirit offers the particularising force which guarantees that hypostasisation in Christ will not end up in an absorption of the many into the one, in the loss of otherness.[110]

The church, then, is a community of people who are ontologically united with the Son and to each other through the Holy Spirit, and yet each person remains a unique, unrepeatable, and free entity. Indeed, for Zizioulas, true community is only possible when both uniqueness and union are maintained by the Holy Spirit.[111] Lossky writes along similar lines when he suggests that "the human persons who form the hypostases of this unified nature [of Christ] are not suppressed. They are not mingled or one with the divine Person of Christ."[112] Where Lossky differs from Zizioulas is in his attribution of the uniting of humans to Christ as the work of the Son and not the Spirit. Lossky maintains that with regard to the establishment of the church, "the work of Christ unifies; the work of the Holy Spirit diversifies. Yet one is impossible without the other."[113] The New Testament, however, lends more weight to Zizioulas's identification of the Spirit as the one who unifies.[114] In this regard, Calvin also sees integration in the work of the Son and of the Spirit: "To sum up, the Holy Spirit is the bond by which Christ effectually unites us to himself."[115]

---

110. Zizioulas, *Communion and Otherness*, 75–76. See also his *Lectures*, 139. Note that Zizioulas's reference to 2 Corinthians 13:13 may be a typographical error, as that verse refers to "the communion of the Holy Spirit"; perhaps he means 2 Corinthians 3:17.

111. Zizioulas, *Lectures*, 139.

112. Lossky, *Mystical Theology*, 165–66.

113. Lossky, *Mystical Theology*, 167.

114. For example, John 3:5–8; 1 Corinthians 2:16; 12:13; Ephesians 2:18, 22; 4:3, 4; Romans 8:14–17. See Fee, *People of God*, 66–73, 81; Pannenberg, *Systematic Theology*, 451–52; Cole, *He Who Gives Life*, 216–21.

115. Calvin, *Institutes*, iii.1.1 (McNeill, 538). "But he unites himself to us by the Spirit alone. By the grace and power of the same Spirit we are made his members, to

Zizioulas, however, puts forward an unusual idea concerning Mary, Jesus's mother. Building upon Jesus's birth narratives which attribute his conception to the Holy Spirit (Matt 1:18; Luke 1:35), Zizioulas suggests that the Spirit enabled Mary to respond to God's call in true freedom, and that when she gave her consent, she represented humanity at a critical point in salvation history. According to Zizioulas, Mary's decision, made in the freedom of the Spirit, ensured the unforced agreement of humanity to God's plan of salvation.

> The role of the Holy Spirit in Christ's conception is therefore essential . . . The complete and proper expression of human freedom came at last in the unforced "yes" given by the Virgin Mary to God's call to carry through this mystery of Christ. Mary could have refused to take part in such a plan that utterly conflicts with our self-directed logic, but her reply was not "no" but "yes." *Her consent was the free consent of humankind to the initiative of God.*[116]

> *In the presence of the Spirit*, the Virgin Mary is able to decide in complete freedom, and thus the incarnation of Christ takes place in true creaturely freedom. The Spirit ensures that what is created is not crushed by the presence of what is uncreated. The contribution of the Holy Spirit is therefore to allow each agent to act as a person, unconstrained by all limits and pressures.[117]

This, however, is a speculative and unsubstantiated interpretation of the incarnation. Zizioulas's commitment to the idea of freedom may be driving this interpretation. By proposing that it is not only Christ who makes his decision for the cross in freedom, but that his mother Mary must also agree on behalf of all humanity to God's salvation plan, Zizioulas sets up *both* Christ and Mary as humanity's representatives. This has no biblical basis, and brings to mind the papal doctrine of the immaculate conception of Mary, which is equally speculative. Nevertheless, Zizioulas's core concept regarding the Spirit as the liberating Spirit has biblical purchase.

---

keep us under himself and in turn to possess him"; Calvin, *Institutes*, iii.1.3 (McNeill, 541).

116. Zizioulas, *Lectures*, 104; italics added.

117. Zizioulas, *Lectures*, 107; italics added.

Spirit of the Eschaton

For Zizioulas, the Spirit is the Spirit of community and freedom because he is none other than the Spirit of the *eschaton*. "Hence the first fundamental particularity of pneumatology is its eschatological character. The Spirit makes of Christ an eschatological being, the 'last Adam.'"[118] Through the Son and the Spirit, God the Father brings to fruition his creative intention, the cosmic realm in which God is all in all, and in the pneumatic Christ, humanity attains true personhood, indwelt by the eschatological Spirit, in right relationship with God and one another, each free in their uniqueness. Even now, the community of those who believe in Jesus Christ stands on earth as the forerunners of God's eschatological kingdom. The Spirit-indwelt church of Christ exists to declare to the world that God's *eschaton* is real, believable, and impending. The roots of this new humanity lie not in the past, but in the future.[119]

It is unsurprising therefore that Zizioulas asserts that the Eucharist not only celebrates the centrality of Christ's sacrifice, but also constantly brings to mind the coming eschatological kingdom. Indeed, just as the church is the ecclesial icon of the God's kingdom, the Eucharist stands as its liturgical icon.

> In the form of the Eucharist all creatures are brought together and recapitulated in Christ. The Eucharist manifests and substantiates within time the identity of this assembly in the form of the Church. When we want to speak of the actual lived experience of the Church we have to start from the Eucharist, for this is where the Church appears. The Eucharist is the free coming together of all parts into their proper relationships and so into the good order of the whole in which each creature is liberated from the limits given by its own nature. This liberation is the eternal will of the Father which the Son has substantiated and which the Spirit now makes possible for us to share.[120]

Through the Spirit, the Eucharist becomes a celebration that transcends time and space, so that it is "both a historical *and* an eschatological event."[121] Thus Zizioulas counters what he perceives is a christomonic tendency in Western celebration of the Eucharist, by emphasizing its

---

118. Zizioulas, *Being as Communion*, 130.

119. Zizioulas, *Being as Communion*, 58–59. "Man appears to exist in his ecclesial identity not as that which he is but that which he *will* be; the ecclesial identity is linked with eschatology, that is, with the final outcome of his existence"; Zizioulas, *Being as Communion*, 59.

120. Zizioulas, *Lectures*, 137–38.

121. Zizioulas, *Lectures*, 153.

pneumatic significance.¹²² When the church gathers together in the Eucharist, Zizioulas suggests that the Holy Spirit mediates the presence of Christ in the elements, and also unites believers in Holy Communion.¹²³ He goes on to propose that it is through the unifying and liberating Spirit that every eucharistic gathering embodies, not simply *part* of the universal church, but the *whole* church of Christ, offering up itself to God.¹²⁴ Even as Christ through the Spirit becomes "the one and the many," similarly each local eucharistic assembly, through the Spirit, embodies the universal church, "the one" that is simultaneously "the many." Zizioulas draws upon John 17:20–23 as the biblical foundation for his vision of the eucharistic union of the body of Christ, set free from its locality in time and space. The unity of the church exists in absolute reality despite its present fractured form simply because Christ wills it, and the church is united, not of itself, but *in Christ through the indwelling Spirit*. According to Zizioulas, the true paradigm for the church is not to be formulated from an understanding of its past, but from its eschatological future. Although the church's earthly history contradicts its true unity, Zizioulas's ecclesial vision is exciting, and it has certainly reinforced his own ecumenical motivation and endeavor. In short, the church *is* united—now let us live out our God-given unity.

In summary, Zizioulas presents the Holy Spirit as the eschatological life-giving God who ensures true community and freedom, who guarantees personhood, who unites humanity in Christ and with each other while maintaining their distinct hypostases, and whose pervading presence within the church signifies God's coming kingdom and *eschaton*. Jesus Christ lives by the power of the Holy Spirit throughout his earthly history, and, according to Zizioulas, it is through the Spirit that Christ transcends historical space and time. How then does he envisage the Spirit's relationship to the dying Christ at Golgotha?

5.4 Zizioulas's *Pneumatologia Crucis*

It must first be said that Zizioulas himself does not use the term "*pneumatologia crucis*," and he does not, like Moltmann, explicitly construct models to explain the possible role of the Spirit at the cross of Jesus Christ. Rejecting

---

122. Zizioulas, *Eucharistic Communion*, 74–75.

123. Zizioulas, *Eucharistic Communion*, 75.

124. Zizioulas, *Being as Communion*, 147–55. Zizioulas's insistence on the centrality of the bishop in eucharistic liturgy is well recognized and has been controversial, but as this concept bears no direct relevance to the present study, it will not be discussed here.

the idea that the Spirit is the "bond of love" or the unifying force between the Father and the Son, whether in the economy or within the Trinity, he emphasizes instead that the Spirit unites *humanity to Christ*. His pneumatic Christology presupposes that the Son is never without the Spirit, and his Trinitarian outlook insists upon the participation of the whole Trinity in every major work of God. Indeed, Zizioulas's insistence on the thoroughly pneumatic character of Christology precludes any theological options that see Jesus dying as a solitary being, the Son abandoned by the Spirit at the cross. In such a scenario, an impossibility in Zizioulas's theology, Jesus bereft of the Spirit is no longer the anointed Messiah, the Christ. It is this firm conviction concerning the Spirit's uninterrupted presence with and in the Son at the cross that provides the framework for Zizioulas's *pneumatologia crucis*.

In Zizioulas's view, the Spirit does more than passively indwell the Son at the cross. Zizioulas's consistent portrayal of Christ as a corporate being leads to the notion that Christ died on the cross as the *inclusive* representative of humanity. That is, Christ not only died on behalf of humanity, but more importantly, humanity died with and in Christ. Zizioulas asserts that it is through the active work of *the Spirit* that humanity is united with Christ. Thus, without the presence and activity of the Spirit at the cross, Christ's destruction of sin and death could not have been achieved. The Spirit, working with the Son, ensures God's redemption and transformation of fallen humanity. In other words, without the active participation of the Spirit at the cross, humanity would not have been saved.

Zizioulas's understanding of the work of the Son and the Spirit at the cross may be deduced from the following passages:

> The Cross of Christ, and especially the idea of his descent into Hades, are the only way to communion with God. Only in utter incapacity can human capacity be realized.[125]

> The Spirit therefore not only resides within Christ and renders him "Christ" (the One anointed by the Spirit), but also, by passing through those crucial points in the course of Christology—which are the major decisions, the major steps that were taken, i.e., the conception, the testing by Satan, the Cross, the Resurrection—all render Christology an expression of liberty, in which Man now participates freely because Christ—as a human and not only as God—makes all these decisions freely, in order to implement God's plan with all the consequences that it entailed.[126]

125. Zizioulas, "Human Capacity," 439.

126. Zizioulas, *Lessons*, E.6 ("Salvation"). Zizioulas's theological students compiled his lectures with his permission and supervision, and made the document freely

> The Spirit is present at Gethsemane, where the all-important decision to drink the cup, despite all its horror, is taken. The Spirit enables the Lord's free decision to go to the cross, and the Spirit raises Christ from the confines of death. The resurrection and the defeat of death is the Spirit's act in transcending all limits, and all dissolution and death.[127]

> This other way was the incarnation of the Son in the now fallen creation, something which required the Son, mankind, and all creation to pass through death and emerge from it in order to reach that union.[128]

The Holy Spirit always acts *through* Christ, because Christ is the point where all mankind and all creation are gathered up and brought into living communion with God on whom there are no confines. The incarnation is therefore not just about Christ's *receiving* the Holy Spirit, but also about Christ *giving* the Holy Spirit to all mankind . . .[129]

Implied within Zizioulas's statements above are three important theological insights. First, Christ's death was absolutely necessary for the redemption of humanity and creation. However, this insight, obvious and undisputed for Western traditions of the atonement, becomes problematic when it is set within the context of Zizioulas's understanding of mortality as largely the consequence of disrupted union with God, since the incarnation itself would have resolved that issue. Second, the Spirit indwelt the Son throughout "the conception, the testing by Satan, the Cross, the Resurrection," and through the Spirit's work, "the Son, mankind, and all creation" passed through the cross and emerged from death to life.[130] Zizioulas proposes that when Jesus of Nazareth died on the cross at Golgotha, fallen humanity and corrupted creation died with him, and when he rose from the dead, new humanity and new creation rose with him. Third, new life in the Spirit is christologically defined. Here Zizioulas asserts that God's eschatological freedom in the Spirit, and full personhood, can be found only in Christ. These theological insights are elaborated below.

---

available in 2005 at http://www.oodegr.co/english/dogmatiki1/perieh.htm.

127. Zizioulas, *Lectures*, 107.

128. Zizioulas, *Lectures*, 133. "This other way" refers to God's plan to achieve his goal of *theosis* despite humanity's rebellion.

129. Zizioulas, *Lectures*, 108.

130. Zizioulas, *Lectures*, 133.

Christ's Necessary Death

Zizioulas maintains that the Son experienced death, humanity's "abyss of absence" and "Hades," and that God's plan of redemption required him to do so.[131] "However difficult and counterintuitive it was to say that it was truly God who suffered all these things, the Church nevertheless insisted that the Son of God was fully involved in this sorrow, suffering and death."[132] Zizioulas accepts that Christ really suffered and really died. Since the Son is God and therefore eternal, Zizioulas asserts that the Son freely chose to die a human death. "In taking on human flesh, the Son took on death and suffered the pain of the cross and death."[133] This emphasis on Christ's death is central to Western soteriology. It is surprising, however, for Zizioulas to affirm it so strongly. Why is it that Christ's *death* is necessary to overcome death? In addressing this question Zizioulas prefers an ontological explanation over the idea that Christ died to pay the penalty for humanity's sin.[134] He states categorically that "the belief that death entered the world as punishment for disobedience and the fall" is a misconception.[135]

For Zizioulas, it seems that *mortality* itself is the key problem. In his view, death represents humanity's failure to remain united to the life-giving God. "The salvation of the world must be salvation from death."[136] He offers two possible explanations for the necessity of Christ's death, both from an ontological perspective. First, Zizioulas sees Christ's death as "an extreme and incomprehensible act of freedom and love"; the divine Christ "suffered because he took human nature and remained obedient to its confines."[137] That is, Christ died because he fully integrated himself into our fallen humanity, and since our fallen condition is mortal, he too dies.[138] In his death however, and more importantly in his resurrection, Christ then corrected the ontological failure caused by humanity's rebellion against God. "The overcoming of death as the acute ontological form of absence—in and

---

131. Zizioulas, "Human Capacity," 439.
132. Zizioulas, *Lectures*, 109.
133. Zizioulas, *Lectures*, 148.
134. Zizioulas, *Lectures*, 102–6.
135. Zizioulas, *Lectures*, 102. It must be said, however, that Zizoulas's perspective on the atonement does not adequately take into account Pauline insights (e.g. Rom 3:24–25; 1 Cor 15:3; 2 Cor 5:15, 21; Gal 3:13).
136. Zizioulas, *Lectures*, 102.
137. Zizioulas, *Lectures*, 110.
138. "Since it was the Son rather than the Spirit who entered our life and became incarnate, it is he rather than the Spirit who bears the dissolution and death that are the outcome of our history"; Zizioulas, *Lectures*, 148.

through death alone—is, therefore, in the light of Christology a capacity given to humanity in its incapacity."[139] Ironically, God used death as the paradoxical instrument of life-giving salvation.

This account does not, however, explain satisfactorily why Christ's death was needed to deal with mortality, if it is indeed purely a problem of ontological failure. Zizioulas's own assertion that death is the direct consequence of disrupted communion with God would seem to lead to the conclusion that the incarnation should have been sufficient in itself to reconnect humanity to God without the need for Christ to die. Since Zizioulas insists that Christ only ever exists as a corporate person, implying that at his birth he was united with humanity through the work of the Spirit, does not that unity constitute life-giving unity with God in the person of the Son? Obviously not. If *theosis* had been fully achieved at the incarnation, mortality as an ontological problem would have been resolved then and there, and Christ's death at the cross is superfluous. The New Testament emphasis on the cross, however, clearly indicates that the Son's incarnation did not by itself achieve reconciliation between God and humanity, but that it was only the beginning of the salvation process.

Second, Zizioulas also suggests that Christ's bodily death is necessary in order to deal with a tension within each human arising from the fall, namely, a conflict between otherness (particularity, represented by the hypostasis) and communion (the shared human nature):

> For the body is paradoxically the vehicle of otherness and communion at the same time. With the body we affirm and realize our particularity, and with the body we establish communion with other particular beings. If the body makes us particular beings not by bringing us into communion with other particular beings but by separating us from them, there is a conflict between otherness and communion experienced through the body. But such a conflict is not part of the body by definition; it is only a result of the fact that the body has been turned into a carrier of death. If the sting of death is removed from it, it ceases to perpetuate the conflict between particularity and nature and becomes the point where communion and otherness meet. This means that the conflict between *hypostasis* and nature cannot be resolved until death is conquered for all and for ever. Those who wish to remove or undermine this conflict already in our actual historical experience, and try to accommodate nature happily in personal existence, must turn a blind eye to the seriousness of death and consequently to the crucial importance of the

---

139. Zizioulas, "Human Capacity," 439.

resurrection both as an historical event in the person of Christ and as the eschatological destiny for all humanity.[140]

This second ontological explanation seems, however, to see the fall in terms of a malalignment between particularity and communion, in short, a perversion of true personhood (in Zizioulan terms). While he is correct in determining that human perversity is so integrated and deeply rooted within the being of every human that nothing short of death puts an end to it, his attribution of that corruption to relational failure *alone* seems altogether too narrow. Zizioulas appears to have ignored the covenantal framework of human-divine communion, a framework that is painfully detailed in Israel's history. Christ died as the only possible solution to human perversity and rose from death to bring about a total renewal of humanity. Humanity's sin, however, is our failure to acknowledge, worship, and obey God as God. Malaligned relationships, and our evil actions, are the *result* of that failure, not the root of the sin itself.

Furthermore, Zizioulas's ontological explanations for Christ's death do not fully account for the *character* of Christ's death. If his death was all that was required to solve the human problem, then why not die as an old man, in comfortable surroundings? Why the betrayal, the trial, the torture, and a form of execution exclusively reserved for sedition against the emperor? The judicial features of Christ's death remain important and cannot be ignored. The moral and judicial implications of sin are thoroughly biblical concepts. Death is described as *earned* wages of sin (Rom 6:23). The sacrificial system of the Mosaic tabernacle and the Jerusalem temple attests to the idea that acceptance into God's holy presence comes at a high price, through death and blood. There can be no human-divine communion without death and blood, and this principle is fulfilled in Christ to whom all the ritual sacrifices of Israel point (Heb 9:11–28). The cover upon the ark of the covenant, named *kappōret* in Hebrew and *hilastērion* in Greek (Exod 25:22; Lev 16:2; Heb 9:5),[141] represented the place of meeting between God and Israel. Significantly, Paul identified *Christ* as God's ultimate *hilastērion* (Rom 3:25), meaning that it is in Christ, the true mercy seat (of which the ark was merely a representative), that God-human communion is finally accomplished. This communion takes place, as it did in the earthly sanctuary, through death and blood, because of the fall. Christ's institution of the Eucharist incorporates this same principle (1 Cor 11:23–26; Mark 14:22–24; Matt 26:26–28; Luke 22:19–20). By limiting the significance of salvation to the reversal of mortality, Zizioulas is in danger of downplaying Christ's work in dealing with the

---

140. Zizioulas, *Communion and Otherness*, 62.
141. In the LXX, כַּפֹּרֶת is consistently translated as ἱλαστήριον.

tragic reality of humanity's sin nature. The Augustinian insight that fallen humanity is predisposed to sin[142] does not feature greatly in Zizioulas's ontological reflection. Interestingly, Athanasius, one of the fathers from whom Zizioulas draws his theology, recognizes that Christ "offered up his sacrifice also on behalf of all, yielding his Temple to death in the stead of all, in order firstly *to make men quit and free of their old trespass . . .*"[143]

Furthermore, humanity's sinful propensity is also part of the ontological corruption of God's creation, in addition to mortality. This slavish tendency to sinful behavior has infected all humanity (Rom 5:12; 7:14). Sin affects the very core of our being as humans and is not merely surface rust to be scraped away. While sinful rebellion against God and his laws result in just punishment, sinfulness also, unfortunately, becomes ingrained and inherently part of our human nature. *By his death, Christ destroyed sin*—he paid the just penalty for our sinful actions, *and* he put an end to the sin nature in humanity when corrupt humanity died with him (Rom 6:6, 7). *By his resurrection, Christ destroyed death*, and rising with him, new humanity shares his new life in the Spirit (Rom 6:8–11; 8:1–4). The cure for sin is death; the cure for death is rebirth in the Spirit. In other words, Christ has successfully dealt with humanity's ontic corruption in its entirety. Zizioulas's ontological accounts of Christ's salvific death would be greatly strengthened by addressing *both* mortality and sin. From this wider perspective, God's pronouncement in Genesis 2:17, "you shall die," signifies not only the fatal consequence of humanity's separation from the living God (Gen 3:23), but also God's just response to sinful actions and sinful human nature. Zizioulas's view of Christ as a corporate being does, however, assist in our understanding that Christ embodied mortal and sinful humanity at the cross, and when he died, we died with him, and when he rose, we rose with him.

This broader ontological account of the cross may explain not only why Christ had to die, but also why he had to die the way he did. From the gospel narratives, the timing of his death was associated with the Passover, a celebration of remembrance of Israel's redemption from slavery in Egypt.[144] The early Christians understood that Christ was God's ultimate Passover lamb for the redemption of the whole world.[145] The context of his death reveals not only its redemptive purpose (the Passover), but its judicial nature (a public trial and execution), its rootedness in rejection (the Jewish religious

---

142. Augustine, "Enchiridion," xxvi–xxvii (*NPNF* 1/3:246).

143. Athanasius, "On the Incarnation," xx.2 (*NPNF* 2/4:47), italics added.

144. Mark 14:1, 12; Matt 26:17; Luke 22:1, 7–15; John 13:1, 28.

145. For example, John 1:29, 36; Acts 8:32; 1 Cor 5:7; 1 Peter 1:19; Heb 9:11–14; Rev 5:6–13, 21:9, 14.

authorities) and betrayal (Judas and Peter), and its cursed state (crucifixion; Deut 21:23; Gal 3:13). One might say that in the crucified Christ, God was rejected and betrayed, and that in the crucified Christ, sinful humanity was judged, condemned, and executed. In the risen crucified Christ, humanity is redeemed, renewed, and reconciled with God, and thereafter is indwelt by the life-giving Spirit of Christ and of God.

Zizioulas rightly stresses, however, that the salvation process does not end with Christ's death on the cross, although "the cross is the only way to the resurrection."[146] Indeed, he is critical of those who focus on the crucifixion without a balanced emphasis on the resurrection.[147] Uncomfortable with the attribution of suffering to the immanent Trinity as an eternal characteristic, a tendency which Zizioulas believes flows from a fixation on the crucifixion to the exclusion of the resurrection, he insists that Christ's resurrection is as important to the redemptive work as his death.[148] Hence, Zizioulas repeatedly uses the phrases "*pass through death*" or "*pass through the cross*" to indicate that Christ's death and resurrection are two sides of the same coin.[149] As he reflects on the theological significance of Christ's resurrection for humanity and creation, once again, Zizioulas has the corporate Christ, the pneumatic Christ, in view. The cross was never the goal of salvation, but its crucible, and out of its hellish depths emerged, *in Christ*, the new Spirit-indwelt humanity. It bears repeating Zizioulas's statement: "This redemption, this liberation from the boundaries of the created status, is the work of the Holy Spirit . . ."[150]

The Pneumatic Cross of Christ

Zizioulas emphasizes that the Spirit indwelt Jesus of Nazareth throughout his earthly sojourn, during his birth, ministry, death, and resurrection. This is the reason Jesus bears the title "'Christ" or "Messiah," which means the "anointed one": "[T]he Holy Spirit is not the one who *aids* us in bridging the distance between Christ and ourselves, but he is the person of the Trinity

---

146. Zizioulas, "Human Capacity," 431. "Needless to say that in this case without the Resurrection the Cross of Christ can have no relevance whatever for ontology, since to stop with the Cross would imply that death—and non-existence—continues to be an ultimate possibility for being"; Zizioulas, "Human Capacity," 444.

147. Zizioulas, *Lectures*, 133–35.

148. Zizioulas, *Communion and Otherness*, 63, n. 145; *One and the Many*, 129; *Lectures*, 109–10, 134; *Lessons*, E.6 ("Salvation").

149. Zizioulas uses these phrases altogether six times in four pages of the section entitled "The Church of God," in *Lectures*, 132–35.

150. Zizioulas, *Lessons*, E.6 ("Salvation").

who actually realizes in history that which we call Christ, this absolutely relational entity, our Saviour."[151]

Since Zizioulas is convinced that Christ is never without the indwelling Spirit, in what way then does he envisage the Spirit's involvement at the cross? Zizioulas makes three assertions. First, the indwelling Spirit empowered Christ to freely accept and to endure the cross. Second, the Spirit did not suffer and die with Christ, but supported him through the agony of death. Third and most importantly, through the power of the Spirit, humanity and creation were embodied *in* Christ and participated in his death and resurrection.

A. The Spirit Empowered Christ

Zizioulas suggests that the Holy Spirit "stands by the Son and finally sustains him through all the trauma that comes with his involvement in fallen creation."[152] The Spirit enabled Christ to endure the suffering brought about by the latter's identification with fallen humanity. Zizioulas proposes that in the garden of Gethsemane, the Spirit ensured that Christ's decision to go to the cross was made in absolute freedom:

> The Spirit therefore not only resides within Christ and renders him "Christ" (the One anointed by the Spirit), but also, by passing through those crucial points in the course of Christology—which are the major decisions, the major steps that were taken, i.e., the conception, the testing by Satan, the Cross, the Resurrection—all render Christology an expression of liberty, in which Man now participates freely because Christ—as a human and not only as God—makes all these decisions freely, in order to implement God's plan with all the consequences that it entailed.[153]

> The Holy Spirit carries this plan through, supporting the Son through the pain of this exchange and union, in which the Son takes on the fallen state of creation. The Holy Spirit stands with Christ in all the decisions by which he affirms his freedom, and he liberates the Son from the consequences of his giving himself to us. The Spirit, who sustains all freedom, ensures that Christ's decisions are free.[154]

151. Zizioulas, *Being as Communion*, 110–11.
152. Zizioulas, *Lectures*, 148.
153. Zizioulas, *Lessons*, E.6 ("Salvation").
154. Zizioulas, *Lectures*, 106.

Zizioulas maintains that Jesus did not *become* Christ after rising from the dead, but was Christ from his very conception, and that Christ took on "the fallen state of creation" not as creation's substitute, but in union with it. In addition, the indwelling of the Spirit ensured that all Christ's decisions were made in complete freedom.[155] This is important to Zizioulas because he is convinced that Christ's "yes" to God, even to death on a cross, was made "on behalf of all humans," and humanity's unforced agreement was necessary to the success of God's redemptive plan.[156] While the Son is free because he is God, and therefore all his decisions are made in perfect freedom, Zizioulas asserts that humanity's participation in the cross required humanity's agreement, freely given. For that, the indwelling power of the Holy Spirit was necessary, because true human freedom exists only through the presence of the Spirit. Christ is both God and human. It was the human "yes" that was required of him, humanity's representative. Thus, according to Zizioulas, Christ's free "yes" to the cross signified humanity's free "yes" to God's final solution to sin and death. Zizioulas is convinced that when Jesus of Nazareth died, he died as the Spirit-indwelt Christ, and not as someone abandoned by the Spirit. On the contrary, Zizioulas clearly gives the Holy Spirit a very significant role in the cross-resurrection event:

> *The Spirit* is present at Gethsemane, where the all-important decision to drink the cup, despite all its horror, is taken. *The Spirit* enables the Lord's free decision to go to the cross, and *the Spirit* raises Christ from the confines of death. The resurrection and the defeat of death is *the Spirit's* act in transcending all limits, and all dissolution and death.[157]

> This redemption, this liberation from the boundaries of the created status, is the work of the Holy Spirit, which manifested itself firstly in the Person of Christ—because the Spirit resurrected Christ—and thereafter passed on, into mankind, again as a gift and an energy of the Holy Spirit.[158]

---

155. Zizioulas, *Lectures*, 106–7.
156. Zizioulas, *Lectures*, 107.
157. Zizioulas, *Lectures*, 107; italics added.
158. Zizioulas, *Lessons*, E.6 ("Salvation").

b. The Spirit Did Not Suffer and Die with Christ

Although Zizioulas is convinced that the Holy Spirit was present in Christ right through his ordeal on the cross, giving him the power to endure it, and raising him from death, Zizioulas is adamant that the Spirit himself did not suffer and die with Christ:

> This was the life that the Son entered in the incarnation. Since it was the Son rather than the Spirit who entered our life and became incarnate, it is he rather than the Spirit who bears the dissolution and death that are the outcome of our history. The Spirit stands by the Son and finally sustains him through all the trauma that comes with his involvement in fallen creation.[159]

Zizioulas affirms that the Spirit maintained his close support of the suffering Christ, and yet paradoxically also insists that the Spirit remained transcendent throughout the cross event. This is not surprising given his reluctance to attribute suffering to the immanent Trinity. In his writings, Zizioulas never describes the Spirit, even in the economy, as someone who suffers. On the other hand, while Moltmann agrees with Zizioulas that the Spirit empowers the incarnate Son, Moltmann insists that the Spirit did indeed suffer empathetically with the Son.[160] Zizioulas, in contrast, emphasizes the transcendence and freedom of the Spirit, particularly over history.[161] He sees the Son voluntarily involving himself in history, while the Spirit ensures that the Son is liberated from history's linearity and the boundaries of time and space.[162] Zizioulas distinguishes between the immanent and the economic Trinity, and while he accepts that the economic Trinity reveals truths about the immanent Trinity, he rejects the idea that this revelation is entire and exhaustive.[163]

Nonetheless, Zizioulas's assertion that the Holy Spirit did not die with Christ is incontrovertible. Moltmann agrees.[164] While Lyle Dabney suggests that the work of the Spirit was abnegated at the cross,[165] and Bruce Mc-

---

159. Zizioulas, *Lectures*, 148.
160. Moltmann, *Spirit of Life*, 62–65. See chapter 4, §4.4 of this book.
161. Zizioulas, *Being as Communion*, 180.
162. Zizioulas, *Being as Communion*, 130.
163. Zizioulas, *Communion and Otherness*, 201.
164. "On Golgotha the Spirit suffers the suffering and death of the Son, without dying with him"; Moltmann, *Spirit of Life*, 64.
165. "On the cross, the *negation of the Son* means the *ab-negation of the Spirit*"; Dabney, "Naming the Spirit," 56.

Cormack believes that both the Father and the Holy Spirit abandoned the Son at the cross,[166] no one has yet presented a model of *pneumatologia crucis* that features the death of the Spirit. Importantly, there is no indication in the New Testament, explicit nor implicit, that this may have occurred. On the contrary, the Spirit is affirmed as "life" (Rom 8:2, 6, 10), "life-giver" (John 6:63; Rom 8:11),[167] "living water" (John 7:38, 39), and "eternal" (Heb 9:14). These descriptors and metaphors emphasize the inextinguishable vitality of the Holy Spirit as life itself. It is also worth noting that against McCormack's idea that the Spirit may have abandoned the Son at the cross, Zizioulas states clearly that when the Son freely empties himself of glory, undertaking the fate of the fallen world, "[h]is relationship with the Father and the Spirit is not broken."[168] Hence, Zizioulas not only rejects the idea that the Spirit abandoned the Son at the cross, but he also denies that the Father abandoned the Son. This latter notion was popularized by Moltmann, based on Jesus's cry of derelicition (Mark 15:35), and it has become quite entrenched in contemporary Christology. Zizioulas's insistence that the Father and the Spirit are *always* with the Son does raise the logical possibility, however, that they experienced the Son's suffering at the cross. Scripture is admittedly silent on this point, while we may conjecture that the intimate unity of the Trinitarian persons leads to that notion.

c. Humanity and Creation Died and Rose with Christ

The concept that Christ died and rose as a corporate being, embodying humanity in his journey through the cross and resurrection, is the key concept that differentiates Zizioulas's *pneumatologia crucis* from those of Taylor and Moltmann. Humanity participates in Christ's death and resurrection, according to Zizioulas, through the power of the Holy Spirit:

> Why is it the Holy Spirit who raises Christ from the dead? Christ is God, so death could never have held him, so why is there this need for the Spirit? The Holy Spirit makes the whole incarnation an expression of the freedom in which, because of Christ, man now participates. The Spirit who liberates all that is created from trials and from deterioration and death, has in Christ passed

---

166. "No death in God-abandonment can occur unless the Son is finally abandoned by both Father and Spirit"; McCormack, "Loud Cries and Tears," 55.

167. τὸ πνεῦμά ἐστιν τὸ ζωοποιοῦν (John 6:63); τὸ πνεῦμά . . . ζωοποιήσει καὶ τὰ θνητὰ σώματα ὑμῶν (Rom 8:11).

168. Zizioulas, *Lectures*, 109.

into humanity. Once dissolution and death are transcended in Christ, the Holy Spirit makes Christ that body within which all mankind begins to experience freedom from death. The Spirit makes Christ's resurrection the liberation from death, not just for Jesus but for all humanity.[169]

The Holy Spirit has made Christ the universal being in whom the boundaries of the created are transcended. Christ ceases to be an individual and has become the truth of human existence, so his life has universal reach. He has broken out of the nature-determined constraints that make him merely one person, separated from nature from all other persons. As Christ took on the fate of creation, creation is taking on the fate of Christ, being liberated from its confines and liberated . . . Christ has broken through these boundaries for created mankind, not as one person alone, but in the Holy Spirit, for all. The Holy Spirit makes Christ *the Christ* by making him inclusive of all humanity.[170]

Whatever the Pauline phrase "you have put on Christ" means in the Bible . . . it cannot be unrelated to putting on incorruption and immortality, since it involves the baptizand's burial and *resurrection* with Christ (surely not a moral and metaphorical resurrection, but an ontological one).[171]

If we see salvation as deliverance not only from social and moral evil but also from corruption and death, thus giving it ontological content, then we necessarily link human existence and the human person with "how God is" since He alone has immortality by nature. This of course, is not achieved through a Platonic flight from history, but *by participation in the Cross of Christ and His Resurrection.* The path is Christology, a Christology that is translated existentially into ecclesiology, into our participation in the Body of Christ in the Spirit.[172]

Although the Church and the whole economy now took a path that passed through the cross, the end of that path remained as it had been from the beginning, the union of the created with the uncreated God. The Church goes through the cross and

---

169. Zizioulas, *Lectures*, 107–8.
170. Zizioulas, *Lectures*, 108.
171. Zizioulas, *One and The Many*, 35.
172. Zizioulas, *One and The Many*, 40; italics added.

travels on until all the discipline of the cross is transformed into the attributes of the *eschaton*, the resurrection.[173]

These five passages are indicative of Zizioulas's vision of the cross as the event at which, through the power and work of the Spirit, the corporate Christ takes on the death and dissolution of fallen creation, then overcoming death, breaks free into the liberation of the *eschaton*, bringing all humanity with him. The Spirit not only empowers Christ as he bears the full consequence of humanity's rebellion, but the Spirit simultaneously maintains the embodiment of humanity within Christ throughout the cross event. The Spirit subsequently raises Christ from death, and with him, humanity. "Why is it the Holy Spirit that raises Christ from the dead?" Zizioulas asks.[174] His answer—not that Christ is unable to rise from the dead himself, since he is God,[175] but because it is the Spirit's particular task to unite humanity to Christ, so as to ensure that redemption of all humanity becomes possible, and to raise the new humanity spiritually reborn in Christ. Indeed, it is the re-creation of *humanity* that requires the life-generating power of the Holy Spirit. If Christ died as an individual (an impossibility according to Zizioulas's Christology), he could have risen from death by himself, since he is the Son of God.[176] But the death and re-creation of *humans in Christ* required the work of the Spirit.

Drawing upon Zizioulas's thoughts and integrating them with Paul's in Romans 3:25, one may perhaps envisage Christ, Son of God, to be the very place, the mercy seat, the *hilastērion*, the crucible within which this momentous work of the Spirit occurred, in accordance with the will and plan of the Father. Only the holy Son of God was able to bear all humanity through this great exchange; only the second Adam, representing fallen humanity, was able to accept the full penalty for sin, to bring the first Adamic choice to disobey God to its legal conclusion, death, so that the Spirit can now bring new life into being in the second Adam. There are two notable observations regarding the death and resurrection of humanity in Christ. First, although Christ's death and resurrection has taken place in history, meaning that this

---

173. Zizioulas, *Lectures*, 133.

174. Zizioulas, *Lectures*, 107.

175. "He was raised from the dead by the Holy Spirit. The biblical witness is clear that it was the Father who raised the Son through the Holy Spirit. It is not enough to say that it was Christ's divine nature that overcame death . . . The idea that it was by his divine nature that Christ overcame death was introduced by Pope Leo I in the council of Chalcedon, against Cyril's insistence that agency can be attributed only to persons, not to natures"; Zizioulas, *Lectures*, 148–49.

176. Jesus asserts that he has the power to lay down his life, and *also* the power to take it up again (John 10:17–18).

event occurred in a particular place and in a particular time, Christ saves humans from all ages and places. Thus, while the cross event is an event in history, its reach and impact breaks free from the limits of time and space. If this were not so, then those in the twenty-first century and not living in Jerusalem would be excluded from Christ's redemptive death and resurrection. Paul would also have been incorrect to imply that Abraham, living centuries before Jesus, was saved, and to hold him up as God's model of faith for Christ's followers (Rom 4:3, 13–25). The cross event is therefore both historical and eternal. The eternality of the cross event is the work of the eternal Holy Spirit (Heb 9:14) who unites humanity to Christ, humans from all ages and all places.

Second, just as the risen Christ is the same Christ who was crucified, but whose humanity is no longer from the old order but from the *eschaton*, likewise we who died and rose with him remain ourselves, and yet we are no longer our old sinful selves but we are now the new humans belonging to God's realm (Rom 8:1–17). This is a miraculous paradox that defies analogical description. Money laundering assumes the complete exchange of notes, while washing of clothes removes dirt, but the clothes themselves are unchanged. Here, we are no longer our old selves—we are reborn—and yet we are still distinctly and uniquely ourselves. This is the work of the Holy Spirit in Christ.

New Life in the Spirit in Christ

For Zizioulas, new life in the Spirit can only be found in Christ. Since it is only through participation in the corporate Christ, through his death and resurrection, that humanity is given the Holy Spirit, it follows that Zizioulas does not envisage new life in the Spirit apart from Christ. "The Holy Spirit always acts *through* Christ, because Christ is the point where all mankind and all creation are gathered up and brought into living communion with God on whom there are no confines."[177] Furthermore, he states that "it is extremely dangerous for the unity of the Economy to speak of a special 'Economy of the Spirit.' With regards to the Church in particular, any such view would make it difficult to understand the biblical assertion that the Church is the Body of Christ and not of the Spirit."[178] Zizioulas is adamant that salvation does not exist outside Christ. On the other hand, he sees *all creation*, not only humanity, redeemed through Christ, in order to be brought into communion with God:

177. Zizioulas, *Lectures*, 108.
178. Zizioulas, *One and The Many*, 77.

The result of this, was that the Spirit, who liberates the created from trials and temptations such as deterioration and death, has hereafter passed into human nature, through Christ. And since deterioration and death are transcended in the Person of Christ, through the energy of the Holy Spirit—since these things are happening to Christ—the Person of Christ is thereafter rendered a Body, on which all of mankind becomes a partaker of the Holy Spirit. Thus, Christ ceases to be an individual; He becomes a universal existence, which took upon it the fate of fallen creation and is now taking upon it the fate of redeemed creation—of creation which is now liberated from its limits (because that is what liberation implies: a liberation from its former boundaries). This redemption, this liberation from the boundaries of the created status, is the work of the Holy Spirit, which manifested itself firstly in the Person of Christ—because the Spirit resurrected Christ—and thereafter passed on, into mankind, again as a gift and an energy of the Holy Spirit. This is why Christ—that universal being in whom the boundaries of the created are transcended—this Christ is the One who imparts or realizes the transcending of the created's boundaries for all of mankind, not as the person Christ alone, but through the Holy Spirit, by imparting the Holy Spirit.[179]

This is a very wide and all-encompassing vista of the scope of God's salvation. While Zizioulas generally signifies the church when speaking of the corporate Christ, in many places in his writings, the passage above being an example, he includes "all of mankind" and "creation" within the Spirit-indwelt body of Christ. His frequent juxtaposition of the church and humanity/creation can be confusing. It is perhaps in his interpretation of the Eucharist that this apparent confusion is resolved. The Eucharist is for Zizioulas the liturgical expression and celebration of the eschatological rebirth of creation, a participation in "the order of the new world."[180] He asserts that through the Eucharist, the church, with Christ as her head, stands as the "priest of the world," offering creation back to God through the Spirit. Believers in Christ act with him as God's royal priesthood.[181] "The fundamental character of the Eucharist consists in the fact that it is a gathering and an act and that *the whole mystery of Christ* (the *totus*

---

179. Zizioulas, *Lessons*, E.6 ("Salvation").

180. Zizioulas, *Eucharistic Communion*, 32.

181. "The Eucharistic synaxis accomplishes this priestly act and it is in this sense that all the faithful who participate in the Eucharist are a 'royal priesthood' (1 Pet. 2:9; cf. Rev. 5:10)"; Zizioulas, *Eucharistic Communion*, 33.

Christus)—the salvation of the world—is revealed in it, lives in it and is concentrated in it."[182]

This eucharistic vision of the world does not exclude and reject the world but instead sees the world in God's eschatological light, the world as it *should* be, and of which the church is its forerunner. In the Eucharist, the "now-and-not-yet" tension is acknowledged, for much of the world is still hostile to Christ. For this reason, Zizioulas believes that the eucharistic celebration should be restricted to those committed to Christ. Nevertheless, the hostile world is the same world that Christ died and rose to save, and in the Eucharist, the people of God bring this very world into God's presence. "In this vision of the Eucharist the world receives sacramental significance and ceases to be a field separate from the Church."[183]

A theological dilemma that immediately arises from Zizioulas's universal view of the scope of Christ's salvific work is the question whether faith in Christ is then necessary for salvation. Furthermore, what is the eternal fate of those who die without volitionally committing themselves to Christ because of lack of opportunity or understanding? Are they to be regarded as part of Christ's body albeit involuntarily? Zizioulas does not appear to address these questions. Perhaps it is not surprising that Clark Pinnock, who sees the Spirit as the Son's coworker in the Father's mission for redeeming humanity, and shares with Zizioulas the conviction that all humanity dies and rises in Christ at the cross through the power of the Spirit,[184] champions the inclusivist understanding of salvation.[185] Unfortunately, the destiny of the unevangelized is too broad and complex to be addressed here.

5.5 Summary

Zizioulas's theology is driven by his ecumenical passion, modelled after the Eucharist, and viewed through the lens of relational ontology. For Zizioulas, authentic personhood is defined in ontological terms of freedom, uniqueness, and unrepeatability, as well as in relational terms of being-in-community. His conviction that true personhood exists only in community is underpinned by a concept which appears in much of his work namely, his "one and many" motif. This motif informs his Trinitarian theology, Christology, pneumatology, and ecclesiology. For Zizioulas, therefore, Christ is always the corporate Christ who, through the power

---

182. Zizioulas, *Eucharistic Communion*, 124.
183. Zizioulas, *Eucharistic Communion*, 33.
184. Pinnock, *Flame of Love*, 94–97.
185. Pinnock, *Wideness in God's Mercy*, 157–68.

of the Holy Spirit, embodies within himself all humanity, and is simultaneously "the one" and "the many." The Spirit ensures both the unity and the distinctiveness of each human in Christ. Zizioulas maintains that it is the corporate pneumatic Christ, not the individual man, Jesus, who undertook the redemptive journey through death to life, who died and rose at Golgotha. It is only through humanity's participation in the death and resurrection of Jesus Christ, through the power of the Holy Spirit, that the ontological corruption that has pervaded all humanity may be completely dealt with, so that God's eschatological goal for creation, communion, may be achieved. For Zizioulas, Christ is not Christ without the Spirit, neither does he envisage the Spirit separate from Christ.

6

Pneumatologia Crucis—A Biblical Basis

THE COGENCY OF ANY theological idea in Christian doctrinal development is measured to a great extent by its rootedness, consistency, and alignment with Scripture. Is the concept of a *pneumatologia crucis* consistent with the biblical witness? The Epistle to the Hebrews may provide the only direct reference to the role of the Holy Spirit in the soteriological work of Christ. In this chapter I argue for a biblical foundation for a *pneumatologia crucis* by examining the pneumatology of Hebrews, paying particular attention to Hebrews 9:14, and by interpreting *Yom Kippur* ("Day of Atonement") through a christological lens. In addition, I contend that there is additional support for a *pneumatologia crucis* in the New Testament in its use of pneumatic covenantal language, and in the unifying role given to the Holy Spirit.

6.1 Pneumatology in Hebrews

Why mention the Holy Spirit in Hebrews? If this question seems to flow against the stream of a pneumatological study and to undermine its agenda, we must, from the outset, acknowledge that the focus in Hebrews is Christology and not pneumatology. It is a carefully crafted theological argument which draws heavily upon the sacred writings of Israel. The author,[1] how-

---

1. While the authorship of Hebrews has been attributed to several candidates over the centuries, among them Paul, Barnabas, Apollos, Luke, Silvanus, Prisca, and Aquila, the masculine ending of the self-referential participle διηγούμενον ("I am telling," Heb 11:32) supports male authorship. Ruth Hoppin posits that the participle of Hebrews 11:32 may be neuter rather than a masculine, or a deliberate alteration of an original feminine participle; Hoppins, "Priscilla's Letter," 147–48. As her argument does not seem entirely convincing, and as the gender of the author of the Epistle is not germane to this study, I shall use the masculine pronoun.

ever, is no armchair theologian engaging in an intellectual exercise, but is responding to a Christian community in crisis who, because of religious persecution, is in grave danger of apostasy.[2] "As a true pastor, who understands their peril and their fears, he displays a combination of firmness and tenderness."[3] While resembling a letter in its ending, this document has the rhetorical features of a sermon.[4] The author's aim is to establish beyond doubt in the minds of the recipients of this letter that Jesus is the mediator of God's new covenant, that he is God's definitive and perfect atonement sacrifice and therefore the *only* sacrifice that matters in God's salvation plan, all other sacrifices being typological "shadows" or "copies." It is in *Christ* that God's promises to Israel are fulfilled. The author of Hebrews sees Israel's Scripture as a record of a history of promise. He sees both continuity and discontinuity in the way God speaks through Israel's prophets and through his Son, but "Christ is the final content of God's word."[5] Thus, history is seen in the light of eschatology, and the central reference from which Israel's history with God should be understood is Jesus, not Moses. While the focus of Hebrews may be Christology, the author's context is clearly eschatological.[6] He believes that he and his hearers live "in *these* last days" (ἐπ' ἐσχάτου τῶν ἡμερῶν τούτων, Heb 1:2) meaning that they were *already* living in the eschatological age even while they looked forward to the coming of God's sabbath "rest" (Heb 4:9–11).

In a radical reversal of theological perspective, the author of Hebrews reinterprets Israel's cultic sacrifices from a christological vantage point, thus understanding the past from the present, and the present from the future. While it seems natural to see the significance of Jesus's death through the hermeneutical grid of Israel's cultic sacrificial system, which to a significant extent he does, the author strongly asserts that, really, it should be the other way around. Thus, the Exodus tabernacle and its cultic sacrifices, and by implication the Jerusalem temple and its sacrificial system, have always been patterned after the heavenly sanctuary and Christ's perfect sacrifice.[7]

---

2. DeSilva, *Perseverance in Gratitude*, 25, n. 73; Koester, *Hebrews*, 42–46; Allen, *Lukan Authorship*, 2010, 1–39. Morna D. Hooker suggests that the word "crisis" may be overstating the exegetical evidence, but nonetheless agrees that Hebrews was written to warn the community of dangers confronting it; Hooker, "Christ the 'End,'" 192–93.

3. O'Brien, *Hebrews*, 9.

4. O'Brien, *Hebrews*, 25.

5. Hughes, *Hebrews and Hermeneutics*, 56, 36–74.

6. Scot D. Mackie asserts that "Hebrews is one of the most eschatologically oriented books in the New Testament"; Mackie, "Eschatological Experience," 94.

7. Heb 8:2, 5–6; 9:23–26. σκιά ("shadow," Heb 8:5), τὰ ὑποδείγματα ("the patterns," Heb 9:23), ἀντίτυπα τῶν ἀληθινῶν ("antitype/copy of the real things," Heb 9:24).

Thus, according to the author of Hebrews, the Levitical sacrificial system not only imitates (imperfectly) the high priesthood and atoning sacrifice of Jesus, but draws its spiritual significance from him. This approach is radical because humans experience and interpret history in a unidirectional way, past to future, not the future to the past. Jesus, as Messiah, is not simply to be "added on" as the finishing touch to an ongoing method of sanctifying sinners, but he is instead *the centerpiece* in God's strategy for bringing creation to its eschatological destiny.[8] In other words, *Christ* is the reality that the Aaronic priesthood and ritual sacrifices attempt to convey. The Levitical sacrifices may possibly be viewed as pedagogical rehearsals leading up to the real event at Golgotha, so that Israel and the rest of humanity "get it" when Christ dies and rises from the dead. Thus the "rehearsals" and the "real event" share the same covenant paradigm, but where the former involve stand-ins (for both priest and sacrifice), the latter involves the *real* high priest and sacrifice. The entire Levitical sacrificial system may also, perhaps, be understood as a complex enacted metaphor for Christ's atoning work, just as Israel's prophets often physically dramatized their messages for greater emphasis and effect.[9]

The author of Hebrews supports his christological perspective of Israel's cultic sacrifices by highlighting the divine sonship and high priesthood of Jesus Christ. He makes the following points:

Jesus is the Incarnate Son of God

a. He is the reflection of God's glory and the exact imprint of God's being (Heb 1:3).

b. He is called God and Lord (Heb 1:8, 10).

c. He possesses an indestructible life (Heb 7:16) and like God, he is eternal (Heb 1:8, 12; 7:24–25, 28; 13:8).[10]

d. He is God's agent in creation and he continues to sustain it by his powerful word (Heb 1:2–3, 10).[11]

---

8. Hooker, "Christ, the 'End,'" 208.

9. For example, Jeremiah 13:1–11 and Ezekiel 4, 5.

10. Inherent uncreated eternality is the attribute that defines divinity in both Jewish and Hellenistic theology; Bauckham, "Divinity of Jesus Christ," 16, 31.

11. Terry J. Wright suggests that the Son's "sustaining" activity refers to his high priestly role rather than to his creative role. Hence, Christ preserves the *relationship* between God and creation. Wright correctly acknowledges, however, that both roles are in view and not one in exclusion of the other; Wright, "Seal of Approval," 144–45.

e. He is heir to "all things," signifying that creation was made for him (Heb 1:2) just as "all things" exist for and through God (Heb 2:10).

f. He is the final and definitive spokesperson for God (Heb 1:2).

g. His ministry and authority in God's "house" as Son are superior to Moses's ministry and authority as servant (Heb 3:1–6).

h. Yet he is fully human, ontologically and experientially, and thus a suitable representative for humanity (Heb 2:14, 17–18).

i. Although fully human, Jesus is holy, sinless, flawless, and perfect (Heb 2:10; 4:15; 5:9; 7:26–28; 9:14).

j. As partners with Christ, believers share in his firstborn sonship (Heb 3:14; 12:23, cf. 1:6) even as Jesus shares in our fragile humanity (Heb 2:14–18; 4:15).

Jesus is Humanity's Eternal High Priest

a. He is the mediator of the new and definitive covenant, of which the promised inheritance is not land, but the eternal kingdom of God (Heb 8:6; 9:15; 12:28).

b. The covenant is mediated through his blood (Heb 9:12; 10:10, 29; 13:12, 20) and redemption through his death (Heb 2:9, 14–15).

c. He is the eternal, perfect, sinless high priest, and sacrifice (Heb 6:20; 7:24, 8:1–2; 9:14).[12]

d. His is a once-only sacrifice, offered within the true heavenly sanctuary, and in the definitive *Yom Kippur* (יוֹם כִּפּוּר, "Day of Atonement"; cf. Lev 16), with eternal benefits for humanity (Heb 5:9; 9:11–12, 24–28; 10:10–14).

---

12. Harold W. Attridge discerns a "severe antimony" which puts into tension "the affirmations about the Son's status as High Priest," attributing the portrayal of what he considers unrelated roles of sonship and high priesthood to different ecclesiastical traditions or a response to different polemical situations; Attridge, *Epistle to the Hebrews*, 25–26. Perhaps this is too extreme a view, since participation in Christ (μέτοχοι . . . τοῦ Χριστοῦ, Heb 3:14) and the formation of the heavenly "assembly of the firstborns" (ἐκκλησία πρωτοτόκων, Heb 12:23), is achieved by the Son's high priestly work. Bruce McCormack sees no contradiction or incompatibility in Jesus's divine sonship and high priestly roles: "The 'Son' is not another or different subject than the subject who makes purification; he is the same subject viewed from a different angle"; McCormack, "Loud Cries and Tears," 59.

e. Having completed atonement for humanity, he sits with God in heaven and lives to intercede eternally for believers (Heb 7:25; 8:1–2), just as he continues to sustain "all things" by his powerful word (Heb 1:3).

In concord with the Fourth Gospel, the author of Hebrews opens his sermonic letter with a lofty exordium, introducing the preexistent Son of God with a brief resume of his divine status and his key achievements, and at the same time previewing his core message. The author presents a high Christology that is both protological and eschatological, citing and freely recontextualizing Old Testament scriptural passages for his own theological purposes, recasting many in the form of divine address about, to, or from Jesus.[13] He begins his letter by declaring confidently that Jesus is the eschatological form of God's Word, and boldly goes on to interpret Scripture christologically.[14] Despite making few direct references to Jesus's resurrection,[15] it is evident that Jesus's exaltation, divine sonship, and eternality are presupposed by the author and declared outright without attestation. These presuppositions, in fact, form the base for the author's christological argument.[16] He speaks about Jesus's indestructible life and exalted heavenly status as truth indisputably accepted by his hearers. If they shrink away from Christ, it is not because they have doubts about the reality of his resurrection but because of an inadequate understanding of the primacy and complete efficacy of his atoning death, and the eschatological significance of his resurrection and exaltation. In other words, the author of Hebrews insists that Jesus did not die because of tragic circumstances, and that he is resurrected and exalted not because he is a sinless person, but in order that through his death and resurrection God achieves complete cleansing of human sin and reconciliation with humanity.

How does the death and resurrection of Jesus impact the traditional practice of cultic sacrifices? Jesus was a Jew. In the gospel accounts, Jesus

---

13. Attridge, *Hebrews*, 24. As a methodological principle, the author of Hebrews chooses scriptural passages with direct speech, perhaps to emphasize his theme of "God is speaking."

14. Hughes, *Hebrews and Hermeneutics*, 8; DeSilva, *Perseverance in Gratitude*, 32.

15. The only direct reference is in Hebrews 13:20. The paucity of such references to Jesus's resurrection, in contrast to references to his exaltation, has been noted. Attridge, *Hebrews*, 406; Koester, *Hebrews*, 104; Peterson, *Hebrews and Perfection*, 70. Yet it is clear that this paucity is not because the resurrection is in doubt since the embodied Jesus cannot be living an indestructible life as humanity's eternal high priest in heaven if this event did not occur, but simply because the resurrection is *not* in doubt. The author is addressing believers, not non-believers. David Moffitt argues that Jesus's resurrection is present in the text and in the author's theological argument as a category even if not in precise phraseology; Moffit, "If Another Priest Arises," 68–79.

16. Koester, *Hebrews*, 104.

himself asked a leper he had healed to comply with the Mosaic regulations for health certification, including the offering of an appropriate sacrifice (Mark 1:44; Matt 8:4; cf. Lev 14:1–32). In the early days of their ministry, the apostles themselves were often in the temple (Acts 2:46; 3:1; 5:12, 21); Paul participated in purification rites and sacrificial offerings in the temple (Acts 21:26). "Why should loyal Jews who were now convinced that Jesus is God's Messiah cease to worship God in the traditional ways, or abandon their observance of the Torah? The picture in Acts is entirely believable."[17] Could not one be a Jew in the traditional sense and affirm the salvation offered by Jesus? While Hebrews does not address circumcision and kosher food laws, perhaps because they were not an issue for *Jewish* Christians,[18] the author's answer is adamantly negative with regards to the continued practice of offering animal sacrifices, against which he pitches a carefully argued, carefully evidenced, and impassioned critique. He rejects any compromise on this matter. Hays comments: "the author of Hebrews is not interested in a blanket abolition of the Mosaic Torah. Rather, his concern focuses narrowly on the cultic practice of offering sacrifices for sins under the first covenant, particularly on the Day of Atonement, as Heb. 9 will show."[19] Not that the author denies the value of cultic sacrifices in Israel's past relationship with her God, but he contends that with Jesus's sacrificial death, there is no longer further need for ritual sacrifices for sin. The author's frequent use of Israel's Scripture to argue his theological position affirms the validity of previous prophetic insights concerning God's holiness and human sin, the need for atonement and the reliability of divine promises made to Israel, but he insists that there is a clear distinction between that which is a temporary earthly copy and that which is the eternal (thus permanent) heavenly reality. The inadequacy of animal sacrifices, despite their regularity and frequency, to atone for human sin and to cleanse the inner conscience is contrasted with the complete efficacy of the once-only sacrifice of God's Christ.

The author of Hebrews presents a strong and comprehensive argument that Jesus is *the definitive mediator* between God and humanity. It would seem that his case is sufficiently persuasive without recourse to references to the Holy Spirit. Lindars observes that "there is no emphasis on the Spirit, and in fact the Spirit plays no part in the argument of the letter."[20] Even stronger is Swete's comment: "In Hebrews there is no theology of the Spirit."[21] Indeed

---

17. Hooker, "Christ, the 'End,'" 190–91.
18. Hays, "No Lasting City," 154; O'Brien, *Hebrews*, 11.
19. Hays, "No Lasting City," 161.
20. Lindars, *Theology of the Letter*, 55–56.
21. Swete, *Spirit in the New Testament*, 249, quoted by Emmrich, *Pneumatological*

it is notable that the author of Hebrews does not mention the Holy Spirit even when it seems pneumatologically appropriate to do so. For example, the author does not, like other New Testament writers, mention the Spirit's involvement in Jesus's incarnation, baptism, earthly ministry or resurrection, nor does he refer to the Spirit when he applies enthronement psalms (Pss 2 and 110) to Jesus's appointment as Son of God (Heb 1:5). Moreover, when the author exhorts his suffering congregation to maintain faith in Jesus Christ in the face of persecution by walking them through Israel's hall of faith (Heb 11) in order to encourage them to imitate these spiritual heroes, at no point does he remind them that the Holy Spirit will help them through this time of trial and weakness, as do the gospel writers (Mark 13:11; Luke 12:12; John 14:26; 16:13) and Paul (Rom 8:26–28).

The observation of both Lindars and Swete concerning the paucity of references to the Holy Spirit in Hebrews is correct. Yet this is the puzzle: in a document which is "consciously beautifully written, carefully constructed, theologically profound and powerfully argued"[22] in which Jesus as divine Son and humanity's high priest is in focus, why then mention the Holy Spirit at all? What is the purpose of these references to the Spirit? How does the attestation of the Holy Spirit lend weight to the author's christological argument, or help to dissuade persecuted and ostracized Christians from withdrawing from this new and "illicit" sect and returning to the legal umbrella and practices of their religious tradition?[23]

Of the eight phrases in Hebrews which contain the singular noun πνεῦμα, seven phrases have been understood to refer to the Holy Spirit, while the eighth (Heb 4:12) refers to the human spirit.[24] The seven pneumatological phrases are shown below, and except for Hebrews 9:14 where a few manuscripts have ἁγίου instead of αἰωνίου, all these phrases have no known textual variants. Five of these seven phrases are hermeneutically unambiguous and have not been controversial as references to the Holy Spirit, irrespective of the presence or absence of the article—Hebrews 1:4 (πνεύματος ἁγίου), 3:7 (τὸ πνεῦμα τὸ ἅγιον), 6:4 (πνεύματος ἁγίου), 9:8 (τοῦ πνεύματος τοῦ ἁγίου), and 10:15 (τὸ πνεῦμα τὸ ἅγιον). The two other phrases are

---

Concepts, 1.

22. O'Brien, *Hebrews*, 1.

23. Hooker suggests that this epistle was written when Jewish Christians were being expelled from the synagogues for the claims they made about Jesus, and they were excluded from ceremonies centered on the Jerusalem temple, assuming it was not yet destroyed; "Christ, the 'End,'" 189, 191. The discussion concerning whether Hebrews was written before or after 70 CE does not materially impact this study.

24. See appendix 1 for verses in full, in Greek (*NA28*) and English (*NRSV*).

probable references to the Holy Spirit—Hebrews 9:14 (πνεύματος αἰωνίου), and 10:29 (τὸ πνεῦμα τῆς χάριτος).

In regard to Hebrews 10:29, there is a general consensus that the phrase τὸ πνεῦμα τῆς χάριτος ("Spirit of grace") refers to the Holy Spirit, since it is more likely that the one "insulted" (ἐνυβρίσας) is a person rather than a "spiritual" attribute.[25] John Owen makes this interpretation explicit in his commentary on this verse: "The Holy Spirit of God promised and communicated under the gospel by Jesus Christ from the Father, as the author and cause, actually communicating and applying of all grace unto the souls of them that believe, is this Spirit of grace."[26] It is the meaning of the phrase πνεύματος αἰωνίου ("eternal s/Spirit") in Hebrews 9:14 that has been contentious, and this will be examined in detail in the next section.

Contrary to the conclusion drawn by Lindars and Swete, it is my contention that the references to the Holy Spirit, while few, are not arbitrary but intentional, and that with them the epistle accomplishes the following: first, affirmation of divine authority for the author's radical and christological interpretation of Israel's Scripture; second, confirmation that faith in *Jesus* and in his atoning work is the requirement for covenant membership in God's eschatological kingdom; and third, assurance for those accustomed to regular temple sacrifices as the core expression of covenantal worship that Jesus's *singular* offering has *eternal* efficacy, so that they are not disobeying God by ceasing to offer these sacrifices.

Pneumatic Authority for New Perspectives and Insights

The author of Hebrews draws upon the Holy Spirit's authority for his message by affirming that the divine Spirit who spoke in the past through the prophets of Israel is the *very same Holy Spirit* who is the source for his new insights. This is shown by his pneumatic perspective of Psalm 95 (Heb 3:7), and of the relationship between the earthly and heavenly sanctuaries (Heb 9:8).

Although the author identifies David as the psalmist of Psalm 95 (Heb 4:7), he attributes its true source to the Holy Spirit (Heb 3:7).[27] That this

25. For example, Calvin, *Epistle of Paul*, 149; Owen, *Exposition*, 546–47; Westcott, *Epistle to the Hebrews*, 331; Attridge, *Hebrews*, 295; Koester, *Hebrews*, 453; O'Brien, *Hebrews*, 379; Lindars, *Theology of the Letter*, 57; Emmrich, *Pneumatological Concepts*, 15. DeSilva, however, translates the phrase τὸ πνεῦμα τῆς χαρίτος as "the spirit of favour"; he focuses his attention on the contrast between ὕβρις and χάρις but makes no comment on the significance of the word πνεῦμα; *Perseverance*, 344, 349–50.

26. Owen, *Exposition*, 546.

27. Lindars, *Theology of the Letter*, 57; O'Brien, *Hebrews*, 140. "Identifying the Spirit as the speaker fits Hebrews' earlier account of the community's own experience";

Spirit is none other than the Spirit *of God* is made clear by the author's declaration from the outset that it is *God* who spoke through Israel's ancestors and prophets (Heb 1:1). Furthermore, he finishes his christological interpretation of Psalm 95 with his affirmation that "the word of God is living and active" (Heb 4:12). Importantly, the contemporizing of the Holy Spirit's utterance with the present tense verb λέγει ("speaks" or "is speaking"), and the repeated stress on the word "today" (Heb 3:7, 13, 15; 4:7), both emphasize the urgency and relevance of the psalmist's (or Holy Spirit's) words for the author's hearers.[28] "The author of the epistle to the Hebrews thus opens a channel of communication from the Spirit to the audience, which in this specific form (recycling of Old Testament oracles), constitutes a unique application of the concept of the "today," suggests that the Holy Spirit himself is speaking through the words of this epistle. Perhaps that is precisely what the author intends to convey. If so, the author implicitly lays claim to pneumatic inspiration, in line with Israel's prophets.[29] The community is urged therefore to consider seriously the epistle's warnings, since the source of its message is none other than the Holy Spirit who is addressing the hearers in their present time and current situation.

In Hebrew 9:8, the author asserts that it is the *Holy Spirit* who "indicates" (δηλοῦντος, present participle, literally "the one clarifying" or "the one showing") that the very layout of the earthly tabernacle, with its separation between the innermost "Holy of Holies" (Ἅγια Ἁγίων) and the outer "Holy [Place]" (Ἅγια; Heb 9:2–3), points to the inaccessibility of God's presence to all humans but the high priest (Heb 9:6–7). It is the Holy Spirit who reveals the significance of this inaccessibility—it demonstrates the inadequacy of the Levitical sacrificial system to completely cleanse human sin and fully restore God-human relations (Heb 9:9–10). This Spirit-inspired insight critiques the Mosaic tabernacle from a christological perspective. Once again, pneumatic authority is invoked. As in Hebrews 3:7, the author uses the present tense, perhaps to emphasize once more the contemporaneity of the Spirit's elucidation. Emmrich notes, "Here the Spirit functions as

---

Koester, *Hebrews*, 263.

28. "The mention of the Spirit in 3:7, however, has mainly to do with the way the Spirit *continues* to speak through the text, making it a living word of God (4:12–13)"; Koester, *Hebrews*, 254. "Even more striking is that the Spirit's speaking is in the present: 'Just as the Holy Spirit says.' This is not only a stylistic variant, for the subsequent interpretation of the psalm stresses the contemporaneity of its voice"; Johnson, *Hebrews*, 113. See also O'Brien, *Hebrews*, 140, 312. Other New Testament writers invoke the divinely authoritative speech of the Holy Spirit (Acts 13:2; 21:11; 1 Tim 4:1; Rev 2:7, 11, 17, 29; 3:6, 13, 22; 14:13, 22:17).

29. One can almost hear in the author's impassioned plea, the prophetic words, "Thus says the LORD!"

the interpreter of scripture, in that he reveals the true significance of Yahweh's tent of meeting and the sacerdotal service on the Day of Atonement."[30] Interestingly, although Lindars sees a minor role for the Holy Spirit in this epistle, he too affirms:

> The elaborate ceremonies of atonement do not in fact establish the relationship with God which belongs to the Messianic age. The annual entry of the high priest into the Holy of Holies never gets beyond an atoning rite which ought to result in removing the barrier created by sin, but fails to do so. Hebrews sees the two chambers as symbolical, and attributes this to the *Holy Spirit* (verses 8–9).[31]

In Hebrews 3:7 and 9:8, the author uses the articular τὸ πνεῦμα τὸ ἅγιον, and as mentioned, there no known textual variants for this phrase in either verse, so that there is little doubt that the divine Spirit is in view. Thus, according to Hebrews, in the last days God speaks through his Son (Heb 1:2) *and* through his Spirit.[32] In Hebrews 3:7 and 9:8, the author could have written "God says" and "God indicates" without affecting his christological argument. Yet he appears to spotlight the Holy Spirit as the subject of these actions, and in doing so, he acknowledges the agency of the Holy Spirit in divine revelation, not only in past but continuing into the present time. John Owen asserts that it is the Holy Spirit who was the very architect of the Mosaic tabernacle, who appointed the priests, and who constituted the entire sacrificial system, and it is the very same Spirit who continues to reveal their true christological significance:

> For he who by his authority and wisdom disposed of the worship of God under the Old Testament, so as it might typify and represent things afterwards to come to pass and be revealed, is so, and none other. He who doth these things, and can do them, is he in whom we believe, the *Holy Spirit*. And as he is the immediate author and appointer of all divine worship, so there are characters of his wisdom and holiness on all the parts of it.[33]
>
> How eminent was the divine wisdom of the Holy Ghost in the structure and order of this tabernacle! What provision of

---

30. Emmrich, *Pneumatological Concepts*, 27.
31. Lindars, *Theology of the Letter*, 87, italics added.
32. It is interesting to note that in Revelation, while the seven churches are directly addressed by the risen Jesus, the divine messages are what "the Spirit is saying" (τὸ πνεῦμα λέγει) (Rev 2:7, 11, 17, 29; 3:6, 13, 22).
33. Owen, *Exposition*, 235.

instruction for the present and future use of the church was laid up and stored in them! . . . He alone in whose divine understanding the whole mystery of the incarnation of the Son of God and his mediation did eternally reside, could institute and appoint these things. And to instruct us unto a humble adoration of that wisdom, is the framing of the whole fabric and the institution of all its ordinances, contained in the sacred record for the use of the church.[34]

If, as Owen's reading of Hebrews suggests, the Holy Spirit is the designer of the tabernacle, priesthood, and ordinances of the covenant (old and new), then it is not surprising that it is the Holy Spirit who indicates that the way into the inner sanctuary is temporarily restricted (Heb 9:8) until the appearance of its true high priest, Jesus Christ (Heb 9:12; 10:20).

Eschatological Efficacy of Christ's Sacrifice

In his epistle, the author appears to address doubts among his hearers regarding their salvation and membership in God's eschatological kingdom. How can they be absolutely sure that faith in Jesus Christ is all-sufficient for redemption from sin, and for inclusion as members of God's holy people? How indeed can the public execution of one man replace and even supersede the entire sacrificial system divinely constituted centuries ago? Compared to a rigorous, complex, and detailed system of animal sacrifices that regulated Israel's covenantal relationship with God, the shameful death of one Jew on a Roman cross must have seemed woefully inadequate.

Hebrews asserts that creation and redemption have the same one goal—the inclusion of humans into God's eschatological sabbath "rest," a metaphor for access into God's presence (Heb 4:1–11; 10:19–22; 12:22–24). Entry into God's sabbath rest is designated the sole privilege of those who are "partners" (μετόχοι, Heb 3:14) with Christ, that is, those whose faith in him remains firm to the end. As "partners" with Christ, believers have unimpeded access into the heavenly sanctuary, whereas prior to the Christ event, only the anointed high priest may enter the earthly innermost sanctuary, and even then, only for a brief moment once a year, representing the whole Israelite community. But can Jewish followers of Christ be confident that that they have indeed become inheritors of God's promise of salvation, without participating in the ritual requirements of the Mosaic law? According to Hebrews, the assurance lies in the concrete reality of their pneumatic experiences—their foretaste of the eschatological Spirit. The "time to set

---

34. Owen, *Exposition*, 236.

things right" (καιροῦ διορθώσεως, Heb 9:10) has been initiated with the arrival of Jesus about whom God himself testified by signs, wonders, and various miracles, and by the distributions of the Holy Spirit (Heb 2:4).[35] "The presence of miraculous occurrences and profound spiritual experiences in early Christian communities were . . . seen as eschatological consequences of the Christ event."[36] The author reminds his hearers that as believers in Jesus, they have *already* received the proleptic guarantee of their future eschatological inheritance. Jesus "tasted" death (Heb 2:9) so that believers can "taste" "the heavenly gift" and "the goodness of God's word and the powers of the age to come" (Heb 6:4, 5). As Holmes rightly observes, "Hebrews operates with a semi-realized eschatology."[37]

Importantly, through partnership with Christ (μετόχοι τοῦ χριστοῦ/), they have "become partners of the Holy Spirit" (μετόχους γενηθέντας πνεύματος ἁγίου, Heb 6:4).[38] Their partnership in the Holy Spirit reminds them that, having already received God's eschatological promise (Heb 2:4), they can confidently approach God in his sanctuary (Heb 10:19–22).[39] "[T]

---

35. Although πνεύματος ἁγίου μερισμοῖς in Heb 2:4 has often been interpreted as "distributions of *gifts* of the Holy Spirit," Allen and Witherington translate the phrase as "distributions of the *Spirit*," notwithstanding the fact that Witherington emphasizes the acts and manifestations of the outpoured Spirit; Allen, "Forgotten Spirit," 56; Witherington III, *Letters and Homilies*, 137. The word μερισμός ("division") is rare in the LXX and New Testament. In every instance, that which is being divided is clearly stated in the immediate context, e.g. land (Josh 11:12; 13:14; Micah 7:12; Ezek 48:29), people (Ezra 6:18; Luke 12:51, 52), between soul and spirit (Heb 4:12). In Heb 2:4, only the Holy Spirit is mentioned, so that a more logical interpretation is that it is the *Spirit* who is being distributed rather than "gifts," recalling the Pentecost event. The following clause κατὰ τὴν αὐτοῦ θέλησιν (literally, "according to his own will") may be a deliberate subversion of κατὰ τὴν γραφὴν Μωυσῆ (literally, "according to the writing of Moses") in Ezra 6:18. Thus, the author of Hebrews may be indicating that God distributes the Holy Spirit according to his own divine prerogative, and not that God distributes spiritual gifts selectively.

36. Mackie, "Eschatological Experience," 94.

37. Holmes, "Death in the Afternoon," 241.

38. Partnership in Christ and the Holy Spirit defines those who are "partners in a heavenly calling" (κλήσεως ἐπουρανίου μέτοχοι; Heb 3:1). That partnership, however, also implies the mutual sharing of divine discipline (παιδείας . . . μέτοχοι; Heb 12:8). The noun μέτοχος describes a close companion or business partner (see Luke 5:7) and is a motif used frequently in Hebrews (Heb 1:9; 3:1, 14; 6:4; 12:8). "Hebrews recalls the charismatic vitality of the early mission (Heb. 2:4) and conversion is still understood as coming to share in the Spirit and in the illumination and eschatological powers by which the Spirit manifests himself"; Dunn, *Christ and The Spirit*, vol. 2, 19.

39. This resembles Paul's argument to the Galatian Christians—since their own spiritual experiences show that they have already received the promised Spirit through faith in Christ, why should Gentiles resort to Jewish circumcision and the Mosaic law? (Gal 3:2–4)

he Spirit, by both its gift and presence, is the one who marks out and testifies to the presence of the new age."[40] In this new age, which has come through Jesus the "firstborn" (τὸν πρωτότοκον, singular, Heb 1:6), believers become the "assembly of the firstborns" (ἐκκλησία πρωτοτόκων, plural, Heb 12:23). Through Christ, believers have been given the status and privileges that belong to the divine Son himself, including entry into God's royal presence. While all believers are called "sons" of God (υἱοί, Heb 2:10) and "brothers" of Jesus (ἀδελφοί, Heb 2:11), they are not placed in a hierarchy of sibship; instead, they are all seen as "firstborns." This undeserved privilege is the outcome of their partnership in Christ and the Holy Spirit. However, their partnership in Christ is not to be regarded as something separate from their partnership in the Holy Spirit, as though believers belong to two different families. Indeed, it is the family of the *one* triune God to whom they belong. This new Spirit-indwelt humanity, the community of the "firstborns" of God the Father, is created in Christ "through the cross" (Eph 3:16). "For through him [Christ] both of us [Jews and Gentiles] have access in one Spirit to the Father" (Eph 3:18).

The author refers to real and tangible pneumatic experiences that his hearers can identify in their lives as Christians. Instead of suggesting that they *shall* have such experiences *because* they believe in Jesus and are saved, he is pointing to the *fact* of their experiences of the Holy Spirit as proof of their having *already* obtained a relationship with God as his children and heirs through Christ. "If these 'confirmations' have not occurred among them, then Hebrews' entire argument is empty and abstract."[41] Therefore, after having experienced the foretaste of eschatological life, if they were now to turn away from Christ, they would be guilty of trampling underfoot the Son of God, treating as unholy (κοινὸν, "common") the blood of the covenant by which they were made holy, and insulting the Spirit of grace (τὸ πνεῦμα τῆς χάριτος) (Heb 10:29). According to Hebrews, the Holy Spirit is the one who is witness to God's new covenant (Heb 10:15–16) which, having been promised in the past through prophetic proclamation (Jer 31:31–34), is reiterated afresh.[42] Indeed, through God's grace the new covenant has been fulfilled by Christ (Heb 2:9). Once again, the use of the present tense, "testifies" (μαρτυρεῖ), emphasizes the continued witness of the Spirit to the new covenant, from the time of Jeremiah to the author's present day. That

40. Allen, "Forgotten Spirit," 58.

41. Johnson, *Hebrews*, 89.

42. When Jeremiah 31:31–34 is first cited in Hebrews 8:8–12, the subject of λέγει in verse 8 is presumed to be God from the identification of "I" as "God" in verse 10, and some translations (e.g. *NRSV*, *NIV*) have "God says" rather than the literal "he says" (e.g. *KJV*, *ESV*). In Hebrews 10:15, however, it is clear that the Holy Spirit is the speaker.

the Holy Spirit "testifies *to us*" (μαρτυρεῖ δὲ ἡμῖν) indicates that the author and his hearers are the direct recipients of that divine testimony,[43] "since the promises of the new covenant are for this community—and ultimately for other believers as well."[44]

It is not surprising that the role as witness to the new covenant is attributed to the Holy Spirit who is, after all, the one who sanctifies the sanctuary. The Mosaic tabernacle (מִשְׁכָּן, *miškān*) or tent of meeting (אֹהֶל־מוֹעֵד, *'ōhel-mōʿēd*) was holy because God dwelt (שָׁכַן, *šākan*) within its innermost sanctuary, and in which he held formal meetings (מוֹעֵד, *mōʿēd*) with Israel's representatives. Interestingly, the LXX translates the phrase "tent of meeting" as "the tent of testimony" (ἡ σκηνὴ τοῦ μαρτυρίου). The author of Hebrews, who quotes from the LXX, may be drawing upon this terminology when he speaks about the Holy Spirit's attestation of the new covenant. It is the eschatological Spirit who affirms and guarantees God's new covenant in Christ, and who is experienced as the indwelling presence, love, and power of God. Paul envisages the Spirit "bearing witness (συμματυρεῖ) with our spirits that we are children of God" (Rom 8:16), and in 1 John 5:6, the writer affirms that "the Spirit is the one that testifies (τὸ μαρτυροῦν), for the Spirit is the truth." According to Hebrews, if the hearers reject this new covenant and attempt to return to the old, they treat the divine Son, his blood by which they were made holy, and the Spirit of God's grace, as dirt. As Owen asserts:

> Yea, they who look for and trust unto any other, they fall into that sin for which there is no remission provided in this covenant, nor shall any other offering be accepted for them for ever; for they despise both the wisdom and grace of God, the blood of Christ, and the witness of the Holy Ghost; whereof there is no remission.[45]

---

43. "ἡμῖν associates the writers with the readers (cf. ἐσμέν in v.10 and προσερχώμεθα in v.22). It thus prepares for the quotation from Jeremiah to be applied, more closely than in chap. 8, to the readers' situation"; Ellingworth, *Commentary on Hebrews*, 512. Note the author's use of the present tense μαρτυρεῖ, as in Hebrews 3:7 (λέγει), and 9:8 (δηλοῦντος). "[B]ecause many of his verbs of introduction are in the present tense, the hearer experiences these voices [from scripture] as God's speech to the present and not simply to the past"; Johnson, *Hebrews*, 23.

44. O'Brien, *Hebrews*, 358.

45. Owen, *Exposition*, 497.

Eternal Efficacy of Christ's Sacrifice through the Spirit

The third issue that the author of Hebrews seems to be addressing is the uncertainty that while Christ's act of atonement is sufficient to cleanse sins of the past, it may not cover sins committed after conversion and baptism.[46] Lindars sees this as an important pastoral concern, because the hearers "knew from their Jewish past that atonement for sin is constantly attended to in Jewish liturgy" and were therefore tempted to return to the Jewish community.[47] Along similar lines, Allen postulates that the recipients of Hebrews may have been Jewish priests who have converted to Christianity, and who are being drawn back to the continual temple sacrifices because of guilt over post-baptismal sins.[48] Without such ongoing sacrifices, how can Christians be confident that their post-baptismal sins are atoned for? This is a reasonable question for Jews accustomed to the sin and guilt offerings prescribed for ritual and moral infractions, and the whole burnt offering offered twice a day, each and every day (or "continually," *tāmîd*, תָּמִיד, Exod 29:42), as a perpetual sign of the relationship between God and Israel, throughout all generations (Exod 29:38–42). The sacrifices of the annual Day of Atonement, instituted to address the sins of the whole Israelite community, was to be performed "as an everlasting statute" (לְחֻקַּת־עוֹלָם, *lᵉḥukkaṯ-ʿôlām*, Lev 16:34). The Levitical cultic term עֹלָה ("whole burnt offering," *ʿōlâh*), links the continual twice daily sacrifices to the concept of עוֹלָם ("eternal," *ʿôlām*). Prior to the formal institution of the Levitical sacrificial system, Noah's animal whole burnt offerings (עֹלֹת, *ʿōlōṯ*), is followed by God's proclamation that he will never again resort to wholesale destruction of living creatures (Gen 8:20–21). The whole burnt offerings signified the *eternality* of God's covenant relationship with Israel, and therefore needed to be presented every day, throughout the year, and throughout the generations. The idea that God's covenant with Israel is "eternal" is deeply rooted in Israel's ancestral narratives, particularly in the Noahic (Gen 9:12, 16), Abrahamic (Gen 13:14; 17:7–8), and Davidic covenants (2 Sam 7:13, 16). After negotiating a treaty with Abimelech at Beersheba, Abraham calls upon YHWH, "the eternal God" (אֵל־עוֹלָם, *ʾēl-ʿôlām*, Gen 21:33; θεὸς αἰώνιος in the LXX).

The author of Hebrews asserts that Christ has become the source of eternal salvation and redemption (Heb 5:9; 9:12) through an eternal covenant (Heb 13:20) for those who believe in him. Through Christ they receive

---

46. Lindars, *Theology of the Letter*, 13–14.
47. Lindars, *Theology of the Letter*, 14.
48. Allen, *Lukan Authorship*, 256–57.

an eternal inheritance (Heb 9:15). Hence, the author claims that only Christ achieves, through his singular action, that which the entire, ongoing, Levitical sacrificial system aimed to achieve. How has Christ accomplished this? It is my contention that the author answers this important question by stating that Christ offered himself "through the *eternal* Spirit" (διὰ πνεύματος αἰωνίου, Heb 9:14).[49] The following section examines this key phrase textually, exegetically, and theologically.

6.2 "Through Eternal Spirit" in Hebrews 9:14

Textual Issues

The majority of Greek manuscripts have the phrase διὰ πνεύματος αἰωνίου, although a substantial few substitute αἰωνίου with ἁγίου.[50] There are no other variants apart from διὰ πνεύματος αἰωνίου and διὰ πνεύματος ἁγίου. Significantly, the phrase in 𝔓[46] (ca. 200), the earliest extant manuscript of Pauline writings, is πνεύματος αἰωνίου (see appendix 2).[51] The major codices Vaticanus (fourth century), Sinaiticus (fourth century), Alexandrinus (fifth century), and Claromontanus (sixth century) have αἰωνίου (appendix 3a–d). Interestingly, in Codex Sinaiticus, a second hand (ℵ2) has written the word ἁγίου at the margin next to the word αἰωνίου in the text. In the Greek-Latin diglot, Codex Claromontanus, it is not only clear that the word αἰωνίου has been written by a second hand (D2) over the original word (very possibly ἁγίου), but on the opposite page containing the Latin translation, the phrase *Spiritum sanctum* has remained unchanged (appendix 3d). John Chrysostom (347–407) used a Greek text with ἁγίου in Hebrews 9:14 for his homilies.[52] Thus it appears that although the original adjective was αἰωνίου, the

---

49. Emmrich is convinced that Heb 9:14 "expresses the central thought of the epistle to the Hebrews"; *Pneumatological Concepts*, 1.

50. ἁγίου is attested in ℵ2, D*, P, 81, 104, 326, 365, 629, 630, 2464, Vulgate and some Coptic manuscripts, but the weightier textual evidence is for αἰωνίου which is present in all other manuscripts; *NA28*, 671.

51. Kenyon, *Chester Beatty Biblical Papyri*, plate 30. Although it is the scholarly consensus that Hebrews was not written by Paul, in some manuscripts it was included among Pauline Epistles; see O'Brien, *Hebrews*, 2–9.

52. Chrysostom, *Homilies on Hebrews*: xv.5 (*NPNF* 1/14:440); the Greek text was obtained from Migne, *PG* 63, col. 119 (page 218 of the digitized book from https://books.google.com.au/books?id=aIbHbKSijYQC&pg=PR5&lpg=PR5&dq=Ad+Homilias+S.+Joannis+Chrysostomi:+In+Epistolam+Ad+Hebraeos&sourc e=bl&ots=YqlKy2rUdL&sig=ACfU3U1jku8wK_5UogMwHyTpmjglTEgW-g&hl=en&sa=X&ved=2ahUKEwj657zoseXhAhWIfnoKHRcwD9AQ6AEwB3oECA cQAQ#v=onepage&q=Ad%20Homilias%20S.%20Joannis%20Chrysostomi%3A%20

alternate ἁγίου had found its way into the Greek text by the fourth century, initially as a gloss in the margin (e.g., Codex Sinaiticus), and subsequently into the main text (e.g. John Chrysostom's Greek text, and Codex Claromontanus before ἁγίου was overwritten with αἰωνίου). In Latin translations, it was rendered "*sanctum.*" By the time the Vulgate was compiled in the sixth century using Jerome's translations (Old Testament, Gospels, and Acts), and Old Latin translations of the rest of the New Testament, *Spiritum sanctum* had become the accepted phrase. It was about a thousand years later, when Desiderius Erasmus (ca. 1449–1536) produced his Greek New Testament in 1516 that αἰωνίου reappeared (appendix 4).[53] It is important to note that the variant ἁγίου does not appear in any extant manuscripts of the Syrian New Testament (Peshitta),[54] which have been dated between the fifth and eleventh centuries.[55] The Peshitta has the phrase "through eternal Spirit," *daḇrūḥā-dalʿālam*.[56]

In the New Testament, the phrase διὰ πνεύματος αἰωνίου is used only once, in Hebrews, whereas διὰ πνεύματος ἁγίου appears four times, always without the article, and clearly referring to the Holy Spirit in all four passages.[57] It is therefore not difficult to understand the scribal substitution of ἁγίου for αἰωνίου, especially when the phrase was widely understood to refer to the Holy Spirit. As Metzger explains, "It was no doubt to be expected that, confronted with the rather unexpected phrase πνεύματος αἰωνίου, copyists would replace the adjective with ἁγίου, but there was no reason for their replacing ἁγίου with αἰωνίου."[58] Ellingworth asserts

---

In%20Epistolam%20Ad%20Hebraeos&f=false).

53. Although Codex Vaticanus has αἰωνίου, the manuscript may have been inaccessible to many scholars prior to its appearance in the Vatican Library's earliest catalogue of 1475. It is likely that it was in Caesarea and Constantinople until the Council of Florence (1438–1445), after which it was brought to Italy. The Codex was consulted by Erasmus for his Greek New Testament; Metzger and Ehrman, *Text of the New Testament*, 67.

54. *NA28*, 671.

55. Vellum manuscripts obtained from the Syrian monastery of St. Mary Deipara in the Desert of Nitria, Scete, are presently housed in the British Library—relevant manuscripts are Add MS 14448 (6th–7th c.), 14470 (5th–6th c.), 14474–481 (5th–11th c.). The Syrian Christian tradition maintains that the Peshitta has origins in the first century, based on the belief that the Gospels were first written in Aramaic; see http://www.peshitta.org/initial/peshitta.html.

56. For a useful analysis of Hebrews 9:14 in the Peshitta, see http://www.dukhrana.com/peshitta/analyze_verse.php?lang=en&verse=Hebrews+9:14&source=ubs&font=Estrangelo+Edessa&size=125%.

57. Acts 1:2; 4:25; Rom 5:5; 2 Tim 1:14.

58. Metzger, *Textual Commentary*, 598.

that while αἰωνίου is the original, ἁγίου is a correct gloss.⁵⁹ It is significant that *all* editions of the Latin Vulgate have the phrase *per Spiritum sanctum* in place of *per Spiritum aeternum*.⁶⁰ In the Vulgate, Hebrews 9:14 reads: "*quanto magis sanguis Christi qui per Spiritum sanctum semet ipsum obtulit inmaculatum Deo emundabit conscientiam vestram ab operibus mortuis ad serviendum Deo viven.*"

Exegetical Issues

The most important exegetical question concerning the phrase διὰ πνεύματος αἰωνίου in Hebrews 9:14 is whether πνεῦμα refers to the Holy Spirit, or to some other "spirit." The factors to consider are the absence of the article, the function of the preposition διά, the author's use of πνεῦμα in the epistle, and the pneumatological context of Hebrews 9:6–14.

A. Absence of the Article

Does the absence of the article in διὰ πνεύματος αἰωνίου preclude a reference to the Holy Spirit? Westcott suggests: "The absence of the article from πνεῦμα αἰώνιον marks the spirit here as a power possessed by Christ, His 'Spirit.'"⁶¹ However, an examination of the kindred phrase διὰ πνεύματος ἁγίου, which appears four times in the New Testament (Acts 1:2; 4:25; Rom 5:5; 2 Tim 2:2), shows that the phrase, while anarthrous, unambiguously refers to the Holy Spirit in all their contexts. The article is inserted when the phrase is not accompanied by an adjective (διὰ τοῦ πνεύματος, appearing in Acts 11:28; 21:4; 1 Cor 2:10; 12:8; Eph 3:16),⁶² and this latter phrase refers to the Holy Spirit in all five cases. Wallace states, "There is no need for the article to be used to make the object of a preposition definite."⁶³ While this does not signify that all anarthrous nouns governed by prepositions are definite, Wallace also states that those with qualifying adjectives are definite.⁶⁴ Hence, Witherington is correct in his assertion concerning διὰ πνεύματος

---

59. Ellingworth, *Commentary on Hebrews*, 457.
60. *NA28*, 671.
61. Westcott, *Epistle to the Hebrews*, 261.
62. In Eph 3:16, a personal pronoun is attached (διὰ τοῦ πνεύματος αὐτοῦ, "through his [the Father's] Spirit").
63. Wallace, *Greek Grammar*, 247; Harris, *Prepositions and Theology*, 69–82.
64. Wallace, *Greek Grammar*, 247, n. 80.

αἰωνίου that "with the adjectival modifier the noun becomes definite."[65] Fee asserts that in the Pauline corpus, the absence of the article does not rule out a reference to the divine Spirit, and that both articular and anarthrous forms of the genitive πνεύματος are used when referring to the Holy Spirit.[66] Moreover, Wallace observes that the singular πνεῦμα qualified by the adjective ἅγιον does not require the presence of the article to be definite, because "the expression πνεῦμα ἅγιον is monadic and refers only to the Holy Spirit."[67] Although αἰωνίου rather than ἁγίου is most probably the adjective modifying πνεύματος in Hebrews 9:14, the point being made here is that πνεῦμα without the article does not exclude a reference to the Holy Spirit, and context has to be taken into consideration. Interestingly, William Estius (1542–1613) asserted *"in Graeco codice non additur articulus, nihil probat"* ("in Greek books, the non-addition of the article proves nothing"),[68] insisting that *"per Spiritum aeternum"* in Hebrews 9:14 should be understood as *"per Spiritum sanctum."* The scribal substitution of ἁγίου for αἰωνίου is understandable, since the phrase διὰ πνεύματος ἁγίου is more frequent than διὰ πνεύματος αἰωνίου, a *hapax legomenon*. Indeed, the variant form ἁγίου (the *only* other form) strengthens rather than weakens the case for the Holy Spirit as the true referent of the phrase διὰ πνεύματος αἰωνίου.

B. Function of ΔΙΑ

In general, the preposition διά, when used with a genitive, is used to convey the sense of time ("throughout," "during"), space ("moving through"), instrumental means ("through"), manner ("through"), agency ("by," "through") or cause ("by virtue of").[69] According to Attridge, the genitival διά in Hebrews frequently refers to the means by which or the agency by whom something is done.[70]

---

65. Witherington III, *Letters and Homilies*, 270.

66. Fee, *God's Empowering Presence*, 18.

67. Wallace, *Greek Grammar*, 248.

68. Estius, *In epistolam B. Pauli Apostoli ad Hebraeos commentarius*, n. 212; quoted in McGrath, *Eternal Spirit*, 21–22; my translation. Estius (Willem Hessels van Est) was a Roman Catholic scholar and Dutch immigrant to France. His commentary on the Pauline Epistles *In omnes Divi Pauli et Catholicas Epistolas Commentarii* was based on his lectures at the University of Douai, and published posthumously in 1614–15. Although he may be accused of bias towards the Vulgate rendition of Heb 9:14, he accepted that διὰ πνεύματος αἰωνίου was the original Greek phrase, and his grammatical insight is valid.

69. Wallace, *Greek Grammar*, 368–69.

70. Attridge, *Hebrews*, 245; he cites Heb 9:6 and 13:5 as examples of the *temporal*

There are four prepositional phrases beginning with διά in Hebrews 9:11–14, a pericope describing Christ's high priestly work; the first part (Heb 9:11–12) deals with Christ's entry into the heavenly tabernacle, and the second (Heb 9:13–14) contrasts Christ's sacrifice with the Levitical sacrifices.[71] The preposition διά in the first prepositional phrase διὰ τῆς μείζονος καὶ τελειοτέρας σκηνῆς ("*through* the greater and more perfect tent," Heb 9:11) functions spatially to convey Christ's movement through the heavenly tabernacle into the inner sanctuary (εἰς τὰ ἅγια, Heb 9:13). In the second and third prepositional phrases, οὐδὲ δι᾽ αἵματος τράγων καὶ μόσχων ("not *through* the blood of goats and bulls"), and διὰ δὲ τοῦ ἰδίου αἵματος ("but *through* his own blood," Heb 9:12), διά conveys the instrumental means by which purification is made, contrasting the limited cleansing by animal blood compared with the complete cleansing by Christ's blood. In regard to the fourth prepositional phrase, διὰ πνεύματος αἰωνίου ("*through* eternal Spirit," Heb 9:14), opinions regarding the function of διά correspond to the variety of interpretations of the expression πνεύματος αἰωνίου. For example, Wescott, for whom the phrase relates to Christ rather than to the Spirit, sees διά functioning instrumentally, and that Christ offers himself through, or by means of, his own spirit.[72] Attridge attaches both spatial and instrumental functions to the preposition. He suggests that Christ's self-offering took place "in the spiritual realm," and also that "the spirit most likely refers to Christ and to the interior or spiritual quality of his spiritual act. Christ's self-offering was thus made with that portion of his being that was most truly himself."[73] Witherington, who also sees διά functioning instrumentally, suggests on the other hand that "God's eternal Spirit, that is, the Holy Spirit, was the *means* by which the human Jesus' blood was offered to God."[74] John Owen, however, argues that διά in Hebrews 9:14 carries the sense of personal agency, and maintains that "the eternal Spirit was not an inferior instrument whereby Christ offered himself, but he was the principal efficient cause in the work."[75] Owen explains that he uses the term "principal efficient cause" to mean nothing less than the status as divine Creator. He insists that the Holy Spirit is not a passive instrument through whom Christ acts, but Christ's coworker in the accomplishment of the redemptive sacrifice. In alignment with Owen's position, O'Brien

---

use of διά with the genitive.

71. Koester, *Hebrews*, 412; McGrath, *Eternal Spirit*, 89; Wescott, *Epistle to the Hebrews*, 262.

72. Westcott, *Epistle to the Hebrews*, 261.

73. Attridge, *Hebrews*, 251.

74. Witherington III, *Letters and Homilies*, 270.

75. Owen, *Exposition*, 303.

concludes "that the Holy Spirit anointed Jesus as high priest for every aspect of his ministry, including his death."[76] Interestingly, the phrase διὰ πνεύματος ἁγίου in Romans 5:5 exemplifies the use of διά as personal agency,[77] and it is the Holy Spirit who is clearly the agent.[78] Furthermore, according to Harris, if "a preposition is followed by two anarthrous substantives, both in the genitive, the preposition always seems to qualify the former."[79] Applying this here, the correct understanding of the phrase διὰ πνεύματος αἰωνίου is "through S/spirit who/which is eternal," rather than "through eternity which is spiritual"—διά qualifies πνεύματος, and αἰωνίου qualifies πνεύματος. This helps narrow the hermeneutical options by clarifying that the adjective αἰωνίου refers to "S/spirit" and not to Christ, and weakens the idea that the phrase refers to an eternal spiritual realm within which Christ made his offering.

c. πνεῦμα in Hebrews

Relevant to the exegesis of διὰ πνεύματος αἰωνίου in Hebrews 9:14 is a review of the other eleven references to πνεῦμα in the rest of Hebrews.[80] The plural πνεύματα of Hebrews 1:7 and 1:14 may be translated either as "spiritual beings" or as "winds," that is, as entities, but the contexts of these passages do not allow this noun to be interpreted as an adjectival attribute, quality, or characteristic. Similarly, in Hebrews 12:9, God is the Father of "spirits" (τῶν πνευμάτων) rather than of abstract "spirituality," because *personal relationship* is in focus—the author compares his hearers' relationship with their human parents (literally, "fleshly fathers") with their relationship with God their heavenly Father. In Hebrews 12:22–23, the author lists those who will be residing in the eschatological "city of the living God"—the angels, the assembly of the firstborns, God the Father, Jesus the mediator of the new covenant, and the "spirits of the righteous" (πνεύμασιν δικαίων). It seems very unlikely that, among all the persons the author expects to meet when he arrives in God's city, are abstract "righteous attributes/qualities" rather than personal "spirits of the righteous." In Hebrews 4:12, where the author asserts that God's word is able to divide "soul from spirit, joints from marrow," the

---

76. O'Brien, *Hebrews*, 324–25.

77. BDAG, 180. Similarly, διὰ πνεύματος ἁγίου in Acts 1:2; 4:25; 2 Thess 2:2; and 2 Tim 1:14.

78. Fee, *God's Empowering Presence*, 493–98.

79. Harris, *Prepositions and Theology*, 44. Harris uses 2 Cor 3:18 to illustrate his point: ἀπο κυρίου πνεύματος is not "by the Spirit of the Lord" but rather "by the Lord who is spirit/the Spirit." The two nouns may also be appositional genitives.

80. Heb 1:17, 14; 2:4; 3:7; 4:12; 6:4; 9:8; 10:15, 29; 12:9, 23.

parallelism between the paired nouns "soul and spirit," "joints and marrow" clearly show that constituents of human existence are in view.[81] In this context, ψυχή and πνεῦμα are seen as basic elements of a living human, so that translating πνεῦμα as an attribute, "spirituality," seems incongruent. Witherington insists that in Hebrews, all instances of "spirit" in the singular (except in Heb 4:12) refer to the Holy Spirit.[82] Since it appears that nowhere in Hebrews does the noun πνεῦμα describe an abstract "spirituality," but instead is used to refer to the divine Spirit or to angelic or human spirit(s), it seems inconsistent that in verse 9:14 the phrase διὰ πνεύματος αἰωνίου means "through the eternal spirituality/divinity" of Christ.

D. Pneumatological Context of Hebrews 9:6–14

In Hebrews 9:6–14, the author parallels and contrasts the earthly cultic sacrifices (Heb 9:6–10) with Christ's sacrifice (Heb 9:11–14), repeating several key words and concepts like "tent," "high priest," "blood," "complete/perfect/spotless,"[83] "worship," "holy," "cleanse," and "eternal," emphasizing the transience and inadequacy of animal sacrifices in the light of Christ's eternal and perfect sacrifice of himself.[84] The literary symmetry between these two passages becomes obvious when they are placed beside each other (see appendix 5).[85] A significant point of difference between the old ritual sacrifices and Christ's own sacrifice concerns access into the heavenly sanctuary. Although the high priest goes into the innermost "Holy of Holies" of the earthly tabernacle once a year, the author does not consider this to be a genuine entrance

---

81. "Soul and spirit" refer to the immaterial elements that animate a human, and "joint and marrow" refer to the material; Koester, *Hebrews*, 274; O'Brien, *Hebrews*, 177. "Thus the four in combination offer a general view of the sum of man's powers in his present organisation. The divine revelation penetrates all. No part of human nature is untouched by it." Westcott, *Epistle to the Hebrews*, 103.

82. Witherington III, *Letters and Homilies*, 270.

83. The word ἄμωμον used of Christ in Heb 9:14 carries both ideas of "clean" and "perfect." For example, the Hebrew word תָּמִים is rendered τέλειος or "perfect" (Gen 6:9; Deut 18:13), and also ἄμωμον or "spotless" (Lev 22:21) in the LXX. Any blemish is considered an imperfection. Peterson observes that in Israel's cultic terminology in the LXX, the verb τελειοῦν is closely related to verbs like καθαρίζειν and ἁγιάζειν; Peterson, *Hebrews and Perfection*, 23–24, 146–47, 150–3.

84. Vanhoye observes a concentric literary pattern in Hebrews with its central focus on the comparison between the old and new covenants in Hebrews 8:1—9:28. At the very heart of this section is the contrast between the ancient ritual and the perfect sacrifice of Christ (9:1–10 and 9:11–14); Vanhoye, *Structure and Message*, 76, 92–95.

85. The parallelism between Heb 9:6–10 and 11–14 appears in many places to be inverse rather than direct.

into God's true sanctuary. Indeed, while the earthly structure was still operational, the Holy Spirit indicates that "the way to the Holies" was not yet revealed (τοῦτο δηλοῦντος τοῦ πνεύματος τοῦ ἁγίου, μήπω πεφανερῶσθαι τὴν τῶν ἁγίων ὁδὸν, Heb 9:8). When Christ appeared, as the eschatological high priest ("the high priest of the good things to come," Heb 9:11), he entered into "the Holies" through his own blood. The author contrasts Christ's once-for-all offering with that of earthly high priests who go into the earthly sanctuary once a year to offer, not their own blood, but the blood of animals on their own behalf, and on behalf of the community (Heb 9:11). The author also makes the point that the earthly sacrifices only cover *unintentional* sins of the people (τῶν τοῦ λαοῦ ἀγνοημάτων, Heb 9:7), implying that not all their sins are addressed. Moreover, while earthly sacrifices may effect outward cleansing of the flesh (σάρξ), only Christ's blood cleanses the inner conscience (συνείδησις, Heb 9:13–14). Note that it is *the Holy Spirit*, according to the author, who discloses this important insight.

The Holy Spirit is closely linked with the new covenant and the heavenly sanctuary. It is the Holy Spirit who functions as the witness to the new covenant that is secured through Jesus's blood (Heb 10:15), and it is the Holy Spirit who reveals that the earthly tabernacle is provisional and anticipatory (Heb 9:8). Indeed, it is the *Holy Spirit* who discloses the full significance of the Levitical sacrificial system in the light of the Christ event: "The readers [of Hebrews] are living in 'the span between the two ages', in which the old order has actually been superseded by the work of Christ and will shortly disappear (Heb 8:13)."[86] With regard to the "Holy of Holies," it is only right that God's *Holy* Spirit, whose very indwelling presence makes the sanctuary *holy*, is the one who prevents all but the true anointed one (the "Christ") from entering it. Leviticus asserts repeatedly that ultimately it is *God* who makes the people "holy" (Lev 20:8; 21:8, 15, 23; 22:9, 16; cf. 1 Thess 5:23). In the Lukan birth narrative, the *Holy Spirit* "overshadows" (ἐπισκιάσει) Mary, ensuring that the child in her womb is *holy* (Luke 1:35). The verbs ἐπισκιάζω and σκιάζω are used in the LXX to describe the overshadowing wings of the cherubim attached to the cover of the ark of the covenant (Exod 38:8), and to the appearance of the pillar of cloud over the desert tabernacle (Exod 40:37; Num 9:18, 22) and over the eschatological Mount Zion (Isa 4:5), signifying God's presence and protection.[87] It is the presence of God's Holy Spirit that makes something, some place or someone holy. In Hebrews, the author's important theme of "holiness" is perhaps more apparent in the

---

86. Peterson, *Hebrews and Perfection*, 133.

87. In Psalm 90:4 (LXX; Ps 91:4 in English versions), the verb ἐπισκιάσει is used to describe God's protection of Israel, rather like a parent bird embracing the nation with its wings.

Greek text than in English translations, as many Greek words with the same stem ἁγι- are translated in English into different sounding words, e.g. "holy," "sanctify," "sanctuary," "consecrate." Indeed, the author's emphasis on "holy" (ἁγία) in Hebrews 9 is particularly striking—this chapter alone contains six of the twelve uses of the term in the epistle.[88] The ἅγιος theme linking Christ's *sanctifying* blood, the *sanctuary* or *Holy of Holies* that represents God's presence, and the *Holy Spirit* may indicate an intentional theological linkage being drawn by the author that establishes the divine source, location, character, and manner of Christ's salvific work on the cross.

In short, from the textual and exegetical standpoints, it seems reasonable to affirm that when Christ offered himself as a spotless perfect sacrifice on humanity's behalf, his offering is made διὰ πνεύματος αἰωνίου, "through the eternal *[Holy]* Spirit." The theological interpretation of this phrase over the centuries has not, however, been consistent.

Theological Aspects

A. History of Theological Interpretation

As an exhaustive investigation of all theologians who commented on Hebrews 9:14 would be beyond the scope of this study, I will highlight only key theologians in order to sketch in broad-brush strokes the history of interpretation of Hebrews 9:14, particularly during the early centuries of Christianity, and at the time of the Reformation when alternate interpretations appeared.

In his study of the exegetical history of Hebrews 9:14, John McGrath observed that from the time of the Greek and Latin fathers up until the Reformation, διὰ πνεύματος αἰωνίου/ἁγίου was understood to refer to the Holy Spirit.[89] He notes that while ἁγίου is firmly established in Catholicism, Protestant exegetes in the Reformation acknowledged αἰωνίου as the original adjective. Although McGrath is himself Roman Catholic, he concedes that the textual evidence strongly favors αἰωνίου.[90] Nonetheless, he is entirely convinced that the author of Hebrews is referring to the Holy Spirit when he uses the phrase διὰ πνεύματος αἰωνίου.

Among the early theologians who showed some interest in the phrase διὰ πνεύματος αἰωνίου in Hebrews 9:14 were Ambrose of Milan (340–397), John Chrysostom (347–407), Theoderet of Cyrus (393–ca. 460) and Thomas

---

88. Heb 2:11 (two uses); 9:2, 3, 12, 13, 24, 25; 10:14; 12:14; 13:11, 12.

89. McGrath, *Eternal Spirit*, 2, 5–16.

90. The latest 1979 edition of the Vulgate has *per Spiritum sanctum*.

Aquinas (ca. 1225–1274). All four understood the phrase to refer to the Holy Spirit, although it must be noted that John Chrysostom had the variant adjective ἁγίου in his Greek text,[91] and possibly Thomas too.[92] Both Ambrose and Theoderet not only understood the phrase διὰ πνεύματος αἰωνίου to refer to the Holy Spirit, but used the adjective αἰωνίου to affirm the eternality of the Holy Spirit, and thus the Spirit's divinity and equal ranking with the Father and the Son, as shown in the following quotations:

> But the Apostle also shows that the Holy Spirit is eternal, for: "If the blood of bulls and of goats, and the sprinkling the ashes of an heifer sanctifieth to the purifying of the flesh, how much more the blood of Christ, who through the eternal Spirit offered Himself without spot to God?" Therefore the Spirit is eternal. (Ambrose of Milan)[93]

> Nor was he content with the name, but he sets forth also the manner of the offering. "Who" (he says) "through the Holy Spirit offered Himself without spot to God," that is, the victim was without blemish, pure from sins. For this is [the meaning of] "through the Holy Spirit," not through fire, nor through any other things. (John Chrysostom)[94]

> That is why the blessed Paul calls him [the Holy Spirit] eternal and existent without beginning: "If the blood of bulls and of goats and the ashes of a heifer sprinkling the unclean, sanctifies to perfection, how much more shall the blood of Christ, who offered himself through the Holy Spirit?" (Heb. 9:13–14). Thus, if the Holy Spirit is eternal and God is eternal also, the conclusion is evident. Nevertheless, we leave to the laborious to gather all the testimonies about the Holy Spirit, which proclaim him as God and Lord and rank him together with the Father and the Son: as for us, we move on to the conclusion of our present teaching. (Theoderet of Cyrus)[95]

---

91. Chrysostom, "Ad Homilias," *PG* 63, col. 119.

92. Aquinas, *Super Epistolam*, 444; *Summa Theologiae*, III.66.12. Thomas wrote in Latin but cited the Greek.

93. Ambrose, "To the Emperor Gratian," i.8.99 (*NPNF* 2/10:106).

94. Chrysostom, "Homilies on Hebrews," xv.5 (*NPNF* 1/14:440).

95. Theoderet, *De Trinitate*: 27 (*PG* 75:1190); "Holy and Vivifying Trinity," in *Theoderet of Cyrus*, 136. Interestingly, Theoderet translated the phrase using the word ἁγίου, but then explained the significance of the phrase with αἰωνίου in mind. Pásztori-Kupán posits that Theoderet probably had αἰωνίου in the text before him, but by mistake, wrote the word ἁγίου in his discussion.

Then the Apostle mentions three things, which show the efficacy of Christ's blood: first, he shows whose blood it is, namely, it is Christ's. From this it is evident that His blood cleanses: "For he will save his people from their sins" (Mt. 1:21). Secondly, the reason why Christ shed His blood, because this was done by the Holy Spirit, through Whose movement and instinct, namely, by the love of God and neighbour He did this: [*quia hoc fuit Spiritus sanctus, cuius motu et instinctu, scilicet charitate Dei, et proximi, hoc fecit.*] "When he shall come as a violent stream which the spirit of the Lord drives on" (Is. 59:10). But the Spirit cleanses: "If the Lord shall wash away the filth of the daughters of Sion, and shall wash away the blood of Jerusalem out of the midst thereof, by the spirit of judgment and by the spirit of burning" (Is. 4:4). Therefore, he says, who by the Holy Spirit offered himself [*per Spiritum sanctum obtulit semetipsum*]: "Christ has loved us and has delivered himself for us, an oblation and a sacrifice to God for an odor of sweetness" (Eph. 5:2). Thirdly, he describes His condition, because He is without blemish: "It shall be a lamb without blemish, a male, of one year" (Ex. 12:5); "What can be made clean by the unclean?" (Sir. 34:4). (Thomas Aquinas)[96]

John McGrath credits (or blames) the Reformers, particularly Theodore Beza (1519–1605), for introducing the idea that the phrase refers to Christ's divinity rather than to the Holy Spirit. He rightly points out that Martin Luther (1483–1546), in his commentary on Hebrews, equated "through *eternal Spirit*" with "through *faith*" by paralleling Hebrews 9:14 with Romans 3:5, perhaps to shore up his argument that salvation comes only through Christ, more specifically through faith in Christ.[97] Luther writes:

Indeed, it was not enough either to believe that it [the blood of Christ] was shed for the remission of sins unless they believe that it was shed for the remission of their own sins. Behold, only the blood of Christ that was shed makes the conscience clean through faith in the Word of Christ. Therefore here, too, the apostle has previously mentioned "the blood of Christ, who through *the Holy Spirit* offered Himself." And Rom. 3:25 speaks of Him "whom God put forward as an expiation *through faith in His blood*."[98]

McGrath's suggestion, though, that John Calvin (1509–1564) interprets πνεύματος αἰωνίου as a reference to Christ's divinity rather than

---

96. Aquinas, *Super Epistolam*, 444.
97. McGrath, *Eternal Spirit*, 5–6.
98. Luther, *Luther's Works*, 210.

the Holy Spirit is inaccurate, as is his claim that "What this spirit of Christ means to Calvin is not perfectly clear."[99] Indeed, Calvin explicitly asserts that Christ's death must be evaluated (*aestimanda*) not from its external act but from the Spirit's power (*a Spiritus virtute*) and as the outcome of the Spirit's efficacy (*ex efficacia Spiritus*):

> He [the author of Hebrews] now shows clearly how the death of Christ is to be regarded; not from its external act but from the power of the Spirit. Christ suffered as man, but in order that His death might effect our salvation it came forth from the power of the Spirit. The sacrifice of eternal atonement was a more than human work. *He calls the Spirit eternal so that we know that the reconciliation which he effects is eternal* [*Et ideo Spiritum vocat aeternum ut sciamus reconciliationem, cuius est effector, aeternam esse*].[100]

Calvin not only understands *Spiritum aeternum* to refer to the Holy Spirit, but also explains that the *eternal* efficacy of Christ's atoning work is attributed by the author of Hebrews to the *eternal* Spirit. A closer reading of his commentary shows that for Calvin, the fullness of the Holy Spirit's anointing is an important factor that differentiates between the eschatological perfection and superiority of Christ's high priesthood and sacrifice *vis-à-vis* the Levitical system. For example, Calvin also clearly asserts that *because* Christ was consecrated by the *Holy Spirit*, Christ's priesthood is made *eternal*:

> Because Christ is the eternal Priest He ought to be distinguished from Aaron by the manner of His institution. This is done in that it was not Moses, a mortal man, who consecrated him but the Holy Spirit [*Quia non Moses homo mortalis ipsum consecravit, sed Spiritus sanctus*], and that not with oil, nor with the blood of goats, nor by the outward show of vestments, but by the heavenly power [*sed coelesti virtute*] which the apostle contrasts with the weak elements. We see, therefore, how the eternity of

---

99. McGrath, *Through the Eternal Spirit*, 10–11. Contrary to McGrath's view, Calvin uses the phrase *Spiritus virtute* elsewhere to refer to the power of the Holy Spirit (see Calvin's comment on Heb 7:15, quoted below.)

100. Calvin, *Epistle of Paul*, 121. (The italicization of the last English sentence is added.) Latin phrases were obtained from Calvin, *In Epistolam Ad Hebraeos*. The "s" in "*Spiritus/um*" is capitalized in Calvin's 1549 publication and in Tholuck's 1963 edition, but not in the 1896 version edited by Baum-Cunitz-Reuss which was used by McGrath in his study.

the priesthood is shown in Christ [*Videmus ergo ut aeternitas sacedorii in Christo commendata feurit*].[101]

Concerning the word "eternal" (עוֹלָם), Calvin maintains that:

When Christ arises, and an everlasting priesthood is conferred on Him, we shall find no end to His age to allow of a termination in a given period of time. We must, therefore, take this word to mean nothing else than eternity [*Ita nihil hac voce quam aeternitas intelligi debet*]. The force of the phrase לעולם must always be judged in this context.[102]

Calvin argues that Christ is greater that all Israel's patriarchs because he has the *fullness* of the Holy Spirit:

Because the Father has released the power of His Spirit much more abundantly in the reign of Christ [*quia ergo multo uberius sub Christi regno potentiam Spiritus sui exseruit Pater*], and has likewise poured out His mercy on mankind, this prominence brings it about that the small portion of grace [i.e., the Spirit] which he bestowed on the fathers under the Law becomes of no account.[103]

Importantly, Calvin envisages Christ as the *Spirit*-anointed heavenly high priest[104] who offered to God the perfect sacrifice of himself. It is Christ's very adornment with the Holy Spirit rather than with external priestly vestments that makes him (and his sacrifice) superior to the Levitical priesthood (and their sacrifices):

In Christ everything is far superior. He Himself is not only pure and blameless but is the fountain of all holiness and justice and is made a High Priest by a heavenly oracle not for the short space of mortal life but forever. To ratify this an oath is interposed. He appears adorned with all the gifts of the Holy Spirit to the highest perfection [*Prodit in medium omnibus Spiritus sancti donis ad summam perfectionem ornatus*].[105]

---

101. Calvin, *Epistle of Paul*, 98; commenting on Heb 7:16.

102. Calvin, *Epistle of Paul*, 98; commenting on Heb 7:17.

103. Calvin, *Epistle of Paul*, 112; commenting on Heb 8:10.

104. "A visible symbol of this sacred anointing was shown in Christ's baptism, when the Spirit hovered over him in the likeness of a dove . . . For the Spirit has chosen Christ as his seat, that from him might abundantly flow the heavenly riches of which we are in such need." Calvin, *Institutes*, ii.15.5 (McNeill, 500).

105. Calvin, *Epistle of Paul*, 141; commenting on Heb 10:22.

Indeed the death of Christ was life for the whole world, and that is surely supernatural. The apostle is referring not so much to the particular properties of human nature but rather to the hidden power of the Spirit [*non humanae tantum naturae proprietatem, sed potius arcanam vim Spiritus respicit.*[106]

Interestingly, Calvin proposes that the Levitical sprinkling of blood prefigured Christ's cleansing of sinners with his sacrificial blood *by the heavenly power of the Spirit*:

> What was fulfilled in Christ by the hidden, heavenly power of the Spirit [*Quod arcana et coelesti Spiritus virtute impletum est in Christo*] was in His case foreshadowed by oil, by various vestments, by the sprinkling of blood, and by other earthly rites.[107]

> When there was a sprinkling of hyssop and scarlet wool there is no doubt that this represented the mystical sprinkling that comes by the Spirit [*Quod autem ex hyssopo adspergillum hebat, et lana coccinea, non dubium est, quin mysticam adsperginem, quae fit per Spiritum, repraesentaverit.*].[108]

To sum up, Calvin understands the Holy Spirit's role at the cross in three ways—first, as the eschatological indwelling of the divine Spirit who anoints Christ as God's perfect and true high priest, second, as the heavenly power through whom Christ presents the offering of himself to God, and third, as the power through whom Christ cleanses sinners with his blood.

McGrath's comments concerning Theodore Beza's interpretation of πνεύματος αἰωνίου are correct, but do need to be nuanced. McGrath cites Beza's 1582 Greek-Latin New Testament although his quotation is actually taken from Beza's 1559 edition. In this 1559 edition, each page carries two parallel columns, the Greek text on the left, and Beza's own Latin translation on the right.[109] Here, Beza translates διὰ πνεύματος αἰωνίου as "*per Spiritum aeternum*" (note the capitalized "S"). In subsequent editions, however, Beza included the Latin Vulgate in a parallel column to the right. This three-column format is used in his 1582 edition with the Vulgate translation "*per Spiritum sanctum*" alongside his own translation "*per Spiritum aeternum.*"[110] Nevertheless, McGrath correctly asserts that Beza understood the phrase to refer to Christ's divinity rather than to the Holy Spirit: "Theodore assigns

106. Calvin, *Epistle of Paul*, 105; commenting on Heb 8:2.
107. Calvin, *Epistle of Paul*, 97–98; commenting on Heb 7:15.
108. Calvin, *Epistle of Paul*, 126; commenting on Heb 9:20.
109. Beza, *Novum Domini*, 751.
110. Beza, *Iesu Christi*, 362.

the infinite efficacy of the sacrifice to "Divinity's union with humanity," and that "It was not only union *with* the divinity but guidance [*gubernavit*] *by* the divinity that conferred the infinite efficacy."[111] This view is based upon Beza's 1559 annotation:

> Nam Spiritus aeterni appellatione, <u>Divinitatis cum humanitate coniuncta</u> efficacitateum infinitatum intelligo, quae totum hoc sacrificium <u>gubernavit</u>.[112]

> ["I understand the appeal to eternal Spirit as *Divinity's union with humanity*, for infinite efficacy, by which the whole sacrifice is *guided*."][113]

In his 1582 edition however, Beza writes:

> Nam Spiritus aeterni appellatione, <u>Deitatis im humanitate assumpta</u> efficacitateum infinitatum intelligo, quae totum hoc sacrificium <u>consecrauit</u>.[114]

> ["I understand the appeal to eternal Spirit as *Deity assumed in humanity*, for infinite efficacy, by which the whole sacrifice is *consecrated*."][115]

Beza's comment on Hebrews 9:14 remains unchanged from his 1582 edition onwards, and this shows that he had the incarnation in mind. For Beza, *Spiritus aeterni* refers to deity (God-ness) or divine nature, in Jesus, and not to the Holy Spirit. In the religious, social and political context of the Reformation impulse and polemical stance against the Roman papacy, it is understandable that the discovery (or recovery) of ancient Greek biblical manuscripts differing in places from the Latin Vulgate provided new hermeneutical opportunities. The traditional Vulgate translation of Hebrews 9:14 was challenged by this discovery of the phrase διὰ πνεύματος αἰωνίου in early manuscripts. With regard to Beza's modification of his annotation on Hebrews 9:14, however, and his inclusion of the Latin Vulgate in subsequent editions, one only can speculate that this may have been in response to criticism concerning his departure from tradition.

While McGrath is correct in determining that Beza understood the "eternal Spirit" of Hebrews 9:14 as Christ's divinity rather than as a reference

---

111. McGrath, *Eternal Spirit*, 12.
112. Beza, *Novum Domini*, 751; underlining added.
113. My translation.
114. Beza, *Iesu Christi*, 363; underlining added.
115. My translation.

to the Holy Spirit, he inaccurately aligns John Owen (1616–1683) with Beza in this matter.[116] A closer examination of Owen's commentary on this passage in *An Exposition of the Epistle to the Hebrews* (1674) reveals that, on the contrary, he states that the term "the eternal Spirit" not only refers to Christ's eternal Spirit, meaning "the divine nature acting in the person of the Son," *but also* to "the Holy Ghost in him."[117] This is in keeping with his Christology that sees the Son's divine nature and the Spirit-controlled human nature coexisting in one person. Owen maintains that while Jesus Christ's high priesthood and sacrificial offering involved his entire *person*, it was only his human nature that was the sacrifice.[118] Owen distinguishes between the term "the Spirit of Christ" (by which he means the Son's divinity), and "the Holy Spirit." It is helpful to quote Owen at some length:

> Some copies read, "by the eternal Spirit"; some, "by the Holy Spirit"; the latter is the reading of the Vulgar translation, and countenanced by sundry ancient copies of the original. The Syriac retains "the eternal Spirit"; which also is the reading of the most ancient copies of the Greek. Hence follows a double interpretation of the words. Some say that the Lord Christ offered himself unto God in and by the acting of the *Holy Ghost in his human nature*; for by him were wrought in him that fervent zeal unto the glory of God, that love and compassion unto the souls of men, which both carried him through his suffering and rendered his obedience therein acceptable to God as a sacrifice of a sweet-smelling savour: which work of the Holy Spirit in the human nature of Christ I have elsewhere declared. Others say that his own eternal Deity, which supported him in his sufferings and rendered the sacrifice of himself effectual, is intended. But this will not absolutely follow to be the sense of the place upon the common reading, "by the eternal Spirit"; for the Holy Spirit is no less and eternal Spirit than is the Deity of Christ himself. The truth is, both these concurred in, and were absolutely necessary unto the offering of Christ. The acting of his own eternal Spirit was so, as unto the *efficacy and effect*; and the Holy Ghost was so, as unto the *manner* of it. Without the first, his offering of himself could not have "purged our consciences from dead works." No sacrifice of any mere creature could have produced that effect. It would have had in itself a worth and dignity whereby we might have been discharged of sin unto the glory of God. Nor without the subsistence of the human nature

116. McGrath, *Eternal Spirit*, 31–32.
117. Owen, *Exposition*, 304.
118. Owen, *Exposition*, 304.

in the divine person of the Son of God, could it have undergone and passed through unto victory what it was to suffer in this offering of it.[119] ... That Christ should thus offer himself unto God, and that by the eternal Spirit, is the centre of the mystery of the gospel.[120]

In his commentary on Hebrews, Owen affirms that *both* interpretations of "eternal Spirit," that is, as the Son's own divinity and as the Holy Spirit, are valid. It is interesting, however, that in an earlier work, *Death of Death in the Death of Christ* (1650), he asserts in no uncertain terms that the phrase διὰ πνεύματος αἰωνίου refers *only* to the Holy Spirit:

In his [Christ's] *oblation*, or passion (for they are both the same, with several respects—one to what he suffered, the other to what he did with, by, and under those sufferings), how "by the Eternal Spirit he offered himself without spot to God," Heb. ix.14: whether it be meant of the offering himself a bloody sacrifice on the cross, or his presentation of himself continually before his Father—it is by the Eternal Spirit. The willing offering of himself through that Spirit was the eternal fire under this sacrifice, which made it acceptable to God. That which some contend, that by the eternal Spirit is here meant our Saviour's own Deity, I see no great ground for. Some Greek and Latin copies read, not, as we commonly, Πνεύματος αἰωνίου, but Πνεύματος ἁγίου, and so the doubt is quite removed: and I see no reason why he may not as well be said to offer himself through the Holy Spirit, as to be "declared to be the Son of God, according to the Spirit of holiness, by the resurrection from the dead," as Rom. i.4; as also to be "quickened by the Spirit," 1 Pet. iii.18. The working of the Spirit was required as well in his oblation as resurrection, in his dying as quickening.[121]

Although Owen's interpretation of the phrase διὰ πνεύματος αἰωνίου seems to have broadened over the intervening two decades between one publication and the other, it is obvious that common to both works is his conviction that the Holy Spirit was involved in Christ's sacrificial offering at the cross. Furthermore, as alluded to earlier, Owen asserts that the preposition διὰ "denotes a concurrent operation, when one works with another. Nor doth it always denote a subservient, instrumental cause, but sometimes that which is *principally efficient*, John i. 3; Rom. xi. 36; Heb. i. 2. So it doth here; the

---

119. Owen, *Exposition*, 303-4.
120. Owen, *Exposition*, 307.
121. Owen, *Death of Death*, I.v, 178.

eternal Spirit was not an inferior instrument whereby Christ offered himself, but he [the Spirit] was the principal efficient cause in the work."[122]

Thus, Owen maintains that the Holy Spirit was an active agent during Christ's passion and death. Having made such a clear affirmation that the Holy Spirit's participation was not minor but that "he was the principal efficient cause in the work,"[123] that the Holy Spirit filled Christ with faith and trust in God, and love and compassion for his church, and empowered him to submit voluntarily to the will of God,[124] and that "the working of the Spirit was required as well in his *oblation* as resurrection, in his *dying* as quickening,"[125] it is a pity that Owen does not expound in detail the nature of that participation. Nonetheless, Owen offers two useful metaphorical suggestions, first, that the Spirit may function as the "eternal fire" through whom Christ offers himself.[126] This is a reference to the Israelite ritual burning of sacrificial offerings,[127] and to the perpetual fire that was to be kept burning on the altar, day and night (Lev 6:12–13). Indeed, no ritual sacrifice is complete without burning at least some part of the offering. Although Owen himself does not explore this pneumatological concept much further, it is clear that fire is closely associated with theophany in the Old Testament,[128] and with the eschatological Spirit in the New Testament.[129] Interestingly, theophanic "fire" (אֵשׁ, *ēš*) in the Old Testament is often accompanied by "wind" (רוּחַ, *rûaḥ*),[130] and even more intriguingly, the fiery divine figure in the vision of Ezekiel 8:2–3 is identified with a spirit, or associated with the s/Spirit.[131]

---

122. Owen, *Exposition*, 303.

123. Owen, *Exposition*, 303.

124. Owen, *Exposition*, 307.

125. Owen, *Death of Death*, I.v, 178, italics added.

126. Owen, *Death of Death*, I.v, 178.

127. There are forty-five references to "offering by fire" (אִשֶּׁה), a term which signifies the burning of sacrificial offerings on the altar, in Exodus (four references—29:18, 25, 41; 30:20), Leviticus (twenty-seven references, e.g. 1:9, 13, 17; 2:3, 9, 16, etc.), and Numbers (fourteen references, e.g. 15:3, 10, 14, 25, etc.). The Passover lamb is always roasted over "fire" (אֵשׁ; Exod 12:8–10). The practice of burning sacrificial offerings predates the setting up of the tabernacle (Genesis 8:20; 22:6–7).

128. Gen 15:17; Exod 3:2–4; 13:21–22; 19:18; Lev 9:24; 10:2; Num 9:15–16; 11:1–3; Deut 4:12, 15, 24; 5:4–5, 22–26; 9:3, 10; 10:4; 18:16; 2 Sam 22:13; 1 Kings 18:38; 2 Kings 2:11; 6:17; 2 Chr 7:3; Pss 18:8, 12; 21:9; 50:3; 97:3; Isa 4:5; 29:6; 66:15; Ezek 1:4, 13, 27; 8:2; Zech 2:5.

129. Matt 3:11; Luke 3:16; Acts 2:2–4, 17–19; Rev 1:14, 7; 4:5.

130. 2 Sam 22:9–13, 16; 1 Kgs 18:38; 2 Kgs 2:11; Ps 18:8–15; 50:3; Isa 29:6; 66:15; Ezek 1:4.

131. The singular noun רוּחַ has been translated as "a spirit" (*TNK*), "the spirit"

Second, Owen suggests that "the eternal Spirit of Christ was the altar whereon he offered himself. This supported and bore it [the sacrifice] up under its sufferings, whereon it was presented unto God as an acceptable sacrifice." [132] By using the term "Spirit of Christ" here rather than "Holy Spirit," Owen refers to the other interpretation of "eternal Spirit," namely, Christ's divinity. In other words, in applying the Levitical sacrificial metaphor to the cross, Owen envisages Christ's humanity as the sacrifice, Christ's divinity as the altar, and the Holy Spirit as the consuming fire. This tantalizing idea is examined more closely in the next chapter. According to McCormack, Owen develops "a pneumatologically responsible two-natures Christology" in which the divine Logos and the Spirit-controlled human nature are united in the one person of Christ.[133] This differentiates Owen's understanding from Christologies that focus on the Logos without reference to the Spirit, and from Spirit Christologies that seem to see no role for the Logos. Owen emphasizes that "Messiah" and "Christ" are terms that by definition entail an anointment by the Holy Spirit. Jesus is *Christ* because he received "the full communication of the Spirit unto Him, not by measure, in all his graces and gifts." [134] While this pneumatic chrismation is to be regarded as one entire work, Owen points out that Jesus was anointed by the Spirit at several points in his life—his birth, his baptism, *his death*, and his ascension, and that it is through Jesus *Christ*, the Spirit-anointed Messiah, that believers receive the Holy Spirit from the Father.[135] In short, John Owen asserts the vital importance of the Holy Spirit in the life, ministry, death, and resurrection of Jesus Christ. He sees in Hebrews 9:14 that which alludes to the participation of the Holy Spirit at the cross of Christ.

While John McGrath's remarks regarding Protestant interpretation of the phrase διὰ πνεύματος αἰωνίου in Hebrews 9:14 may be too sweeping, it is true nevertheless that as the Roman church's monopoly on biblical hermeneutics was increasingly questioned, Protestant scholars rightly rejected the Vulgate translation "*Spiritum sanctum*" in favor of "*Spiritum aeternum*" on textual grounds. In so doing, many (but not Calvin or Owen) put forward a variety of alternative interpretations that precluded a reference to the Holy Spirit. Their main reasons for rejecting the Holy Spirit as the referent of the phrase are first, the absence of the article, and second, the adjective "eternal"

(*NAB*, *NRSV*), "the Spirit" (*ESV*, *NIV*, *TNIV*). The *NRSV* and *NAB* identify "the spirit" with the fiery figure.

132. Owen, *Exposition*, 305.
133. McCormack, "Loud Cries and Tears," 40.
134. Owen, *Work of the Holy Spirit*, 392.
135. Owen, *Work of the Holy Spirit*, 392–93.

instead of "holy."[136] I have argued in the exegetical section above that in regard to the singular noun πνεῦμα, the presence or absence of the article, by itself, does not distinguish between a reference to the Holy Spirit or to other meanings of "spirit"; the phraseology and context are important. Concerning the adjective αἰωνίου, on the basis of the pneumatological context of Hebrews, and from the reflections of Ambrose of Milan, Theoderet of Cyrus, John Calvin, and John Owen, I have argued that although the description "eternal" is used, the phrase διὰ πνεύματος αἰωνίου refers to the Holy Spirit.

Among those who are convinced that the referent of Hebrews 9:14 is indeed the Holy Spirit, Dunn elaborates "that Christ was enabled to offer himself up in death by the power of the eternal Spirit"[137] while Bruce alludes to the Spirit-anointment of the Isaianic servant of the Lord.[138] Emmrich, highlighting passages from Jewish pseudepigrapha, Josephus, Qumran, and rabbinic literature that link the bearers of the office of high priest with the Holy Spirit, suggests that the role of the Spirit in Christ's work of atonement is *amtscharisma* or specific "gifting for priestly office."[139] McGrath proposes that Christ's self-offering takes place within the Pauline paradigm of the law of the Spirit, and that Christ's blood becomes "the vehicle of the Spirit of grace."[140] Barth consistently interprets the phrase πνεύματος αἰωνίου to mean the Holy Spirit, highlighting the sanctifying work of the Spirit at the cross.[141] He asserts that Jesus is "the spiritual man, i.e., the true and exalted royal man who lives by the descent of the Spirit of God and is therefore wholly filled and directed by him . . . And it is again as this wholly sanctified man that 'through the eternal Spirit he offered himself without spot to God' in His death (Heb. 9:14)."[142] Although Albert Vanhoye somewhat confusingly translates πνεύματος αἰωνίου both as "the eternal Spirit" and as "an eternal spirit,"[143] in his detailed explanation he specifies that it is "the Holy Spirit with which he [Christ] was filled." Vanhoye also suggests that "Jesus permitted the Spirit of God to penetrate his human existence through and through, including even his tragic death, and to transform everything into a perfect offering."[144] As John Owen did

---

136. See Westcott, *Epistle to the Hebrews*, 261–62.
137. Dunn, *Christ and The Spirit*, vol. 2, 19.
138. Bruce, *Epistle to the Hebrews*, 205.
139. Emmrich, *Pneumatological Concepts*, 1–16.
140. McGrath, *Eternal Spirit*, 97–98, 102.
141. Barth, CD, II/2, §33, 102; IV/1, §59, 277, 309; IV/2, §64, 324; IV/4, §75, 29.
142. Barth, CD, IV/2, §64, 324. See chapter 7, §7.1 in this book.
143. Vanhoye, *Structure and Message*, 67, 94.
144. Vanhoye, *Structure and Message*, 67–68.

before him, Vanhoye also postulates that the phrase may be an allusion to the perpetual fire (*"feu continuel"*) of Israel's sacrificial altar, stating, "And in fact the true 'fire from heaven' can only be the Holy Spirit who alone is capable of bringing about the sacrificial transformation."[145]

Among those who interpret the phrase διὰ πνεύματος αἰωνίου to mean something other than the Holy Spirit, some suggest that it refers to Christ's divinity (following Beza),[146] or his human will,[147] soul,[148] ethical character,[149] spirituality,[150] or the heavenly tabernacle in which he offered himself to God.[151] Other interpretations include a spirit of determination or obedience,[152] Christ's inner disposition,[153] or the spiritual realm of God's existence.[154] Another rather creative interpretation is Joachim Jeremias's idea that Jesus's spirit was separated from his body at the time of his death, and identifies πνεύματος αἰωνίου with Jesus's spirit that became the medium for presenting the sacrificial blood in the presence of God, after which his spirit was reunited with his body.[155] These various interpretations have in common the view that πνεύματος in Hebrews 9:14 is related to Christ and not to the Holy Spirit. Although I have argued that a reference to the Holy Spirit is more likely on exegetical grounds, pneumatological context, and history of theological interpretation, nevertheless, among these alternate interpretations, the ideas that the phrase refers to Jesus's spirit or to the resurrected Jesus, are worthy of more detailed rebuttal.

---

145. Vanhoye, *Structure and Message*, 68; Vanhoye, "Esprit éternel et feu du sacrifice en He 9,14," 263–74; cited in Emmrich, *Pneumatological Concepts*, 2.

146. "In men the 'spirit' is, as has been said, that by which they are capable of connexion with God. But in Christ, who did not cease to be the Son of God by becoming man, the 'spirit' is to be regarded as the seat of His Divine Personality in His human Nature." Westcott, *Epistle to the Hebrews*, 262.

147. De Ribera, *Commentarius in epist.* (1598), n. 431; Tena, *Commentaria et disputationes* (1661), 405; both cited in McGrath, *Eternal Spirit*, 17–19.

148. Salodense, *Paraphrasis in onmes* (1589), n. 197; Poli, *Synopsis Criticorum Aliorumque* (1712), 1250; both cited in McGrath, *Eternal Spirit*, 41–42.

149. Lünemann, *Critical and Exegetical Handbook*, 329–30; McGrath, *Eternal Spirit*, 38–41.

150. Attridge, *Hebrews*, 251.

151. H. Grotius, *Annotationes in Novum Testamentum, II* (1756), 897; cited in McGrath, *Eternal Spirit*, 28–29.

152. Moffatt, *Epistle to the Hebrews*, 124.

153. Bonsirven, *Saint Paul: épître aux Hebreux* (1943), 390; cited in McGrath, *Eternal Spirit*, 43–44.

154. Johnson, *Hebrews*, 236; Attridge, *Hebrews*, 251.

155. Jeremias, "Zwischen Karfreitag und Ostern:" (1949), 194–201; cited in Emmrich, *Pneumatological Concepts*, 2.

First, the idea that Christ offers his disembodied spirit to God contradicts the assertion of the author of Hebrews that "we have been sanctified through the offering of the *body* (σώματος) of Jesus Christ once for all" (Heb 10:10). Emmrich, who is convinced that Hebrews 9:14 "expresses the central thought of the epistle to the Hebrews,"[156] contends that if the author meant to refer to Jesus's spirit he would have inserted the personal pronoun "his," so that the prepositional phrase would have been διὰ πνεύματος αὐτοῦ αἰωνίου.[157] Lindars rightly observes that "Hebrews nowhere contrasts Jesus' spiritual nature with his human nature. In fact, he is most insistent that Jesus died as a member of the human race, and this is essential to his high priestly character (2:10–18)."[158] Indeed, there is no sense in Hebrews of a body-spirit dualism. The metaphorical "division" (μερισμός) between "soul" (ψυχή) and "spirit" (πνεῦμα) portrayed in Hebrews 4:12 is a rhetorical device to demonstrate the utmost ability (ἄχρι, "as far as") of God's word to differentiate between inseparable elements of humanity, signifying the extent of the divine reach into every crevice of the inner human. Such a "division" is not applied between "*body*" and "spirit." When the author of Hebrews states that "Christ did not enter a sanctuary made by human hands, a mere copy of the true one, but he entered into heaven itself, now to appear before God on our behalf" (Heb 9:24), there is no intimation that only his spirit entered the heavenly sanctuary, leaving his body behind, or even the idea that his spirit offered up his body.

Second, can Christ's offering be understood as one that occurs *after* he has been raised from the dead, so that the "eternal Spirit" refers to the *resurrected* Christ? While this is an attractive proposition, from the standpoint of Hebrews and the passion narratives, it is unlikely. When animal sacrifices are compared with Christ's sacrifice, it is his *death* that is in focus, not his resurrection. According to the author of Hebrews, it is the sacrificial *death* and *blood* that accomplishes redemption from covenantal transgression (Heb 9:15–22). As the mediator of the new covenant, Christ "has appeared once for all at the end of the age to remove sin by the sacrifice of himself" (Heb 9:26). That Christ rose from the dead is affirmed in no uncertain terms (Heb 13:20), but that is *after* his atoning sacrifice. "When he had made purification (ποιησάμενος) for sins, he sat down (ἐκάθισεν) at the right hand of the Majesty on high" (Heb 1:3) and again, "But when this priest had offered (προσενέγκας) for all time one sacrifice for sins, he sat down (ἐκάθισεν) at

---

156. Emmrich, *Pneumatological Concepts*, 1.

157. This is not a strong argument, because the personal pronoun is sometimes implicit in the absence of αὐτοῦ, e.g. John 11:33; 13:21; Matt 27:50; cf. Luke 23:46.

158. Lindars, *Theology of the Letter*, 57–58.

the right hand of God" (Heb 10:12).[159] Wallace notes, "To sit at God's right hand meant that the work was finished, and this could not take place *until* the sin-cleansing was accomplished."[160] The resurrected Christ, sitting on his heavenly throne, lives eternally as humanity's high priest and intercessor (Heb 7:24–25). His second appearance on earth will be at the end of human history, to bring to fulfillment the salvation that he has inaugurated (Heb 9:28). Hebrews 9:14 is set within the context of Christ's sacrificial offering, and does not, at that point, refer to the resurrected Christ. Indeed, Christ's bodily resurrection points to the *result* of the perfect effectiveness of his sacrifice, giving him, and humanity with him, victory over sin and death. The veil of the innermost sanctuary was torn immediately after (Mark 15:38; Matt 27:51) or even just before Christ died (Luke 23:45), that is, while he still hung on the cross and *before* he was resurrected. In his commentary on Hebrews, John Owen insightfully points out:

> For by the entrance of the high priest into the most holy place with blood the Holy Ghost did signify that the way into it, namely, for believers to enter by, was only the one true sacrifice which he was to offer and to be. And accordingly, to give an indication of the accomplishment of this type, when he expired on the cross, having offered himself unto God for the expiation of our sins, the veil of the temple, which enclosed and secured this holy place from any entrance into it, was rent from the top to the bottom, whereby it was laid open into all, Matt. xxvii. 51. And an evidence this is that *the Lord Christ offered his great expiatory sacrifice in his death here on earth, a true and real sacrifice; and that it was not an act of power after his ascension, metaphorically called a sacrifice,* as the Socinians dream. For until that sacrifice was offered the way could not be opened into the Holies; which was immediately after his death, and signified by the rending of the veil. This is ὁδὸς τῶν ἁγίων, the only way whereby we enter into the most holy place, the gracious presence of God, and that with boldness.[161]

---

159. ποιησάμενος ("having made") and προσενέγκας ("having offered") are aorist adverbial participles, and the main verb is the aorist ἐκάθισεν ("he sat"). When both adverbial participle and its main verb are aorist, the action of the participle may be antecedent to or contemporaneous with the action of the main verb; Wallace, *Greek Grammar*, 624. NIV and ESV use the word "after" for ποιησάμενος, and NAB uses the participle clause "when he had accomplished."

160. Wallace, *Greek Grammar*, 624. Interestingly, Wallace nuances his own grammatical observations in regard to aorist participle ποιησάμενος in Heb 1:3, by seeing an additional, though secondary, causal force in the use of that participle.

161. Owen, *Exposition*, 240; italics added.

The tearing of the veil, whether actual or metaphorical, indicates that the Synoptic Gospel writers were convinced that the barrier separating humanity and God was destroyed even as Jesus died on the cross, signifying that Christ's sacrificial offering of himself fulfilled humanity's covenantal obligations, and reconciliation between God and humanity was successfully established. In John 19:30, Jesus's words "It is finished" (τετέλεσται) are spoken just as he dies; for the Fourth Evangelist, the offering of Christ, the humanity's paschal lamb, occurred *on the cross*.[162] The use of the verb τελέω and the perfect tense leaves little room for doubt that with Christ's death, according to the Fourth Evangelist, atonement has been accomplished. Hence the view that it was the *resurrected* Christ that offered himself as the atonement sacrifice is untenable. Furthermore, in the Day of Atonement liturgy, the sacrificial offerings are offered on the altar *outside* the sanctuary. The high priest then sprinkles some of the sacrificial blood in the sanctuary and on the ark of the covenant as a *cleansing* ritual; thereafter the sacrificial offerings are burned (Lev 16). All components of the ritual sacrifices, including the banishment of the sins of the people with the live goat, contribute to an understanding of Christ's self-offering on the cross. *Every* aspect of the atonement is accomplished on the cross before the veil is torn (Heb 10:20; cf. Mark 15:38; Matt 27:51; Luke 23:41), signalling that reconciliation between God and humanity has been effected in Christ through the power of the Spirit.

In summary, from the textual evidence, exegetical analysis, and an examination of the history of theological interpretation of Hebrews 9:14, there is considerable support for the notion that the phrase διὰ πνεύματος αἰωνίου refers to the Holy Spirit, and not to Jesus's divinity or to his human spirit, or to an ethical principle of courageous determination, or to some spiritual dimension. If, however, it is indeed the *Holy Spirit* whom the author of Hebrews is referring to when he uses the phrase διὰ πνεύματος ἀιωνίου, it is still unclear why he chooses the adjective *"eternal"* when he generally uses "holy" in other references to the divine Spirit.

B. 'ETERNAL' SPIRIT—THEOLOGICAL IMPLICATIONS

It must be said at the outset that the theme of *eternality* is significant in Hebrews. The author repeats the "eternal" theme an impressive nineteen times in the epistle, through the phrases εἰς τὸν αἰῶνα and εἰς τὸ διηνεκές, and

---

162. The meaning of the clause that follows, παρέδωκεν τὸ πνεῦμα ("he gave up his/the spirit") has been contentious, and is examined in chapter 7, §7.2, in this book. Whether τὸ πνεῦμα here refers to Christ's spirit or breath, or to the Holy Spirit, does not affect the impact of the word τετέλεσται.

the adjective αἰωνίου/ίαν.[163] Right at the beginning, the author takes pains to portray Jesus as God's Son whose preexistence (Heb 1:2, 10) and eternality (Heb 1:11-12) are attestations of his divinity. That the Son is the agent through whom God made τοὺς αἰῶνας ("the ages"; Heb 1:2)[164] is echoed in his appointment as God's agent of eternal redemption (αἰωνίαν λύτρωσιν; Heb 9:13) for humanity. Would not, however, the Son's own divinity be sufficient to ensure the eternality of his sacrifice without the need to invoke the eternality of *the (Holy) Spirit*?

Hebrews 9:14 itself has been recognized as an *a-minori-ad-maius* ("from lesser to greater") argument,[165] and as mentioned earlier, the structure of Hebrews 9:11-14 appears to be a complex parallelism that contrasts the Levitical animal sacrifice with Christ's self-offering while maintaining continuity through the motifs of "blood" and "eternal" (appendix 5). The temporal repetitive Levitical offering of the blood of goats and bulls can only cleanse the "*flesh*," whereas Jesus Christ's once-only offering of himself cleanses our "*consciences*." McGrath insightfully observes that the author's argument would be complete even with the omission of that phrase "διὰ πνεύματος αἰωνίου."[166] Yet its authenticity is undeniable given the textual evidence. In other words, it is more likely that "through eternal Spirit" qualifies Christ's self-offering rather than his spotlessness (ἄμωμον). If Christ's sinlessness was the focus of that phrase rather than his self-offering, then the phrase "through *Holy* Spirit" would seem more appropriate. Moreover, Jesus Christ *already* comes to the sacrificial altar ἄκακος ἀμίαντος ("blameless, pure," Heb 7:26), and this is the precondition of his acceptability as the perfect sacrifice for humanity, just as animals chosen for sacrificial offerings must also be without defect (Lev 1-4).[167] Jesus Christ is the spotless and perfect human, representing humankind before God, accepting the covenantal consequences of our sin—death. At this momentous watershed in human history, Hebrews 9:14 suggests that Jesus Christ's offering of himself to God

---

163. Occurrences in Hebrews: εἰς τὸν αἰῶνα (nine occurrences, 1:8; 5:6; 6:20; 7:17, 21, 24, 28; 13:8, 21); εἰς τὸ διηνεκές (four occurrences, 7:3; 10:1, 12, 14); αἰωνίου/ίαν (six occurrences, 5:9, 6:2, 9:12, 14, 15, 13:20). In Revelation the phrase εἰς τὸν αἰῶνα appears twelve times, only in the plural form εἰς τοὺς αἰῶνας, as a technical term for "eternity."

164. τοὺς αἰῶνας in Hebrews 1:2 is translated "the world/s" or "the universe" in all English translations except *NJB* which retains "the ages."

165. McGrath, *Eternal Spirit*, 94.

166. McGrath, *Eternal Spirit*, 94.

167. While it is tempting to see a reference to Spirit Christology in Heb 9:14, i.e., the Spirit enables Jesus to remain sinless during his earthly life, this probably overreads the passage.

involved the Holy Spirit in some way. But then again, why emphasize the *eternality* of the Spirit?

O'Brien, stating that "the Holy Spirit anointed Jesus as high priest for every aspect of his ministry, including his sacrificial death," explains that "the adjective *eternal* suggests an eschatological dimension to the Spirit's activity, linking the expression with the *eternal redemption* he has obtained for us (v.12)."[168] Thus the phrase διὰ πνεύματος αἰωνίου helps to strengthen the author's argument that Christ's single act of sacrificial atonement secures "eternal salvation" (σωτηρίας αἰωνίου; Heb 5:9), "eternal redemption" (αἰωνίαν λύτρωσιν; Heb 9:12), and "the eternal inheritance" (τῆς αἰωνίου κληρονομίας; Heb 9:15) for humanity. It is the *eternal* quality of Christ's sacrifice and his permanent priesthood that ensure the superiority and finality of the new covenant over the old. The old covenant was, in the light of the cross, always an imperfect shadow of the new (and true) covenant. This *eternality* of Christ's offering is inseparably united with the *singularity* of his sacrificial act, *through the eternal Spirit*.[169] Christ only died once, and only needs to die once (Heb 9:12, 25–28; 10:10–14), because that one act has an eternal reach through the Spirit. Ellingworth points out that the author's use of the aorist προσήνεγκεν in Hebrews 9:14 emphasizes that Christ's self-offering is a single act rather than a continuous one.[170] Furthermore, on grammatical grounds, the adjective is part of a prepositional phrase headed by διά, so that πνεύματος and αἰωνίου are inseparable. Therefore, it is clear that the eternal quality of Christ's sacrifice is attributed to the Spirit and not to Christ.

While Christ's death is a single event in time and space, its efficacy for humanity is eternal and complete. Hence, Christ's sacrifice supersedes the continual Levitical sacrifices which, according to Hebrews, are transitory and imperfect imitations of Christ's eternal sacrifice, mere earthly hints at eternality. Significantly, this eternal reach of Christ's sacerdotal act is effected *through the Spirit* rather than through the Son's own eternality. "[I]t was the power of the eternal Spirit which made Christ's unique sacrifice

---

168. O'Brien, *Hebrews*, 324–25.

169. The author of Hebrews stresses the singularity of Christ's act by the repeated use of ἅπαξ, three times in 9:26–28. Ἐφάπαξ, which gives added emphasis to the notion of "once," is used only in Hebrews to refer to Christ's self-sacrifice (Heb 7:27; 9:12; 10:10), and by Paul (Rom 6:10; 1 Cor 15:6); see Ellingworth, *Commentary on Hebrews*, 319.

170. Ellingworth, *Commentary on Hebrews*, 457. In concord with Ambrose and Theoderet, Erickson argues for the full divinity of the Holy Spirit on the basis that Heb 9:14 testifies to the Spirit's eternality; Erickson, *Christian Theology*, 874.

eternal in its effect."[171] Hebrews seems to suggest that while the eternality of the Son is crucial for the permanence of Christ's high priestly role, it is the eternality of the Spirit that ensures the *eternal scope* of Christ's atonement, comprehensively cleansing humanity of sin across space and time. Thus, the author of this epistle assures all its hearers that those who trust in Christ, no matter when or where they live, or who they may be, are redeemed by him and share his royal status as God's firstborn Son. This eternal redemption is effected by Christ through the work of the Holy Spirit. Although the author of Hebrews does not himself elaborate on the Spirit's actions at the cross, he draws pneumatology and Christology together in the atoning sacrifice of Christ, providing a biblical basis for the theological development of a *pneumatologia crucis*.

6.3 Pneumatic Sacrificial Metaphors in the New Testament

Apart from Hebrews 9:14, there are two other biblical passages that allude to the Spirit's involvement in sacrificial metaphors in the New Testament, and which may convey additional support for an active role for the Holy Spirit at the cross. They are Romans 15:15-16 and 1 Peter 1:2.

Romans 15:15–16

> Nevertheless on some points I have written to you rather boldly by way of reminder, because of the grace given me by God to be a minister of Christ Jesus to the Gentiles in the priestly service of the gospel of God, so that the offering of the Gentiles may be acceptable, *sanctified by the Holy Spirit* [ἡγιασμένη ἐν πνεύματι ἁγίῳ].

Paul sees himself as Jesus Christ's minister (λειτουργὸν Χριστοῦ Ἰησοῦ) in the sacred service of God's gospel (ἱερουργοῦντα τὸ εὐαγγέλιον τοῦ θεοῦ) to the Gentiles, offering Gentile believers to God as an acceptable offering *sanctified by [the] Holy Spirit* (ἡγιασμένη ἐν πνεύματι ἁγίῳ).[172] There are

---

171. Ellingworth, *Commentary on Hebrews*, 457.

172. Irrespective of whether the genitive τῶν ἐθνῶν is to be understood as an objective genitive (the Gentiles are the offering—the view of most scholars) or as a subjective genitive (the Gentiles are doing the offering—the view of Witherington), the offering has been made holy by or in the Holy Spirit; Witherington III, *Paul's Letter*, 355. It is clear from Romans 12:1 that the offering is nothing else than the believers themselves, although the priestly terminology used by Paul of himself in Romans 15:16 tends to

no known manuscript variants for the phrase ἡγιασμένη ἐν πνεύματι ἁγίῳ which is uniformly understood to refer to the Holy Spirit;[173] note that the word πνεῦμα is anarthrous here. As ἡγιασμένη is a singular feminine passive participle, it is clearly related to ἡ προσφορά ("the offering," singular), so that the Gentiles are viewed as one entity.[174] This offering of the Gentiles is "made *holy*" by the "*Holy* Spirit." "The Holy Spirit is the source of sanctification, and therefore the offering of the Gentiles which is made by Paul, in the role of priest, is said to be made acceptable to God by the Holy Spirit and not by the observance of the law."[175]

Paul's use of sacrificial imagery in his choice of cultic language (λειτουργὸς, "tabernacle/temple servant or minister," and ἱερουργοῦντα, "one acting as a priest"), is, according to Morris, "a striking way of affirming that the proclamation of the gospel is a solemn and sacred act."[176] This sacrificial metaphor is used in the context of Paul's strong emphasis in Romans on covenant membership,[177] and his conviction that Jesus Christ has perfectly fulfilled humanity's covenantal obligations through his sinless life, and through his death (Rom 5:9–11). Paul is at pains to demonstrate that God's Abrahamic covenant with humanity, as provisionally represented by the Mosaic law and Israel, has been ratified in Jesus Christ. This is also the essential message of Hebrews. Membership access into God's covenant community is no longer based on Abrahamic descent, circumcision, and adherence to the Mosaic law, but on faith in Christ. Membership is now open to all humanity, by faith in Christ.

Proof that one has secured this covenantal membership is demonstrated by the very presence and power of the eschatological Spirit (God's "badge" of covenant membership) in the lives of the believers (Rom 8).[178]

---

include him in the process.

173. Fitzmyer, *Romans*, 711–12; Holland, *Romans*, 458; Robert Jewett, *Romans*, 906–8; Kruse, *Paul's Letter*, 537–38; Morris, *Epistle to the Romans*, 512; Moo, *Epistle to the Romans*, 889–91; Murray, *The Epistle to the Romans*, 208–10; Schreiner, *Romans*, 766–67. These commentators translate the preposition ἐν as "by" although Jewett prefers "in."

174. Holland, *Romans*, 458.

175. Origen, *Epistle to the Romans* v. 214, 216; cited in Bray, *Ancient Christian Commentary*, 360–61.

176. Morris, *Epistle to the Romans*, 511. The verb λειτουργεῖν ("to serve") is commonly, although not exclusively, used as a cultic term for priestly service in the tabernacle/temple in the LXX translation of Exodus, Numbers, and 1 and 2 Chronicles. Although ἱερουργοῦντα is a *hapax legomenon* in the New Testament, ἱερουργίαν in 4 Macc 3:20 refers to temple service; the noun ἱερόν itself means "temple."

177. Holland, *Romans*, 22–23.

178. See also Gal 3:2. As Dunn asserts, "The (eschatological) transformation of

Paul is adamant that covenant membership through faith in Christ is not about an incremental enhancement in one's conduct and ethics, or even about a progressive upward transcendence into holiness, but a total and radical transformation that can only be described in terms of death and rebirth, that is, participation in Christ's death on the cross of Golgotha, and in his resurrection (Rom 6:5–8). It is not that believers *claim* Christ's sacrificial death as their own, but that they *themselves* have participated in his death. It is *because* they have died with him that they can be assured of their being raised with him (Rom 6:5). Christ's representation is inclusive, not exclusive.[179] Paul stresses this very point in order to assert that in dying with Christ their sin-controlled old humanity died, so that the power of sin and death over them is broken, and through the very Spirit who raised them in Christ, they are now empowered to live holy lives as children of God (Rom 8:11).[180] Christ is much more than a victorious exemplar for humanity—he is the very basis for victory. Indeed (or as Paul writes, "therefore"), having been raised with Christ through the Holy Spirit, the believers are now to present themselves, as the new Spirit-filled covenant community, to God as one[181] living, holy, and pleasing sacrifice (θυσίαν ζῶσαν ἁγίαν εὐάρεστον τῷ θεῷ; Rom 12:1).[182] This is the way the new covenant community worships God, not through ongoing animal sacrifices, but the presentation of themselves to God, as God's eschatological Spirit-indwelt people. Calvin writes concerning Romans 15:16:

> Now as the ancient victims were dedicated to God, having been externally sanctified and washed, so these victims are consecrated to the Lord by the Spirit of holiness, through whose power, inwardly working in them, they are separated from this world. For though the purity of the soul proceeds from faith in the word, yet as the voice of man is in itself inefficacious and lifeless, *the work of cleansing really and properly belongs to the Spirit.*[183]

---

traditional Jewish categories and cultic distinctives is striking. Not only is the priestly ministry of Paul 'out in the world,' but the offering breaches the fundamental cultic distinction between Jew and Gentile which prevented Gentiles from even getting near the great altar of sacrifice in the Temple (the law which forbade Gentiles to go beyond the Court of the Gentiles was firmly established and unyielding)." Dunn, *Romans 9–16*, 860–61.

179. Pannenberg, *Systematic Theology*, 429–37.

180. See also Galatians 2:19 and Colossians 2:12; 3:3.

181. θυσίαν ("offering" in the accusative) is singular.

182. Dodd and Witherington observe that the sacrificial metaphor of Romans 15:16 is echoed in Romans 12:1; Dodd, *Epistle of Paul*, 226; Witherington III, *Paul's Letter*, 355.

183. Calvin, *Commentaries on Romans*, 524, italics added.

Believers are holy and acceptable sacrifices to God because through Christ, they are made holy by the Holy Spirit, on the basis of Christ's atoning death. Romans 15:16 parallels Hebrews 9:14 in its use of pneumatic sacrificial metaphors, although in Hebrews, Jesus Christ is the high priest who offers himself, whereas in Romans, Paul is the priest offering the Gentiles to God. The concept of Christ as humanity's high priest is unique to Hebrews. In Romans, Paul sees himself as the mediating priest, bringing the Gentile community to God as an offering to God, made holy ("set apart," "consecrated," "sanctified") by the Holy Spirit.[184] This offering, however, only takes place "in Christ," as Paul's teaching in Romans precludes any independent access to God apart from Christ. Having been raised with Christ through the Spirit, the covenant community remains in the presence of God as a "living" sacrifice, no longer dead, but alive with Christ into eternity (Rom 5:21; 6:23; cf. Eph 2:5–6).

1 Peter 1:1–2

> Peter, an apostle of Jesus Christ, to the exiles of the Dispersion in Pontus, Galatia, Cappadocia, Asia, and Bithynia, who have been chosen and destined by God the Father and *sanctified by the Spirit* [ἁγιασμῷ πνεύματος] to be obedient to Jesus Christ and to be sprinkled with his blood: May grace and peace be yours in abundance.

Although Michaels wisely cautions against deriving a comprehensive theology from 1 Peter because of its brevity and lack of support from a larger corpus,[185] Achtemeier correctly perceives that the controlling metaphor in 1 Peter is "the Christian community." This new community of God does not arise in a vacuum, but is predicated on God's covenant with Israel. "1 Peter relies on the writings of the people of Israel for language to describe the new people of God."[186] The specific focus of 1 Peter, as Elliott explains, is "the innocent suffering of Christian believers and the dilemma this presented concerning the believers' relation to and behavior among hostile outsiders."[187] In 1 Peter 1:1–2, the author[188] employs Israel's cultic language

---

184. Likewise, in 2 Corinthians 3:6, Paul declares himself a minister of God's new covenant in the Spirit of life.

185. Michaels, *1 Peter*, lxvii, lxxv.

186. Achtemeier, *1 Peter*, 69.

187. Elliot, *1 Peter*, 104.

188. The contentious authorship of 1 Peter, whether authentically Petrine or otherwise, is not relevant here; the masculine pronoun will be used in this study as the

to emphasize that the Christian community are God's new "chosen" ones (ἐκλεκτοῖς) even as the people of Israel were "chosen" (ἐξελέξατο) out of all the nations to be God's treasured possession, to be a holy people (λαὸς ἅγιος), set apart for YHWH, their God.[189] This new divine call and election is a major theme in 1 Peter.[190]

The prepositional phrase εἰς ὑπακοὴν καὶ ῥαντισμὸν αἵματος Ἰησοῦ Χριστοῦ is hermeneutically problematic. The *NRSV* translation above interprets εἰς as telic, and understands the genitive Ἰησοῦ Χριστοῦ to be related to both ὑπακοὴν and ῥαντισμὸν αἵματος. This interpretation entails making the genitive Ἰησοῦ Χριστοῦ objective in regard to ὑπακοὴν, but possessive in regard to ῥαντισμὸν αἵματος, a methodology which Achtemeier rejects as "something of a grammatical monstrosity and surely confusing to the reader/listener."[191] Options which render εἰς as telic and Ἰησοῦ Χριστοῦ as *subjective* for both ὑπακοὴν and ῥαντισμὸν αἵματος ("for Jesus Christ's obedience and sprinkling of blood by him"), or *objective* ("to obey and sprinkle Jesus Christ with blood") make little theological sense. Agnew suggests that εἰς should be understood to be causative—the believers are sanctified by the Spirit *because of* Jesus Christ's obedience and sprinkling of his blood.[192] While there is some merit to Agnew's view, this prepositional phrase so closely parallels Israel's covenantal language of obedience and blood sacrifice (Exod 24:7-8; Lev 16:14-19; cf. Heb 9:19-20; 12:24), that many regard the genitive Ἰησοῦ Χριστοῦ to be linked only to ῥαντισμὸν αἵματος, and not to ὑπακοὴν—thus "the believers are sanctified by the Spirit for obedience, and for sprinkling with the blood of Jesus Christ."[193] This translation fits better grammatically, as both ὑπακοὴν and ῥαντισμὸν are nouns in the accusative case, and are objects of the preposition εἰς. Page asserts, "The combination of obedience and blood-sprinkling in both Exod. 24 and 1 Pet. 1:2 lends strong support for the view that our author had the scene at Sinai in mind when he wrote 1 Pet. 1:2."[194] The difference

---

traditional attribution is to Peter.

189. Deut 7:7; 10:15; 14:12 (LXX).

190. 1 Peter 1:1, 15; 2:4, 6, 9-10, 21; 5:13.

191. Achtemeier, *1 Peter*, 87.

192. Agnew, "1 Peter 1:2," 69-70. This view is endorsed by Elliot and Green; Elliot, *1 Peter*, 319-20; Green, *1 Peter*, 20.

193. This is the translation selected by *KJV, NKJV, NAB,* and *NET*. See Achtemeier, *1 Peter*, 88-89; Michaels, *1 Peter*, 11-12; Schreiner, *1, 2 Peter, Jude*, 55; Ben Witherington III, *Letters and Homilies*, 71-73; Page, "Obedience and Blood," 295-97.

194. Page, "Obedience and Blood," 296. 1 Peter 1:2 uses the noun ὑπακοή, a cognate of the verb ἀκούω which is the term used for "obey" in Exod 24 (LXX). The noun ῥαντισμός is a cognate of the verb ῥαίνω ("I sprinkle") which is a cultic term for blood

between the Exodus narrative and 1 Peter 1:2, however, is the source of the blood. In the former, the blood is of bulls, while in the latter, the blood of Christ. Since the shedding of Christ's blood is a reference to his death, the author of 1 Peter links the *Spirit*'s sanctifying activity with the fulfillment of the covenant by Christ on the cross.

1 Peter envisages the new covenant community as a holy priesthood and God's "spiritual household" (οἶκος πνευματικός). Believers are sanctified priests offering "spiritual sacrifice'" (πνευματικὰς θυσίας) through Jesus Christ (1 Peter 2:5, 9). Like Romans and Hebrews, 1 Peter asserts that the community of believers in Christ have been elected as God's new chosen people according to God's foreknowledge (κατὰ πρόγνωσιν θεοῦ). It is YHWH, God of Israel, who is doing the choosing, although "God" is now defined by Father, Spirit, and Jesus Christ.[195] The fundamental principles of God's relationship with humanity, taught through the Mosaic law and the Levitical sacrificial system, have not been overturned, but continue as the basis of humanity's redemption in Jesus Christ and new life in the Spirit. In Hebrews, Romans, and 1 Peter, the Holy Spirit's work through Israel's ancestors, prophets, priests, and kings, is brought to fruition in Christ, and continues in and through the new covenant community. Yet the "new" covenant is rooted in the "old." Indeed, there is only one definitive covenant that God makes with humanity, the covenant fulfilled in Jesus Christ, of which the Noahic version may be regarded as the idea, the Abrahamic version the sketch, and the Mosaic version the draft.[196]

6.4 The Spirit in Covenantal Christology

On the basis that Jesus's first disciples perceived his identity, ministry, death, and resurrection through the lens of Israel's covenantal paradigm, it is my contention that the corporate character of the high priesthood

---

sprinkling (Exod 29:21; Lev 4:17; 5:9; 14:16, 27; 16:14–19; Num 19:4, LXX). The term ὕδωρ ῥαντισμοῦ is used for the "water of purification" made with the ashes of a red heifer (Num 19, LXX). In contrast, 1 Peter sees Christ's *blood* as that which purifies when sprinkled (ῥαντισμὸν αἵματος Ἰησοῦ Χριστοῦ). Although both authors of 1 Peter and Hebrews use cognates of the verb ῥαίνω, Snaith is correct that in Exod 24:8, Moses vigorously "splashes" (κατεσκέδασεν) rather than "sprinkles" the blood over the people; Snaith, "Sprinkling of Blood," 23–24.

195. Although it would be anachronistic to see the Trinity as a doctrine espoused by 1 Peter, a nascent understanding of the triune nature of God seems to emerge from this epistle.

196. The Davidic promise can be considered, within this metaphor, a supplementary clause to the overall covenant.

juxtaposed against the New Testament depiction of pneumatic union with Christ, may provide further clues to an understanding of the Spirit's role at the cross of Christ.

The High Priest Foreshadows the Corporate Christ

The portrayal of the high priesthood in Exodus and Leviticus makes it clear that the high priest always represents God's people. He does not stand in God's presence as an individual, but embodies the nation, as his highly symbolic breastplate, shoulder pieces, and turban plate signify (Exod 28:6–38).[197] The names of the twelve tribes of Israel are professionally carved onto the two precious stones inserted into his shoulder pieces, six names on each stone, which are "engravings of a seal" or "seal engravings" (פִּתּוּחֵי חֹתָם, pitûḥê ḥōṯām, Exod 28:11). Likewise, each of the twelve precious stones embedded into the breastplate carries the name of one of the twelve tribes, and again the term "seal engravings" (פִּתּוּחֵי חוֹתָם) is used for the inscribed names (Exod 28:21). The high priest's turban carries a gold plate in the front upon which is inscribed, not the names of Israel's tribes, but the words "holy to YHWH" (קֹדֶשׁ לַיהוָה, qōḏeš la-yhwāh, Exod 28:36), and these words are also called "seal engravings" (פִּתּוּחֵי חֹתָם, Exod 28:36). Alongside each thrice repeated term is an explanation for their function.

The seals of the shoulder pieces and the breastplate are memorial stones that represent all twelve Israelite tribes before God (Exod 28:12, 29). The inscription on the turban is a seal that refers to the whole nation of Israel, and not to the high priest as an individual: "It shall be on Aaron's forehead, and Aaron shall take upon himself any guilt incurred in the holy offering that the Israelites consecrate as their sacred donations; it shall always be on his forehead, in order that they may find favour before the Lord" (Exod 28:38).[198] In the Old Testament, the seal represents the authority of the person whose name is engraved upon it (e.g. 1 Kgs 20:8; Neh 10:1; Esth 8:8; Jer 32:10).[199] "This threefold reference may not be coincidental but intentional, to emphasize the importance of that which is written and has a permanent character."[200] The precious stones and golden turban plate are themselves not of primary importance. The focus is on the *inscriptions* that have been engraved upon

---

197. Sarna, *Exodus*, 183.

198. "'Set apart for Yahweh' refers not alone, indeed not even primarily to Aaron and his successors, as v.38 makes plain. It is Israel that is 'set apart for Yahweh'"; Durham, *Exodus*, 388.

199. Millard, "חתם," 325; BDB, 368; HALOT, 364.

200. Cassuto, *Book of Exodus*, 384.

them—the names of the twelve tribes, and the phrase "holy to YHWH." The names of the twelve tribes appearing on the high priest's shoulder pieces and on the twelve stones of his breastplate clearly indicate that the high priest represents the twelve tribes of Israel when he stands before God. That the twelve tribes are seen, not as separate groups of people, but as *one* holy people (קָדֵשׁ, singular) before God, is indicated by the words engraved into his turban plate. Thus, any ritual infractions of the people are borne by the high priest. The corollary also applies—when the high priest sins, he confers guilt upon the entire nation (Lev 4:3); this latter ruling particularly emphasizes the inclusive nature of the high priest's representation. Importantly, the high priest carries upon himself the names of Israel (as twelve tribes) and God (YHWH), as the formal identification of the two parties who are bound by the covenant represented by the Mosaic law, the ark of the covenant and the tabernacle. This role and responsibility is the high priest's alone; none of the other priests or Levites bear such insignias.

Interestingly, the LXX renders חֹתָם ("seal") as σφραγίς,[201] and this same Greek term is used in the New Testament to describe God's pneumatic seal of ownership upon those who belong to Christ (2 Cor 1:22; Eph 1:13; 4:30).[202] "[The] seal is a metaphor for the Spirit, by whom God has marked believers and claimed them as his own."[203] The Holy Spirit is described as the one who applies God's seal (ἐσφραγίσθητε τῷ πνεύματι τῆς ἐπαγγελίας τῷ ἁγίῳ, Eph 1:13), or who *is* God's seal as Gottfried Fitzer maintains: "The Holy Spirit as the pledge of the inheritance is now the seal with which the believer is marked, appointed and kept for the redemption."[204] Rodney Thomas concurs: "The seal is the Holy Spirit; it is not baptism and is not linked by the author in any concrete fashion to baptism. With this possession of the Spirit in the present came the guarantee of future salvation."[205] Fee also asserts, "there can be little question that the Spirit himself is the

---

201. "Σφραγίς occurs *ca.* 25 times in the LXX, always, except in Exod. 35:22, translating *ḥôṯām*"; Schramm, "σφραγίς," 316. "In literal usage a seal referred to a stamped impression in wax or clay, signalling ownership and authenticity, and carrying with it the protection of the owner"; Fee, *People of God*, 55. See also Thomas, "Seal of the Spirit," 155–59. The "seal" is a key motif in Revelation, functioning as the stamp of divine authenticity and authority (Rev 7:2), as the divine security lock preventing access or escape (Rev 5–6; 8:1; 10:4; 20:3; 22:10), and as the defining mark of divine possession (Rev 7:3–8, 9:4). Although the Holy Spirit is not associated with the "seal" motif in Revelation, the Spirit is the source of divine speech (Rev 2–3; 14:3; 22:17).

202. Arnold, *Ephesians*, 92–93.

203. Fee, *People of God*, 55.

204. Fitzer, "σφραγίς, σφραγίζω, κατασφραγίζω," 949.

205. Thomas, "Seal of the Spirit," 165. So also the *NIV* and *TNIV*, which have "you were marked in him with a seal, the promised Holy Spirit" in Eph 1:13.

'seal,' the mark of ownership."²⁰⁶ The Spirit is the one who is "promised" (τῆς ἐπαγγελίας). The Spirit is the down payment that guarantees eschatological inheritance (ὅ ἐστιν ἀρραβὼν τῆς κληρονομίας, Eph 1:14). One might even say that the Holy Spirit *is* the inheritance, as Galatians 3:14 seems to imply: "in order that in Christ Jesus the blessing of Abraham might come to the Gentiles, so that we might receive the promise of the Spirit through faith." The author of Hebrews reminds his hearers that they have already received a portion of their eschatological inheritance because they "have tasted the heavenly gift, and have shared in the Holy Spirit" (Heb 6:4), so that rejecting Christ and the new covenant of which they are already a part of, is retrograde and nonsensical.

Hebrews maintains that the Levitical high priesthood foreshadows Christ's high priesthood, and since the earthly high priest embodies the whole nation of Israel as a holy people set apart for God, it is reasonable to affirm that Christ's high priesthood is also corporate in nature, so that he stands before God as the embodiment of all who belong to God. The Levitical seals carry the names of the covenant partners, Israel and YHWH. Christ also bears in himself the names of the covenant partners, humanity and God—because he is simultaneously Son of Man and Son of God. Indeed, Jesus is explicity identified as the bearer of God's "seal": "For it is on him [the Son of Man] that God the Father has set his seal (τοῦτον γὰρ ὁ πατὴρ ἐσφράγισεν ὁ θεός; John 6:27)." Jesus wore no sacred vestments and bore no visible seals on his person, but perhaps the Levitical seals foreshadow the true seal, the Holy Spirit. As our high priest, Christ bears, not physical seals, but more importantly, the full measure of the true eschatological seal, the Holy Spirit (John 3:34). All four gospels concur that John the Baptist identified the coming Messiah as the one who baptizes with the Holy Spirit (Mark 1:8; Matt 3:11; Luke 3:16; John 2:33). The efficacy of Christ's high priesthood (and atoning sacrifice) is demonstrated in the indwelling presence of the promised Holy Spirit in each and every one who belongs to him, and therefore to God (Rom 8:9), regardless of race, gender, and social status (Gal 3:28).²⁰⁷ This gift of the Holy Spirit is mediated specifically through the risen Christ (John 20:22; Acts 2:33).

If the physical seals on the shoulder pieces, breastplate, and turban of the high priest's garments signify the corporate nature of the Levitical high priesthood, then it seems reasonable to conclude that it is the Holy Spirit (the true "seal") who confers upon Christ's high priesthood its corporate nature. Thus Jesus Christ, the Spirit-anointed true high priest of the covenant,

---

206. Fee, *God's Empowering Presence*, 669.
207. Macchia, *Justified in the Spirit*, 135–37, 141–46, 310–11.

carries in himself the whole pneumatic eschatological community before God —those who are "holy to YHWH." Perhaps this is why Paul regularly addresses Christian converts as "saints" (ἅγιοι),[208] precisely because they have already received the pneumatic seal as God's holy people. The presence of the indwelling eschatological Spirit confirms and authenticates their heavenly citizenship and divine lineage. It is also important to note that in contrast to the physical seals which only the high priest bears, the Holy Spirit—God's pneumatic seal—is given to *every individual believer in Christ*, not to promote individualism, but on the contrary, to unite all believers in one Spirit and one body (Eph 4:4).

Union with Christ

The theme of union with Christ is an important New Testament concept. It is "right at the centre of the Christian doctrine of salvation"[209] and is "a characteristic and distinctive trait within Paul's theology."[210] This theme is expressed through several metaphors, for example, the vine and its branches (John 15:1–8), the body and its parts (Rom 12:5; 1 Cor 12:12–27; Eph 1:22–23; 2:15–16; 4:4, 12, 15–16; 5:29; Col 1:18; 2:19; 3:15), the temple (1 Cor 3:16–17, Eph 2:21–22), and marriage (Eph 5:31–32). The core concept that threads through all these metaphors is the union of diverse plurality into one common whole without homogenizing diversity, or to employ John Zizioulas's catchphrase, "the one and the many."

For example, Paul envisages the believers, *united together*, as the temple (ὁ ναός, 1 Cor 3:16–17; ναὸς ἅγιος, Eph 2:21), and contrasts them to the idol temple (τὸ εἰδωλῖον, 1 Cor 3:16–17). It is interesting to observe that for Paul, all the believers together (he uses the plural "you"), form the ναός, which is a singular noun. Indeed, in the Pauline corpus, when ναός is used in this way, it is only in the singular—believers are not seen as separate individual temples, but as integrated parts of one temple in Christ. Interestingly, the Fourth Evangelist portrayed Jesus himself as the temple (John 2:19–22; cf. Mark 14:58; Matt 27:40), and in Revelation, the eschatological temple, ναός, is none other than God and the Lamb.

The theme of union with Christ is also expressed explicitly in John 17:21–24. Jesus prays that those who believe in him may be brought into the union that he shares with his Father: "As you, Father, are in me and I am in you, may they also be in us," and "I in them and you in me, that they

---

208. For example, Rom 1:7; 1 Cor 1:2; 6:2; 2 Cor 1:1; 13:12; Eph 1:1; Phil 1:1, etc.
209. Letham, *Union with Christ*, 1.
210. Dunn, *Theology of Paul*, 397.

may become completely one." The Greek καθώς which is translated with the word "as," indicates that the union of the Father and the Son, which is so profoundly intimate that the Johannine Jesus can assert that he and his Father are "one" (ἕν, John 10:30), is the very kind of union that he prays will exist between believers and God.

Moreover, the idea that believers are united to Christ is frequently conveyed by the prepositional phrases "in Christ" (ἐν Χριστῷ), "in the Lord" (ἐν κυρίῳ), "into Christ" (εἰς Χριστόν), and "with Christ" (σὺν Χριστῷ), including similar phrases using pronouns for Christ, and phrases that use compound σὺν- words in relation to Christ. There are seventy-three occurrences of the exact phrase ἐν Χριστῷ in the Pauline corpus.[211] Dunn notes that outside of the Pauline corpus, the phrase ἐν Χριστῷ only appears in 1 Peter.[212] While the preposition ἐν is flexible and notoriously wide in its range of usage,[213] in his careful and comprehensive study, Constantine Campbell concludes that "the notion of 'sphere' appears to be one of the key uses of ἐν within the Pauline idiom. It also seems prudent to accept that the phrase ἐν Χριστῷ denotes a personal relatedness."[214] Campbell identifies nine passages which he categorizes under the contextual subtheme "new status *in Christ*," that "express the locative notion of being within the realm or sphere of Christ."[215] These passages communicate the concept that because believers are "in Christ," they participate in his history, his status, and his entitlements. They are united in him (Rom 12:5; Gal 3:28), and in his death (1 Cor 15:18), resurrection (Rom 6:11; 1 Thess 4:16), righteousness (Rom 8:1; 2 Cor 5:17), and sonship (Gal 3:26; Eph 3:6). To these nine passages may be added others which Campbell places under different subcategories, but which nevertheless convey the idea of union with Christ (1 Cor 1:2, 30; 2 Cor 5:19; Eph 1:3-4; 2:6, 10; 4:32; Col 1:28). Closely aligned with this theme of union with Christ is Paul's portrayal of Christ as the second Adam (Rom

---

211. Campbell, *Union with Christ*, 67.

212. Dunn, *Theology of Paul*, 396. The three occurrences in 1 Peter (1 Peter 3:16; 5:10, 14) do not add significantly to the theme of union with Christ.

213. For example, *BDAG* lists twelve main uses—location, state or condition, extension toward a position/condition, limit, means/instrument, agency, circumstance, connection, manner, causality, temporal marker, composition; *BDAG*, 326–29.

214. Campbell, *Union with Christ*, 73.

215. These nine passages are Rom 6:11; 8:1; 12:5; 1 Cor 15:18; 2 Cor 5:17; Gal 3:26, 28; Eph 3:6; 1 Thess 4:16. Campbell examines the contexts in which the phrase ἐν Χριστῷ appears in the Pauline corpus, and groups them under eight subcategories: "things achieved for/given to people *in Christ*," "believers' actions *in Christ*," "characteristics of those *in Christ*," "faith *in Christ*," "justification *in Christ*," "new status *in Christ*," "*in Christ* as periphrasis for believers," and "Trinity *in Christ*"; *Union with Christ*, 73–141.

5:14; 1 Cor 15:22, 45) through whom God's gift of righteousness by grace becomes available to all.

The phrases εἰς Χριστόν and εἰς αὐτόν feature less prominently in the Pauline corpus. Of the fourteen instances in which the phrase εἰς Χριστόν appears, only two may relate to the theme of union with Christ, namely in Romans 6:3 (ἐβαπτίσθημεν εἰς Χριστὸν Ἰησοῦν) and Galatians 3:27 (εἰς Χριστὸν ἐβαπτίσθητε), in which the phrase concerns "baptism into Christ." While some scholars understand the phrase in a referential sense (that is "baptised with reference to Christ"),[216] the overwhelming majority maintain that the phrase signifies union with Christ,[217] whether or not the term "baptism" itself is understood metaphorically, or to water baptism or Spirit baptism. Dunn, for instance, points out that in Romans 6:3, "baptized into Christ" follows immediately after the imagery of Christ as the second Adam, and in Galatians 3:27, the phrase is accompanied by the metaphor of "putting on Christ."[218] He concludes that "[i]n both cases some sort of identification or sense of bound-up-with-ness is implicit."[219] The phrase εἰς αὐτόν, where the antecedent is Christ, appears in only four instances within the Pauline corpus, of which one, Ephesians 4:15, relates to the theme of union with Christ (αὐξήσωμεν εἰς αὐτὸν τὰ πάντα, ὅς ἐστιν ἡ κεφαλή, Χριστός; "may grow up in all things into Him who is the head—Christ," NKJ). This latter passage employs the metaphor of biological growth to describe the maturing relationship between the believer and Christ; εἰς here conveys the sense of location ("in Christ") as well as the goal ("into Christ") towards which this maturing process is directed. "The condition that is reached through growing *into him* reflects incorporation into Christ. This is clear from the context in which Paul is unfolding the metaphor of believers belonging to the *body* of Christ, which is explicitly referenced through the description of Christ as *Head*. The corporate metaphor of *body* is key for Paul's communication of the incorporation in which believers partake with Christ."[220]

---

216. Cranfield, *Critical and Exegetical Commentary*, 301; Käsemann, *Commentary on Romans*, 166.

217. Bird, *Romans*, 196–98; Dodd, *Epistle of Paul*, 86–88; Fitzmyer, *Romans*, 429–32; Jewett, *Romans*, 397–401; Murray, *The Epistle to the Romans*, 214; Morris, *Epistle to the Romans*, 246–50; Moo, *Epistle to the Romans*, 194–97; Sanday and Headlam, *Commentary on Romans*, 153–57; Schreiner, *Romans*, 302, 306–7; Nygren, *Commentary on Romans*, 232–36; Osborne, *Romans*, 150; Dunn, *Theology of Paul*, 404; Campbell, *Union with Christ*, 207–8; Letham, *Union with Christ*, 6, 43, 87, 138.

218. Dunn, *Theology of Paul*, 404.

219. Dunn, *Theology of Paul*, 405.

220. Campbell, *Union with Christ*, 212.

There are eleven instances of the phrases σύν (τῷ) Χριστῷ, σύν κυρίῳ, and σύν αὐτῷ in the Pauline corpus which assert that *with Christ* believers have died (Rom 6:8; Col 2:20), have gained new life (2 Cor 13:4; Col 2:13; 3:3), have received all God's gifts (Rom 8:32), and can look forward to the fullness of resurrection life in the *eschaton* (Phil 1:23; Col 3:4; 1 Thess 4:14, 17; 5:10).[221] Furthermore, there are eleven additional instances in which compound σύν- words convey the theme of union with Christ and "a sharing in Christ's death and life"[222] in bold, and sometimes graphic, terms:

1. With Christ I have been crucified (Χριστῷ συνεσταύρωμαι) (Gal 2:19)
2. We were therefore buried with him (συνετάφημεν οὖν αὐτῳ) (Rom 6:4)
3. (Our old humanity) was crucified with (συνεσταυρώθη) [him] (Rom 6:6)
4. We died with Christ (ἀπεθάνομεν σὺν Χριστῷ) (Rom 6:8)
5. We shall live with him (συζήσομεν αὐτῳ) (Rom 6:8)
6. Having been buried with him (συνταφέντες αὐτῳ) (Col 2:12)
7. In whom you were also raised up with (ἐν ᾧ καὶ συνηγέρθητε) (Col 2:12)
8. [God] made us alive with him (συνεζωοποίησεν ὑμᾶς σὺν αὐτῳ) (Col 2:13)
9. [God] made [us] alive with Christ (συνεζωοποίησεν τῳ Χριστῷ) (Eph 2:5)
10. [God] raised [us] with (συνήγειρεν) [Christ] (Eph 2:6)
11. [God] seated [us] in/with Christ Jesus (συνεκάθισεν . . . ἐν Χριστῷ Ἰησοῦ) (Eph 2:6).

These passages describe believers as having participated in the cross event in close intimacy with Christ, or to use Dunn's phraseology, "bound-up-with" Christ. The choice of verb tenses is interesting. In Galatians 2:19, "crucified with" is in the perfect passive indicative, and as such alludes to a completed action in the past, with continuing effect in Paul's present.[223] The verbs "crucified with," "buried with," and "died with" in Romans 6:4–8 are

---

221. Campbell, *Union with Christ*, 217–36.

222. Dunn, *Theology of Paul*, 402.

223. "To be united with Christ is to be united with Christ on the cross—'I have been crucified with Christ—the tense indicating not an event in the past finished and done with, but an event whose consequences still hold—'I have been crucified in Christ, and am still hanging there with him' (Gal. 2:20; so also Rom. 6:5)." Dunn, *Christ and the Spirit*, vol. 2, 351.

in the aorist indicative, amplifying the meaning of "baptized into Christ" (Rom 6:3), as are the verbs "raised with," and "made alive with" in Colossians 2:12–13, and the verbs "made alive with," "raised with," and "seated with" in Ephesians 2:5–6.[224] These aorist verbs, as they are in the indicative mood, express actions in the past. The aorist passive participle συνεταφέντες (having been buried with) in Colossians 2:12 describes an action that is prior to or contemporaneous with the action of the indicative verb συνηγέρθητε (you were raised up with), which is also aorist passive.[225] The key events that are alluded to in these passages are Christ's death, resurrection, ascension, and exaltation. Paul's ethical argument in Romans 5–6 hinges on the theological understanding that, in some real way, the believers' old sin-addicted humanity has died with Christ, and their new Spirit-led humanity has risen with him, so that they no longer have recourse to their old way of life. They have, as it were, burned the proverbial boat. They have left the old "flesh" kingdom behind, and have been transferred, in Christ, to the realm of the Spirit. If dying and rising with Christ is viewed in purely abstract terms, as a metaphorical concept that exists only in thought with no substance or relation to lived life, then at best, Paul's argument is weak, and at worst, his theological basis for a complete and paradigmatic revolution in ethics is completely undermined.

The plethora of prepositional phrases and compound σύν- words that allude to the union of believers with Christ throughout the Pauline corpus does, unfortunately, make it extremely difficult to include within this study a comprehensive exegetical examination of all the relevant passages. Nevertheless, this bountiful harvest strongly affirms the importance of the concept of union with Christ for Pauline theology. From the perspective of the corporate role of the Levitical high priest and its significance for Christology, the idea that believers are united with Christ is altogether unsurprising. Indeed, Letham prefers to use the term "union with Christ" rather than the terms "substitute" and "representative" to describe the way in which believers are redeemed:

> As both substitute and representative, Christ is seen as distinct from those who benefit from what he did. A substitute is, by definition, another person than the one he replaces. A representative, similarly, acts on behalf of another. While his actions are legally accounted as those of the one he represents, the two

---

224. There are no recorded textual variants for συνεσταύρωμαι (in Gal 2:19), συνεσταυρώθη, συνεσταυρώθη, ἀπεθάνομεν (in Rom 6:4–8), συνεταφέντες, συνηγέρθητε, συνεζωοποίησεν (in Col 2:12–13), and συνεζωοποίησεν, συνήγειρεν, and συνεκάθισεν (in Eph 2:5–6).

225. Wallace, *Greek Grammar*, 555.

are distinctly separate persons. The concept of union takes us a stage further than either of these two metaphors. In this case, all that Christ did and does we do, since we are one with him. The "otherness" of a substitute or representative is in the background. Not only does Christ act in our place as substitute, and on our behalf as our representative, but because of the union sustained between Christ and ourselves, his actions *are* ours.[226]

Dunn sees in 2 Corinthians 5:14–15, yet another allusion to the union of believers with Christ, particularly in verse 14, ὅτι εἷς ὑπὲρ πάντων ἀπέθανεν, ἄρα οἱ πάντες ἀπέθανον ("that one has died for all, therefore all have died"). While some understand οἱ πάντες to refer only to believers in Christ and not to all people,[227] Dunn interprets the phrase to include the whole of humanity.[228] However, he understands οἱ ζῶντες in verse 15 to include only those who believe in Christ, arguing that while *all* sinful humanity died with Christ on the cross, only those who identify with Christ and with his death, rise with him. In other words, as Dunn sees it, Christ's inclusive and universal representation of all humanity in his death does not equate to universal salvation for all. It is worthwhile to quote Dunn at some length:

> 2 Cor 5:14 now becomes clearer as one of the most explicit expressions of Paul's understanding of Jesus as representative man—"one man died for all; therefore all humankind (*ho pantes*) has died." When we talk of Christ as representative man we mean that what is true of him in particular is true of men in general. When we say Adam is representative man in his fallenness, we mean that *all men* are fallen. So when Paul says Christ died as representative man he means that there is no other end possible for men—all humankind dies, as he died, as flesh, as the end of sinful flesh, as the destruction of sin. Had there been a way for fallen man to overcome his fallenness and subjection to the powers, Christ would not have died—Christ as representative man would have shown men how to overcome sinful flesh. His death is an acknowledgement that there is no way out for fallen men except through death—no answer to sinful flesh except its destruction in death. "Man could not be helped other

---

226. Letham, *Union with Christ*, 62–63.

227. See Barnett, *Second Epistle*, 292–93; Hughes, *The Second Epistle*, 195; Kistemaker, *2 Corinthians*, 188–89.

228. Furnish agrees: "But the grammar requires us to give the *all* in this statement the same universal scope as the *all* in the preceding one: just as Christ has died for all without exception, so all without exception have died"; *2 Corinthians*, 327.

than through his annihilation."²²⁹ Only through death does the New Man emerge in risen life. In other words, if we may follow the train of thought a little further, Christ's identification with fallen men is up to and into death. But there it ends, for death is the end of fallen men, the destruction of man as flesh—Christ died, all died. Beyond death he no longer represents all men, fallen man. In his risen life he represents only those who identify themselves with him, with his death (through baptism), only those who acknowledge the Risen One as Lord (2 Cor. 5:15). Only those who identify themselves with him in his death are identified with him in his life from death.²³⁰

In agreement with Dunn's position, Fee paraphrases 2 Corinthians 5:14-15 thus: "then we must own up to the fact that Christ's death for all people means that everyone has come under God's sentence of death; and that means further that the only people who currently live are those brought to life by Christ to live for him and his purposes."²³¹ Fee perceives the use of the language of the "new" and "the old" in 2 Corinthians 5:16-17, and together, he suggests that verses 14-17 portray the passing of the old order, and the establishment of the new. Along the same lines Linda Belville writes: "But by *all* does he mean all believers or all people? The contrast between *one* and *all* suggests that the term is to be taken in the broadest sense. Even so, while Christ may have died for all humanity, it is only the believers who reap the benefits."²³² Hulitt Gloer comes to a similar conclusion, stating, "In the one sense, of course, he is referring to both . . . In the final analysis, however, Paul is speaking of those who have accepted Christ."²³³ Interestingly, Gloer also asserts that "Paul has moved beyond a merely substitutionary view of the significance of Christ's death. On the basis of v.14c, however, it is possible to suggest that Paul has moved even beyond the notion of representation to the idea of participation."

---

229. Dunn quotes Karl Barth here, citing Berkwouer's *The Triumph of Grace in the Theology of Karl Barth*, 135.

230. Dunn, *Christ and the Spirit*, vol. 1, 196.

231. Fee, *God's Empowering Presence*, 331; similarly, Guthrie, *2 Corinthians*, 305–6.

232. Belleville, *2 Corinthians*, 150; so also Garland, *2 Corinthians*, 278–80; Martin, *2 Corinthians*, 131–32.

233. Gloer, *2 Corinthians 5:14-21*, 35. "Our destiny is determined by our participation with Christ in his death to the old and resurrection to the new"; Gloer, *2 Corinthians 5:14-21*, 186.

Pneumatic Union with Christ

Given that union of believers with Christ is a significant New Testament theme, is there biblical support for a role for the *Holy Spirit* in this union? A detailed examination of 1 Corinthians 6:11, 15–19, 12:12–13, and Ephesians 2:16–18 seems to indicate that the answer is affirmative.

A. 1 Corinthians

In the context of challenging a Christian community that was fissured by sectarian loyalties, whose thought and life were still shaped by contemporary Corinthian culture and worldview, Paul holds up to them the central tenet of the gospel—Christ crucified and risen—as the foundational and pneumatic bedrock for ethical, ecclesial, and social conduct. This central tenet is counterculturaI, but must replace their Corinthian worldview. The believers are to consider themselves, not as competing parties or individuals, but as one body, united to Christ in the Spirit. Diversity is acknowledged, but seen as complementary, not competitive. As part of Christ's body, with the Holy Spirit indwelling them, they cannot therefore participate in idol worship and immoral behavior.

1 Corinthians 6:11

καὶ ταῦτά τινες ἦτε·
ἀλλ' ἀπελούσασθε,
ἀλλ' ἡγιάσθητε,
ἀλλ' ἐδικαιώθητε
    ἐν τῷ ὀνόματι τοῦ κυρίου Ἰησοῦ Χριστοῦ[234] καὶ
    ἐν τῷ πνεύματι τοῦ θεοῦ ἡμῶν.

And this is what some of you used to be.
    But you were washed,
    you were sanctified,
    you were justified
        in the name of the Lord Jesus Christ and
        in the Spirit of our God.

---

234. There are textual variations of the name Ἰησοῦ Χριστοῦ which do not affect the overall meaning of the verse; *NA28*, 527.

Referring to behaviors that Paul asserts should not characterize those who belong to God's eschatological kingdom (1 Cor 6:1–10),[235] he reassures his hearers that although they were participants in such conduct prior to conversion, that they have now been washed clean (ἀπελούσασθε),[236] made holy/set apart (ἡγιάσθητε), and put right (ἐδικαιώθητε). These three verbs are each headed by the strong adversative ἀλλά,[237] and are related to the parallel prepositional clauses "in the name of the Lord Jesus Christ," and "in/by the Spirit of our God." The repeat of the preposition ἐν emphasizes that all three activities are attributed to the name of Jesus Christ, as well as to the Spirit of God.[238] "The effects of baptismal washing, sanctification, and justification are thus related explicitly to the activity of the Holy Spirit; cf. 1 Tim 3:16."[239] As to whether the aorist middle ἀπελούσασθε refers specifically to the water baptism,[240] or more broadly to the conversion experience,[241] Anthony Thiselton rightly points out that this cleansing is about the "wiping clean of the slate once-for-all," emphasizing the conversion experience to which water baptism points.[242] More importantly, this cleansing is carried out in the name (that is, through the authority and power) of Jesus Christ, and by the activity of the Holy Spirit.[243] Since Paul is arguing for a paradigmatic shift in the foundational worldview of his hearers, the idea of being washed clean, set apart and put right (with God), refers to nothing less than a total and utter break with their past habits and perspectives. Such a radical

---

235. The extensive conversation regarding what Paul signifies by μαλακοὶ and ἀρσενοκοῖται, and his views on homosexuality, is not relevant to this present discussion, and therefore will not be discussed here.

236. Ἀπελούσασθε is an aorist middle verb, and can mean "you have washed yourselves"; *BDAG*, 117.

237. "The *structure* of the sentence seems certain. It begins with three verbs, each introduced with the strong adversative 'but,' which gives additional force to the 'once you were, but now you are not' emphasis of the sentence"; Fee, *First Epistle*, 271.

238. "[T]he two prepositional phrases are to be understood as modifying all three verbs." Fee, *First Epistle*, 271.

239. Fitzmyer, *First Corinthians*, 258. Fitzmyer highlights the triadic reference to God (the Father), Jesus Christ, and the Spirit of God.

240. Fitzmyer, *First Corinthians*, 258; Garland, *1 Corinthians*, 216.

241. Dunn, *Baptism in the Holy Spirit*, 121; Fee, *First Epistle*, 271–72.

242. Thiselton, *First Epistle to the Corinthians*, 454.

243. Fee, *God's Empowering Presence*, 129. He points out that the verbal metaphors of salvation "washed," "justified," and "sanctified" are attributed to the Spirit elsewhere in the Pauline corpus, e.g., "wash" (Titus 3:5), the cognate noun "righteousness/justification" (2 Cor 3:8–9; Gal 5:5), "sanctified" (1 Thess 4:7–8; 2 Thess 2:13; Rom 15:16); Fee, *God's Empowering Presence*, 130.

change is based on the work of Christ *and* the Spirit.[244] "The source of being *set apart as holy* and *put right in your standing* is sharing Christ's identity (ἐν τῷ ὀνόματι τοῦ κυρίου Ἰησοῦ Χριστοῦ), and being 'glued' (κολλώμενος, 6:17) to the Lord as one (ἕν, v. 17). Incorporation in *one body* and *one Spirit* (6:17–19) is *by the Spirit of our God* (6:11), interpreting ἐν as a preposition of instrument or agency here."[245]

1 Corinthians 6:15–19

οὐκ οἴδατε ὅτι τὰ σώματα ὑμῶν μέλη Χριστοῦ ἐστιν;

ἄρας[246] οὖν τὰ μέλη τοῦ Χριστοῦ ποιήσω πόρνης μέλη; μὴ γένοιτο.

οὐκ οἴδατε ὅτι ὁ κολλώμενος τῇ πόρνῃ ἓν σῶμά ἐστιν;

ἔσονται γάρ, φησίν, οἱ δύο εἰς σάρκα μίαν.

ὁ δὲ κολλώμενος τῷ κυρίῳ ἓν πνεῦμά ἐστιν.

Φεύγετε τὴν πορνείαν.

> πᾶν ἁμάρτημα ὃ ἐὰν ποιήσῃ ἄνθρωπος ἐκτὸς τοῦ σώματός ἐστιν·
>
> ὁ δὲ πορνεύων εἰς τὸ ἴδιον σῶμα ἁμαρτάνει.

ἢ οὐκ οἴδατε ὅτι τὸ σῶμα[247] ὑμῶν ναὸς τοῦ ἐν ὑμῖν ἁγίου πνεύματός ἐστιν

> οὗ ἔχετε ἀπὸ θεοῦ, καὶ οὐκ ἐστὲ ἑαυτῶν;

Do you not know that your bodies are members of Christ?

> Should I therefore take the members of Christ and make them members of a prostitute? Never!

Do you not know that whoever is united to a prostitute becomes one body with her?

> For it is said, "The two shall be one flesh."

---

244. This idea is the central message of Frank Macchia's *Justified in the Spirit*.

245. Thiselton, *First Epistle to the Corinthians*, 455.

246. Some later manuscripts substitute ἄρας ("take away") with ἄρα ("therefore") but the far greater textual weight is with the participle ἄρας which is the reading in the significant majuscules 𝔓46, Codex Sinaiticus, Alexandrinus, Vaticanus, Ephraemi, and Claromotanus, and the miniscule 33, among others; *NA28*, 528.

247. Some manuscripts have the plural τὰ σώματα in place of the singular τὸ σῶμα, but the weightier textual witness is with the latter; *NA28*, 528.

> But anyone united to the Lord becomes one spirit with him.
>
> Shun fornication!
>
> Every sin that a person commits is outside the body;
>
> but the fornicator sins against the body itself.
>
> Or do you not know that your body is a temple of the Holy Spirit within you,
>
> which you have from God, and that you are not your own?

In 1 Corinthians 6:12–20, Paul addresses the Corinthian believers' habit of visiting prostitutes. Underlying this practice, based upon the Stoic slogan "food for the stomach and the stomach for food, and God will destroy them both" (1 Cor 6:13)[248] seems to be the view that "all bodily functions are generally equal, and basically irrelevant for the life of the future."[249] The Corinthian believers appear to have followed the dualistic perspective of the wider community, and detached bodily actions from the spiritual state, so that eating and sex are both seen as activities that are confined to transient earthly existence with no consequence for heavenly life. In his counterargument, Paul states that τὸ δὲ σῶμα οὐ τῇ πορνείᾳ ἀλλὰ τῷ κυρίῳ, καὶ ὁ κύριος τῷ σώματι ("the body is not meant for fornication but for the Lord, and the Lord for the body," 1 Cor 6:13), affirming the close relationship between "the body" and "the Lord." While food itself is not the issue, unless consumed in the context of pagan worship and in the presence of new converts (1 Cor 8:7), Paul quotes from Genesis 2:24 to assert that sexual intimacy not only involves the body but signifies personal relationship, and according to Paul, even a casual sexual encounter with a prostitute constitutes a form of union. Since believers are members of Christ's body, such practice is tantamount to uniting Christ's body with that of prostitutes (ὁ κολλώμενος τῇ πόρνῃ ἓν σῶμά ἐστιν, 1 Cor 6:15–16). This is a situation that Paul utterly rejects (μὴ γένοιτο). Instead, Paul declares that whoever is united with the Lord is *one spirit* with him (ὁ δὲ κολλώμενος τῷ κυρίῳ ἓν

---

248. τὰ βρώματα τῇ κοιλίᾳ καὶ ἡ κοιλία τοῖς βρώμασιν, ὁ δὲ θεὸς καὶ ταύτην καὶ ταῦτα καταργήσει. The *NRSV*, *RSV*, *NEB*, *ESV*, and 1984 *NIV* attribute the second clause to Paul, whereas *TNIV* and 2011 *NIV* include it within the slogan. The latter approach is supported by the majority of recent scholarship, e.g., Ciampa and Rosner, *First Letter to the Corinthians*, 252–55; Collins, *First Corinthians*, 239; Conzelmann, *1 Corinthians*, 110, n. 17; Fee, *First Epistle*, 274; Fitzmyer, *First Corinthians*, 264; Garland, *1 Corinthians*, 230; Thiselton, *First Epistle to the Corinthians* 462–63. Those who exclude the second clause as part of the slogan: Moffatt, *First Epistle of Paul*, 67; Robertson and Plummer, *Critical and Exegetical Commentary*, 123.

249. Fee, *First Epistle*, 280.

πνεῦμά ἐστιν). The two clauses beginning with the substantive participle ὁ κολλώμενος are rhetorical parallels, so that "prostitute" is contrasted with "Lord," and "one body" is contrasted with "one spirit." Importantly, the idea that believers are "one body" with Christ is equated with the idea that believers are "one spirit" with him. The word "spirit" in verse 17 is more likely to indicate the Holy Spirit rather than Jesus's human spirit, since in the following verse 19, Paul reminds his hearers that their bodies are the temple of the indwelling Holy Spirit (ναός τοῦ ἐν ὑμῖν ἁγίου πνεύματός), repeating his earlier assertion that together they are God's temple (ναός; singular), the dwelling place of the Spirit of God (πνεῦμα τοῦ θεοῦ οἰκεῖ ἐν ὑμῖν; 1 Cor 3:16).[250] Indeed, in his commentary on verse 19, Conzelmann makes the following insightful observation: "The pneumatological grounding of the paraenesis links up with v.17, but in so doing strongly modifies the thought. In v.17 it is a question of the *pneumatic body of Christ*; in v.19 it is a case of the earthly body as the dwelling place of the Spirit."[251]

1 Corinthians 12:12–13

Καθάπερ γὰρ

    (A) τὸ σῶμα <u>ἕν</u> ἐστιν

        (B) καὶ μέλη πολλὰ ἔχει,

        (B´) πάντα δὲ τὰ μέλη τοῦ σώματος πολλὰ ὄντα

    (A´) <u>ἕν</u> ἐστιν σῶμα,

οὕτως καὶ ὁ Χριστός

καὶ γὰρ <u>ἐν</u> ἑνὶ πνεύματι

    ἡμεῖς πάντες εἰς <u>ἓν</u> σῶμα ἐβαπτίσθημεν,

        εἴτε Ἰουδαῖοι εἴτε Ἕλληνες

        εἴτε δοῦλοι εἴτε ἐλεύθεροι, καὶ

    πάντες <u>ἓν</u> πνεῦμα ἐποτίσθημεν.[252]

---

250. Ciampa and Rosner, *First Letter to the Corinthians*, 260–61; Fee, *God's Empowering Presence*, 133; Garland, *1 Corinthians*, 235; Thiselton, *First Epistle to the Corinthians*, 469.

251. Conzelmann, *1 Corinthians*, 112; italics added.

252. There are three alternative readings of the last clause in verse 13: a) the addition of the preposition εἰς is added after πάντες; b) the substitution of πνεῦμα with πόμα; c) the substitution of πνεῦμα ἐποτίσθημεν with σῶμα ἐσμεν. The first variant does not affect the overall meaning of the clause, while the second variant appears mainly in later manuscripts; and the third variant is only present in Codex Alexandrinus; *NA28*, 542. In view of these variants, Collins holds the minority view that this clause may refer

For just as

    (A) the body is *one*

        (B) and has many members,

        (B′) and all the members of the body, though many,

    (A′) are *one* body,

so it is with Christ.

For in the *one* Spirit

    we were all baptized into *one* body

        Jews or Greeks,

        slaves or free, and

    we were all made to drink of *one* Spirit.

Verse 12 is structured in a chiasm, while verse 13 contains a Semitic parallelism.[253] The chiasm in verse 12 emphasizes the unity of the body of Christ while acknowledging the diversity of its members (A and A′—one body; B and B′—many members). In verse 13 the clause πάντες εἰς ἓν σῶμα ἐβαπτίσθημεν (literally, "into one body we were all baptized") parallels the clause πάντες ἓν πνεῦμα ἐποτίσθημεν (literally, "one Spirit we were all made to drink/were drenched"),[254] "where both clauses make essentially the same point."[255] This parallelism juxtaposes baptism into "one body" (meaning the body of Christ as indicated in verse 12), with drinking or being drenched in "one Spirit." Reading verse 12 and 13 together, it is clear that the repeated emphasis is on "one" (ἕν). According to Garland, "In 12:13, Paul explains how 'we' (he includes himself) as many different individuals are all part of this one body of Christ. We were all baptized in the one Spirit into one body and were all given one Spirit to drink (cf. Gal 3:26-28)."[256] Dunn, who translates the verb ἐποτίσθημεν as "we were drenched" rather than "we were made to drink," sees its close link to the verb ἐβαπτίσθημεν:

"Here clearly the element into which the baptisands are baptised is the Spirit—just as in the Baptist's original metaphor ('in Holy Spirit and

---

to the Eucharistic cup rather than to baptism or conversion; Collins, *First Corinthians*, 463.

253. Fee, *First Epistle*, 666-69; Ciampa and Rosner, *First Letter to the Corinthians*, 590-3.

254. The aorist passive ἐποτίσθημεν may also mean "we were drenched." The *passive* form of the verb ποτίζω appears in the LXX and New Testament only here and in Ezekiel 32:6, where the land is "drenched" (ποτισθήσεται) with blood.

255. Fee, *First Epistle*, 670.

256. Garland, *1 Corinthians*, 590.

fire') and in the formulation in Acts ('in Holy Spirit')—'baptized in Spirit' denoting the experience of the Spirit to which the rite of baptism in water pointed."[257]

In support of this position, Fitzmyer writes, "Through the 'one Spirit' (already mentioned in 12:9, 11) all Christians have been plunged into or immersed in 'one body', i.e. into Christ."[258] Kistemaker concurs and supplies the evocative term, "spiritual saturation."[259] In this passage, the baptismal metaphor is used to describe the believer's pneumatic union into the body of Christ. As Thiselton explains: "The previous verse [verse 12] had concluded with ὁ Χριστός as the focus of unity. Paul amplifies this unity by speaking of the common agency and experience of *one Spirit* and *one body* as focused in the very baptism that proclaimed and marked their turning to Christ and their new identity as the people of the Spirit."[260]

The preposition ἐν in the phrase ἐν ἑνὶ πνεύματι at the beginning of verse 13 has been understood as locative ("in," e.g. *ESV, NRSV, NJB, NAB*) or instrumental ("by," e.g. *CEB, KJV, NASB, NAU, NIV, NKJ*). Fitzmyer comments that the force of this preposition is not clear, and he himself seems to have both senses in view.[261] Scholars appear fairly evenly divided.[262] Some suggest that having two prepositional clauses "*in* one Spirit" and "*into* one body" sound harsh,[263] Carson points out that this "harshness" relates to the English language, but "the combination of Greek phrases nicely stresses exactly the point that Paul is trying to make: *all* Christians have been baptised in *one* Spirit; *all* Christians have been baptised into *one* body."[264] Dunn, with the concurrence of Carson and Fee, observes correctly that when the verb βαπτίζειν is associated with ἐν in the LXX, the preposition consistently has locative force, and "always indicates the element in which the baptisand is immersed," and in all six NT passages that refer to Spirit baptism (Mark

---

257. Dunn, *Christ and the Spirit*, vol. 2, 114.

258. Fitzmyer, *First Corinthians*, 477; cf. Moffat, *First Epistle of Paul*, 186.

259. Kistemaker, *1 Corinthians*, 431.

260. Thiselton, *First Epistle to the Corinthians*, 997; the emphases are original. Thiselton endeavors to keep both meanings of the aorist passive ἐποτίσθημεν, "made to drink" and "was drenched," by translating the verb as "we were given to drink our fill"; *The First Epistle to the Corinthians*, 1000–1001.

261. Fitzmyer, *First Corinthians*, 477–78.

262. For example: locative force (Barrett, *First Epistle to the Corinthians*, 288; Collins, *First Corinthians*, 462; Conzelmann, *1 Corinthians*, 212, n. 17; Fee, *First Epistle*, 671); instrumental force (Ciampa and Rosner, *First Letter to the Corinthians*, 591–92; Kistemaker, *1 Corinthians*, 429; Moffat, *First Epistle of Paul*, 184–85); both senses (Fitzmyer, *First Corinthians*, 477–78; Garland, *1 Corinthians*, 590–91).

263. For example, Green, *I Believe*, 141; Kistemaker, *1 Corinthians*, 429.

264. Carson, *Showing the Spirit*, 47.

1:8; Matt 3:11; Luke 3:16; John 1:33; Acts 1:5; 11:6) "the Spirit is the element used in the Messiah's baptism in contrast to the water used in John's baptism."[265] In keeping with this usage, Dunn is thus convinced that ἐν also has a locative force here. In his detailed examination of the preposition ἐν in 1 Corinthians 12:13, Harris agrees, pointing out that although the phrases ἐν πνεύματι and ἐν τῷ ἑνὶ πνεύματι can express the agency of the Spirit in Paul (Rom 2:29; 1 Cor 12:3, 9; 14:16; Eph 2:22; 3:5; 4:30), he too argues that the locative force is the correct understanding here:

> The focus on the verse is on believers' common and universal experience (πάντες . . . πάντες) of the Spirit that creates unity out of diversity (cf. v.12). Verse 13 explains how the many diverse parts of the body are constituted a single entity—it is by their immersion in one and the same Spirit (ἐν ἑνὶ πνεύματι) and by their deriving spiritual nourishment from a single source, the Spirit (ἓν πνεῦμα).[266]

Interestingly, Garland suggests that the two views may not be mutually exclusive, and that "[t]he point is that every Christian has been made part of one body and immersed in (or by) the Spirit."[267]

It is important to note in 1 Corinthians the "one body" that Paul refers to is primarily the *body of Christ* (σῶμα Χριστοῦ, 1 Cor 12:27) of which all believers are inseparable members. This ecclesial community differs from groups that follow the teaching and example of their founders, but which cannot be described as sharing their founders' existence and life. Paul is making his appeal to the Corinthian church for unity, based not upon *loyalty* to Christ, but on their very *participation* in Christ himself. This participation surpasses all factional loyalties. Indeed, being part of σῶμα Χριστοῦ is much more deeply rooted, integral, connected, and vital than just being loyal. Even as parts of the human body cannot separate themselves from the body and function or survive independently (1 Cor 12:14–18), the ecclesial community cannot and does not exist apart from Christ (cf. John 15:1–8). Believers are one with Christ and one with each other by being members of σῶμα Χριστοῦ, in the Spirit. Furthermore, the close association of Christ and Spirit here and elsewhere,[268] especially in 1 Corinthians 12:13 where

---

265. Dunn, *Baptism in the Holy Spirit*, 128; Carson, *Showing the Spirit*, 47; Fee, *First Epistle*, 671.

266. Harris, *Prepositions and Theology*, 230–31.

267. Garland, *1 Corinthians*, 591.

268. For example, Romans 8:2, 9–10; 1 Corinthians 15:45; Ephesians 1:13. The juxtaposition of participation in Christ and participation in the Holy Spirit is also seen in Hebrews (3:14; 6:4) and in Ephesians (2:18, 22; 4:4).

baptism into the body of Christ is said to be in the Spirit, indicates that the Spirit has a vital role in the constitution of σῶμα Χριστοῦ.

B. Ephesians

Whether Ephesians is from Paul's hand or not, its message remains relevant to our understanding of Christology and the involvement of the Holy Spirit in the body of Christ. The purpose of the document and its destination are areas of considerable debate, although the general consensus is that it was written for broad readership, possibly a circular letter or homily to be read to churches in Asia Minor,[269] and with a particular focus towards Gentile believers.[270] Lincoln suggests that the writer may be responding to a general crisis affecting Christians living in a first-century Hellenistic environment and cosmic worldview, lacking a sense of cohesiveness and communal identity, and unsure how to live as authentic followers of Jesus Christ.[271] O'Brien, who accepts Pauline authorship, proposes that "[c]osmic reconciliation and unity in Christ are the central message of Paul's Letter to the Ephesians."[272] In line with these views, Arnold suggests that this letter was written "to a large network of local churches in Ephesus and the surrounding cities to affirm them in their new identity in Christ as a means of strengthening them in their ongoing struggle with the powers of darkness, to promote a greater unity between Jews and Gentiles within and among the churches of the area, and to stimulate an ever-increasing transformation of their lifestyles into a greater conformity to the purity and holiness that God has called them to display."[273]

Ephesians 2:16–18

καὶ ἀποκαταλλάξῃ

τοὺς ἀμφοτέρους ἐν <u>ἑνὶ σώματι</u> τῷ θεῷ

διὰ τοῦ σταυροῦ,

---

269. Arnold, *Ephesians*, 29, 45; O'Brien, *Ephesians*, 49–57; Lincoln, *Ephesians*, lxxxi–lxxxiii; Schnakenberg, *Epistle to the Ephesians*, 29. Thielman, however, recently argues for the authenticity of the Ephesian destination, based on his view that leaving out the destination, as is the case in some ancient manuscripts like 𝔓46, renders the Greek text "unintelligible"; Thielman, *Ephesians*, 13.

270. O'Brien, *Ephesians*, 50; Lincoln, *Ephesians*, lxxxiv.

271. Lincoln, *Ephesians*, lxxxiv–lxxxvi.

272. O'Brien, *Ephesians*, 58. "Certainly one theme on which most commentators agree is unity"; Hoehner, *Ephesians*, 102.

273. Arnold, *Ephesians*, 45.

ἀποκτείνας τὴν ἔχθραν ἐν αὐτῷ.
καὶ ἐλθὼν εὐηγγελίσατο εἰρήνην ὑμῖν τοῖς μακρὰν
καὶ εἰρήνην τοῖς ἐγγύς
ὅτι δι' αὐτοῦ
ἔχομεν τὴν προσαγωγὴν
οἱ ἀμφότεροι ἐν <u>ἑνὶ πνεύματι</u> πρὸς τὸν πατέρα.[274]

and might reconcile
both groups to God in *one body*
through the cross,
thus putting to death that hostility through it.
So he came and proclaimed peace to you who were far off
and peace to those who were near;
for through him
both of us have access in *one Spirit* to the Father.

Fee observes parallelism between verse 16 and verse 18: διὰ τοῦ σταυροῦ ("through the cross") corresponds to δι' αὐτοῦ "through him"), τοὺς ἀμφοτέρους ("both," accusative case) corresponds to οἱ ἀμφότεροι ("both," nominative case), and ἐν ἑνὶ σώματι τῷ θεῷ ("in one body to God") corresponds to ἐν ἑνὶ πνεύματι πρὸς τὸν πατέρα ("in one Spirit to the Father"). Here again, there is a clear juxtaposition of "one body" with "one Spirit." Thus, being united into one body is equivalent to being united in (or by) one Spirit, and the unified community in Christ has been given access to God himself. The subject of the verb ἀποκαταλλάξῃ is Christ (Eph 2:13, 15), who has reconciled both groups (Jew and Gentile) into one body through his death on the cross, destroying the hostility between the two, "that he might create in himself (ἐν αὐτῷ) one new humanity (καινὸν ἄνθρωπον) in the place of two" (Eph 2:15). "The usage here closely resembles 1 Cor 12:13, where all believers (including Jew and Gentile) are 'immersed' in the one Spirit so as to form the one body of Christ (cf. v.15)."[275] That Christ's sacrificial death is the *grounds* for the reconciliation and pneumatic union of the two groups is clear from this passage,[276] especially when the preposition διά in the phrases διὰ τοῦ σταυροῦ and δι' αὐτοῦ is understood to

---

274. There are minor textual variants for this passage: ἑαυτῷ instead of αὐτῷ in verse 16, deletion of εἰρήνην in verse 17, and none in verse 18; *NA28*, 593. These alternate readings do not affect the meaning of the passage.

275. Fee, *God's Empowering Presence*, 684.

276. Lincoln, *Ephesians*, 146; Thielman, *Ephesians*, 172; Hoehner, *Ephesians*, 383.

have instrumental force.²⁷⁷ Interestingly, Schnackenburg suggests that διά may also have a locative nuance here, and that the cross is "the place of reconciliation."²⁷⁸ Paul identifies Christ as the ἱλαστήριος put forward by God for humanity's redemption (Rom 3:25; in the LXX, the word ἱλαστήριος is used consistently to render כַּפֹּרֶת, *kappōret*, the term given to the cover of the ark of the covenant; cf. Heb 9:5),²⁷⁹ so that there is support for Schnackenburg's view. Moreover, the emphasis on Christ's blood (Eph 2:13), "flesh" (Eph 2:14), the term "in himself" as the domain within which this one new humanity has been created (Eph 2:15), and the term "one body" is used in the specific context of the cross (Eph 2:16), seems to suggest that this reconciliation has taken place, not only *because* of the death of Christ, but *in* it. In his death, the enmity is itself put to death (Eph 2:16). As Fee insists, the term "in one body" "can only be locative."²⁸⁰ Schnackenburg understands the term "one body" in this epistle to mean the church, united to and in Christ by the "unifying power" of the Spirit.²⁸¹ He writes:

> The Church is thereby pulled into the immediate vicinity of the Cross, *exists in fact in the Crucifixion-event*. In that Christ dies on the cross, the Church is born; in that he gives himself for us as a sacrifice (5:2) he proves his love for the Church (5:25), becomes in fact the redeemer of his Body, the Church (5:23). So close is the connection of the Church to Christ that *she already appears in the Cross as a New Creation*, the one redeemed humanity.²⁸²

> The approach to the Father which is opened for us through Christ takes place "in one single Spirit" . . . The Christ who brought peace through his Cross brings together those formerly separated into a single Body (2:16) and leads them by one single Spirit, the divine Spirit (3:16) ever closer (2:22) to the Father.²⁸³

In other words, Schnackenburg sees all believers united in the body of Christ *at the cross*, and he also emphasizes that this unity is *in the one Spirit*. Furthermore, he suggests that the church, the new redeemed humanity, was

---

277. Arnold, *Ephesians*, 165–66; Fee, *God's Empowering Presence*, 682–84; Schnackenburg, *Epistle to the Ephesians*, 116; Thielman, *Ephesians*, 174.

278. Schnakenburg, *Epistle to the Ephesians*, 117.

279. See Exod 25:17–22; Lev 16:2, 13–15; Num 7:89.

280. Fee, *God's Empowering Presence*, 684.

281. Schnackenburg, *Epistle to the Ephesians*, 119. Hoehner concurs; *Ephesians*, 382.

282. Schnackenburg, *Epistle to the Ephesians*, 117; italics added.

283. Schnackenburg, *Epistle to the Ephesians*, 118–19.

born at the cross, in the death of Christ. This significant insight seems consistent with the message of Ephesians 2:16-18. While Christ is the subject of the reconciliation and the creation of this new redeemed humanity within himself (Eph 2:15-16), yet it is ἐν ἑνὶ πνεύματι ("in one Spirit"; Eph 2:18) that the new united humanity has access to God, and this unity that has been forged by and in Christ is described as τὴν ἑνότητα τοῦ πνεύματος ("the unity of the Spirit"; Eph 4:3). Moreover, heading the list of seven "ones" (Eph 4:4-6), emphasizing a key theme of Ephesians, *unity*, is the phrase ἓν σῶμα καὶ ἓν πνεῦμα ("one body and one Spirit").

In Ephesians, reconciliation and the creation of one new humanity in Christ involves God the Father, Son and Holy Spirit. The author of the salvation plan for humanity is *God* (Eph 1:3-12; 2:4-10; 3:7-12). *Christ* is the one in whom the salvation plan is executed; the concept of "in Christ," "in him," "in whom," "through Christ," and similar phrases appears forty-three times in Ephesians. The redeemed community becomes God's temple in the *Spirit* (Eph 2:22); it is in or by the Spirit that believers are sealed for the day of redemption (Eph 1:13; 4:30), and believers are urged not to grieve the Spirit (Eph 4:30). The exhortation to ecclesial unity in the creedal hymn of Ephesians 4:4-6 may allude to a nascent Trinitarian understanding.[284] This then strengthens the possibility that the cross event itself may be thoroughly Trinitarian.

6.5 Summary

In this chapter, I argue for a biblical foundation for a *pneumatologia crucis*, on the basis of a pneumatological reading of the Epistle to the Hebrews, and on the textual, exegetical, and theological examination of Hebrews 9:14, with support from Romans 15:16, 1 Peter 1:2, 1 Corinthians 6:11, 15-19, 12:12-13, and Ephesians 2:16-18.

In the Epistle to the Hebrews, the author presents Jesus Christ as God's perfect high priest who is both divine and human, who ministers in the true heavenly sanctuary, and who is also the perfect covenantal sacrifice. The Aaronic priesthood, Levitical sacrificial system, and earthly tabernacle are enacted metaphors for Christ and the heavenly sanctuary. The Holy Spirit who spoke through Israel's ancestors, prophets, and leaders, and who sanctifies the tabernacle and Holy of Holies, is the one who reveals that Israel's cultic sacrifices must be understood in the light of Christ's atoning work, not the other way around. It is the Holy Spirit who reveals that the barrier between the holy God and sinful humanity has finally been breached through Christ's

---

284. O'Brien, *Ephesians*, 280; Fee, *God's Empowering Presence*, 704-5.

perfect, pure, and sinless sacrifice of himself. That Christ's sacrifice has succeeded, where others have been inadequate, is evidenced in the pneumatic experiences of the author's listeners. They are the new covenant community in Christ. In Hebrews 9:14, Christ offered himself to God "through [the] eternal Spirit." The textual evidence is in favor of διὰ πνεύματος αἰωνίου as the original reading rather than διὰ πνεύματος ἁγίου, and I argue that the long-held tradition attributing this phrase to the Holy Spirit is correct. Unlike all earthly sacrifices, Jesus Christ's atoning sacrifice involves the participation of the Spirit of the "Holy of Holies." The term "eternal" is used to contrast the transience and repetitiveness of the Levitical sacrifices with the "once only" and permanent efficacy of Christ's atoning sacrifice. The term "eternal" also reveals the comprehensive reach through space and time of Christ's redemptive sacrifice, and the absolute thoroughness of humanity's cleansing from sin and evil. Therefore, all those who put their faith in Christ can have utter and complete confidence that their relationship with their holy God has been perfectly and permanently restored. It is through God's eternal Holy Spirit whom Christ, Son of God and Son of Man, offers himself. Jesus is the perfect, acceptable sacrifice through whom, finally, a right relationship is restored between God and humankind.

Romans 15:16 and 1 Peter 1:2, like Hebrews 9:14, are passages set in the context of the affirmation of the covenant in Jesus Christ, and its significance for the new covenantal community. All three passages employ the Levitical sacrificial system as their controlling metaphor. While Romans 15:16 envisages Paul as priest rather than Christ as the high priest, nevertheless Paul asserts that his offering of the Gentile believers to God has been made holy by the Holy Spirit. In 1 Peter 1:2, the Spirit's sanctifying activity is linked with Christ's atoning work on the cross, with the suggestion that the Spirit sprinkles Christ's sacrificial blood on believers. Unity in the Spirit is a key theme for both 1 Corinthians and Ephesians. In 1 Corinthians 6:11, the sanctification and justification are attributed to Christ *and* to the Holy Spirit. In 1 Corinthians 6:15–19 and 12:12–13, it is the Spirit who engenders the integration and union of all believers into the body of Christ. In Ephesians 2:16–18, at the cross of Christ, believers are reconciled to God and to one another in one body and one Spirit. From all these New Testament passages there seems to be sufficient support for the Holy Spirit's participation in Christ's atoning work on the cross, and a Trinitarian view of the cross event.

7

Pneumatologia Crucis—A Theological Basis

IF WE MAINTAIN THAT the cross event is at the center of our triune God's redemption strategy, then we are led to consider with all seriousness that God the Father, Son and Holy Spirit were involved at the cross, since the alternative is that some form of Docetism was operative at Golgotha. Our Christian understanding of the cross event centers correctly on the atoning work of Jesus Christ, the Son and Word of God. The Father is, on the one hand, the One who gives up his Son, and on the other, the One whose just satisfaction is secured by the Son's offering of himself. What then is the Spirit's role? Does the Spirit's involvement in this great divine work of reconciliation bypass the cross, moving directly, so it would seem, from Gethsemane to Easter and Pentecost? Is the Spirit active before and after the cross event but not during the event itself? Is the cross event truly Trinitarian?

7.1 Incorporating Barthian Pneumatological Perspectives

It is at this point that the insights of Karl Barth are helpful. He makes some key assertions that, when put together, raise the strong possibility that the Holy Spirit plays a critical role in the salvific work of Christ at the cross. Although Barth himself does not explicitly address the role of the Spirit at the cross, the trajectory of his christological and pneumatological reflections appear to lead, it seems inexorably, towards a *pneumatologia crucis*. These insights include *first*, his insistence that God is essentially and eternally triune and that the reconciling God who reconciles humanity to Godself is one God, who is Father, Son and Holy Spirit; *second*, that God elects humanity in his election of the Son, so that in him, God proclaims God's righteous "No" to humanity's rebellion, godlessness, and sin, but also God's gracious "Yes" to the re-creation of eschatological humanity in Christ; *third*, that the messianic Christ is incarnated in time and history by the Holy Spirit, and is indwelt and empowered by the fullness of the Spirit; *fourth*, that it is through the power of the Holy Spirit that Christ unites humanity to himself; *fifth*, that humanity dies and rises with and in Christ; and *sixth*, that God creates, destroys and re-creates humanity in Christ through the Spirit. One wonders whether Barth would have gone on to explore the pneumatological aspects of the cross event had he written his fifth volume in his *Church Dogmatics*.

The One Triune God

Barth maintains that the doctrine of the Trinity should be placed at the beginning of Christian theology.[1] He asserts, "The doctrine of the Trinity is what basically distinguishes the Christian doctrine of God as Christian."[2] He prefers the term "triunity" (*Dreieinigkeit*) to "trinity" (*Dreifaltigkeit*) in his rejection of any movement towards a tritheistic understanding of God.[3] In order to emphasize the *unity* of Father, Son and Holy Spirit, he employs the term "mode/way of being" (*Seinsweise*). He is careful, however, to distinguish this term from any sense of modalism.[4] Hence, Barth affirms that God is *both* "unimpaired unity" *and* "unimpaired differentiation" in his "threefold mode of being."[5] He rejects the idea that God is any other than God the Father, Son and Holy Spirit. For Barth, God is irreducibly triune, but also, and importantly, one God.

> He is One even in the distinctions of the divine persons of the Father, Son and the Holy Spirit. He is One even in the real wealth of His distinguishable perfections.[6]

> There is no such thing as Godhead in itself. Godhead is always the Godhead of the Father, the Son and the Holy Spirit. But the

---

1. Barth, *CD*, I/1, §8, 296, 300.
2. Barth, *CD*, I/1, §8, 301.
3. Barth, *CD*, I/1, §9, 369.
4. Barth, *CD*, I/1, §9, 382.
5. "The doctrine of the Trinity means, on the other side, as the rejection of Modalism, the express declaration that the three moments are not alien to God's being as God"; Barth, *CD*, I.1, §8, 299.
6. Barth, *CD*, II/1, §31, 445.

> Father is the Father of Jesus Christ and the Holy Spirit is the Spirit of the Father and the Spirit of Jesus Christ.[7]

> The position is not that we have to seek the true God beyond these three moments in a higher being in which He is not Father, Son and Spirit . . . The One who according to the witness of Scripture is and speaks and acts as Father, Son and Spirit, in self-veiling, self-unveiling and self-imparting, in holiness, mercy and love, this and no other God.[8]

Using his paradigmatic prism of "revelation" through which he envisages God as Revealer, Revelation and Revealedness,[9] Barth asserts that genuine revelation about God can never issue from humanity itself or through human effort, but only from God. It is God who freely and graciously reveals Godself to sinful humanity, and even the human ability to receive, recognize and respond to God's revelation is only ever possible as a gift from, and through the work of, the Holy Spirit in human hearts. According to Barth, God is not knowable to humans without God's miracle of grace.[10] Furthermore, "All these things, faith, knowledge and obedience, exist for man 'in the Holy Spirit.'"[11] The features of Barth's Trinitarian theology that are relevant to the concept of a *pneumatologia crucis* are first, his Christocentric and covenantal Trinitarianism, second, his understanding that the Spirit unites the Godhead, and third, his commitment to the principle *omnia opera trinitatis ad extra sunt indivisa*.

A. Christocentric and Covenantal Trinitarianism

Barth gives the Trinity the primary place in his doctrine of God. His Trinitarian theology, however, is clearly Christocentric and covenantal, even as his Christology is Trinitarian. For Barth, Jesus Christ is always the Son of the Father, and always the Spirit-indwelt Christ. "[T]he heart of the Church's dogmatics . . . has a circumference, the doctrine of creation and the doctrine of the last things, the redemption and consummation. But the covenant fulfilled in the atonement is its centre."[12] As Barth sees it, from eternity the triune God freely and graciously determines to be "Emmanuel," "God with

---

7. Barth, *CD*, II/2, §33, 115.
8. Barth, *CD*, I/1, §9, 382.
9. Barth, *CD*, I/1, §8, 295.
10. Barth, *CD*, II/1, §26, 129.
11. Barth, *CD*, I/1, §12, 453.
12. Barth, *CD*, IV/1, §57, 3.

us"—this is the core of the Christian message, "always in such a way that it is primarily a statement about God and only then and for that reason a statement about us men."[13] What is this covenant? It is none other than the "fellowship which originally existed between God and man, which was then disturbed and jeopardised, the purpose of which is fulfilled in Jesus Christ and the work of reconciliation."[14] As such, the covenant represents the relationship between God and humanity, a relationship formed and filled by the phrase, "God with us."

The covenant is rooted in a faithful God who wills to be always a "God with us." It is God who initiates the covenant, guarantees it, and brings it to fruition. Barth rightly perceives that the covenant, in all its iterations, is a covenant of grace.[15] The covenant is God's resounding "Yes" to humanity.[16] The covenant may have been given its formal shape at Mount Sinai, but it originates in God's eternal election of humanity, and it is fulfilled in the history of Jesus Christ. Humanity is God's covenant partner, but not God's *equal* covenant partner. No human will, exertion, or endeavor contributes to the foundation and maintenance of the covenant. Humanity's part in the covenant is to answer God's "Yes" with its own "Yes," that is, in a response of faith, love, and obedience. Instead, humanity becomes the covenant breaker, turning away from God in their effort to be their own gods. God's counterresponse to humanity's rebellion is reconciliation through atonement. "Jesus Christ is the atonement."[17] Reconciliation takes place in Christ (Rom 5:10; 2 Cor 5:18, 20; Col 1:22). Indeed, Christ is both the atoning sacrifice (ἱλασμός, 1 John 2:2; 4:10) and the *place* of atonement or mercy seat (ἱλαστήριος, Rom 3:25). Barth correctly asserts, "Jesus Christ is God, God as man, and therefore 'God with us' men, God in the work of reconciliation. But reconciliation is the fulfilment of the covenant between God and man."[18] It is not surprising therefore, that in his covenantal Trinitarianism, Barth is unapologetically Christocentric.

---

13. Barth, *CD*, IV/1, §57, 5.
14. Barth, *CD*, IV/1, §57, 22.
15. Barth, *CD*, IV/1, §57, 23.
16. Barth, CD, IV/1, §57, 40.
17. Barth, *CD*, IV/1, §57, 34.
18. Barth, *CD*, IV/1, §57, 22.

b. Spirit Unites Father and Son

Barth holds firmly to the notion that since the Holy Spirit is common to the Father and the Son, then the Spirit unites them.[19] His strong support for this idea aligns with his firm and uncompromising commitment to the *filioque*, perhaps because Barth rejects any suggestion that the Spirit may be separated from Christ.[20] He insists, for example, that "the work of the Spirit is nothing other than the work of Jesus Christ."[21]

> We have here the root of that recognition on whose basis the Western Church assumed into the creed, in relation to the eternal procession of the Holy Spirit, the *Filioque* as well as the *ex Patre*. Its intention was to recognize the fact that in God's revelation the Holy Spirit is the Spirit of Jesus Christ, that He cannot be separated from Him, that He is only the Spirit of Jesus Christ . . . It is because the Holy Spirit is from all eternity the communion between the Father and the Son, and therefore not only the Spirit of the Father but also the Spirit of the Son, that in God's revelation he can be the communion between the Father and those whom His Son has called to be His brethren.[22]
>
> The *Filioque* expresses recognition of the communion between the Father and the Son. The Holy Spirit is the love which is the essence of the relation between the two modes of being of God.[23]
>
> God the Father and God the Son are together the origin of the Holy Spirit: *Spiritus, qui procedit a Patre Filioque*. It is this which the poor folk in the Eastern Church have never quite understood, that the Begetter and the Begotten are together the origin of the Holy Spirit, and so the origin of their unity. The Holy Spirit has been called the *vinculum caritatis*. Not *although* God is Father and Son, but *because* God is Father and Son, unity exists.[24]

---

19. Hunsinger, "Karl Barth's Doctrine," 180.

20. "Where the Holy Spirit is sundered from Christ, sooner or later He is always transmuted into quite a different spirit, the spirit of the religious man, and finally the human spirit in general." Barth, *CD*, I/2, §16, 251.

21. Barth, *CD*, I/2, §16, 241. "Because the person of Jesus Christ has not only enacted but is and remains our salvation, he is and remains the enduring focus of the Spirit's work"; Hunsinger, "Karl Barth's Doctrine," 181.

22. Barth, *CD*, I/2, §16, 250; also *CD*, I/1, §12, 469–70, 479–80.

23. Barth, *CD*, I/1, §12, 480.

24. Barth, *Dogmatics in Outline*, 44.

Barth's biblical basis for the idea that the Spirit unites the Father and the Son in eternity appears to rest mainly on Romans 8:9 in which Paul identifies the Holy Spirit as "Spirit of God" and "Spirit of Christ." Like Augustine, Barth understands the function of the genitive phrases "πνεῦμα θεοῦ" and "πνεῦμα Χριστοῦ" in terms of "possession" or "source." The context concerns the indwelling, life-giving Spirit—believers in Christ have been raised to life from the deadness of sin by the Spirit who indwells God and Christ. In the verses that follow, "God" is the "Father," and "Christ" is the "Son" (Rom 8:14–17). That the Spirit indwells the Father and the Son, however, does not automatically signify that the Spirit *mediates* between them. Rather, their mutual indwelling may signify *perichoresis*. Perhaps a counterargument may be made that these genitival phrases indicate "relation" rather than "possession" or "source." Thus, instead of seeing the Spirit as "belonging" to the Father and the Son, rather, the Spirit is *related* to God and to Christ. A human analogy may be helpful—if Jane is George's sister and Alice's sister, then she is sister to both, and they are both related to her. This does not mean that if she were not their sister, or simply did not exist, that George and Alice are no longer brother and sister. Neither would it mean that by being sister to both that she originates from both. It may be the tendency to subordinate the Spirit to the Father and the Son, no matter how slight or disavowed,[25] that privileges the "possessive" or "source" hermeneutic for the genitive phrases "πνεῦμα θεοῦ" and "πνεῦμα Χριστοῦ." It is important to note that the Johannine portrayal of Jesus clearly emphasizes the unmediated relationship, even unity, between the Father and the Son.[26] The Holy Spirit is the "other" (but similar, ἄλλος) παράκλητος (John 14:16), sent by the Father at the request of the Son, to dwell in those who put their trust in the Son. Thus, the Son and the Spirit are both sent by the Father. Furthermore, our triune God is one, a point which Barth himself stresses, and God's oneness need not necessarily be dependent on any other unifying principle apart from the fact that God *is* one. God's threeness and oneness are both essential characteristics of God.

The principle that the Holy Spirit is the indwelling Spirit is undeniably biblical. Whether this satisfactorily translates to the concept that the Spirit is the unifying factor between the Father and the Son is not so clear. Nevertheless, this does not detract from the New Testament teaching that the Holy Spirit unites believers to Christ.[27] Barth's commitment to the intra-

---

25. Barth asserts that with respect to God the Father, "in no sense can Christ and the Spirit be subordinate hypostases"; *CD*, I/1, §9, 353.

26. John 5:20, 23, 26; 10:15, 30, 38; 12:49; 14:7, 10–11.

27. See chapter 6, §6.4 in this book.

Trinitarian unitive role for the Spirit is so closely linked to his commitment to the *filioque* that he probably cannot give up one without giving up the other. John Thompson, who studied under Barth, is closer to the mark when he suggests that Barth drew his concept of the unitive function of the Spirit in the Godhead *from* the revelation of the unitive function of the Holy Spirit in the economy rather than the other way around, hinting that Barth may be employing a somewhat circular argument.

> Barth follows Augustine closely here as in so much else and speaks of the Holy Spirit as the union and communion of the Father and the Son, yet at the same time as a distinct person. How does one know this? Again one can only draw from the economy of salvation. The Holy Spirit is the bond of union between God and humanity in Christ Jesus and between Christ and humanity and *these unions in turn reflect how God is in himself*. The Holy Spirit is thus a person in the union and communion of the divine life in the divine and holy love.[28]

It is interesting to note that although Barth adheres firmly to the view that the Spirit unites the Father and the Son in their eternal Trinitarian relations, he does not seem to extend this idea to the cross event. Perhaps this is not surprising, since Barth understands Jesus's death as the fulfilling of God's judgment on humanity in Jesus Christ the Elect, rather than the alienation of God the Son from the God the Father. Moltmann does the opposite.[29] For Barth, it is the sinful human race, united to the Son in Jesus Christ, who is rejected, not the Second Person of the Trinity *per se*.

c. Omnia opera Trinitatis ad extra sunt indivisa

In keeping with the Augustinian principle *omnia opera Trinitatis ad extra sunt indivisa* ("all the outward works of the Trinity are undivided"), Barth insists that while God is triune, God is one God, and as such, God's actions are the actions of the triune God. Indeed, God can meet us and unite Godself to us, *because* God is Father, Son and Holy Spirit.[30] Barth writes:

> Just as Scripture is to be read in context as the witness to God's revelation, just as, e.g., Good Friday, Easter and Pentecost can only say together what they have to say, so we must say that all God's work, as we are to grasp it on the basis of His revelation,

---

28. Thompson, *The Holy Spirit*, 26; italics added.
29. See chapter 4, §4.4, in this book.
30. Barth, *CD*, I/1, §9, 383.

is one act which occurs simultaneously and in concert in all His three modes of being. From creation by way of revelation and reconciliation to the coming redemption it is always true that He who acts here is the Father and the Son and the Spirit.[31]

Although prominence is given to certain acts in relation to the Father, Son or Holy Spirit, Barth insists that this should be done without "the forgetting or denying of God's presence in all His modes of being, in His total being and act even over against us."[32] Thus, the Father is the Creator, but the Son and the Spirit are also Creator with him. Likewise, the Father is not only Creator, but with the Son and the Spirit he is also God the Reconciler and Redeemer. It is not that the terms Creator, Reconciler, and Redeemer refer to three gods or to three parts of one God; these names belong to one triune God. "He is and remains God *unus et individuus* ('one and undivided')."[33] The unity and distinction of the triune God is manifest in God's acts. While Barth emphasizes God's unity, he cautions that God's threefold distinctiveness is also important because the dissolution of the triunity into a "neutral fourth" leads to unacceptable modalistic ideas like patripassianism.[34]

Bearing in mind Barth's insistence that unity and distinction must be held together in constructive tension whenever God's acts are considered, his emphasis on the unity of the triune God at the cross of Christ suggests that a *pneumatologia crucis* may not be incongruent with his Trinitarian theology, as the following statements seem to indicate:

> With the eternal Son the eternal Father has also to bear what falls on the Son as He gives Himself to identity with the man Jesus of Nazareth, thus lifting it [God's judgment] away from us to Himself in order that it should not fall on us. In Jesus Christ God Himself, the God who is the one true God, the Father with the Son in the unity of the Spirit, has suffered what it befell this man to suffer to the bitter end.[35]

> The lonely man of Gethsemane and Golgotha, the lonely God, then comes together with lonely man isolated in his deepest need. Each of us can then say that in this place, even though he is forsaken and alone, he is not forsaken and alone, since the crucified man Jesus Christ, and in Him as the Son of God, God

---

31. Barth, *CD*, I/1, §9, 374–75.
32. Barth, *CD*, I/1, §9, 375.
33. Barth, *CD*, I/1, §10, 395.
34. Barth, *CD*, I/1, §10, 397.
35. Barth, *CD*, IV/3.1, §70, 414.

himself has also stooped down and been forsaken there... There God does not say No to man without bearing and experiencing Himself all the bitterness of this No in order that according to His own will and power He might, in, with and under this no, pronounce to him His own eternal Yes.[36]

Barth's emphasis on the unity of the triune God, his Christocentric covenantal Trinitarianism, and his attribution of a unifying role within the Godhead to the Spirit (rightly or wrongly), together lead almost inevitably as it were to the idea of the Spirit's involvement at Golgotha. Indeed, as the quotations above show, Barth explicitly describes the God who suffers with Jesus Christ on the cross as "the one true God, the Father with the Son *in the unity of the Spirit*." There are, however, other aspects of Barth's theology that also lend support to a *pneumatologia crucis*.

Jesus Christ, the Elect

Following Calvin, Barth affirms that God's gracious work of reconciliation begins with election, and the subject of this election is the triune God.[37] For Barth, "to all eternity, God is the electing God," and "God Himself does not will to be God, and is not God, except as the One who elects."[38] Barth radically departs from Calvin, however, where the identity of the object of the election is concerned. Barth insists that it is *Christ* who is the Elect, not individual humans *per se*. He adamantly disagrees with the Reformed doctrine of the *decretum absolutum* that God elects some humans for salvation and others for damnation by an "absolute decree."[39] Rather, it is Jesus Christ, Son of God, who is himself the Elect. Jesus Christ is not simply the first of a series of elected humans,[40] but the Elect who is "himself the divine election of grace"[41] and "the election of God's covenant with man."[42]

> With Athanasius the decree, or predestination, or election, was, in fact, the decision reached at the beginning of all things, at the beginning of the relationship between God and the reality

---

36. Barth, *CD*, IV/3.1, §70, 416.
37. Barth, *CD*, II/2, §33, 111.
38. Barth, *CD*, II/2, §33, 77.
39. Barth, *CD*, II/2, §33, 67–76, especially 75–76. He labels the Reformed doctrine of predestination "Christless," and remarks, somewhat sarcastically, "The electing God of Calvin is a *Deus nudus absconditus* ['purely hidden God']"; *CD*, II/2, §33, 111, 113.
40. Barth, *CD*, II/2, §33, 110.
41. Barth, *CD*, II.2, §33, 95.
42. Barth, *CD*, II.2, §33, 102.

which is distinct from him. The Subject of this decision is the triune God—the Son of God no less than the Father and the Holy Spirit. And the specific object of it is the Son of God in his determination as the Son of Man, the God-Man, Jesus Christ, who is as such the eternal basis of the whole divine election.[43]

Barth shares with the supralapsarian approach its Calvinistic concern for the primary freedom and supremacy of God, its refusal to separate the divine act of creation from the divine act of redemption, and its determination to see all history, including creation and the fall, in the light of God's eschatological goal—God's glory. He is less convinced by the infralapsarian approach because, in his view, while it portrays a kinder God, it undermines those very concepts that he acknowledges and applauds in supralapsarianism.[44] Nonetheless, Barth rejects the classical supralapsarian portrayal of a God who, for the sole purpose of self-glorification, predestines from eternity one group of humans for salvation and another group for damnation, and for this very purpose, creates a world in which evil rules, so that humans will fall and need redemption;[45] in crude vernacular—the idea that God wants to be a hero, like a firefighter who sets fires in order to be commended for putting them out and rescuing people. In Barth's more refined terminology, the classical supralapsarian approach is "most dangerous."[46]

Common to both supra- and infralapsarianism, according to Barth, are four presuppositions. First, the *obiectum praedestinationis* ("object of predestination") is the human *individual*, both elected and reprobate. Second, God's eternal decree of predestination is a fixed deterministic system that humans can only fulfill and affirm. Third, this system is a two-column structure in which God utters God's "Yes" to the elect (who are guided in their lives to election) and "No" to the reprobate (who are similarly guided to perdition). Fourth, there exists behind this fixed system God's hidden *decretum absolutum* ("absolute decree") that expresses God's absolute freedom to allocate humans unconditionally into the two groups.[47] Barth completely rejects all four presuppositions because, in his opinion, they are "not the picture of God in Jesus Christ."[48]

---

43. Barth, *CD*, II/2, §33, 110.
44. Barth, *CD*, II/2, §33, 133–39, 143.
45. Barth, *CD*, II/2, §33, 140.
46. Barth, *CD*, II/2, §33, 140.
47. Barth, *CD*, II/2, §33, 133–34.

48. Barth, *CD*, II/2, §33, 134. Interestingly, the Scriptures speak of a book of life (e.g., Ps 69:28; Rev 3:5; 13:8; 17:8; 20:12, 15) but never of a book of life *and* death, or even a separate book of death.

In place of these presuppositions, Barth sees Jesus Christ as the true *obiectum praedestinationis*, not a rigid *system* but a *person* who is the God-man Jesus Christ, and certainly not a *decretum absolutum* but a God who loves rather than a self-seeking God, a God who creates humanity in order to express God's love.[49] Of critical significance to Barth's doctrine of election is that Jesus Christ is *both* the electing God *and* the elected human, in one person.[50] This is vitally important because Barth asserts that the Son, as Elector with the Father and the Spirit, not only elects himself to be the Elect, but also, as Elector, elects with himself, *his people*.[51] Thus it is not individuals who are elected, or damned, or even groups of people labelled "elect" and "reprobate," but humanity as a whole who are united to Christ in his election. According to Barth, humanity has no salvation apart from Christ, and no assurance of salvation apart from the confidence that in Christ, the original and inclusive Elect, they too are elected. Jesus Christ is the Elect, and also the electing God.[52]

> If Jesus Christ is only elected, and not also and primarily the Elector, what shall we really know at all of a divine electing and our election? But of Jesus Christ we know nothing more surely and definitely than this—that in free obedience to His Father He elected to be man, and as man, to do the will of God. If God elects us too, then it is in and with this election of Jesus Christ, in and with this free act of obedience on the part of His Son. It is He who is manifestly the concrete and manifest form of the divine decision—the decision of the Father, Son and Holy Spirit—in favour of the covenant to be established between Him and us. It is in Him that the eternal election becomes immediately and directly the promise of our election as it is enacted in time, our calling, our summoning to faith, our assent to the divine intervention on our behalf, the revelation of ourselves as sons of God and of God our Father, the communication of the Holy Spirit who is none other than the Spirit of this act of obedience, the Spirit of obedience itself, and for us the Spirit of adoption.[53]

The Trinitarian shape of Barth's doctrine of election is clear from his insistence that election is the decision of the triune God. It is God the Father,

---

49. Barth, *CD*, II/2, §33, 143, 145.
50. Barth, *CD*, II/2, §32, 3.
51. Barth, *CD*, II/2, §33, 77.
52. Barth, *CD*, II/2, §33, 145.
53. Barth, *CD*, II/2, §33, 105–6.

Son and Holy Spirit who is the subject of the election; Jesus Christ is the Elect (and Elector); the Spirit is the power of the Son's obedience and the one who makes humans children of the Father in the Son. Barth points out that humanity is elected insofar as humans are elected in Jesus Christ, who is not only the object but primarily the subject of the election.[54] It is because he is the electing Son of God and Son of Man that the Son has the authority to elect all other humans in his humanity.[55] "The election of man is his election in Jesus Christ, for Jesus Christ is the eternally living beginning of man and of the whole creation. Electing means to elect 'in Him.' And election means to be elected 'in Him.'"[56] By the phrase "in Him," Barth clarifies that he does not simply mean "with Him," "in His company" or even "through Him" or "like Him."[57] "From the very beginning (from eternity itself), there are no other elect together with or apart from Him, but as "Eph. 1:4 tells us, only 'in' Him . . . 'In Him' means in His person, in His will, in His own divine choice, in the basic decision of God which He fulfills against every man."[58] Individual humans, according to Barth, are not elected by God in any other way except "in Christ." There is therefore no primary eternal selection of individuals for glory or perdition, no *decretum absolutum*.

Furthermore, Barth stresses that the election of Jesus Christ is his election for the execution of divine judgment and divine mercy.[59] God's judgment of sinful humanity is just, but "even God's judgement is sustained and surrounded by God's mercy, even His severity by His kindness, even His wrath by His love."[60] In this judgment, both sin and sinner are dealt with. At the cross, sin and evil are destroyed, completely, decisively, and categorically. According to Barth, evil exists only as an illicit, irrational, alien anomaly, a shadow to God's light, a parasite with no substantial basis of its own, a "nothingness"—*das Nichtige*.[61] It is not a creature of God, neither is it an eternal uncreated entity. "The existence, presence and operation of 'nothingness' . . . are also objectively the break in the relationship between Creator and creature."[62]

---

54. Barth, *CD*, II/2, §33, 120.
55. Barth, *CD*, II/2, §33, 117.
56. Barth, *CD*, II/2, §34, 195.
57. Barth, *CD*, II/2, §33, 116–17, 121.
58. Barth, *CD*, II/2, §33, 116–17.
59. Barth, *CD*, II/2, §34, 205.
60. Barth, *CD*, II/2, §34, 211.
61. Barth, *CD*, III/3, §50, 289–302, 305. "Nothingness is that which God does not will. It lives only by the fact that it is that which God does not will"; *CD*, III/3, §50, 352.
62. Barth, *CD*, III/3, §50, 294.

Notwithstanding the term *das Nichtige*, Barth does not deny the concrete reality of evil. He perceives that evil derives from, and thrives because of, the breakdown in God-human relations, and that it exists, really exists, as worldly opposition and resistance to God's sovereignty. Barth asserts however, that this evil, this illegitimate "nothingness" which permeates all humans, human organisations and structures, is annihilated in the death of the Son of Man on the cross.[63] "Nothingness is the past, the ancient menace, danger and destruction, the ancient non-being which obscured and defaced the divine creation of God but which is consigned to the past in Jesus Christ, in whose death it has received its deserts, being destroyed with this consummation of the positive will of God which is as such the end of His non-willing. Because Jesus is Victor, nothingness is routed and extirpated." [64]

At the cross, not only are sin and evil dealt with, but the sinner is put to death. This is the fulfillment of God's judgment on human disobedience—"you shall die" (Gen 2:17). Without dealing with the sinner herself and her propensity to sin, there cannot be reconciliation. The debt of sin may be repaid and forgiven, but the problem of the sinner remains. Thus, the proclamation, "You must be born from above (John 3:7)." But rebirth implies the death of the old. This death (and rebirth) takes place in Jesus Christ. Barth asserts, "The election of the man Jesus means, then, that a wrath is kindled, a sentence pronounced and finally executed, a rejection actualised."[65] "That the elected man Jesus had to suffer and die means no more and no less than that in becoming man God makes Himself responsible for man who became his enemy, and that He takes upon Himself all the consequences of man's action—his rejection and death."[66]

Nevertheless, the extermination of evil and death of the sinner in Jesus Christ the Elect is not the final outcome of the righteous judgment of God. It is the very fact that Christ "is the only-begotten Son of God who can suffer death but *cannot be holden of death, who by His death must destroy death*,"[67] and who rises from the dead to return to sit at his Father's right, that humanity is redeemed and exalted "in Christ," and *only* "in Christ."

> He [God] decrees the rejection of the evil-doer, but in predestinating Himself to union with the Son of Man in His Son He decrees that this rejection should be lifted from man and laid

---

63. Tan, "Humanity's Devil," 151–52.
64. Barth, *CD*, III/3, §50, 363.
65. Barth, *CD*, II/2, §33, 122.
66. Barth, *CD*, II/2, §33, 124.
67. Barth, *CD*, II/2, §33, 125, italics added.

upon Himself. In spite of man's unworthiness in himself, He wills and affirms and loves man, yet in so doing He does not will the continuance of man in His unworthiness. He wills rather that man should be exalted, and that (by the power of His grace) he should have a share in His own worthiness.[68]

In presenting Christ as the true *obiectum praedestinationis* who is the One addressed by God's "Yes" and "No," Barth overturns the Reformed understanding that divine predestination involves a predetermined dualistic categorization of humans into elect and reprobate groups. Instead, in Jesus Christ the Elect, God pronounces his righteous judgment against *das Nichtige* in all its forms, and against sinners themselves. This is a "No" that must be fully implemented *in order that God's "Yes" can be declared*. Matthias Grebe correctly discerns a universalistic trajectory in Barth's doctrine of election.[69] However, while on the one hand Barth asserts that all humans are enclosed within the work of Christ on the cross, on the other hand Barth divides humans into two groups, "the elect" and "the rejected,"[70] whom he also terms "the called" and "the uncalled."[71] By these terms, Barth signifies that only some are made aware of their election, and who are "called." Barth attributes this "calling" to the Holy Spirit.[72] Only those whose hearts and minds have been opened by the Holy Spirit to the truth of Christ are named, by Barth, "the elect"; only they receive the twofold work of the Spirit: proclamation and faith, and are able to acknowledge the salvation afforded them by Jesus Christ.[73]

Drawing from Israel's ancestral history, Barth highlights the principle that God selects some individuals and not others. For example, God chooses Abel and not Cain, Isaac and not Ishmael, Jacob and not Esau, and that certain individuals are chosen, for instance, Noah, Abraham, Moses, Aaron, David, and the prophets.[74] Furthermore, Barth sees parallels in the ritual liturgy of

68. Barth, *CD*, II/2, §34, 192.
69. Grebe, *Election and Atonement*, 202–7.
70. Barth, *CD*, II/2, §35, 341–409.
71. Barth, *CD*, II/2, §35, 351.
72. Barth, *CD*, II/2, §35, 345–48.
73. "But their calling—the work of the Holy Spirit—is that by means of the community the election of Jesus Christ may be proclaimed to them as their own election, and that they may be assured of their election by faith in Jesus Christ, in who it was brought about. This twofold possibility is the objective difference between the elect and other men. By the free event of proclamation and of faith they are placed in a special situation in relation to others, and in a ministry in which the latter do not stand." Barth, *CD*, II/2, §35, 345.
74. Barth, *CD*, II/2, §35, 341–42.

Leviticus 16 (Day of Atonement), where two goats are presented before God on behalf of the Israelite community. One is chosen for sacrifice as their sin offering, while the other is released into the desert, bearing away their sins to the goat demon, Azazel. For Barth, the sacrificed goat represents "the chosen" or "the elect," while the banished goat represents "the non-elect."[75] This differentiation of humanity into "elect" and "rejected" seems *prima facie* to undermine Barth's own determination that it is primarily Christ who is the *obiectum praedestinationis* rather than individual humans. Barth then clarifies, however, that elect and reprobate humanity are *both* represented by and in Christ. Thus, for Barth *both* goats typify Christ's work, so that Christ is both the Elect and the Rejected.[76] On the other hand, perhaps it is more accurate to see the sacrificed goat as the one representing *sinners*, and the banished goat as the one carrying away their *sins*, so that both goats foreshadow the comprehensive soteriological work of Christ.

Although Barth recognizes an existential difference between "the elect" and "the rejected" among humanity, he emphasizes that without the saving work of Christ, all humans are, in truth, "the rejected." "To be rejected of God is the threat whose fulfilment would be the inevitable lot of every single human life. And it is this threat which in the election of Jesus Christ is diverted to Him, the One, and in that way averted from all others. By permitting the life of a rejected man to be the life of His own Son, God has made such a life objectively impossible for all others."[77] How then does Barth envisage the final destiny of "the rejected"? While he acknowledges that there exists "the rejected" among humans, whose lives bear false witness to the truth in Christ, he asserts that the judgment that is theirs has also been borne by Christ, and that they too have no expectation of eternal damnation. "They may indeed conduct themselves as rejected, but even if they deserved it a thousand times they have no power to bring down on themselves a second time *the sword of God's wrath now that it has fallen.*"[78] For Barth, God's righteous judgment on humanity has already fallen on Jesus Christ at the cross, and therefore no single human exists in anticipation of that judgment. While Grebe infers from Barth's statements a clear universalistic view of salvation, Barth himself seems less certain. Concerning the personal justification of Judas, whom he sees as typifying "the rejected," Barth wisely states, "On the contrary, we are

---

75. Barth, *CD*, II/2, §35, 357–60.

76. "[T]here is only one Rejected, the Bearer of all man's sin and guilt and their ensuing punishment, and this One is Jesus Christ . . . the Lord and Head of both the elect and also of the rejected"; Barth, *CD*, II/2, §35, 346–47, 352–53.

77. Barth, *CD*, II/2, §35, 346.

78. Barth, *CD*, II/2, §35, 349, italics added.

asked to leave this question as one which can only be answered by the Judge who is competent in this matter."[79]

Grebe challenges Barth's typological characterization of the goats in Leviticus 16, and suggests that it is only the sacrificed goat that is representative of Christ's work and not the goat released into the desert, because "God speaks only a *Yes* over Jesus Christ and through him over humanity."[80] He stresses that Christ died for sinful *humanity* and not for *sin*. Indeed, Grebe denies that sin-bearing has any part in the atonement. Not surprisingly, he concludes that Christ is only the Elect, never the Rejected. This does not mean that Grebe agrees with universal salvation. On the contrary, he offers his "participatory atonement" model as an answer to the difficulties inherent in the limited atonement and universalistic positions. In his model Grebe affirms that while Christ does indeed die for all humanity, individual salvation is conditional on having faith in Christ.

> A person's salvation depends on participation in the cross-event through faith. From a New Testament perspective, salvation is not contingent on whether or not the individual is part of an "elect," but instead must be viewed as a free invitation to be in covenantal fellowship with God. Likewise, it is not contingent on whether or not Christ bore a person's sins, but rather on a person's response to the work of Christ, trusting in God's decision over Christ that he or she is elected "in Christ."[81]

It appears that Grebe's "participatory atonement" model is really a form of Arminianism, and does not present a holistic understanding of sin that takes into account both the sinner and his or her sinful actions. The fall is a twofold problem, an ontological problem of the sinner who is corrupt, and the moral problem of sinful acts and events that have come into being. Justice, to be complete and comprehensive, not only requires the miscreant to be comprehensively dealt with, but also directs an appropriate response to the misdeed itself and the damage caused. Grebe's approach does not seem to take into serious enough consideration Barth's profound acknowledgement of the extent of God's "No."

Barth's concept of Jesus Christ as the Elect and the Elector supports the idea of the corporate Christ. It strengthens the notion that when Christ died and rose on the cross, he did so not only as the man Jesus of Nazareth, but also as Jesus Christ, the Elect, with the elect community with and in him. Indeed, Barth's doctrine of election is worthless and meaningless if

---

79. Barth, *CD*, II/2, §35, 484.
80. Grebe, *Election and Atonement*, 94, 99, 251.
81. Grebe, *Election and Atonement*, 251.

it were not so. Nevertheless, while Barth's doctrine of election is insightful and helpful for the direction of the conversation concerning the role of the Spirit at the cross of Christ, it raises further questions. For example, how does this incorporation happen? When does it happen? How is it related to the earthly history of Jesus Christ? Is the incorporation a process or a single event? Does this incorporation happen at the level of impersonal "human nature" or between personal "hypostases"? Some of these questions find answers in Barth's understanding of the pneumatic Christ.

The Pneumatic Christ

Karl Barth's pneumatology is Christocentric, and he frequently points out that the Holy Spirit is the Spirit of Jesus Christ.[82] As George Hunsinger correctly perceives, Barth insists that "[t]he Spirit's abiding content and focus is therefore Jesus himself."[83] Barth's adamant insistence on the *filioque* attests to his commitment to a Christocentric pneumatology. Nevertheless, Barth is equally clear that every aspect of the life and ministry of Jesus Christ, from his incarnation to his resurrection and exaltation, takes place through the work of the Holy Spirit.[84]

> The particular existence of the Son of God as man, and again the particular existence of this man as the Son of God, the existence of Jesus Christ as the Lord who becomes a servant and the servant who becomes the Lord, His existence as the Guarantor of truth is itself ultimately grounded in the being and work of the Holy Spirit. He is *conceptus de Spiritu sancto.*[85]

> Jesus Christ is the Son of God who became man, who as such is One with God the Father, equal to Him in deity, by the Holy

---

82. For example, Barth states, "He is the Spirit of Jesus Christ"; "He is the Spirit of the Lord Jesus"; "He is the Holy Spirit in this supreme sense—holy with a holiness for which there are no analogies—because He is no other than the presence and action of Jesus Christ Himself: His stretched out arm; He Himself in the power of His resurrection"; "Thus the Spirit who makes Christians Christians is the power of this revelation of Jesus Christ Himself—His Spirit. And for this reason, and in this fact, He is the Holy Spirit"; Barth, CD, IV/2, §64, 322–24. Similarly, CD, I.2, §16, 241–51.

83. Hunsinger, *Disruptive Grace*, 160.

84. "His [Jesus's] human existence is peculiarly the work of God the Holy Spirit"; Barth, CD, I/2, §15, 196.

85. Barth, CD, IV/1, §58, 148.

Spirit, in whom the Father affirms and loves Him and He the Father, in a mutual fellowship.[86]

[I]t is important that at least one group in the New Testament tradition understood the human existence of the Son of God, that is, the justification and sanctification of human nature in the person of the Virgin Mary which was indispensable to union with the Son of God, as the work of the Holy Spirit (Matt 1:18, 20; Luke 1:35). It is also important that another series of passages—not 2 Cor 3:17, but 1 Cor 15:45 ("the second Adam was made a πνεῦμα ζωοποιοῦν), John 3:6 ("That which is born of the Spirit, is spirit") and especially the accounts of His baptism in the Jordan—understands His whole being as πνεῦμα, that is, filled and controlled by the Spirit, so that in Heb 9:14 it can already be said of His way to death that διὰ πνεύματος αἰωνίου He offered Himself without spot to God. [87]

For Barth, the work of the Holy Spirit is vital to the very existence of the Son of God as the man Jesus of Nazareth, and also to the existence of the human Jesus as Son of God. It is through *the Spirit* that the Word takes on human nature because, as Hunsinger discerns, Barth attributes to the work of the Holy Spirit the union of disparate realities across the divine-human ontological divide.[88] "Through his hypostatic union with the eternal Son of God, as effected by the Spirit, Jesus is the one truly human being."[89] This Spirit-created union between the eternal Son and human nature in the man Jesus of Nazareth takes place at the incarnation, and the union is maintained throughout the life, ministry, death, and resurrection of Jesus Christ. As Hunsinger rightly perceives, Barth's essentially Chalcedonian Christology leans towards the Alexandrian pole, with less frequent oscillations towards the Antiochene side.[90] Notwithstanding the dialectical shape of his two-nature Christology, Barth affirms that it is through the Spirit that Jesus Christ lives, teaches, performs miracles, dies, and lives again. Jesus Christ is the Spirit-indwelt "wholly sanctified" "spiritual man," that it is the Holy Spirit who empowers and directs him.[91]

---

86. Barth, *CD*, IV/1, §59, 204.
87. Barth, *CD*, IV/1, §59, 309.
88. Hunsinger, *Disruptive Grace*, 169.
89. Hunsinger, *Disruptive Grace*, 160.
90. Hunsinger, *Disruptive Grace*, 136–147; see also Neder, *Participation in Christ*, 73.
91. In the section entitled "The Direction of the Son," Barth identifies the Spirit as the one who directs the Son's life and ministry; *CD*, IV/2, §64, 265–377.

Jesus is the beloved Son of God, and as such He is from the very outset and throughout His existence the spiritual man, i.e., the true and exalted and royal man who lives by the descent of the Spirit of God and is therefore wholly filled and directed by Him.[92]

He [God] gives Him without reserve or limit—the fullness of the Spirit—so that His being as flesh is directly as such His being as Spirit also. *It is as this man who is wholly sanctified*, and therefore not in the form of an individual and sporadic inspiration but in accordance with the comprehensive necessity of His holy humanity, that the Spirit drives Him into the wilderness (Mark 1:12), i.e., to His vicarious conflict against Satan, in fulfilment of the penitence which He has accepted. *And it is again as this wholly sanctified man that "through the eternal Spirit he offered himself without spot to God," in His death (Heb 9:14).* It is as this man that He was "put to death in the flesh" (σαρκί, according to the law to which He bowed when He became and was flesh), but was quickened by the Spirit (πνεύματι, according to the law of His being as life-giving and death-destroying Spirit, 1 Peter 3:18). For as this man He is the Lord who is Himself Spirit.[93]

[A]ccording to the remarkable hymn in 1 Tim. 3:16, He was revealed in the flesh (and therefore in concealment) and justified in the Spirit (as He who was in the flesh). It is in this radical sense that *the Holy Spirit is the Spirit of Jesus Himself.* Because and as He is the Son of God, Jesus is the spiritual man. It is as such that He traverses the way which leads to the cross. But it is also as such that He is revealed and known when He is raised from the dead.[94]

It seems clear, therefore, that for Barth the Holy Spirit does not stand aloof from Jesus Christ during his passion and death. On the contrary, Barth insists that throughout Jesus's passion, death and resurrection, he continues to be the "wholly sanctified man" and the "spiritual man." It does not seem possible that Jesus can be this "wholly sanctified" and "spiritual man" without the real presence of the Spirit with him. It is also noteworthy that Barth consistently interprets the phrase διὰ πνεύματος αἰωνίου in Hebrews 9:14 as a reference to the Holy Spirit.[95] He observes that in the New Testament, the whole history of Jesus Christ is the work of the Holy Spirit including "the

---

92. Barth, *CD*, IV/2, §64, 324.
93. Barth, *CD*, IV/2, §64, 324; italics added.
94. Barth, *CD*, IV/2, §64, 325.
95. Barth, *CD*, II/2, §33, 102; IV/1, §59, 309; IV/2, §64, 323, 324; IV/4, §75, 29.

story of the miraculous birth of Jesus, His baptism, *His death* according to Heb. 9:14,"[96] that "*it was in the power of the Spirit that He went to His death; and it was also in the power of the Spirit that He was raised again from the dead.*"[97] Unsurprisingly, Barth emphasizes the role of the Spirit in raising Jesus from the dead.

> The fact that Jesus Christ was raised from the dead by the Holy Spirit and therefore justified confirms that it has pleased God to reveal and express Himself to the crucified and dead and buried Jesus Christ in the unity of the Father with the Son and therefore in the glory of the free love which is His essence: a revelation and expression which as such—and where the Spirit of God blows, where the Holy Spirit is at work, this does take place necessarily—must consist in the merciful work of creating καινότης ζωῆς (Rom. 6:4) of this One who is dead, in His presentation and exhibition as the One who is alive forevermore.[98]

Philip Rosato observes that although Barth's focus on Christology remains central to his theology, his pneumatological insights progressively become more pronounced particularly in volume IV/2, "where Barth counterweighs his christological pneumatology with a surprisingly well-developed pneumatological Christology."[99] The use of the term "pneumatological Christology" seems a more appropriate term to apply to Barth's reflections about the Holy Spirit vis-à-vis Jesus Christ than the term "Spirit Christology," as he clearly rejects any notion that the Spirit is the focus of Christology, or that the Spirit is the divine principle made incarnate in Christ. To emphasize this point, Barth insists that "it is not this special relationship to the Holy Spirit which makes this man [Jesus] the Messiah and the Son of God. On the contrary, it is because this man is the Messiah and the Son of God that He stands to the Holy Spirit in this special relationship."[100] Perhaps an even more precise term to describe Barth's Son-Spirit framework is "*pneumatic Christology,*" as this affirms Barth's contention that the content and focus of the Spirit is Jesus Christ, the Word and Son of God, while also highlighting his juxtaposed insistence that the Spirit is the power through whom God effects his redemption plan in Christ.[101] Barth's dialectical methodology allows

---

96. Barth, *CD*, IV/4, §75, 29; italics added.

97. Barth, *CD*, IV/2, §64, 323; italics added.

98. Barth, *CD*, IV/1, §59, 309. The phrase "the unity of the Father with the Son" is Barth's reference to the Holy Spirit.

99. Rosato, *The Spirit as Lord*, 121.

100. Barth, *CD*, III/2, §46, 333.

101. Hunsinger, *Disruptive Grace*, 157–60.

him to hold his Christocentric pneumatology and pneumatic Christology together, bringing Christ or the Spirit into the conversational foreground as is relevant to particular stages in his discussion.

The Unifying Spirit

Barth unambiguously ascribes to the Holy Spirit, as the Spirit of κοινωνία, the role of unifier in three overlapping dimensions—intra-Trinitarian, christological, and ecclesial.[102] As alluded to earlier, Barth is committed to the Western concept, attributed to Augustine, that the Holy Spirit, as Spirit of God and Spirit of Christ, unites the Father and the Son in their eternal relations. This idea underpins Barth's vigorous insistence on the theological accuracy of the addition of the *filioque* term to the pneumatological statement of the Niceno-Constantinopolitan Creed. For Barth, as we have seen, this intra-Trinitarian unifying role is the very primordial basis upon which the Spirit's unifying role in the christological and ecclesial dimensions is rooted.[103] The notion that the Holy Spirit is the unitive force within the Trinity is attractive, but it is certainly not as clearly discernible in the Scriptures as Barth suggests. Indeed, it seems more intuitive and speculative than solidly biblical. Putting this tenuous idea to one side, there is nevertheless ample biblical witness to the Spirit's unifying activity in the christological and ecclesial dimensions without recourse to a similar intra-Trinitarian role. According to Barth, Jesus Christ the Elect encloses humanity within himself—it is only in this way that humans are elected by God for salvation. The union between humanity and Christ is effected by the power of the Holy Spirit.[104] For Barth, Christ is the corporate Christ. He insists, however, that "Christ does not merge into the Christian nor the Christian into Christ. There is no disappearance nor destruction of the one in favour of the other."[105] The terms "corporate Christology" and "ecclesiology" almost seem to refer to the same thing, and indeed the metaphor "body of Christ"

---

102. Hunsinger, *Disruptive Grace*, 168–73.

103. See §7.1, 195–97 in this chapter; Thompson, *The Holy Spirit*, 26, 42.

104. Barth, *CD*, IV/3.3, §71, 538.

105. Barth, *CD*, IV/3.3, §71, 539. Neder rightly emphasizes this point in his summary of Barth's views on union with Christ, but he may not have given sufficient weight to the role of the Spirit; *Participation in Christ*, 78–79. Barth asserts quite clearly that "As Jesus Christ speaks with man in the power of the Holy Spirit, His vocation is *vocatio efficax*, i.e., effective to set man in fellowship with Himself," and "What is the nature of this fellowship of Christians with Jesus Christ if we have correctly understood it as the relationship of discipleship and possession, and finally as the powerful work of the Holy Spirit?"; *CD*, IV/3.3, §71, 538, 539.

is key to both dimensions, but perhaps these terms may be distinguished by their different focus. Corporate Christology focuses on Christ, while ecclesiology focuses on the believing community of Christ. Nonetheless, in both spheres the Holy Spirit is the agent of unity.

Barth strongly affirms that the incarnation of Jesus Christ is a creative act of the Holy Spirit, one that is paralleled only by the resurrection.[106] He accepts the birth narratives in Matthew and Luke as authentic accounts of "an event occurring in the realm of the creaturely world in the full sense of the word,"[107] and that they describe "the genuine birth of a genuine man."[108] Barth is convinced that Jesus of Nazareth was miraculously born without a human father, and from a mother who, being a virgin, should not have been able to conceive by herself, [109] and even if she could, she should certainly not have been able to give birth to a *male* child.[110] He also dismisses modern attempts to explain the birth in scientific terms.[111] Barth repeatedly refers to the creedal phrase *conceptus de Spiritu Sancto* ("conceived by the Holy Spirit").[112] He asserts that this phrase is biblically rooted and unambiguously identifies the Spirit as "God, God Himself, God in the fullest and strictest sense of the term . . . He and no other and nothing else is the Holy Spirit by whom Jesus Christ was conceived according to his human nature, in order to be born of the Virgin Mary,"[113] "a pure divine beginning."[114] Barth carefully points out that Jesus Christ's divine sonship does not begin at the incarnation, but *because* he is Son of God, his birth is a direct pneumatic act:

> It [the formula *conceptus de Spiritu Sancto*] states that the conception of Jesus Christ prior to His birth of the Virgin Mary was the work of God the Holy Spirit. To that extent it was a miraculous birth and as such the sign of the incarnation of the

106. Barth, *CD*, I/2, §15, 182.
107. Barth, *CD*, I/2, §15, 181.
108. Barth, *CD*, I/2, §15, 186.
109. Barth, *CD*, I/2, §15, 194.

110. Only the father carries the Y gene that is fundamental to maleness, so that even if parthenogenesis was operative, biology dictates that Mary can only produce female offspring.

111. Barth, *CD*, I/2, §15, 197.

112. For example, *CD*, I/2, §15, 181, 185, 196–197, 200–202. The phrase "*conceptus de Spiritu Sancto*" (τὸν συλληφθέντα ἐκ πνεύματος ἁγίου in Greek) is from the Apostle's Creed. In the Niceno-Constantinopolitan Creed, the corresponding phrase is "*incarnates est de Spiritu Sancto*" (σαρκθέντα ἐκ πνεύματος ἁγίου).

113. Barth, *CD*, I/2, §15, 197.
114. Barth, *CD*, I/2, §15, 198.

eternal Word. The formula *conceptus de Spiritu Sancto* thus fills in the blank, as it were, indicated by the formula *natus ex Maria virgine*. It indicates the ground and content, where the latter indicates the form and shape, of the miracle and sign.[115]

The man Jesus of Nazareth is not the true Son of God because He is conceived by the Holy Spirit and born of the Virgin Mary. On the contrary, because He is the true Son of God and because this is an inconceivable mystery intended to be acknowledged as such, therefore He is conceived by the Holy Spirit and born of the Virgin Mary.[116]

Since the Holy Spirit brings about the incarnation, Barth reasons that it is the Spirit who enables the union of incompatible, opposite realities—divine and human. "Through the Spirit flesh, human nature, is assumed into unity with the Son of God."[117] "In the Holy Spirit we know the real togetherness of God and man."[118] The incarnation, and the Holy Spirit's role in it, is thus, for Barth, foundational for an understanding of Christology and ecclesiology. With respect to Christology, it is the Holy Spirit who holds together both natures of Jesus Christ[119] and who makes possible the whole human existence of God the Son.[120] With respect to ecclesiology (and corporate Christology), it is the Holy Spirit who unites humanity to Christ and therefore to God.[121] Hence, according to Barth, the Holy Spirit's role in the incarnation provides a firm biblical and theological basis to name the Spirit as the unitive agent and power that makes Christ, Christ; the Christian, Christian; and the church, the body of Christ. Without the Holy Spirit's work, Creator and creature cannot be united in the way that Jesus Christ is understood to be *vere Deus vere homo* ("very God, very man"), and in the way that humans can become children of God.[122]

---

115. Barth, *CD*, I/2, §15, 196. Barth takes care to clarify that *conceptus de Spiritu Sancto* does not mean that a marriage took place between the Holy Spirit and Mary, or that "Jesus Christ is the Son of the Holy Spirit according to his human existence"; *CD*, I/2, §15, 200. Barth accepts the Virgin birth as fact, that it took place miraculously through the power of the Holy Spirit, asserting that we may ever understand the "how"; *CD*, I/2, §15, 201.

116. Barth, *CD*, I/2, §15, 202.

117. Barth, *CD*, I/2, §15, 199.

118. Barth, *CD*, I/2, §16, 246.

119. Barth, *CD*, I/2, §15, 199; *CD*, IV/1, §59, 309; *CD*, IV/3.1, §69, 357.

120. "His human existence is peculiarly the work of God the Holy Spirit"; Barth, *CD*, I/2, §15, 196.

121. Barth, *CD*, I/2, §16, 241–42.

122. Barth, *CD*, I/2, §15, 200.

> The very possibility of human nature's being adopted into unity with the Son of God *is* the Holy Ghost. Here, then, at the fontal point in revelation, the Word of God is not without the Spirit of God. And here already there is the togetherness of the Spirit and Word. Through the Spirit it becomes really possible for the creature, for man, to be there and to be free for God. Through the Spirit flesh, human nature, is assumed into unity with the Son of God.[123]

> The work of the Holy Spirit, however, is to bring and hold together that which is different and therefore, as it would seem, necessarily and irresistibly disruptive in the relationship of Jesus Christ to His community, namely, the divine working, being and action on the one side and the human on the other, the creative freedom and act on the one side and the creaturely on the other, the eternal reality and possibility on the one side and the temporal on the other. His work is to bring and to hold them together, not to identify, intermingle into the other, but to co-ordinate them, to make them parallel, to bring them into harmony and therefore to bind them into a true unity.[124]

As Hunsinger notes, "The mutual indwelling of Christ's two natures, established by the Spirit in the incarnation, serves as the backdrop for his uniting of Christ with the church."[125] Rosato accurately pinpoints Barth's *"incarnational analogy"* as the pneumatic thread that ties together his Christology and ecclesiology. [126]

> By defending the Church's teaching on *conceptus de Spiritu Sancto*, Barth reaffirms not only the Spirit's prior and unequalled role in uniting the Word of God to the human nature of Jesus, but also the Spirit's subsequent and parallel function of uniting human nature itself to the Word of God through the faith of believers. On the grounds of his understanding of the incarnation, Barth can affirm that the very union between God and man is the Holy Spirit. This is true primarily of Jesus Christ, but also of the believer.[127]

---

123. Barth, *CD*, I/2, §15, 199; italics added.
124. Barth, *CD*, IV/3, §72, 761.
125. Hunsinger, *Disruptive Grace*, 168.
126. The term "incarnational analogy" is a term coined by Rosato, not Barth, but it aptly describes Barth's application of the theological implications of the incarnation for anthropology, Christology and ecclesiology; Rosato, *The Spirit as Lord*, 67.
127. Rosato, *The Spirit as Lord*, 68.

Barth places great emphasis on the Spirit's noetic work,[128] but also describes the Spirit's unifying activity using ontological language.[129] He affirms that it is through the power of the Holy Spirit that a real union between the human and divine natures of Christ exists, a union which does not dissolve one into the other but which preserves the distinction of each,[130] a union which is eternal and irrevocable. Jesus Christ, Son of God, now lives in embodied form:[131]

> Through the Spirit flesh, human nature, is assumed into unity with the Son of God. Through the Spirit this Man can be God's Son and at the same time the Second Adam and as such "the firstborn among many brethren" (Rom. 8:29), the prototype of all who are set free for His sake and through faith in Him.[132]

> In His presence and activity in the promise of the Spirit, if it is really His promise of the Spirit and the power of His resurrection, there can be no question of a restitution of the separation between divine and human being which is done away in His incarnation. It was not in such separation, but in the unity of His divine and human natures, that he went to heaven, and entered into the mystery of the living God, and now lives at the right hand of God the Father Almighty.[133]

Likewise, it is the Spirit who calls the church of Christ into being. According to Barth, the Spirit's unifying work in the ecclesial dimension corresponds to his role in the incarnation (incarnational analogy), and as the bond between the Father and the Son in the Trinity (bond of love analogy).

---

128. For example, Barth, *CD*, I.2, §16, 222, 232–40, 242–50, 277. "The reason, and the only reason, why man can receive revelation in the Holy Spirit is that God's Word is brought to his hearing in the Holy Spirit"; *CD*, I.2, §16, 247. "The work of the Holy Spirit is that our blind eyes are opened and that thankfully and in thankful self-surrender we recognize and acknowledge that it is so: Amen"; *CD*, I.2, §16, 239.

129. Rosato's criticism that Barth limits the Spirit "merely to the noetic task of illumining for the Christian his fully attained salvation" is an overstatement; *The Spirit as Lord*, 160. Thompson correctly maintains that Barth's theology typically combines ontology (being) and dynamic (action), corresponding to his understanding of God as Being in action; Thompson, *The Holy Spirit*, 106.

130. Barth, *CD*, IV/3.2, §72, 761.

131. Although Barth views the incarnation as the work of the Spirit, he is unambiguous that the subject of Jesus Christ is the eternal Son, the Word. "The man Jesus has his existence—*conceptus de Spiritu Sancto*—directly and exclusively in the existence of the eternal Son of God"; Karl Barth, *Credo*, 60.

132. Barth, *CD*, I/2, §15, 199.

133. Barth, *CD*, IV/3.1, §69, 357.

In regard to his incarnational analogy, Barth highlights two things—the *union* of human nature to the Second Person of the Trinity, a union in which the two natures remain distinct, and the essential work of the *Holy Spirit* in bringing about this union. Both aspects together become the ground and framework for the unity of humanity to the Son who becomes the corporate Christ, the Elect in whom humanity is elected by the triune God for salvation,[134] and the ecclesial community which becomes the body of Christ.[135] Through the work of the Holy Spirit, creatures are united with the Creator, without any dissolution of their individual and unique hypostases.[136]

> It is this freedom of the Holy Spirit and in the Holy Spirit that is already involved in the incarnation of the Word of God, in the assumption of human nature by the Son of God, in which we have to recognize the real ground of the freedom of the children of God, the real ground of all conception of revelation, all lordship of grace over man, the real ground of the Church. *The very possibility of human nature's being adopted into unity with the Son of God is the Holy Ghost.*[137]

Barth also applies here the "bond of love" concept as a way of emphasizing that the work of the Spirit in uniting humanity to the Son arises in *love* and *peace*. This union is about eschatological reconciliation, a joyful coming home to a loving God, and not primarily about defeat and dissolution:

> [The Holy Spirit] is the *vinculum pacis* (Eph. 4:3), the *amor*, the *caritas*, the mutual *donum* between the Father and the Son, as it has often been put in the train of Augustine. He is thus the love in which God loves Himself (i.e., loves Himself as the Father and as the Son, and) as the Father loves the Son and as the Son loves the Father.[138]

> Just as the Holy Spirit, as Himself an eternal divine "person" or mode of being, as the Spirit of the Father and the Son (*qui ex Patre Filioque procedit*), is the bond of peace between the two, so in the historical work of the reconciliation He is the One who constitutes and guarantees the unity of the *totus Christus*, i.e., of

---

134. Barth, *CD*, I/2, §15, 199; italics added.
135. Barth, *CD*, I/2, §16, 242.
136. Barth, *CD*, I/2, §16, 215.
137. Barth, *CD*, I/2, §15, 199; italics added.
138. Barth, *CD*, I/1, §12, 470.

> Jesus Christ in the heights and in the depths, in His transcendence and in His immanence.[139]

> In short, the Holy Spirit is the bond of peace (Eph. 4:3), by which Christ has bound us to Himself and united us to Himself, just as already and on high He is the *vinculum pacis* in which the Father and the Son are united. Therefore, the work of the Spirit is nothing other than the work of Jesus Christ . . . As the Spirit of Jesus Christ who, proceeding from Him, unites men closely to Him *ut secum unum sint* ["so that they might be one with Him"].[140]

Interestingly, Barth uses different terms for the human reality which the Spirit binds to Jesus Christ. When referring to Christ as an individual he uses the term "human nature," and when he refers to the christological community, he uses the terms "men" (which includes women), or "us." As discussed earlier, Barth's Christology is Chalcedonian with a tilt towards the Alexandrian position. His use of the terms "men" or "us" when describing the pneumatic union of humans to Christ shows that he has people in view, not an amorphous human principle or substance. While he sees individuals in community and not in isolation, nonetheless, it is human beings who are united to the Son of God in his humanity. This is important when considering Barth's affirmation that believers have died and risen with and in Jesus Christ—this will be examined in the next section. Barth attributes to the Holy Spirit the unitive agency and power that unites the divine and human natures of Christ, and that unites human beings to Christ. In other words, for Barth, pneumatology is foundational for both Christology and ecclesiology.

Humanity Dies and Rises in Christ

Barth writes in no uncertain terms that humanity dies and rises with Jesus Christ. He makes two points. First, the divine judgment on humanity, God's unfaithful covenant partner, is inevitable and certain. No solution to humanity's predicament bypasses God's righteous judgment. Second, it is only in Christ that such a solution exists, and it is necessary for humans to be united to Christ in order to benefit from it. It is in dying and rising with and in Christ that humans participate in God's eschatological kingdom.

---

139. Barth, *CD*, IV/3.2, §72, 760.
140. Barth, *CD*, I/2, §16, 241.

A. Inevitable Judgment

According to the Genesis accounts, God's judgment for the disobedience of the first humans was death (Gen 2:17; 3:3). Having been denied access to the tree of life, mortality became a constant feature of human life (Gen 3:22–24). The Old Testament prophets envisaged Israel's salvation in the form of the restoration of king, land, and temple, rather than eternal life.[141] "Evidence from the Hebrew Scriptures indicates that Israel did not dwell on the question of the after-life until late in the OT period."[142] Even the "new earth" and "new heaven" of Isaiah 65:17 promised national restoration for Israel, and mortal lives fully lived rather than everlasting life.[143] In the intertestamental period, there developed the idea of a future resurrection of all the dead, followed by a divine accounting of individuals, with the expectation that some would be rewarded and others punished.[144] Hopes for the full restoration of Israel's power and prestige, and retribution for her enemies, gradually gave some way to the hope for life beyond the earthly sphere, as centuries of political oppression continued unabated. The view of death, in the form of the end of earthly life, was increasingly viewed as a passage to some other form of existence, whether pleasant or unpleasant.[145] In first-century Palestine, the notion of life after death was therefore not original. Among the first Christians, who were predominantly Jews, there was also a common expectation of a divinely appointed "Last Day," a time of accountability for all humanity, a time and event in which even the dead participated by being brought to life again (John 11:24).[146] The New Testament writers differentiated between the "first" and "second death." Although this two-stage view of death is most prominent in Revelation,[147] its concept is evident elsewhere in the New Testament.[148] This two-stage view of life is the presupposition for Jesus's demand that his disciples give him priority above everything and everyone, even life itself, because he guaranteed that they would not die the second death if they believed him—that is, he claimed he had the authority

---

141. Gowan, *Eschatology*, 5–6, 21–27, 122.

142. Osborne, "Resurrection," 896. See also Sanders, *Paul and Palestinian Judaism*, 125.

143. Johnston, *Shades of Sheol*, 221–24.

144. White, "Resurrection of the Dead," 1017–18; Johnston, "Death and Resurrection," 445.

145. Osborne, "Resurrection," 897–98; Sanders, *Paul and Palestinian Judaism*, 125–26, 142.

146. White, "Resurrection of the Dead," 1018.

147. Rev 2:11; 20:6, 14; 21:8.

148. Matt 10:28; Luke 12:4–5.

to give them eternal life.[149] The New Testament accounts of his ability to bring humans back from the dead, and even more spectacularly, his own resurrection, gave credence to his claim.

With respect to this two-stage understanding of death, how may the death pronounced on humanity in Genesis 2:17 be understood? When he writes about Jesus's death on the cross, Barth has in view both stages of death, although he refers primarily to the second death, which is final and eternal.[150] Hence, according to Barth, Jesus Christ not only experiences the physical death that occurs to all mortal creatures, but also the second death which constitutes the divine judgment pronounced over humanity.[151] "[I]n death we are confronted not only with death itself but also with God; with the very God who is in the right against us and against whom we have done wrong . . . Our end is not a tolerable evil, but the great and serious and intolerable evil, to the extent that in our opposition to God we draw upon ourselves God's opposition to us."[152] If Barth is right, this means that the death that God pronounces on humanity in Genesis 2:17 falls, not at the end of human history on the "Last Day," but in first-century Jerusalem on Jesus of Nazareth, Son of God and Son of Man, God's Elect. On Golgotha, Jesus Christ drank the *whole* cup of divine wrath,[153] and was baptized by the fire of judgment that was humanity's fate.[154] Balthasar concurs: "It is not a matter of just any suffering, but the Old Testament sinking beneath the destroying flood (Isa. 43:2; Ps. 42:8, 68:2ff, etc.). But what unrolls in our context is the *krisis* on the world as a whole (John 12:31), the wholly objective event of judgement, wherein the sin of the world is, in the fullest

---

149. For example, Mark 10:30; Matt 25:46; Luke 18:30; John 3:15–16, 36, 4:14, 6:54, 10:28, etc.

150. Barth, *CD*, III/2, §47, 602–3.

151. Barth, *CD*, III/2, §47, 604–5. "The death of Jesus Christ is unnatural and is determined by God as the proper way of dealing with sinful humanity. By being unnatural, Jesus Christ's death consists of the fullness of God's judgement and wrath . . . This death is described by Barth as no other than the atonement"; Lauber, *Descent into Hell*, 26.

152. Barth, *CD*, III/2, §47, 607–8.

153. Mark 14:36; Matt 20:22; 26:39; Luke 22:42; 18:11. "This was the unique cup which made Jesus shrink back in fear. This is the unique baptism of which He was afraid"; Barth, *CD*, III/2, §47, 603.

154. Mark 10:38–39; Luke 12:50. The fire of divine judgment is a frequent motif in Old and New Testament writings, for example, Gen 19:24; Num 11:1; 16:35; Deut 4:24; 32:22; Ps 28:21; Isa 10:17; 30:30; 31:9; 33:10–14; 66:15–16; Mark 9:43, 48; Matt 3:10–12; 13:40–42; Luke 3:9, 16–17; John 15:6; Rev 18:8; 19:20; 20:9–10, 15.

way possible, laid bare."[155] But by his obedience, humanity is given a second birth, a new beginning, in Jesus Christ:

> There is no mistaking the fact that here man is made to hear a sharp and overwhelming divine No. But there is also no mistaking the fact that this No is enclosed within God's creative, reconciling, and redeeming Yes to man. The Law that binds man is certainly established and proclaimed here, but its divine validity and divinely binding power are due no less certainly to its character as the Law of the covenant and as a form of the Gospel. A condemnation is undoubtedly pronounced and executed at this juncture, but in this very condemnation reconciling grace is clearly displayed, as in the decisive execution of this condemnation on the Cross at Golgotha. Death appears here unmistakably as the meaning and goal of his death.[156]

> In the eternal election of the one man Jesus of Nazareth, God, merciful in his judgement, appoints for man a gracious end and a new gracious beginning. *He makes him die in order that he may truly live.* He makes him pass in order that he may acquire a real future. The purpose of the election of this One is God's righteous and saving will *to deal with man's need at its very root* and show this man the supreme favour by taking his place in the person of this One, taking away from man and upon himself the bitterness of man's own end, and bringing upon man the whole joy of the new beginning. Thus the election of the One is his election to death and to life, to passing and to new coming.[157]

B. In Christ

The idea that reconciliation and redemption take place in Christ, and are only possible in Christ, is important to Barth. This idea underpins his radical doctrine of election which identifies Jesus Christ as "the Elect" in whom humanity is elected. In Christ, sinful humanity has received the divine judgment proclaimed at the beginning of human history. This judgment entailed death, the second death. Barth asserts that Jesus Christ died not only for us

---

155. Balthasar, *Mysterium Paschale*, 123–24.
156. Barth, *Evangelical Theology*, 93.
157. Barth, *CD*, II/2, §34, 260.

(*pro nobis*) as our substitute (*extra nos*), but also as our inclusive representative, enclosing us in his death and resurrection.[158]

> According to [Rom. 6] v. 3 they are certainly to remember that their own dying as sinners took place, and from which, since it was followed by the resurrection of Jesus Christ from the dead, there is opened up the prospect of their own new life beyond this point of nullity . . . Done away once for all in the death of Christ, their existence as sinners is behind them; before them there is only a walk in newness of life corresponding to the raising of Jesus Christ from the dead.[159]

> It [the New Testament community] is "in Christ'—the Crucified and Risen—and Christ is in it. In His death its own death and that of the world is, in fact, already past, and in His life its own life and that of the future world is before it.[160]

> The justification which took place in the resurrection of Jesus Christ confirmed and revealed in what sense God was right in His death—not surrendering but asserting His right against sinful men who, as such, were judged in the death of their Representative, *being destroyed and necessarily crucified and dying with Him*; but also not surrendering His right over these men as His creatures, and therefore re-establishing and maintaining it. The death of Jesus Christ preceded His resurrection . . . This is the sequence and correspondence of the death of Jesus Christ and His resurrection. This is how they are with and after one another the basic events of the alteration of the human situation in which there took place the reconciliation of the world with God.[161]

The old is completely done away with; there is no going back. The world has ended, even though it lives on as though it has not.[162] In that sense, Barth insists that *all* humans have died the second death in Christ, although this second death is not yet actualized in each human's history. Humanity has been reconciled to God in Christ through his death (Rom 5:10).

---

158. Barth, *CD*, I/1, §10, 387; I/2, §16, 261; III/2, §45, 304; IV/4, §75, 117–18. In Lauber's otherwise excellent study on Barth's perspective of Jesus's death, he focuses mainly on Barth's understanding of Christ as the substitute for humanity on the cross, and only glances at Barth's exposition of Christ as the inclusive Elect of God; Lauber, *Descent into Hell*.

159. Barth, *CD*, IV/4, §75, 117–18.

160. Barth, *CD*, IV/1, §59, 311.

161. Barth, *CD*, IV/1, §59, 310–11.

162. Barth, *CD*, IV/1, §57, 77.

Judgment *has* been carried out, and it has been carried out *in Christ*.[163] It is only on that basis that reconciliation can occur, a reconciliation that Paul maintains has taken place at the cross (Rom 5:10). Resurrection is the outcome of reconciliation and demonstrates unequivocally that reconciliation has been achieved. We are reconciled to God not through Christ's resurrection, but through his death. But if the old-world order (and old humanity) has died in Christ, then there is no returning to it; only the new-world order (and new humanity) truly and really exists.[164]

> This means that the event of the end of the world which took place once and for all in Jesus Christ is the presupposition of an old man, and the event of the beginning of the new world which took place once and for all in Jesus Christ is the goal of the new man, and because the goal, therefore the truth and power of the sequence of human existence as it moves towards this goal. The world and every man exist in this alteration. Note that it is not dependent upon whether it is proclaimed well or badly or even at all. It is not dependent upon the way in which it is regarded, upon whether it is realized and fulfilled in faith or unbelief. The coming of the kingdom of God has its truth in itself, not in that which does or does not correspond to it on earth.[165]

C. Pneumatic Death and Rebirth in Christ

Barth does not directly address the specific role of the Holy Spirit at the cross, nor does he use the term *pneumatologica crucis*. He does, however, insist that humanity dies and rises with and in Christ, who is God's Elect. Barth also asserts that the Spirit unites humanity to Jesus Christ, and that the Spirit is with the Son throughout his passion, death, and resurrection. Hence, it is through the power of the Spirit that humanity dies and rises in union with Jesus Christ. Not only does the Spirit maintain this unity between humankind and Christ as he undergoes crucifixion, death, and resurrection, it is the Spirit the life-giver through whom God raises Jesus Christ from the dead, and through whom he brings all the children of God who are created in the risen Christ.[166]

---

163. Barth, *CD*, IV/1, §59, 222.
164. Barth, *CD*, IV/1, §57, 76.
165. Barth, *CD*, IV/1, §59, 312.
166. Barth, *CD*, I/2, §18, 369.

To this Barth adds an intriguing idea. According to Barth, the Holy Spirit not only unites humanity with Christ in the latter's death, but the Spirit is also the Judge—not only is the Spirit the Comforter, but also Judge. The Spirit is Judge with the Father and the Son:[167]

> For only by the knowledge of that revelation, the knowledge of Jesus Christ, do we learn that God is a hidden God. Similarly, it is by the same Holy Spirit by whom God takes up His abode in us and makes us His temple, that God and man are separated with such power and finality, that their unity can no longer be understood except as the unity of the free grace of God with His unconditional adoration by man. We have only to look at it strictly to see that there is not the slightest contradiction between the offices of the Holy Spirit as Comforter and as Judge, between the unity and the distance which He creates . . . The Holy Spirit puts God on one side and man on the other. And then He calls this God our Father and man the child of this Father . . . The miracle does not cease to be a miracle. It will remain a miracle to all eternity of completed redemption.[168]

In the first instance, the Holy Spirit, as Judge, reveals to humans that they are "rebels against this Lord, as unthankful for his kindness, as resisters of His call."[169] This activity is in line with Barth's view of the noetic work of the Spirit in bringing humans to faith in Christ, and as such, is theologically unsurprising. Second, according to Barth, the Holy Spirit, as Judge, and perhaps because of his utter holiness, separates humanity from God so completely that it is only by God's free grace that this distance is overcome. Yet it is the work of the Holy Spirit that the very distance he creates is overcome. Third, Barth attributes to the Holy Spirit, as Judge, the power that makes it possible for humanity to die with Christ. This is a death which Barth determines as the unavoidable first step to redemption, yet it is beyond human capability. This death is not "a natural and self-evident starting-point" nor a work which is in human hands to fulfill.[170] "No, the starting-point, dying, destruction, putting off the old man, being dead, this too is obviously outside the range of our own possibilities . . ."[171] The death that Barth refers to here is the second death. This death is nothing short of

---

167. Barth, *CD*, IV/1, §59, 218–24.
168. Barth, *CD*, I/2, §16, 245.
169. Barth, *CD*, I/2, §16, 245.
170. Barth, *CD*, IV/1/2, §16, 261.
171. Barth, *CD*, IV/1/2, §16, 261.

hell itself.¹⁷² No human being has the power to commit eternal suicide, only temporal suicide. Barth explicitly sees the Holy Spirit as the one through whom humanity is destroyed and raised anew in Christ.

> Of itself the world cannot punish itself: but according to John 16:8f *it is the Comforter, the Holy Spirit, who will punish them, who shall "judge them and kindle a fire"* (Isa. 4:4). The judgement upon man is not his [humanity's] own but God's business.¹⁷³

> But God plunges us into this despair when He reveals Himself to us, *when His Word is made flesh and the judgement of our flesh by the Holy Spirit*, who opens our eyes and ears and therefore kindles our faith. When that occurs, the Christian life begins. We are born and live as the children of God.¹⁷⁴

Thus, in addition to the identification of the Holy Spirit as the one who unites humanity to Christ in his death, Barth also proposes that it is the Holy Spirit who carries out God's judgment on humanity, like the sanctifying fire which consumes the sacrificial offering. Then, and only then, when both sinner and sin are fully and eternally dealt with at the cross, does the Spirit of life regenerate humanity with Christ at the resurrection.

To sum up, Barth's commitment to God's Trinitarian existence and unity of action as Father, Son and Holy Spirit, his radical revisioning of election and predestination in christological terms, his understanding of the Spirit-filled and Spirit-directed messianic Christ, his assertion that humanity is elected insofar as it is united by the Spirit to Christ, the Elect, his affirmation with Paul that humanity dies the second death with Christ, and rises as God's Spirit-born children, and his insight that the Spirit is the divine judge with the Father and the Son, may lead toward a possible Barthian *pneumatologia crucis*. It is highly improbable that Barth would ever consider that the Spirit takes a leave of absence just when Christ is dying on the cross, to wait on the sidelines until his agony and death are complete before springing into action once more, to bring him to life.

7.2 Towards a Multifaceted *Pneumatologia Crucis*

In this section, a summary of the three main positions on the role of the Spirit at the cross championed by John V. Taylor, Jürgen Moltmann, and

---

172. Barth, *CD*, III/1/2, §47, 603.
173. Barth, *CD*, I/2, §16, 262; italics added.
174. Barth, *CD*, I/2, §18, 373; italics added.

John D. Zizioulas are presented, with a brief overview of the core concepts, strengths, and weaknesses of each perspective. All three positions use Hebrews 9:14 as a key text, understanding "through eternal Spirit" as a reference to the *Holy Spirit*. We have seen in chapter 6 that such an understanding is most likely given the manuscript evidence, the early and long hermeneutical tradition, and the pneumatological context of Hebrews. Together with Barth's pneumatological reflections, they provide the building blocks for a multifaceted *pneumatologia crucis*.

Spirit as "Bond of Love"

The "bond of love" position is based upon two premises. The first is the idea, attributed to Augustine, that the Holy Spirit unites the Father and the Son in their eternal relations.[175] The second is the understanding that Jesus's cry of dereliction at the cross (Mark 15:34; Matt 27:46) not only represents God's abandonment of humanity, but more importantly, the Son's abandonment by the Father. According to this model, in humanity's place, the Son experiences the godforsakenness which is the divine judgment for sin. Hence an intra-Trinitarian rupture is seen to occur between the Father and the Son at the cross. However, just as the Holy Spirit unites the Father and the Son in eternity, so the Spirit unites the Son and the Father in their separation at the cross.

The strengths of this perspective are twofold. It frames the cross event as a thoroughly Trinitarian event in which Father, Son and Spirit participate, and it also emphasizes God's love for sinful humanity as the motivation for Christ's suffering, death, and resurrection. No longer is the Father seen as the wrathful God who must be satisfied by Christ's sacrifice of himself, but instead, is envisaged as the grieving Father who loses his Son.

However, there are considerable problems with this position, mainly due to the tenous biblical foundation for its underlying premises. First, and most importantly, while there is ample biblical support for the Spirit's role in uniting believers to Christ and with each other,[176] and for the love between the Father and the Son,[177] there is no explicit support for the idea that the Spirit is the personification of that love, or that the Spirit mediates

---

175. "The Holy Spirit also, whether we are to call Him that absolute love which joins together Father and Son, and joins us also from beneath, that so that it is not unfitly said which is written, 'God is love'"; Augustine, "On the Holy Trinity," vii.4.6 (*NPNF* I/3:108).

176. 1 Cor 12:12–13; Eph 2:18; 4:4–6; 1 John 3:24b.

177. Mark 1:11; John 3:35; 5:20; 14:31; 15:9, 10.

between the Father and the Son. The employment of Romans 8:9 as the exegetical basis for the concept that the Spirit unites the Father and the Son in eternity is not altogether convincing. Moreover, the Johannine witness emphasizes the unmediated intimacy between Jesus and his heavenly Father (John 10:30: "The Father and I are one"; 10:38: ". . . that the Father is in me and I am in my Father"; 14:11: "Believe me that I am in the Father and the Father is in me").

Second, the idea of a rupture in the Father-Son relationship at the cross may have been read back into the cry of *godforsakenness*. The words are more in keeping with the wretched cry of the creature to its Creator than the cry of a son against his father. All three synoptic accounts of Jesus's struggle as he prayed to his Father at Gethsemane end in his determination to be obedient to his Father's will. Jesus Christ the Son went to Golgotha at one in purpose with his Father, and they remained united in this purpose through his death and resurrection.

Third, the "bond of love" image of the Spirit tends to depersonalize the Holy Spirit, and to subordinate the Spirit to the Son and the Father. This metaphor limits the Spirit to a relatively passive role vis-à-vis the Father and the Son, and fails to take into account the biblical witness to the freedom, dynamism, power, and authority of the Spirit seen in John, Acts, Romans, and Revelation. Notwithstanding its influential footprint on a contemporary understanding of the role of the Spirit at the cross, the "bond of love" concept, as it stands alone, is inadequate at best, and misleading at worst. Nevertheless, if the "bond of love" idea is applied, not to the relationship between the Father and the Son, but that between Christ and humanity, it aligns better with the biblical witness and makes a stronger contribution to *pneumatologia crucis*.

Spirit as Coworker with the Son

The second perspective sees the Holy Spirit as an active co-participant in the Son's soteriological work, not only in the noetic or subjective sense *after* the cross event, but also *during* Jesus's passion, death, and resurrection. According to this position, the Spirit's participation involves indwelling and empowering Jesus Christ, empathetically suffering with him, accompanying him through the portal of death (yet without dying with him), and raising him from the dead.

The strengths of this second position are threefold. First, it is better aligned with the biblical portrayal of the Spirit's prominent involvement at key points of the Son's messianic mission, namely, Jesus's birth, baptism, ministry, and resurrection. Jesus is described as being filled with the Spirit (Luke 4:1, 14; John 3:34). The Lukan account highlights that Spirit anointment is that which defines Jesus's messiahship and mission (Luke 4:18–21; cf. Acts 10:38), and all four gospel accounts assert that Jesus is the Spirit-baptizer, a unique role not attributed to any other biblical character. Indeed, throughout the New Testament, the indwelling of the eschatological Spirit is the *sine qua non* of every disciple of Jesus Christ; it is the Spirit of the Son who ensures that believers are also sons (children) of God (Rom 8:14–16). Thus, this perspective envisages a greater integration of pneumatology and Christology at the cross. Second, the personhood of the Spirit is made clearer here in comparison with the "bond of love" view. The Holy Spirit is seen to be actively working alongside the Son to achieve the Father's plan of salvation, and the Spirit's life-giving role in raising Jesus from the dead and rebirthing the new Spirit-indwelt humanity is adequately acknowledged. Third, the Spirit's participation in the Son's suffering is empathetic, and this is in keeping with the biblical portrayal of a God who suffers with his people (Isa 63:9), and whose Spirit grieves (Isa 63:9; Eph 4:30). This position carefully maintains, however, that the Spirit himself does not undergo death.

The deficiencies of this position, notwithstanding its strengths, are first, that it marginalizes God the Father at the cross so that he almost seems to be *Deus absconditus*. Although it is the Father's will that the Son and the Spirit undertake, the active participants at the cross appear to be mainly the Son and the Spirit. Thus, as it stands, this position is not truly Trinitarian. Second, this perspective does not sufficiently take into account the involvement of humanity at the cross. Jesus Christ is perceived as an individual, suffering and dying *on behalf* of humanity, while humanity itself seems to stand outside the cross event. In other words, Christ is viewed as an exclusive rather than an inclusive representative of humanity at the cross. Although Christ's substitutionary work has strong biblical support, this single view of the atonement does not exhaust the theological reflections of the New Testament writers. For example, Paul also asserts, using insistent and graphic language, that believers themselves participate in Jesus's death and resurrection (Rom 6:3–11; Gal 2:19–20; Col 2:12–14; 3:3), and because Christ died for all, "therefore all died" (ἄρα οἱ πάντες ἀπέθανον; 2 Cor 5:15).

Spirit as Unifier

The third major position on *pneumatologia crucis* emphasizes the role of the Spirit as the one who unites humanity to Christ at the cross. Here, the central idea is that the Spirit is the Spirit of κοινωνία. The Spirit's unifying power not only constitutes Christology (uniting the divine and human natures of Christ), but also *corporate* Christology (uniting humanity to Christ), so that Jesus Christ lives, dies, and rises as the corporate Christ, not as a single individual. This position also asserts that the Holy Spirit is the Spirit of freedom and the Spirit of the *eschaton*. Being the Spirit of freedom, he frees Christ from the limits of time and space, so that the Christ's work on the cross transcends time and space, and as he gathers humanity to Christ, the Spirit ensures that human hypostases remain distinct and unique, and do not dissolve into Christ. Being the Spirit of the *eschaton*, he creates a new humanity whose roots lie in the eschatological future; in Christ, the old humanity is judged and destroyed, and in Christ, the new Spirit-indwelt humanity lives. Salvation is thus understood in both moral and ontological terms. In common with the second perspective of the Spirit as coworker with the Son at the cross, the Spirit is also envisaged as the one who empowers Christ, and who suffers with Christ but does not die with him.

This is probably the strongest theological position with regard to the Spirit's role at the cross. There is ample New Testament support for the Spirit's unifying activity. The union of divine and human nature in the incarnation of the Son occurs through the Spirit's power (Matt 1:18, 20; Luke 1:35),[178] and the union of believers to Christ[179] takes place through the Spirit (1 Cor 6:11–19; 12:12–13; Eph 2:16–18). Aside from its coherence with the New Testament witness, this position also addresses gaps in the preceding two perspectives. First, it pays greater attention to the Pauline concept that believers participate in Christ's death, burial, and resurrection. Humanity is not an onlooker to the Christ event, standing by until it is finished, in order to reap its benefits. The inclusive representation of the corporate Christ addresses both moral and ontological problems of the fall—both sin and sinner are dealt with in Christ. Second, this position affirms that through the eternal Spirit, Christ's work on the cross transcends time and space, reaching out to all humanity in every age and in every location. Third, it envisages with Paul a thoroughly radical and comprehensive renewal of the human being, one who henceforth breathes and lives in the freedom of the Spirit, and one for whom addiction to sin is illogical and nonsensical.

---

178. Although the Johannine account does not describe Jesus's birth, since those who belong to God are born of the Spirit (John 3:5–6), and since Jesus is clearly portrayed as the one upon whom the Spirit remains and who gives the Spirit (John 1:32–33; 20:22), it is reasonable to deduce that the Word became flesh (John 1:14) through the Spirit.

179. John 15:1–8; Rom 12:5; 1 Cor 3:16–17; 12:12–27; Eph 1:22–23; 2:15–16, 21–22, 4:4, 12–16; 5:29–32; Col 1:18; 2:19; 3:15.

One weakness of this position is, however, its trajectory towards universalism. The very notion of the corporate Christ, as described by Zizioulas and Barth, tends to suggest that humanity in its entirety are elected in Jesus Christ the Elect. There are those, of course, who view this concept positively.[180] Here, Dunn's proposal that all die in Christ but only believers rise with him, has merit.[181] Another weakness of this position is one that is shared with the second, namely, the marginalization of the Father's role at the cross. Christology and pneumatology are in the forefront here, while the Father's ongoing participation is less clearly explicated.

Barthian Pneumatological Perspectives

We have seen that Barth himself does not directly address the subject of a *pneumatologia crucis*. Nevertheless, he insists that God is irreducibly the Father, Son and Holy Spirit; that the unifying Spirit is the "bond of love"; that God's actions in the economy are always Trinitarian; that Jesus Christ is the pneumatic Christ; that election should be understood as the election of Jesus Christ; that humanity is united to Christ through the Spirit; and that humanity is judged, destroyed, and reborn in Christ through the power of the Holy Spirit. These views cohere well with many elements in the three major perspectives of the Spirit's role at the cross put forward by Taylor, Moltmann, and Zizioulas. Barth, however, is likely to disagree with the particular application of the "bond of love" idea to the cross event in which he sees *humanity* rejected by *God* in Jesus Christ the Elect, rather than that a rupture occured between the First and Second Persons of the Trinity. Nonetheless, the concepts of the Spirit as unifier and as the Son's coworker at the cross align with his overall pneumatology and Christology. In addition, Barth supplies the valuable insight that the Spirit is not only humanity's teacher and comforter but also, with the Father and the Son, is humanity's *judge*. Since he locates the fulfillment of God's judgment at the cross in Jesus Christ and not at the *eschaton*, this implies that the Spirit is present as divine judge at Golgotha. Although the formal categorization of "Spirit as Judge" as a specific Barthian *pneumatologia crucis* is probably a step too far, this idea is an important contribution to the construction of a multifaceted understanding of the role of the Spirit at the cross of Christ.

---

180. For example, Pinnock, *Wideness in God's Mercy*; Sanders, *No Other Name*.
181. Dunn, *Christ and the Spirit, vol. 1*, 196. See chapter 6; §6.4, in this book.

7.3 The Cross as "Crucible": A New Proposal for a *Pneumatologia Crucis*

The three perspectives of *pneumatologia crucis* viewed each by themselves are deficient in one way or another, but when they are brought together, and integrated with Barth's pneumatological insights, they provide a more comprehensive understanding of the Holy Spirit's role at the cross. The vision of the Spirit as "bond of love," when applied to Christ and humanity rather than between the Father and the Son, dovetails into the concept of the Spirit as the "unifier." Both perspectives derive from the recognition of the Holy Spirit as the Spirit of κοινωνία, and together they emphasize that the horror of Jesus's suffering and death paradoxically expresses the triumph of God's love, grace, and mercy towards sinful humanity. The Spirit indwells Jesus Christ from the time of his birth, and empowers him throughout his ministry, life, passion, and death, enabling him to fulfill his heavenly Father's will. The Father's loving will is to lead us through the death we deserve into eternal life.[182] The human nature that the Son enfolds to himself, that which is creaturely in Jesus Christ, is a Spirit-constituted, Spirit-directed and Spirit-empowered human nature. Through the Spirit, humankind is brought into union with the humanity of Christ. In this way, humankind participates in the recapitulating history of the second Adam, the corporate Christ, a history which traverses the cross and the second death into the resurrection. At the cross, the Spirit not only maintains the unity of humanity with Christ as he dies, is buried, and is raised from the dead, but the Holy Spirit also carries out God's judgment on sin and sinful humanity, in Christ. Hence, through the Son and the Spirit, the triune God achieves reconciliation and communion with his creatures, his eschatological goal for creation.

The crucible, in which metals are melted together and refined by fire, may be helpful as a spatial metaphor in envisaging this synthesis: Jesus Christ is the triune God's "crucible" brought into being by the power of the Holy Spirit, in whom the Spirit unites humanity to the Son, in whom the Spirit executes God's judgment (the annihilation of sin and sinful humanity), and in whom the Spirit re-creates humanity as the Spirit-indwelt human children of God the Father.

In this "crucible" construal, the Spirit carries out four main roles at the cross—as divine power, unifier, consuming fire and life-giver. These functions, of course, are not confined to the cross event, but are in keeping with the Spirit's overall and continuing work in the life of Christ and of Christians.

---

182. "God the Father wills neither our life in itself nor our death in itself. He wills our life in order to lead it through death to eternal life. He wills death in order to lead our life through it to eternal life"; Barth, *CD*, 1/1, §10, 388.

The attribution of these roles to the Holy Spirit is not intended to minimise the co-participation of the Father and the Son, nor is the work of the Spirit limited to these four areas. Nevertheless, a common thread that links these four roles is the view of the Holy Spirit as divine executive. Together with the Son, the Spirit executes the Father's will. The Spirit is involved in all the activities of the Son, not repetitively nor competitively, but complementarily, in order that the Father's will for creation is accomplished.

1. *Spirit as Divine Power*

According to the New Testament narrative, it was through the power of the Holy Spirit that Mary became pregnant with her son Jesus, without any human paternal contribution. Through the power of the Holy Spirit the Second Person of the Trinity took on human form and nature at the incarnation. Jesus was born, Son of God and Son of Man—the God-man. When the adult Jesus was baptized by John at the Jordan, the Holy Spirit descended on him. Jesus's divine sonship was proclaimed and his messianic ministry was inaugurated. Returning from his baptism, full of the Holy Spirit, Jesus was driven out into the desert by the Spirit, to be tempted by the devil. Throughout this encounter, Jesus showed himself to be the obedient and faithful Son of his heavenly Father, refusing to transcend the human condition or to deviate from his commitment to humanity's destiny, refusing to claim his privilege as God's Son bypassing the cross of judgment and reconciliation. Filled with the Holy Spirit, he began his ministry in Galilee.

Through the power of the Spirit, Jesus preached, healed, exorcised demons, raised the dead, and performed miracles. As the second Adam, Jesus Christ, God's Son in human flesh, lived and served in the power of the Spirit, as the firstborn of all humans born of the Spirit. In the Spirit's power, the human Jesus was sinless. Not one of his accusers could charge him with any moral sin except that of perceived blasphemy. Through the power of the Spirit, Jesus Christ endured betrayal, capture, trial, abuse, torture, and crucifixion. Through the power of the Spirit, Jesus Christ bore humanity's judgment and died the second death. Reconciliation took place in Christ through his death (Rom 5:10). Through the power of the Spirit, God raised him from the dead, and because reconciliation was achieved, God raised with him the new humanity. It is important to note that humanity is reconciled to God *at the cross*, and not in the resurrection.

2. Spirit as Divine Unifier

In Christ, the Holy Spirit unites human nature to the Second Person of the Trinity. In Hebrews, one of the important features of Jesus Christ's high priesthood is his becoming in every respect like the people he was born to save, except that he did not sin (Heb 2:17; 4:15; cf. Rom 3:4; 2 Cor 5:21). Calvin asserts that the human nature appropriated by the Son, through the Spirit, was the pure and undefiled prelapsarian human nature.[183] On the other hand, in accordance with the patristic dictum "that which is not assumed is not healed," Barth argues that the human nature appropriated by the Son is fallen human nature, although Jesus himself lived a sinless life.[184] Both are valid perspectives. Calvin is correct that Jesus, as the second Adam, has prelapsarian freedom of choice; he is not caught in the thrall of sin. "He knew no sin" (τὸν μὴ γνόντα ἁμαρτίαν; 2 Cor 5:21), meaning that Jesus had no relationship with sin. It is in his identity as the second Adam that Jesus is tempted to assert his divine sonship prematurely, bypassing his messianic solidarity with humanity, and bypassing the cross. The first humans freely chose to disobey God. In contrast, the second Adam, at every point in his life, freely chooses to obey God. In unity with the Father and the Holy Spirit, Jesus Christ carries out the salvation plan of the triune God in solidarity and union with fallen humanity. Barth, on the other hand, is right to insist that in order to redeem fallen human existence, Christ has to assume it completely. If Christ assumes fallen human nature, then how is he pure and without sin? Barth answers that question with the idea that the Logos, being the subject of Jesus Christ, sanctifies human existence.[185] However, if this is so, and the very union of the Logos with human nature sanctifies it, then what is the need for the cross? If the incarnation is the complete solution to sin, then the atonement is superfluous.

Nevertheless, perhaps both perspectives are valid if the unifying work between the Son and humankind in Jesus Christ is twofold—the Spirit unites prelapsarian human nature to the Son, and then fallen human beings to the incarnate Son. Hendrikus Berkhof, in describing the corporate personality of Jesus, states: "First [the Spirit] creates the One; then he includes

---

183. While Calvin maintains that in Christ, "human likeness was manifest in a lowly and abased condition," and that "the Son of God in human nature had been weak," he stresses that "we make Christ free of all stain not just because he was begotten of his mother without copulation with man, but because he was sanctified by the Spirit that the true generation might be pure and undefiled as would have been true *before Adam's fall*"; *Institutes*, II.13.2, 4; italics added.

184. Barth, *CD*, I.2, §15, 151–56.

185. Barth, *CD*, I.2, §15, 160.

the many in the One. The Spirit rests on Jesus and the Spirit goes out from Jesus. He on whom the Spirit remains, this is he who baptises with the Holy Spirit."[186] Thus the state of the second Adam truly corresponds to that of the first human pair. He has a prelapsarian freedom of choice. The incarnate Son, however, lives kenotically in the fallen human condition, and it is the indwelling Spirit who empowers him to remain sinless. The Spirit not only unites human nature to the Son, but also unites sinful human beings to the incarnate Son, in his humanity. As Zizioulas maintains, individual human hypostases are united to the hypostasis of the incarnate Son, so that he is the corporate Christ. In the corporate Christ, with his death and resurrection, sinful humanity dies, and the new Spirit-indwelt humanity is born. This scenario satisfies Calvin's important assertion that Jesus Christ has prelapsarian freedom of choice, and also Barth's equally important assertion that human existence is completely healed in Christ.

At the cross, Jesus Christ's humanity incorporates ours. As humanity's inclusive high priest, Jesus, God's anointed Messiah or Christ, carries within him the holy people of God before the Father, just as the Israelite high priests bore the names of the twelve tribes of Israel upon their chests and shoulders year after year in the Day of Atonement ritual (Leviticus 16, Hebrews 9). Paul stresses that baptism signifies union with Christ in his death and resurrection (Rom 6:3–5). According to Dunn, in Romans, Paul "insists that the initiating experience of the Spirit brings about not only a belonging to Christ (8:9), not only a sharing in his risen life (8:10), but also a union with Christ the crucified, a sharing in his death," so that being baptized into Christ means being baptized in the Spirit, and vice versa.[187] Therefore, believers are baptized into Christ's death through the Spirit. Thomas Torrance rightly asserts:

> Christ was on the one hand so one with God that what he did, God did, for he was none other than God himself acting thus in our humanity. And therefore there is no other God for us than this God, and no other action of God toward us than this action in which he stood in our place and acted on our behalf. On the other hand, he was so one with us that when he died, for he did not die for himself but for us, and *he did not die alone, but we died in him as those whom he had bound to himself inseparably by his incarnation. Therefore when he rose again we rose in him and with him,* and when he presented himself before the face

---

186. Berkhof, *Doctrine of the Holy Spirit*, 19.
187. Dunn, *Christ and the Spirit*, vol. 2, 115.

of the Father, he presented us also before God, so that we are already accepted of God in him once and for all.[188]

Adoptionist christologies fail to comprehend fully the soteriological importance of the incarnation. They fail because Jesus's death is viewed as the death of an individual human, albeit a vicarious death, and they do not address the underlying ontological problem of sin-tendency in fallen humanity. It is not possible for a human being to bear the sins of billions of people, or to represent all of them in death. No human is able to endure this pneumatic union of all humanity with himself. No human can endure the total fullness of the Spirit. Only God can do so. Only the Logos, the Son of God, is holy, perfect, and mighty enough to be indwelt with the fullness of the Holy Spirit. Only the divine Logos is capable of encompassing every sinful human being who has ever lived within himself, so that God's "No" can be finally and fully uttered, so that sin and evil can be perfectly destroyed, and so that sinful humanity, in whom sin is so deeply rooted that no superficial alteration is ever sufficient, is destroyed. Only the Logos is big enough for the task. But it is a task done with the Holy Spirit. As Barth asserts:

> Everything happened to us exactly as it had to happen, but because God willed to execute His judgement on us in His Son it all happened in His person, as His accusation and condemnation and destruction. He judged, and it was the Judge who was judged, who let Himself be judged. Because He was a man like us, He was able to be judged like us. Because He was the Son of God and Himself God, He had the competence and power to allow this to happen to Him.[189]

Since the redemptive task concerns human beings, only a human can undertake it. For this reason, God becomes human in the Son, to accomplish what humans cannot do on their own. And only God the Spirit can unite human beings and human nature to God the Son in Jesus Christ, so that human nature itself can be re-created, and human beings reborn as children of God the Father. Only the eternal Spirit can reach out to all humans through time and space to unite them with the Son in Christ, so that Christ's once-for-all atonement achieves eternal redemption for humanity (Heb 9:12–15, 26–28).

There is perhaps yet another perspective from which to understand the necessity of the incarnation for the success of God's redemption plan. Although God has supreme power, his Holy Spirit can be "quenched" (1

---

188. Torrance, *Atonement*, 152, italics added.
189. Barth, *CD*, IV/1, §59, 222–23.

Thess 5:19) and "grieved" (Isa 63:9; Eph 4:30). The Creator gives his creatures a voice in their destiny. He does not rape, he woos. The New Testament images of Christ as a head loving and nurturing his body, and as a husband loving and nurturing his wife, provide insights into God's love for his creatures, and his desire to be freely loved in return. The acceptance of God's redemption plan for humanity, which involved the fulfillment of his just judgment (death and separation from God), followed by rebirth into life in the Spirit (intimate communion with God), is a choice that only humans can make for themselves. According to Zizioulas, fallen humanity no longer have the capacity for making that choice.[190] Without the indwelling presence of the Spirit, humans are no longer truly free. Ironically, without rebirth, humans are unable to accommodate the Spirit. In a sense, this is a "catch-22" situation. The incarnation provided an opportunity to resolve this human predicament. Jesus Christ, the only prelapsarian human after the fall who remains truly free because of the indwelling Spirit—and only he had the full indwelling presence of the Spirit prior to the cross (John 3:34; 7:39)—makes the choice to trust and obey his heavenly Father, continually and perfectly. The firmness of his commitment to God is severely tested in the desert after his baptism, but it is most at risk in the garden of Gethsemane. The responsibility for the destiny of entire humanity, both past, present and future, lay in the hands of Jesus the God-human. Through the power of the Holy Spirit, Jesus made the choice, freely, that changed human history, and humanity itself, forever.[191]

3. Spirit as Consuming Fire

It is clear that divine judgment must occur if reconciliation is to succeed, and if humanity is to be reborn. It is also clear that it is God who is the Judge. God is described as a consuming fire (Heb 12:29; cf. Deut 4:24). Jesus anticipated that his earthly ministry would end in a cup of wrath and a baptism of judgment (Mark 10:38; 14:36; Matt 20:22; 26:39; Luke 12:49–50; John 18:11). In the New Testament, divine judgment and hell are very often associated with burning.[192] John the Baptist called for repentance in response to God's impending fiery judgment (Matt 3:10, 12; Luke 3:9, 17), and he associated the Holy Spirit with fire (Matt 3:11; Luke 3:16). At Pentecost, tongues of fire signified the presence of the Holy

---

190. Zizioulas, "Human Capacity," 434–40.

191. Zizioulas, *Lectures*, 107; *Lessons*, E.6 ("Salvation").

192. Some examples include Mark 9:43, 48; Matt 3:12; 5:22; Luke 3:17; 17:29; John 15:6; 1 Cor 3:13; 2 Thess 1:7; Heb 10:27; 2 Peter 3:7, 10–12; Jude 7; Rev 20:9, 14–15.

Spirit (Acts 2:3–4). Interestingly, the notion that the Holy Spirit can be "quenched" (σβέννυμι; 1 Thess 5:19) portrays the Spirit as a fire that can be extinguished. In Isaiah 4:4, the prophet envisaged a future restoration for Israel in which Jerusalem is purged and made holy "by a spirit of judgment and by a spirit of burning" (Isa 4:4). Barth views this phrase as a reference to the Holy Spirit.[193] In Israel's cultic liturgy, *fire* plays a major role, and the primary sacrifices that signify Israel's relationship with YHWH are the "whole burnt offering" (Lev 1:3)[194] and the "sin offering" (Lev 4:3).[195] The entire animal for the whole burnt offering is burned on the altar except for its skin (Lev 1:6–9; 7:8). When the sin offering represents the high priest, or the whole community, a portion of the animal is burned on the altar, while the rest including the hide, flesh, entrails, legs, and dung, are completely burned outside the camp (Lev 4:8–12).[196] The fire on the sacrificial altar is kept burning day and night (Lev 6:12–13). In his commentary on Hebrews 9:14, John Owen's visualization of the Holy Spirit as "the eternal fire" under Christ's sacrifice of himself is not, therefore, so farfetched.[197] Albert Vanhoye also links the image of sacrificial fire to the Holy Spirit.[198] Furthermore, the sanctifying activity of the Holy Spirit is visualized amongst sacrificial metaphors (Rom 15:15–16; 1 Peter 1:2).[199]

The use of fire as a symbol for the Holy Spirit and for divine judgment is not surprising given its important place in Israel's theophanic and covenantal narratives, and in its practical application in Israel's sacrificial rituals. In the Day of Atonement rituals (Lev 16), all the animal sacrifices, both for the sin offering (a bull representing the high priest, and a goat representing the people) and the whole burnt offering (two rams), are slaughtered beside the altar *outside* the sanctuary (Lev 16:6, 11, 23). The high priest then takes some of the blood of the sin offering to be sprinkled on and before the ark of the covenant in the inner sanctuary, as well as on the sacrificial altar outside, in order to purify these areas from his sins and the sins of the people (Lev 16:14–16, 18). Entry into the inner sanctuary can only be made when

---

193. Barth, *CD*, I/2, §16, 262.

194. עֹלָה (*'ōlâh*) in Hebrew, and ὁλοκαύτωμα in Greek.

195. חַטָּאת (*ḥaṭṭā't*) in Hebrew and ἁμαρτία in Greek.

196. Sin offerings representing individual non-ordained Israelites are not completely burned in the way that sin offerings representing the high priest or the whole community are. The idea is that when the high priest sins, his sin brings guilt upon the entire community (Lev 4:3).

197. Owen, *Death of Death*, 178.

198. Vanhoye, *Structure and Message*, 68; "Esprit éternel et feu du sacrifice en He 9,14," 263–74; cited in Emmrich, *Pneumatological Concepts*, 2.

199. See chapter 6, §6.3 in this book.

accompanied by the sacrificial blood of the sin offering. In the sanctuary, atonement having been made and covenantal relationship restored, the high priest then presents the whole people of Israel before God, presumably in prayerful mediation. The slain rams for the whole burnt offering are subsequently burned on the altar (Lev 16:23–25; cf. Lev 1:3–9). Parts of the slain bull and goat for the sin offering are burned on the altar, with the rest of the carcasses completely burned to ashes outside the camp (Lev 16:27; cf. Lev 4:3–12). In addition to these burnt sacrifices, a second live goat is used to signify the departure of sin from the camp, far away into the desert and away from God's people (Lev 16:7–10, 20–22).

If the writer of Hebrews is correct, and these rituals are an interpretive window into the mystery of Christ's atoning sacrifice, then it must be emphasized that Christ's self-offering in the heavenly tabernacle is made at the altar *outside* the sanctuary as the sin offering for the whole of humanity (2 Cor 5:21).[200] By his sacrifice, Christ opens a new and living way for humanity through the curtain (which is identified with Christ's flesh; Heb 10:20) separating God from sinful humanity. *After his sacrifice*, the resurrected Christ enters the heavenly sanctuary with his blood, in order to present the newly created humanity before God, and to prayerfully intercede for them (Heb 9:11–12, 15). The heavenly sanctuary is revealed to be nothing less than God's very own presence. Here Jesus Christ sits beside his Father (Heb 10:12). By way of Christ's sacrificial blood, humanity's access into God's presence is now unhindered by the impenetrable curtain of sin, and open to those who are not anointed priests (Heb 10:19, 29). Other insights into Christ's atoning work in the Day of Atonement liturgy may be seen in the sacrifice of the rams on the altar as the whole burnt offering, in the burning of the remaining parts of the sin offering outside the camp (cf. Heb 13:12–13; Rev 14:20), and the removal of the sin-bearing goat far away from the community (cf. 1 Peter 2:24; Heb 9:28), demonstrating the utter destruction of the sinner and complete exclusion of sin.

In Hebrews, the Holy Spirit's participation occurs at several points. The Spirit calls Christians to attend to the prophetic call for faith and obedience (Heb 3:7), reveals the earthly tabernacle as provisional and anticipatory (Heb 9:8), functions as the witness to the new covenant that is secured through Jesus's blood (Heb 10:15), and is the eschatological Gift as well as the provider of spiritual gifts (Heb 2:4, 6:4). Importantly, it is through the eternal Spirit that Christ makes the offering of himself to God

---

200. The noun ἁμαρτία, rendered "sin" in many English translations, can also mean "sin offering," following the Septuagint translation of Leviticus. Thus in 2 Cor 5:21, Paul uses the word in both ways—although Jesus knew no sin (τὸν μὴ γνόντα ἁμαρτίαν), God made him sin or a sin offering (ἁμαρτίαν ἐποίησεν) on our behalf.

(Heb 9:14). According to the Levitical rituals, the sacrificial procedure involves not only the death of the animal but includes the entire burning up of the sacrifice. It is conceivable, therefore, that the Holy Spirit is involved in Christ's atoning sacrifice.

The covenantal sacrifices enacted in the Levitical rituals are only some of the ways to help understand Christ's sacrifice. Other biblical metaphors include Abraham's near-sacrifice of Isaac (Gen 22:1–14), the Passover lamb (Exod 12:13), the Isaianic servant (Isa 53:4–12), and the good shepherd who lays down his life for his sheep (John 10:11–18). It is likely that all these perspectives put together do not fully explicate Christ's salvific sacrifice.

In the narrative of Abraham's near-sacrifice of Isaac, a father is commanded to sacrifice his beloved "only" son.[201] In the case of Jesus Christ, his heavenly Father not only "gave" (ἔδωκεν, John 3:16), but "gave up" or "handed over" (παρέδωκεν, Rom 8:32) his only Son. These verbs convey some sense of the anguish and horror that any parent would feel in a similar circumstance. Jesus's physical death was brought about by humans. On the other hand, if his atoning death encloses within it the second death of humanity, then this second death could not have been brought about by anyone else but by God himself (Matt 10:28). If Abraham represents God the Father, and Isaac represents Jesus, perhaps the Holy Spirit is represented by the knife that kills, and by the consuming and sanctifying fire that burns. Using more prosaic terminology, if the Father is the subject of humanity's judgment, and humanity (in the incarnate Son) its object, then perhaps the Spirit is its executive. Yet Barth is also correct in stating that Jesus Christ "is the subject and not the object of what happens—the subject even when He is object."[202] In the words of Torrance:

> Jesus Christ is our mediator, who entered into the presence of God who is a consuming fire and we see that judgement and fire upon the cross. But from the cross too there comes the voice of amazing love: the voice of incredible love and mercy and pardon right in the heart of judgement—that is why it is such incredible love.[203]

---

201. In the biblical narrative, Abraham sent Hagar and Ishmael away (Gen 21), so that Isaac was effectively Abraham's "only" son when God commanded Abraham to sacrifice him (Gen 22).

202. Barth, *CD*, IV/1, §59, 235.

203. Torrance, *Atonement*, 85.

Jesus's Cry of Dereliction

At this point it is appropriate to examine Jesus's anguished cry of godforsakenness (Mark 15:34; Matt 27:46). Both synoptic evangelists use the Greek verb ἐγκατέλιπές (literally, "left behind," in the aorist indicative), probably quoting from the LXX version of Psalm 22:1, to depict an experience of abandonment by God. The textual evidence for this word is weighty, although there are minor variations in spelling and word order among the manuscripts. A thorough discussion of the historicity and authenticity of Jesus's cry of dereliction goes beyond the scope of this present study, but for the purposes of my investigation into the Spirit's role at the cross, Mark 15:34 and Matthew 27:46 are accepted as canonical testimonies, together with the corresponding passages in Luke 23:46 and John 19:30.

While Barth, Taylor and Moltmann understand Jesus's cry of dereliction to signify his experience of godforsakenness, there are differences in their interpretation of that cry. For Taylor and Moltmann, Jesus's cry of dereliction signifies a rupture within the Trinity at the cross, a rift between the first and second Persons. Hence the idea of the Spirit as the mediating "bond of love" between the Father and the Son informs Taylor's view of *pneumatologia crucis*, and likewise the second of Moltmann's three perspectives of the Spirit's work at the cross. Zizioulas, of course, disagrees completely with the concept of the Spirit as mediator between the Father and the Son, and has therefore no place in his pneumatology for any "bond of love" role for the Spirit. As for Barth, Jesus's cry is the cry of *humanity* undergoing judgment:

> But the self-humiliation of God in His Son is genuine and actual, and therefore there is no reservation in respect of His solidarity with us. He did become—and this is the presupposition of all that follows—the brother of man, threatened with man, harassed and assaulted with him, with him in the stream which hurries downwards to the abyss, hastening with him to death, to the cessation of being and nothingness. With him he cries—knowing far better than any other how much reason there is to cry: "My God, my God, why has thou forsaken me?" (Mark 15:34). *Deus pro nobis* means simply that God has not abandoned the world and man in the unlimited need of his situation, but that He willed to bear this need as his own, and that He took it upon Himself, and that He cries with man in this need.[204]

---

204. Barth, *CD*, IV/1, §59, 215.

And, of course, the question of the Crucified: Had God forsaken Him? (Mark 15:34) . . . No, God had not really forsaken Him.[205]

Bruce McCormack stands with Taylor and Moltmann against Barth when he affirms that the Son is indeed abandoned. On the other hand, he rejects the idea that the Spirit unites the Father and the Son at the cross. McCormack states that "[i]t will not do . . . to speak of the Spirit as continuing to bind Father and Son together in their separation in death."[206] Instead, he is of the view that the break in relationship occurs between the Son and the other two members of the Trinity, rather than between the Son and the Father. He writes, "no death in God-abandonment can occur unless the Son is finally abandoned by both Father and Spirit."[207] It is important, however, to note that McCormack carefully nuances what he means by the term "Son." With Barth, McCormack asserts that the Second Person of the Trinity is a composite God-human, not only in historic time, but from eternity. "For if the pre-existent Logos is already a 'composite Person,' then the Chalcedonian identification of the 'person' with the pre-existent Logos is upheld."[208] For McCormack, Christ's suffering and death represents the suffering and death of the Son's *humanity*. In other words, the cross is a human experience for the Son. Yet while McCormack emphasizes that "it is God who suffers and dies *humanly*," he also insists that "it is *God* who suffers humanly," and that it is the Second Person of the Trinity who takes the human experience of God-abandonment into his own divine life.[209] With Balthasar, McCormack sees the God-abandonment beginning at Gethsemane when Jesus's fervent prayer to his *Abba* is seemingly unanswered. Jesus then drinks the "cup" that represents "the entry of the sin of the world into the personal existence, body and soul, of the representative Substitute and Mediator."[210] McCormack agrees with Barth and Balthasar that Christ suffered more than the physical death on the cross, and that he endured hell itself, the eternal and complete separation from God that humanity justly deserves. With respect to the Spirit, therefore, and despite the fact that he strongly affirms the formative role of the Spirit for Christology,[211] McCormack suggests

205. Barth, *CD*, IV/1, §59, 239.
206. McCormack, "Loud Cries and Tears," 55.
207. McCormack, "Loud Cries and Tears," 55.
208. McCormack, "Loud Cries and Tears," 48.
209. McCormack, "Loud Cries and Tears," 51, 55.
210. Balthasar, *Mysterium Paschale*, 119–24; McCormack, "Loud Cries and Tears," 54.
211. McCormack, "Loud Cries and Tears," 40.

that when Jesus "gave up the spirit" (παρέδωκεν τὸ πνεῦμα, John 19:30), it is at the point of death when the Spirit departs from him.[212] Interestingly, Balthasar has a different understanding of παρέδωκεν τὸ πνεῦμα; he sees instead that the the Spirit has been set "free" to be breathed into the church by the risen Christ.[213] Barth, however, would probably not agree with either Balthasar or McCormack in this instance, as he insists that "Jesus has the Holy Spirit lastingly and totally," and therefore, "the word 'spirit' is used in a general anthropological sense."[214]

In the Fourth Gospel, while the phrase τὸ πνεῦμα is often used for the Holy Spirit, it is also used to refer to the wind (τὸ πνεῦμα, John 3:8, where there is a clear pun between "wind" and "Spirit"), and to Jesus's human spirit (τῷ πνεύματι without the qualifying pronoun αὐτοῦ, John 11:33; 13:21). It is also significant that in all four gospel accounts, Jesus's final moment is described as his letting out or letting go of πνεῦμα (Mark 15:37, ἐξέπνευσεν, "he expired"; Matt 27:50, ἀφῆκεν τὸ πνεῦμα, "he released the breath/spirit"; Luke 23:46, ἐξέπνευσεν, "he expired"; John 19:30, παρέδωκεν τὸ πνεῦμα, "he handed over the breath/spirit"). Given the physical circumstances of crucifixion in which death occurs by asphyxiation when the victim is no longer able to push himself up to breathe (John 19:31), these descriptive clauses may indicate that Jesus dies when he gives up breathing. In addition, it is a biblical concept that creatures live because they receive breath/spirit from God (Gen 2:7; 6:3, 17) and that they die when God takes it away (Ps 103:29, LXX). Therefore, it is also plausible that the letting go of one's breath or spirit is simply an idiomatic way of referring to death.

McCormack is of the opinion that for Christ to have been completely abandoned by God, both the Father and the Spirit must have departed from him. There are two difficulties with this view. First, it ignores the biblical testimony that Christ's self-sacrifice took place "through the eternal Spirit" (Heb 9:14). As we have seen in chapter 6, on the basis of manuscript evidence, exegesis, and hermeneutical history, this phrase most likely refers to the Holy Spirit. Trevor Hart rightly asserts that Jesus was filled with the Spirit from the time of his conception right up to, and including, the time of his death:

---

212. McCormack, "Loud Cries and Tears," 54–55.

213. "[T]he very emphatic *paredōken to Pneuma* of John, whose meaning is, without any shadow of doubt, that in the unitary event of *krisis* and glorification which is the Cross, the Spirit becomes 'free' in the moment when Jesus breathes his last (cf. John 7:39), and thus can be breathed into the Church, undelayed, by the Risen One (John 20:22)"; Balthasar, *Mysterium Paschale*, 126–27.

214. Barth, *CD*, III.2, §46, 334.

> The transformation or *palingennesia* of humanity did not begin on Golgotha, that is to say, but precisely in the womb of the virgin, and was effected through Jesus' Spirit-filled and enabled responsiveness to his father from moment to waking moment of his life *culminating* in the self-offering to death on the cross.[215]

Second, since McCormack places the moment of the Spirit's departure at the point of Jesus's death (John 19:30; cf. Mark 15:37), then the Spirit was still with Jesus when he experienced and articulated his godforsakenness (Mark 15:34). McCormack, however, insists that Jesus's cry of dereliction signifies the departure of both the Father *and the Spirit* from the Son. It seems then that McCormack has two moments in which the Spirit leaves Christ. This does not seem plausible.

Barth is most likely correct in his interpretation of Jesus's cry of dereliction as the Son's cry *in solidarity* with humanity, as the elect human on whom God's judgment is executed. The proposal put forward in this study is that the event at Golgotha was indeed a Trinitarian event in which the Father is Judge, the Spirit is Executioner, and Christ the Son is the Elect upon whom, with humanity, God's judgment is carried out. Christ is also the *place* of judgment and renewal—the crucible. From the mouth of Jesus, old humanity cries as it dies in Christ the Son. God does not abandon his Son at the cross. On the contrary, God is present at the cross as the awesome judge and all-consuming fire. God is also present there as the loving Redeemer who lays his life down for his sheep. God is *simultaneously* the Judge and the judged, so that in Christ, God bears the very judgment that God pronounces. God is present at the cross as life-taker and as life-giver.

4. Spirit as Life-Giver

Although the moral problem of sin and ontological problem of sinful humanity are resolved in Christ by their annihilation on the cross, God does not allow death to have the last say. Judgment, although righteous and deserved, was never the end goal. Although the resurrection did not take place at the cross but in the tomb, the death and resurrection of Jesus Christ are inseparable events. The very purpose for Jesus Christ's atoning sacrifice on the cross is the re-creation of humanity as children of God, in Christ and through the Spirit. Importantly, the new humanity is given eternal life, the divine life of God himself, ζωή and not merely ψυχή. The Holy Spirit's role here is evident. He is "the Spirit of life" (τοῦ πνεύματος τῆς ζωῆς,

---

215. Hart, "Imagination," 74. The italicization of "culminating" is added.

Rom 8:2) and the one who "makes alive" (ζῳοποιήσει, Rom 8:11; cf. τοῦ ζῳοποιοῦντος, Rom 4:17). The Father raises Jesus (and humanity) from the dead through the power of the Spirit, and this same Spirit, who is both Spirit of God and Spirit of Christ, brings the new humanity into being by his life-giving indwelling presence (Rom 8:11).

Before, during and after the cross event, Jesus Christ is the Spirit-indwelt Son. Without the presence and power of the Spirit in Christ, humanity would not have its sin-debt paid and its sin-nature transformed. From the eternal Son's perspective, he has incorruptible divine life, so that in that sense he does not require the Holy Spirit to raise him up. Interestingly, when Jesus is reported in the Fourth Gospel as saying that he willingly lays his "life" down for his sheep, the noun used is ψυχή rather than ζωή.[216] On the other hand, Jesus calls himself "life" (ἡ ζωή, John 11:25), the "bread of life" (ὁ ἄρτος τῆς ζωῆς, John 6:48), and "the light of life" (τὸ φῶς τῆς ζωῆς, John 8:12). In the New Testament, the noun ζωή is usually used to signify God's life or life with God,[217] and is always the Greek word for "life" used in the phrase "eternal life" (ζωή αἰώνιος). Such a distinction is not observed in the Septuagint, and the Greek noun ζωή (which renders the Hebrew חַי, *ḥay*) is used to signify God's life as well as life in general.[218] In the Fourth Gospel, the difference between the "life" (ψυχή) that Jesus gives up and the "life" (ζωή) that belongs to God (John 5:26), which humanity inherits by Jesus's sacrificial death, seems to suggest that while Jesus gave up his earthly ψυχή, he did not give up his divine ζωή during the process. This distinction in nomenclature may give support to McCormack's assertion that the death Jesus Christ died was a human death; the Second Person of the Trinity did not die at the cross although he experienced humanity's death within himself. In other words, in Christ, our triune God experienced suffering and death. At the cross, the Father and the Spirit did not desert or look away from the Son; they endured each moment with him.

In short, the constructive proposal presented here is an attempt at a multifaceted and biblically informed account of the Spirit's role at the cross. How does this crucible concept of *pneumatologia crucis* relate to atonement theology, to pneumatology itself, and specifically to Amos Yong's foundational pneumatology that motivated this study?

216. For example, compare John 10:11, 15, 17; 15:13, with John 1:4; 3:15–16, 36; 12:25.

217. Some exceptions are Luke 12:15; 16:25; Acts 17:25; 1 Cor 15:19; 1 Tim 4:8; Jas 4:14.

218. The significance of the difference between the Old and New Testament understanding of "life" is a fascinating area of investigation that, unfortunately, lies outside the scope of this study.

7.4 A Crucible *Pneumatologia Crucis* and Atonement Theology

There are several vantage points with which to view Christ's work of atonement, and it is probably true to say that no single perspective, or indeed all of them put together, can fully and comprehensively explicate the mystery of the atonement. Although this study did not set out to construct another atonement model, the crucible construal of *pneumatologia crucis* inevitably relates to atonement theology. It overlaps with aspects of some recent atonement models, particularly with those in which the incarnation and the new covenant are core themes.

Incarnational Atonement Model

Thomas Torrance rightly stresses that the incarnation and the atonement are inseparable, and the person of Jesus Christ cannot be seen apart from his work.[219] He sees the atoning aspect of the incarnation at three levels: first, the assumption of human physicality and nature by the Son at his birth as Jesus of Nazareth, second, the increasing solidarity of Christ with sinners, and third, his union with sinners at the cross.

First, following the patristic dictum that "the unassumed is the unredeemed," Torrance proposes that "in the very act of assuming our flesh the Word sanctified and hallowed it, for the assumption of our sinful flesh is itself atoning and sanctifying action."[220] In agreement with Barth and against Calvin, Torrance asserts that the Word assumed *fallen* human nature. Since Jesus was without sin, Torrance suggests that the Word "sanctified" the human nature that he assumed.[221] There are two objections to this idea, however, namely, that this very act of sanctification seems to bypass the atoning cross, and second, it weakens the idea that Jesus is the second Adam, with the prelapsarian freedom of choice that the first Adam had. It is possible, however, that the "sanctification" of human nature at the birth of Jesus looks ahead to his work at the cross; in other words, this is proleptic sanctification. Otherwise, the very need for the atonement is questionable if fallen human

---

219. Torrance, *Incarnation*, 107–9; Torrance, *Atonement*, 148–50, 182–83.

220. Torrance, *Incarnation*, 63.

221. "That atoning exchange begins right away with the incarnation, with its assumption of our flesh of sin, its condemnation of sin in the flesh, its sanctification of our humanity through the gift of divine righteousness and sanctification of man in Christ"; Torrance, *Incarnation*, 63.

nature, understood in Pauline terms of enslavement to sin, can be sanctified without the cross.

Second, Torrance envisages Jesus's incarnational solidarity with sinners as a *dynamic* process rather than a once-off event at his birth.

> Beginning with his baptism among sinners at the Jordan to fulfil all righteousness, and ending with his baptism in blood on the cross, again among malefactors when he died, the just for the unjust, we see the person of Christ at work in a movement of increasing solidarity with his fellow men and women, increasing solidarity with sinners. Throughout that *growing interpenetration of the Son of Man with sinful man*, the intensity of battle within the person of Christ increases, reaching its culmination in Gethsemane.[222]

According to Torrance, Jesus assumed sinful flesh at his birth, identified with sinners at his baptism of repentance at the Jordan, lived with sinners, sharing their world of beguiling temptations, healing and ministering to them, then finally dying for them and taking on their judgment.

> In this way we see that the whole of his life was an atoning sacrifice, although it is on the cross that at last all the sin of humanity is finally laid upon him, and there through the eternal Spirit he offered himself once and for all in complete and final expiation for the sin of mankind.[223]

Thus, for Torrance, Jesus's person and actions should be seen in the light of the atonement, with his incarnation encompassing not only his birth, but also his deepening identification with human sinners and their sin burden. He stresses that the Holy Spirit was and is active in Jesus from the time of his birth, during his ministry, on the cross, at his resurrection, and in his continuing prayers of intercession for his church.[224] Torrance, however, does not forward any specific detail about the role of the Spirit at the cross aside from solidly affirming that Jesus Christ offered himself through the eternal Spirit.[225] Interestingly, Torrance's juxtaposition of the laying on of humanity's sin upon Jesus and his self-offering through the eternal Spirit raises the possibility of a link between the two processes, or even an identification of these two processes. Who lays humanity's sin upon

---

222. Torrance, *Incarnation*, 106–7; italics added.
223. Torrance, *Incarnation*, 136.
224. Torrance, *Incarnation*, 135–37.
225. Torrance, *Atonement*, 81, 92, 274.

Jesus Christ? While the obvious answer is God, perhaps this coheres with the concept of the Spirit as divine Executioner.

Third, Torrance concurs with Barth and Zizioulas that when Jesus Christ died on the cross and was raised from the dead, he did so in union with sinners. In this way, the growing interpenetration of the Son of Man with sinful man climaxes in Christ's death and resurrection. In the posthumously published work, *Atonement*, Torrance explores the idea that Jesus is both Son of God and Son of Man not only because of the pneumatically constituted hypostatic union between divine and human natures, but also because he is united with human beings at the cross. Having assumed human flesh and the human condition, he is united with humans at the cross, as the corporate Christ.[226] Indeed, Torrance insists that *all* humans are united to Christ in his death *and* resurrection, placing his soteriology firmly at the universalist pole.[227]

> [He] was so one with us that when he died we died, for he did not die for himself but for us, and that he did not die alone, but we died in him with those whom he bound to himself inseparably by his incarnation. Therefore when he rose again we rose in him and with him, and when he presented himself before the face of the Father, he presented us also before God, so that we are already accepted of God in him once and for all.[228]

Although Torrance did not formally name his approach to the atonement as an "incarnational atonement model," nonetheless, it seems appropriate when others have done so.[229] There are clear points of contact between Torrance's incarnational atonement and the crucible *pneumatologia crucis* offered in this thesis. The first is in Torrance's vision of the corporate Christ at the cross, in whom the incarnation not only entails the assumption of human flesh and human nature, but also union with human beings. The second is his affirmation of the Spirit's role in the self-offering of Christ. Torrance also offers a useful dynamic perspective of the incarnation, although he does not make the connection between this deepening solidarity with humanity with the work of the Holy Spirit. Such a connection seems very plausible, given that Christ is the pneumatic Christ. As a modification of Torrance's dynamic incarnational atonement model, the following *schema* is proposed:

---

226. Torrance, *Atonement*, 149–53.
227. Torrance, *Atonement*, 197–200.
228. Torrance, *Atonement*, 152.
229. Habet, *Theology in Transposition*, 182.

1. *Incarnation*—through the Spirit, the Son of God assumes human flesh and nature, and is born as Jesus of Nazareth.

2. *Baptism* at the Jordan—through the Spirit, Jesus, anointed as humanity's Messiah (Christ), assumes human history and covenantal obligations.

3. *Crucifixion*—through the Spirit, Jesus Christ is united with human beings, and assumes humanity's punishment as the (inclusive) Elect.

4. *Resurrection*—through the Spirit, Jesus Christ assumes humanity's eschatological status as the (inclusive) New Adam.

Yves Congar envisages two "successive moments" of the Holy Spirit's descent upon Jesus Christ, namely at his baptism at Jordan, and at his resurrection and exaltation.[230] The above *schema* expands Congar's pneumatic "successive moments" and combines his idea with Torrance's concept of incarnation as a dynamic process. Thus, all major milestones in Jesus's life and ministry are seen as pneumatic events in which a progressive and intensifying *assumptio carnis* culminates in the radical renewal of humanity in Christ, through the power of the Holy Spirit.

New-Covenantal Atonement Model

Michael J. Gorman detects a lacuna in the array of atonement models.[231] Among the traditional perspectives that focus on the atonement as punishment, sacrifice, moral example, or victory over evil powers, Gorman suggests that the New Testament itself often views Christ's atonement in the context of "covenant," more precisely, a "new or renewed covenant." He points out that the atonement is not the ultimate purpose of Christ's death but penultimate, because the ultimate purpose is the birth of a new covenant people of God. In alignment with Torrance's incarnational atonement model, Gorman stresses the inclusive nature of Christ's representation and the participation of humanity in Christ; believers die and are raised up with and in Christ.[232] Importantly, Gorman sees the Holy Spirit's involvement in the whole salvific event of death and rebirth. "The Spirit effects both death and resurrection (Rom. 8:11, 13), accomplishing in believers—as a result of Jesus' death—the covenantal obligations that could not be accomplished among those mastered

---

230. Congar, *Believe*, vol. 3, 166–71.
231. Gorman, *Death of the Messiah*, 1–2.
232. Gorman, *Death of the Messiah*, 66–67.

by sin (Rom. 8:3–4; cf. 2 Cor. 5:21)." [233] Gorman rightly emphasizes that Christ's atoning sacrifice on the cross should be understood in the context of the fulfillment of God's covenant with Israel, resulting in the formation of the eschatological Spirit-indwelt covenant community. This covenant community, rather, this *new*-covenant community, now extends beyond ethnic boundaries to include all people groups. The indwelling Spirit ensures that the presence of God is accessible, in and through Christ, to everyone irrespective of race, gender, and social status.

Gorman also emphasizes the *cruciform* paradigm within which this new-covenant community is to live, serve, and be Christ's witnesses to the world. He is rather less concerned with the mechanics of the atonement than on the results of the atonement, besides providing a refreshing reminder that reconciliation has both vertical and horizontal relational aspects.[234] Whereas many atonement models, in Gorman's opinion, are isolationist, individualistic, and too focused on the penultimate purpose of the cross, he seeks not only to integrate the various perspectives of Christ's atoning work, but also to re-center theological attention onto its ultimate goal—the new-covenant community.[235] Accepting that there are many possible ways of understanding the atonement, he sees in his new-covenant atonement model the intertwining threads of justice, sacrifice, satisfaction, victory, moral example, incarnation, and participation. He highlights the work of the Holy Spirit. Christ's self-sacrifice "effects the new covenant and thereby unleashes the Spirit" who empowers the transformation of the community of Christ into his image.[236] Gorman emphasizes that the eschatological Spirit, promised by the prophets of Israel, ensures that the cross not only saves but changes lives.[237]

There is much in Gorman's new-covenant atonement model that resonates with the crucible concept of *pneumatologia crucis* presented here. In both, God's covenant with Israel (and thereby humanity) is the context within which Christ's atoning sacrifice is understood. Common to both is the importance placed on Christ's high priestly role, and the inclusive nature of his representation. An integrative approach is undertaken in the framing of both concepts, in the recognition that neither the atonement, nor the role of the Spirit at the cross, is monodimensional. The Spirit's participation in the Christ's work of reconciliation is highlighted in both.

---

233. Gorman, *Death of the Messiah*, 67–68.
234. Gorman, *Death of the Messiah*, 4–5, 29–31, 210–11.
235. Gorman, *Death of the Messiah*, 19–22, 26–27.
236. Gorman, *Death of the Messiah*, 58.
237. Gorman, *Death of the Messiah*, 212.

However, in spite of the many points of congruence, there is a significant difference—their focus. Gorman's concern is with the *results* of the atonement, namely the ethical, moral, and spiritual characteristics of the cruciform new-covenant community of Christ, and although he affirms the involvement of the Spirit at the cross, he does not venture into what that involvement may entail. Nonetheless, he is right to balance the upwards with the outwards. The focus of the crucible concept of *pneumatologia crucis* is, on the other hand, the *process*, with its greater stress on the destruction of old humanity and the re-birth of the new humanity in Christ. In terms of outcomes, this crucible concept pushes Gorman's new-covenant atonement model a step further by emphasizing with Barth (and Paul) that the old life is over. The power of sin is broken. The prison doors of addicting habits, practices, and attitudes have been vaporized, and the way forward into the life of freedom in the Spirit lies ahead. These habits, practices, and attitudes still cling, but the way forward is now open, and the indwelling Spirit creates Christ within us, day by day. This is not some self-motivated positive thinking. This is the power of God. Humanity is changed forever, because the God-human freely lay down his ψυχή for us. For all who belong to Christ, while we still live in a time of transition between the old and new aeons, *real change* is now possible in the eschatological Spirit.

If the crucible construal of *pneumatologia crucis* is to be considered as one possible way of understanding *the atonement*, perhaps it sits alongside these two atonement models, with the label "pneumatic-crucible atonement model," emphasizing the vital role of the Holy Spirit at the cross of Christ. As Torrance and Gorman would probably agree, however, no single perspective of the cross can ever claim to be complete. Such is the mystery of the cross.

7.5 A Crucible *Pneumatologia Crucis* and Pneumatology

With respect to pneumatology proper, the specific question raised for the crucible concept of a *pneumatologia crucis* is this: What did Jesus Christ's suffering, death, and resurrection mean for *the Spirit*? The answer appears to be fourfold.

First, it signifies that the *indwelling* Spirit experiences all that Jesus Christ, the Son, experiences. Indeed, through the Spirit, the triune God experiences all that Christ experiences. Without ascribing *kenosis* to the Spirit, this construal denies the impassibility of the Spirit, and therefore the impassibility of God. The Spirit, however, is both transcendent and immanent. In his transcendence, the Spirit empowers and enables Jesus as he surrenders himself to his heavenly Father's will. In his immanence, the Spirit suffers with Jesus, but does not die with him.

Second, since the fulfillment of humanity's covenantal obligation in Christ results in new life in the Spirit, then Christ's sacrifice is the very basis for the outpouring of the Spirit. In other words, without the cross, there would have been no resurrection and no Pentecost. Yet without the Spirit, the cross would have been powerless and meaningless. Without the death of old humanity, there would have been no rising of new humanity, just as the metaphoric seed must die in order for the plant to grow (John 12:24). The provisional revelation of the covenant was given to Israel; the definitive covenant in Christ extends to all humanity. In Christ, the covenant between God and humanity is restored and transformed, so that God's eschatological promise of his indwelling Spirit can come into being (Isa 44:3; Ezek 37:12-14; Joel 2:28-29). For the Johannine community, a clear difference seems to have been discerned in their pneumatic experience before and after the cross event. Prior to the cross, "there was no Spirit, because Jesus was not yet glorified" (John 7:39). Before Jesus's atoning death, the Spirit "remained" with them; after his death and resurrection, the Spirit was "in" them (John 14:17). While few details are given with regard to this difference in their pneumatic experience, doubtless such a difference was perceived. The Spirit's power trickling upon a few select individuals before the Christ event is transformed by Christ's atoning death to become a pneumatic flood upon "all flesh" (Acts 2:2-4, 17-18). To describe this change as a "freeing" of the Spirit is probably hyperbolic;[238] perhaps it is more accurate to see the change occurring in humanity itself, now reborn with far greater receptivity to, and consciousness of, the Holy Spirit, because reconciliation has been achieved in Christ. The reference to Joel 2:28-29 in Acts 2 frames the Pentecost event within an eschatological context. The positive response of thousands from different countries to Peter's message that day also signifies the inauguration of the church's mission to the world by the Spirit of Christ.

Third, if the Spirit is the one who unites humanity to Christ, and through this union old humanity dies with Christ, then in spite of the fact that the Spirit is the *Holy* Spirit, he is not distant from *sinful* humanity, but has the power to gather sinful humanity up *in Christ* for extinction and re-birth. This is a paradox. In the Levitical system, the curtain separating the "Holy of Holies" from the presence of all humans apart from the high priests (accompanied by sacrificial blood) demonstrates the utter separation between a holy God and sinful humanity. Yet, if God saves sinners while they are still sinners (Rom 5:8), and if sinners die and are raised in union

---

238. Balthasar, *Mysterium Paschale*, 126-27.

with Christ (Rom 6:3–5), then the Holy Spirit must be able to access sinful human beings. Perhaps the Spirit does this proleptically, *as the Spirit of Christ*, and therefore as the Spirit of the cross. It is only because of Jesus Christ's atoning work that the Holy Spirit has access into the hearts and minds of unholy sinners. In the light of the eternal election (Eph 1:4–5), God's eschatological Spirit reaches out throughout time and space to all who are elect in Christ (whether this means all humanity or some),[239] while they are yet sinners. In a paradoxical reordering of the *ordo salutis*, these sinners are treated as though they have already been made holy by the eternal redemption of Christ. Perhaps another way of explaining this may be to say that for the Spirit, it is *who* these people are, the elect in Christ, not the moral state they are in, or their location in space and time, that determines their access by the Spirit. The eternal Spirit, for whom neither space nor time are barriers, reigns in history and eternity. Importantly, the Holy Spirit is eternally the Spirit of Christ, and therefore he relates to all humanity as the Spirit of Christ (1 Peter 1:10–11).

These pneumatological insights, if valid, have implications for ethics and mission. As the Spirit of the crucified Christ, the Spirit's transformative goal for all who belong to Christ is the *imago Christi* which, of course, corresponds to the *imago Dei*. The Spirit of the cross is the Spirit of the suffering Servant, and it is Christ's loving, self-sacrificing cruciform character that shapes new humanity. The eternality of the Spirit and his access to sinners through the work of Christ, means that the Holy Spirit has already gone ahead of his human evangelists. It is the Spirit who prepares the way. As the Spirit of Christ, he works to lead the elect to Christ. As the Spirit of Christ, he touches the hearts of sinners. As the Spirit of Christ, the Holy Spirit is, in a sense, "God behind enemy lines."

Fourth, the prevailing apprehension of the Holy Spirit as gentle "guide," "advocate," "comforter," and "encourager" must take into account the other face of the Spirit as the powerful, all-consuming, sanctifying fire. This is an uncomfortable vision of the Holy Spirit. For ancient Israel, where unmediated encounters with God often resulted in death, and the holiness of God was demonstrated in cleanliness, purity, perfection, and separation, the association of God with consuming fire is understandable. In our pluralist, multicultural world, where racial and religious tolerance underpins social harmony, such a view of an exacting and wrathful God is unwelcome.

---

239. The question whether the elect in Christ encompasses all humanity or only some is too vast to address in this limited study. If Barth is right and all humanity has been redeemed, then mission becomes proclamation of good news. If only some are saved, then the gospel is bad news for those who are not, because in Christ, they are already dead, and will not rise with him.

Nevertheless, the Bible does not shirk from warning humanity that "the wages of sin is death"; on the other hand, the good news is that "the free gift of God is eternal life in Christ Jesus our Lord" (Rom 6:23). The holiness of the Holy Spirit characterizes the holiness of God's eschatological kingdom. Those that are made citizens of that kingdom in Christ, and who are adopted as God's own children, must embody this holiness. However, the new humanity is empowered and enabled by the Holy Spirit to do just that. Paul's insistence that the power of sin is broken is based on his conviction that in Christ, the old sin-enslaved humanity is no more, and that the new humanity lives in the realm of the Spirit where love, freedom, and holiness reign (Rom 6:6-23; 8:1-17; 2 Cor 5:14, 17). The Spirit indwells the elect not only to inform, but to engender that very holiness in them. The Spirit's transforming work, however, will not be completed until the *eschaton*.

A Foundational Pneumatology?

Amos Yong's vision of a foundational pneumatology as a theological approach to the plurality of religions in the world provided an impetus for this study. He maintains that the Spirit is universally present and active, and that the Spirit is not only the source of God's life breath and image in every human being, but also the basis for all human relationships and all religions.[240] He offers the concept of the Spirit that flows beyond church and Christ, speaking multiphonically through humanity's many ways of religious expression. The Spirit to whom Yong refers is specifically the Holy Spirit who is poured out at Pentecost on "all flesh," the divinely promised eschatological Spirit.[241] He suggests, therefore, that where the particularity of Christ may be divisive, people from various religious streams may find a common place for discourse and interaction in the Holy Spirit. Veli-Matti Kärkkäinen, in agreement, suggests that "other religions are not salvific as such, but other religions are important to the Christian church in that they help the church to penetrate more deeply into the divine mystery . . . Thus the discernment of the activity of the Holy Spirit within other religions must also bring the church more truthfully into the presence of the triune God."[242] While this appears an attractive proposition for interfaith dialogue, the underlying premise for Yong and Kärkkäinen seems to be that such dialogue can only progress smoothly in a pneumatological milieu, without reference to Christ. This implies that the Holy Spirit can be understood

---

240. Yong, *Beyond the Impasse*, 44-46.
241. Yong, *Beyond the Impasse*, 131.
242. Kärkäinen, *Trinity*, 179.

apart from Jesus Christ. The two questions that this notion raises are, "Do the Spirit and the Son have distinct economies? Is the Spirit sometimes not the Spirit of Christ, but only the Spirit of God?" The issue underlying these questions is the nature of the Holy Spirit's relationship to the Son. Since the first Christians identified Jesus as the Spirit-baptizer, and they experienced the indwelling Spirit only *after* the cross event, I asked, "What is the role of the Spirit at the cross?" If salvation through Christ's atoning sacrifice relates only to Christians and if the cross event was but *one of the many ways* that God seeks to bring humanity to himself, then yes, the Holy Spirit's sphere of activity, and mission, may extend beyond the christological horizon.

The crucible concept of a *pneumatologia crucis* proposed in this study asserts that the Spirit played a key role in the atoning work of Jesus Christ the Son, uniting humanity to Christ in his death and resurrection, executing God's righteous judgment upon humanity, the covenant breaker, in order to re-create a new, Spirit-indwelt humanity in Christ. Thereafter, from the vantage point of human experience, the Spirit of God comes into sharper focus as the Spirit of Jesus Christ, the cruciform Spirit. The Spirit has not changed, we have. In Christ, creation has been reborn, although the fulfillment of its rebirth is in the future. If these pneumatological insights are correct, then the answer to the two questions asked in the paragraph above are "No" and "No." The Spirit and the Son do *not* have separate economies, and the Spirit is always the Spirit of God *and* the Spirit of Christ. There is no other divine Spirit, and Jesus Christ is the only Spirit-baptizer. The Spirit and the Son may have distinct *activities*—for example, it is the Son who is made incarnate, not the Spirit, and it is the Spirit who anoints and empowers, not the Son—but the Son and the Spirit, and indeed the triune God, work together in *one economy, one mission*. This mission is the formation of the new-covenant community. The Spirit's sphere of activity is none other than the sphere of activity of the risen Christ. As the eternal Spirit of Christ, the Holy Spirit works continually to bring sinners to Christ. Macchia insightfully observes:

> This is precisely how Pentecost was severed from the cross—and the Spirit from justification—in Christian theology. This is not meant to deny that the cross is an event of reconciliation in its own right in the sense that God descends there into the abyss to take the godforsaken into the divine bosom. It only means that the goal of the embrace of the cross is the embrace of human hearts and communities through Pentecost, and that the two cannot be separated. If we are ever to recover the ancient

integration of justification and the Spirit, we must heal the breach between the cross and Pentecost.[243]

Yet Amos Yong is also right when he asserts that the Holy Spirit is active beyond the *visible church*. Kärkkäinen distinguishes between ecclesiocentrism and Christocentrism.[244] God's grace extends far beyond the walls put up by humans to separate the insiders from the outsiders. Yong's vision of the global reach of the Holy Spirit is theologically significant and exciting.[245] He is right in relating the vivifying creator Spirit to the Spirit of Christ as one and the same Spirit, and to see the Spirit active in nature, and in all spheres of human experience.[246] Only the vivifying Spirit can breathe new life into sin-dead humanity. He is right when he asserts that the Holy Spirit is the Spirit of the Father and of the Son, Jesus Christ.[247] Yong also affirms the role of the Spirit at the cross,[248] and presents a pneumatological soteriology that acknowledges both Spirit and Logos Christologies.[249] "[T]he Spirit is no less than the Spirit of Jesus."[250] One suspects, however, that for Yong, the Spirit is rather *more* than the Spirit of Jesus. On the one hand, he seeks to present a pneumatology that is both global and Christocentric, while on the other he is concerned that Christians should not be inward looking but be willing to hear the voices that speak from outside their own theological paradigms.[251] These are important goals, and despite the difficulty in holding them together, on the whole, Yong succeeds. He observes that gracious hospitality characterizes the Father, Son and Holy Spirit. Likewise, the community of Christ should be hospitable, genuine, and humble in their dialogical openness to those who hold other beliefs.[252] This is not controversial. However, on the basis of his conviction that the voice of the Holy Spirit may be heard within the teachings of other faiths, and that other religions may be "instruments of the Holy Spirit working out the divine purposes in the world,"[253] he further suggests that interreligious discourse not only helps contextualize the gospel message, but also,

243. Macchia, *Justified in the Spirit*, 162.
244. Kärkkäinen, *Theology of Religions*, 25.
245. Yong, *Spirit Poured Out*, 167–202.
246. Yong, *Spirit Poured Out*, 280–95.
247. Yong, *Spirit Poured Out*, 202, 295.
248. Yong, *Spirit Poured Out*, 111–12.
249. Yong, *Spirit Poured Out*, 109–20.
250. Yong, *Spirit Poured Out*, 295.
251. Yong, *Spirit Poured Out*, 254; Yong, *Hospitality*, 80–84.
252. Yong, *Hospitality*, 118–28.
253. Yong, *Spirit Poured Out*, 236.

"as a practice of mutual transformation,"[254] can inform and help construct Christian theology.[255] Yong's timely, even prophetic, reminder that Christianity's approach to people of other faiths must change as global society changes, seems at this point to bring Christian theologizing a step too close to syncretism, even taking into consideration his welcome cautionary advice on spiritual discernment.[256] It is a fine line between the continual refreshing of the *communication* of the gospel, and changing the gospel itself.

Yong refers to Peter's multilingual audience in Acts 2 to support his view that the Spirit speaks to communities outside the Judeo-Christian sphere.[257] In the Lukan account, however, while the people were from diverse backgrounds, they all heard the *one* message—the gospel of Jesus Christ. This is not interreligious discourse. Notably, they were there to celebrate the *Jewish* festival of Pentecost. Furthermore, those who received the eschatological Spirit were Jesus's disciples who had gathered in the upper room, including all those who accepted their testimony to the risen Jesus, and no one else. Hence, using that particular text to give credence to the notion that the voice of the Spirit can be heard in *other traditions* overreads the narrative. To do so is taking the Spirit out of his christological context. It is separating the Spirit from Christ, and this contradicts the biblical teaching that it is the Son who forms the content of the Spirit's revelation and illumination (John 16:13–14). Indeed, Macchia insists, "There is no critical dialectic between Jesus and the Spirit. He is the king and the Spirit is the kingdom."[258]

Nevertheless, since there are several points of agreement between Yong's foundational pneumatology and the ideas expressed in this thesis, namely, the mutual relationship between Spirit and Logos Christologies, the significant role of the Spirit in the atoning work of Christ, the presence and activity of the Spirit at the cross, the global reach of the Spirit, and the identification of the Creator Spirit with the Holy Spirit, is there room for creative engagement between Yong's perspective of the Spirit's voice among the teachings of other faiths and a crucible conceptualization of the Spirit's role at the cross? Perhaps there is.

The plurality of religions may simply represent an innate human religiosity, a longing for purpose and meaning, even a longing for transcendence. This inner longing may not always be expressed in theistic belief, but

---

254. Yong, *Hospitality*, 158.
255. Yong, *Spirit Poured Out*, 235–66.
256. Yong, *Beyond the Impasse*, 73; *Spirit Poured Out*, 202, 295.
257. Yong, *Spirit Poured Out*, 171–73, 196–201.
258. Macchia, *Justified in the Spirit*, 277.

in human relationships, work, music, art, and culture. On the other hand, if the pneumatological insights presented here are correct, it is plausible that the Holy Spirit has access to sinners everywhere and in every age, *but only on the basis of Christ's atoning work* and *in Christ*. Thus, as the Spirit of Christ, the Holy Spirit spoke proleptically to the prophets of Israel, to prepare a human community for God's definitive revelation, Jesus Christ. That the people of Israel have largely failed to acknowledge him as such is beside the point. It is conceivable that the Holy Spirit, in his divine freedom, may reach out to other communities too. Since the Spirit of Christ points to Jesus Christ, then it is possible that Christward hints have been proleptically given to them, and that such hints have been variously interpreted and articulated. The missiological task then is not to incorporate symbols and insights from other faiths into Christian theology, but rather to seek out the christological clues that the Holy Spirit may have previously implanted, and to use them as bridges to bring these communities to Christ.

7.6 Summary

From the writings of John V. Taylor, Jürgen Moltmann, and John D. Zizioulas, three main perspectives of *pneumatologia crucis* may be discerned, namely, the Spirit as the "bond of love," as coworker with the Son, and as unifier, uniting humanity to Christ. These perspectives, when integrated with the pneumatological reflections of Karl Barth, suggest a multifaceted view of the Spirit's role at the cross, using the metaphor of a crucible. Thus, Jesus Christ is envisaged as the Father's pneumatic crucible in which the Spirit unites humanity to the Son, carries out God's judgment in Christ the Elect, destroying sinful humanity and re-creating a new Spirit-indwelt humanity in him. Jesus Christ not only bears the sins of humanity, but sinful humanity itself, and in this crucible, both sin and sinner are extinguished. Jesus's cry of godforsakenness is a window into the hell of the second death. The Creator Spirit then brings Jesus Christ to life again, and with him, new humanity. Such an understanding of *pneumatologia crucis* implies that the Spirit is intimately present with Christ the Son as he undergoes suffering and death, that the Spirit is God's consuming fire and power in addition to being comforter and advocate, that the resurrection and Pentecost are contingent on the cross event, that as the *Spirit of Christ*, and on the basis of Christ's atoning work, the eternal Spirit is able to access sinful humanity throughout space and time, speaking to individuals, leaders and prophets of Israel, giving Christward hints to people in other communities, and most of all, drawing sinners to Christ. From the viewpoint of Christian life and ethics, the power of enslaving habits and practices has been broken, and there is genuine potential for transformation by the indwelling Spirit. From the viewpoint of missions, having confidence in the Spirit of Christ who prepares the way encourages Christ's earthly witnesses to press on.

8

Conclusion

THIS PRESENT INVESTIGATION INTO the question "What was the role of the Spirit at the cross?" has shown that theologians have offered three main perspectives—a mediatory role (the Spirit as the "bond of love" uniting the Father and the Son in their alienation), a participatory role (the Spirit as the Son's coworker at the cross), and a unifying role (the Spirit uniting believers to the corporate Christ). From the time of the church fathers down to the twenty-first century, the majority of scholars affirm the presence of the Holy Spirit at the cross. However, few have ventured to describe the Spirit's role at the cross in greater depth.

Perhaps the first to consider the Spirit's activity at the cross in more detail was John Vernon Taylor, whose understanding of the Spirit as "communion" leads him to suggest that the Holy Spirit holds the Father and the Son in awareness of each other in the godforsaken agony of the cross, drawing into their embrace some of the people gathered around the dying Jesus. Meanwhile, Jürgen Moltmann develops his ideas about the Spirit's role at the cross over several decades, putting forward three models—that the cruciform Spirit proceeds from the cross event to include humanity, that the Spirit is the "bond of love" uniting the forsaking Father and the godforsaken Son, and that the Spirit is the Son's coworker at the cross. On the other hand, John D. Zizioulas emphasizes that Christ is the corporate Christ, and that through the unifying work of the Holy Spirit, humanity is united to Christ, so that humanity dies and rises with Christ. Karl Barth, who does not specifically address a *pneumatologia crucis*, portrays the Spirit as the one who unites humanity to Christ, the Elect, and who executes God's final judgment on sinful humanity in Christ.

This investigation demonstrates a firm biblical foundation for the idea that the Spirit was with Jesus Christ at the cross, and actively involved. This biblical basis for a *pneumatologia crucis* is derived from the textual, exegetical, and theological examination of Hebrews 9:14 within the broader pneumatological context of Hebrews, together with support from the New Testament use of pneumatic sacrificial metaphors (Rom 15:15–16; 1 Peter 1:1–2), from the typology of the Levitical high priesthood viewed through Christology and pneumatology, from the important concept of union with Christ, and from the role given to the Holy Spirit as the one who unites believers to Christ (1 Cor 6:11, 15–19; 12:12–13; Eph 2:16–18). The Spirit-indwelt Messiah, Jesus, is the incarnate Son who bears both sin and sinful humanity on the cross through the unifying power of the Holy Spirit. In his death and resurrection, old humanity dies and new humanity is reborn into God's eschatological kingdom of the Spirit and eternal life (Rom 6:3–10, 22–23; 8:9–11).

Building upon this biblical foundation, and drawing upon the insights of Taylor, Moltmann, Zizioulas, and Barth, a multifaceted *pneumatologia crucis* is offered. This construal envisages the eternal Holy Spirit having multiple roles at the cross—as the one who empowers the incarnate Son, the one who unites humanity across space and time to the Son in Christ, the one who executes judgment on humanity in Christ, and the one who raises to life, in and with Christ, the new humanity. The metaphor of the crucible is used to portray the Spirit's vital activities at the cross within a Trinitarian context. Hence, Jesus Christ is the Father's pneumatic crucible in whom sinful humanity is united to the Son and destroyed in the consuming fire of the sanctifying Spirit. This destruction is nothing less than the second death, God's righteous and final judgment upon sin and sinner. Within this christological crucible of the incarnate Son, the life-giving Spirit re-creates humanity as the royal children of God the Father, coheirs with Christ in God's eschatological realm.

At the cross, the triunity of God is revealed, as is the incredible extent of the love of God the Father, Son and Holy Spirit for hapless humanity. God the Father is the judge, and also the one who willingly gives up his only Son for sinners. God the Son is the Word through whom all creation is created, who freely and kenotically becomes the sacrificial vessel for humanity and creation. God the Spirit is the one who shapes this God-human vessel, the one who empowers the incarnate Son, the one who unites sinful humanity to the Son, and finally, the one who carries out the judgment that is not only retributive but restorative, so that in Christ's resurrection, God's goal for creation is fulfilled. The cross event also reveals the Spirit of God as the cruciform Spirit of Christ, whose proleptic presence filled

Israel's prophets with God-breathed visions and words, and whose design of the tabernacle and the Levitical sacrificial system provided Israel with a pedagogical resource in preparation for Christ, and whose power and grace works noetically and transformatively, forming Christ in human hearts and minds. The Holy Spirit cannot be separated from the incarnate Son. Pentecost cannot be separated from the cross, because Pentecost would not have been possible without the cross. The Son and the Spirit have a single mission in the world—the Father's mission to bring home, in Jesus Christ, all his children who are lost in the far country.

The practical implications that arise from the conclusions reached in this study chiefly concern Christian ethics and mission. Although these implications deserve careful consideration and further study, only brief statements can be made here. With respect to ethics, a crucible concept of a *pneumatologia crucis* emphasizes that God has accomplished, in Christ and through the Spirit, God's radically effective solution to sin and the sinner. Both are comprehensively dealt with in the inclusive death of Christ, and therefore day-to-day victory over sin is made entirely possible on the real basis of Christ's victory, and through the power of the indwelling Holy Spirit. Jesus Christ is not only the highest moral exemplar, but the pneumatic locus of salvation and transformation. With respect to Christian mission, Christ's human ministers of reconciliation go where the Spirit of Christ has already penetrated, proclaiming a message of reconciliation accomplished. Christ's witnesses implore hearts and minds that are already pneumatically prepared, "Be reconciled!" Through Christ's atoning work, the barrier between a holy God and sinful humanity has been permanently torn asunder, and *all* sinners, throughout time and space, are accessible to the power of the Holy Spirit, the Spirit of Christ—the God behind enemy lines.

APPENDIX I

Pneuma (singular) in Hebrews

2:4

συνεπιμαρτυροῦντος τοῦ θεοῦ σημείοις τε καὶ τέρασιν καὶ ποικίλαις δυνάμεσιν καὶ <u>πνεύματος ἁγίου</u> μερισμοῖς κατὰ τὴν αὐτοῦ θέλησιν

[W]hile God added his testimony by signs and wonders and various miracles, and by gifts of the *Holy Spirit*, distributed according to his will.

3:7

Διό, καθὼς λέγει τὸ πνεῦμα τὸ ἅγιον· σήμερον ἐὰν τῆς φωνῆς αὐτοῦ ἀκούσητε

Therefore, as *the Holy Spirit* says, "Today, if you hear his voice . . ."

6:4

Ἀδύνατον γὰρ τοὺς ἅπαξ φωτισθέντας, γευσαμένους τε τῆς δωρεᾶς τῆς ἐπουρανίου καὶ μετόχους γενηθέντας <u>πνεύματος ἁγίου</u>

For it is impossible to restore again to repentance those who have once been enlightened, and have tasted the heavenly gift, and have shared in the *Holy Spirit*.

9:8

τοῦτο δηλοῦντος <u>τοῦ πνεύματος τοῦ ἁγίου</u>, μήπω πεφανερῶσθαι τὴν τῶν ἁγίων ὁδὸν ἔτι τῆς πρώτης σκηνῆς ἐχούσης στάσιν

By this *the Holy Spirit* indicates that the way into the sanctuary has not yet been disclosed as long as the first tent is still standing.

9:14

πόσῳ μᾶλλον τὸ αἷμα τοῦ Χριστοῦ, ὃς <u>διὰ πνεύματος αἰωνίου</u> ἑαυτὸν προσήνεγκεν ἄμωμον τῷ θεῷ, καθαριεῖ τὴν συνείδησιν ἡμῶν ἀπὸ νεκρῶν ἔργων εἰς τὸ λατρεύειν θεῷ ζῶντι.

[H]ow much more will the blood of Christ, who through the *eternal Spirit* offered himself without blemish to God, purify our conscience from dead works to worship the living God!

10:15

Μαρτυρεῖ δὲ ἡμῖν καὶ <u>τὸ πνεῦμα τὸ ἅγιον</u>· μετὰ γὰρ τὸ εἰρηκέναι·

And *the Holy Spirit* also testifies to us, for after saying . . .

10:29

πόσῳ δοκεῖτε χείρονος ἀξιωθήσεται τιμωρίας ὁ τὸν υἱὸν τοῦ θεοῦ καταπατήσας καὶ τὸ αἷμα τῆς διαθήκης κοινὸν ἡγησάμενος, ἐν ᾧ ἡγιάσθη, καὶ <u>τὸ πνεῦμα τῆς χάριτος</u> ἐνυβρίσας;

How much worse punishment do you think will be deserved by those who have spurned the Son of God, profaned the blood of the covenant by which they were sanctified, and outraged *the Spirit of grace*?

4:12

Ζῶν γὰρ ὁ λόγος τοῦ θεοῦ καὶ ἐνεργὴς καὶ τομώτερος ὑπὲρ πᾶσαν μάχαιραν δίστομον καὶ διϊκνούμενος ἄχρι μερισμοῦ ψυχῆς καὶ <u>πνεύματος</u>, ἁρμῶν τε καὶ μυελῶν, καὶ κριτικὸς ἐνθυμήσεων καὶ ἐννοιῶν καρδίας·

Indeed, the word of God is living and active, sharper than any two-edged sword, piercing until it divides soul from *spirit*, joints from marrow; it is able to judge the thoughts and intentions of the heart.

APPENDIX 2

𝔓⁴⁶ (ca. 200)

Frederick G. Kenyon, *The Chester Beatty Biblical Papyri Descriptions and Texts of Twelve Manuscripts on Papyrus of the Greek Bible: Fasciculus III Supplement—Pauline Epistles* (London: Emery Walker, 1937), plate 30. Image digitally reproduced with the permission of the Papyrology Collection, Graduate Library, University of Michigan; inventory number P. Mich. Inv. 6238; http://www.lib.umich.edu/papyrus-collection;underlining added.

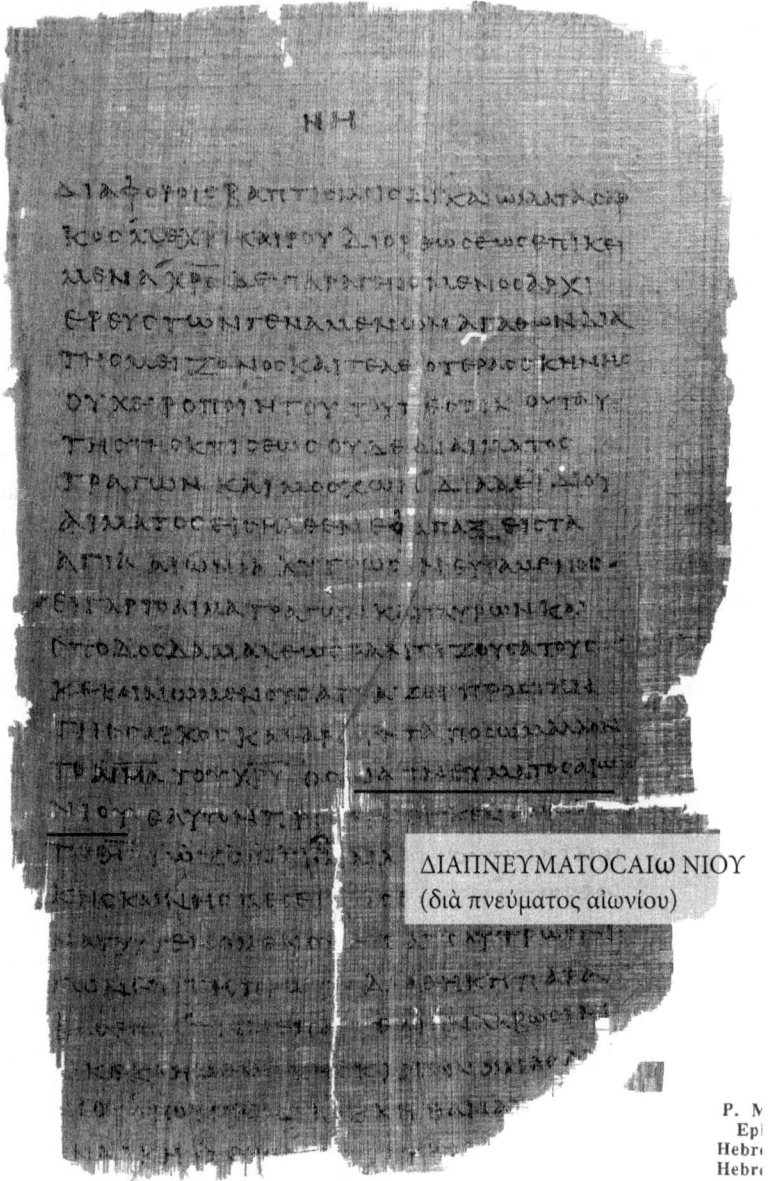

Hebrews 9:10–16

APPENDIX 3A
CODEX SINAITICUS (Hebrews 9:14)

Source: BibleWorks 10

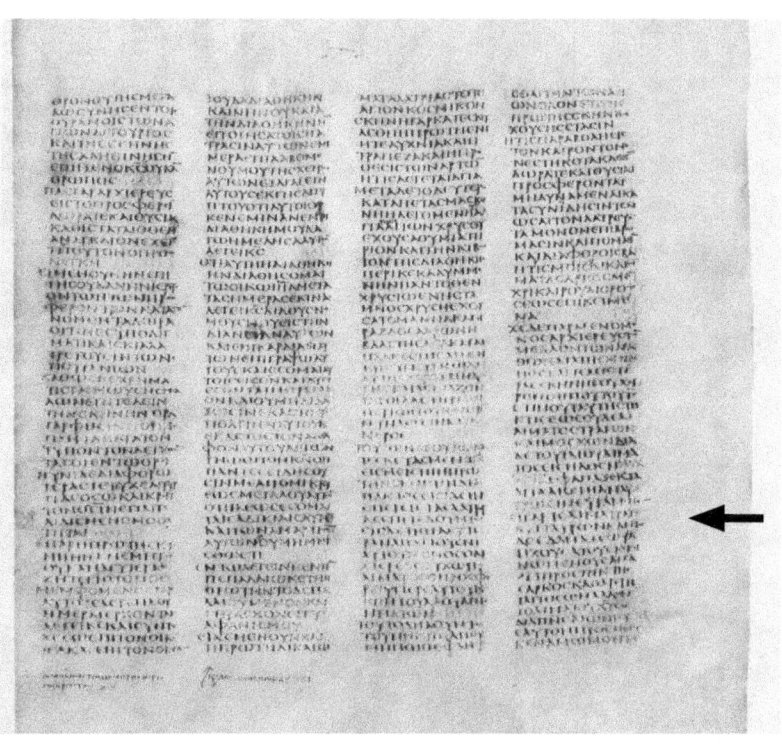

ΑΓΙΟΥ
(ἁγίου)

ΔΙΑ∏ΝΣ
(διὰ πνεύματος)

ΑΙΩΝΙΟΥ
(αἰωνίου)

APPENDIX 3B
CODEX VATICANUS (Hebrews 9:14)

Source: BibleWorks 10

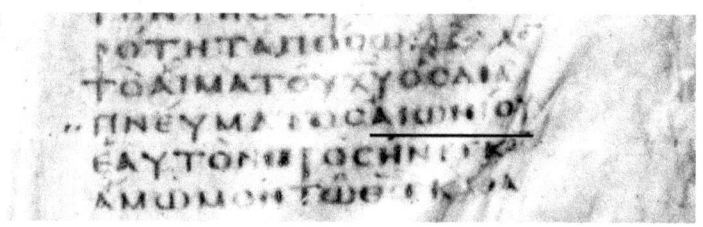

ΠΝΕΥΜΑΤΟC   ΑΙΩΝΙΟΥ
(πνεύματος)   (αἰωνίου)

APPENDIX 3C
CODEX ALEXANDRINUS (Hebrews 9:14)

Source: BibleWorks 10

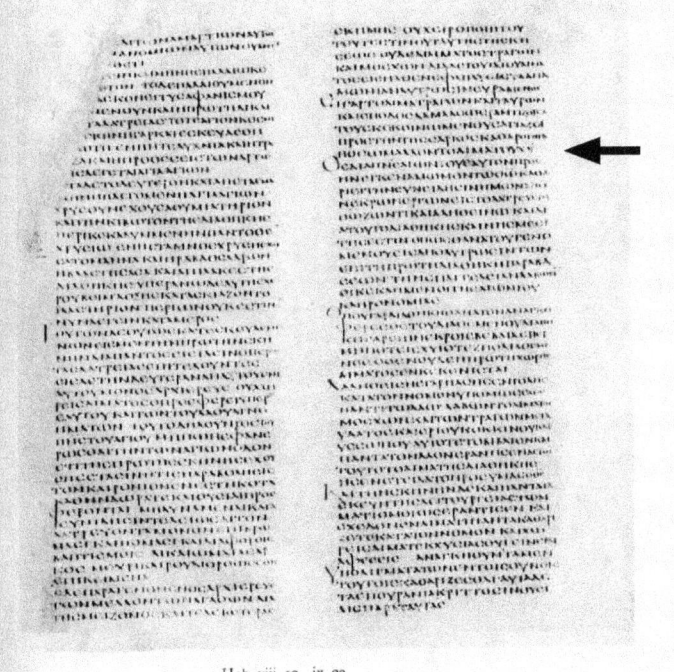

Heb. viii. 12—ix. 23

ΟΣ ΔΙΑ ΠΝΣ   ΑΙΩΝΙΟΥ
(ὅς διὰ πνεύματος)   (αἰωνίου)

APPENDIX 3D

CODEX CLAROMONTANUS
(Hebrews 9:14)

Source: http://gallica.bnf.fr/ark:/12148/btv1b8468311, accessed 19.02.2016; folio 502v, 503r.

OCΔIAΠNC   AIΩNIOY
(ὅς διὰ πνεύματος)   (αἰωνίου)

QUIPERSPMSANCTUM
(*qui per Spiritum sanctum*)

Reproduced with permission from Bibliothèque nationale de France (utilization reference number RDV-1904-001601).

APPENDIX 4

Desiderius Erasmus, *Novum Instrumentum*, 1516 (first edition)

Source: http://images.csntm.org/PublishedWorks/
Erasmus1516_0237b.jpg;accessed 01.03.2016.

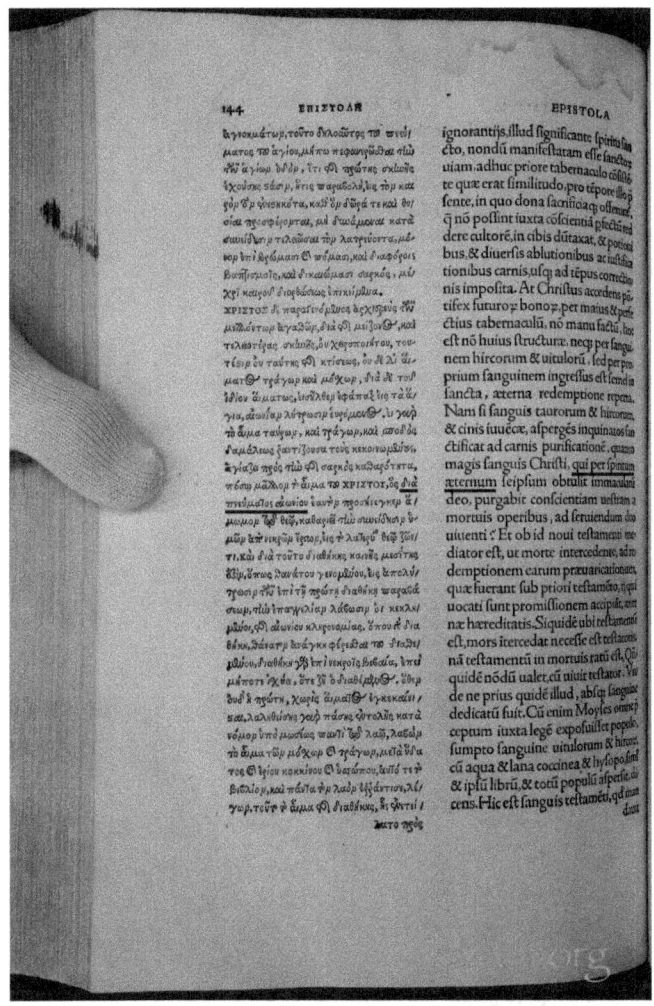

Reproduced with permission from The Lutheran School of Theology, Chicago, USA, and The Centre for the Study of New Testament Manuscripts (www.csntm.org).

APPENDIX 5
Hebrews 9:6–14 (Greek text from NA²⁸; English translation, my own)

⁶ Τούτων δὲ οὕτως κατεσκευασμένων
    εἰς μὲν τὴν πρώτην σκηνὴν
        διὰ παντὸς εἰσίασιν
        οἱ ἱερεῖς τὰς λατρείας
        ἐπιτελοῦντες,

⁷ εἰς δὲ τὴν δευτέραν
ἅπαξ τοῦ ἐνιαυτοῦ μόνος ὁ ἀρχιερεύς,
    οὐ χωρὶς αἵματος ὃ προσφέρει
    ὑπὲρ ἑαυτοῦ καὶ τῶν τοῦ λαοῦ
    ἀγνοημάτων

⁸ τοῦτο δηλοῦντος τοῦ πνεύματος τοῦ ἁγίου,
    μήπω πεφανερῶσθαι τὴν τῶν ἁγίων ὁδὸν
        ἔτι τῆς πρώτης σκηνῆς ἐχούσης στάσιν,

⁹ ἥτις παραβολὴ εἰς τὸν καιρὸν τὸν ἐνεστηκότα,
    καθ' ἣν δῶρά τε καὶ θυσίαι προσφέρονται
    μὴ δυνάμεναι κατὰ συνείδησιν τελειῶσαι τὸν λατρεύοντα,
    ¹⁰ μόνον ἐπὶ βρώμασιν καὶ πόμασιν καὶ διαφόροις
βαπτισμοῖς, δικαιώματα σαρκὸς μέχρι καιροῦ διορθώσεως ἐπικείμενα.

¹¹ Χριστὸς δὲ παραγενόμενος
    ἀρχιερεὺς τῶν γενομένων ἀγαθῶν
    διὰ τῆς μείζονος καὶ τελειοτέρας σκηνῆς
    οὐ χειροποιήτου, τοῦτ' ἔστιν οὐ ταύτης τῆς κτίσεως,

¹² οὐδὲ δι' αἵματος τράγων καὶ μόσχων
    διὰ δὲ τοῦ ἰδίου αἵματος εἰσῆλθεν ἐφάπαξ

    εἰς τὰ ἅγια
        <u>αἰωνίαν</u> λύτρωσιν εὑράμενος.

¹³ εἰ γὰρ τὸ αἷμα τράγων καὶ ταύρων καὶ σποδὸς δαμάλεως ῥαντίζουσα
    τοὺς κεκοινωμένους ἁγιάζει
    πρὸς τὴν τῆς σαρκὸς καθαρότητα,
¹⁴ πόσῳ μᾶλλον τὸ αἷμα τοῦ Χριστοῦ
ὃς διὰ πνεύματος <u>αἰωνίου</u>
    ἑαυτὸν προσήνεγκεν ἄμωμον* τῷ θεῷ,
    καθαριεῖ τὴν συνείδησιν ἡμῶν ἀπὸ νεκρῶν ἔργων
    εἰς τὸ λατρεύειν θεῷ ζῶντι.

⁶ Thus, these having been prepared, into the first *tent*

> regularly enter
>> the priests to complete the worship duties,

⁷ but the *high priest* enters the second [tent] once a year only,

> not without taking *blood* that he offers
>> on his own behalf and for the unintentional sins of the people.

⁸ By this *the Holy Spirit* indicates that

> *the way to the Holies* is not yet revealed
>> as long as the first tent is still standing.

⁹ This is an illustration of the present *time*,

> during which gifts and sacrifices are offered that cannot perfect the *conscience* of the worshiper,

¹⁰ but deal only with food and drink and various baptisms—regulations for the *flesh*,

until the *time* comes to set things right.

¹¹ But Christ having become *high priest* of the coming good things:

> through the greater and more perfect *tent*
>> not made by hands, that is, not of this creation

¹² neither through *blood* of goats and of bulls but through his own *blood* he entered once-for-all

> into the Holies

eternal redemption having secured.

¹³ For if *the blood* of goats and bulls and the sprinkled ash of a heifer

>> makes holy those who are defiled for the cleansing of the *flesh*,

¹⁴ how much more *the blood* of Christ

> who through eternal *Spirit* himself he offered spotless* to God

it cleanses our *consciences* from dead works

for the worship of the living God.

---

*ἄμωμον ("spotless") encompasses both senses of "clean" and "perfect" (Lev 22:21; Gen 6:9; Deut 18:13).

Bibliography

Achtemeier, Paul J. *1 Peter*. Hermeneia. Minneapolis: Fortress, 1996.
Agnew, Francis H. "1 Peter 1:2—An Alternative Translation." *Catholic Biblical Quarterly* (1983) 68–73.
Allen, David L. *Lukan Authorship of Hebrews*. NAC Studies in Bible Theology. Nashville: Academic, 2010.
Allen, David M. "'The Forgotten Spirit': A Pentecostal Reading of the Letter to the Hebrews?" *Journal of Pentecostal Theology* 18 (2009) 51–66.
Ambrose. "To the Emperor Gratian." In *A Select Library of Nicene and Post-Nicene Fathers of the Christian Church*, Series 2, edited by Philip Schaff and Henry Wace, translated by H. de Romestin and H. T. F. Duckworth, 10.93–158. Grand Rapids: Eerdmans, 1891.
Aquinas, Thomas. *Selections from Summa Theologiae, vol. 7: Father, Son and Holy Ghost*. Translated by T. C. O'Brien. London: Eyre and Spottiswoode, 1975.
———. *Summa Theologiae*. http://www.ccel.org/ccel/aquinas/summ.html.
———. *Super Epistolam B. Pauli ad Hebraeos lectura*. Translated by Fabian R. Larcher. https://dhspriory.org.thomas/ssHebrews.htm#93.
Arnold, Clinton E. *Ephesians*. Exegetical Commentary on the New Testament. Grand Rapids: Zondervan, 2010.
Athanasius. "To Bishop Serapion, Epistle I." In *The Letters of Saint Athanasius Concerning the Holy Spirit*, translated by C. R. B. Shapland, 58–149. London: Epworth, 1951.
———. *De Incarnatione—An Edition of the Greek Text*. Edited by Frank Leslie Cross. London: SPCK, 1939.
———. "On the Incarnation." In *A Select Library of Nicene and Post-Nicene Fathers of the Christian Church*, Series 2, edited by Philip Schaff and Henry Wace, translated by A. Robertson, 4.36–67. Grand Rapids: Eerdmans, 1891.
Attridge, Harold W. *The Epistle to the Hebrews*. Hermeneia. Philadelphia: Fortress, 1989.
Augustine. "Enchiridion." In *A Select Library of the Nicene and Post-Nicene Fathers of the Christian Church*, Series 1, edited by Philip Schaff, translated by J. F. Shaw, 3.229–76. Edinburgh: T. & T. Clark, 1887.

———. "On Faith and the Creed." In *A Select Library of the Nicene and Post-Nicene Fathers of the Christian Church, Series 1*, edited by Philip Schaff, translated by S. D. F. Salmond, 3.315–33. Edinburgh: T. & T. Clark, 1887.

———. "On the Gospel of St. John." In *A Select Library of the Nicene and Post-Nicene Fathers of the Christian Church, Series 1*, edited by Philip Schaff, translated by H. Browne, 7.7–193. Edinburgh: T. & T. Clark, 1888.

———. "On the Holy Trinity." In *A Select Library of the Nicene and Post-Nicene Fathers of the Christian Church, Series 1*, edited by Philip Schaff, translated by Arthur W. Haddan, 3.17–228. Edinburgh: T. & T. Clark, 1887.

———. "A Treatise on the Merits and Forgiveness of Sins." In *A Select Library of the Nicene and Post-Nicene Fathers of the Christian Church, Series 1*, edited by Philip Schaff, translated by Arthur W. Haddan, 5.12–79. Edinburgh: T. & T. Clark, 1887.

———. "A Treatise on the Spirit and the Letter." In *A Select Library of the Nicene and Post-Nicene Fathers of the Christian Church, Series 1*, edited by Philip Schaff, translated by Arthur W. Haddan, 5.80–115. Edinburgh: T. & T. Clark, 1887.

Badcock, Gary, D. *Light of Truth and Fire of Love: A Theology of the Holy Spirit*. Grand Rapids: Eerdmans, 1997.

Balthasar, Hans Urs von. *Mysterium Paschale: The Mystery of Easter*. Translated by Aidan Nichols. Edinburgh: T. & T. Clark, 1990.

Barnett, Paul. *The Second Epistle to the Corinthians*. New International Commentary on the New Testament. Grand Rapids: Eerdmans, 1993.

Barrett, Charles K. *The First Epistle to the Corinthians*. Black's New Testament Commentaries. 2nd ed. London: A. and C. Black, 1971.

Barrington-Ward, Simon. "The Right Rev. John Taylor." *The Independent*, February 7, 2001. https://www.independent.co.uk/news/obituaries/the-right-rev-john-taylor-728810.html.

Barth, Karl. *Church Dogmatics*. 4 vols. in 13 parts. Edited by G. W. Bromiley and T. F. Torrance. Translated by G. W. Bromiley et al. London: T. & T. Clark, 1956.

———. *Credo: A Presentation of the Chief Problems of Dogmatics with Reference to the Apostles' Creed*. Translated by J. Strathearn McNab. New York: Charles Scribner's Sons, 1962.

———. *Dogmatics in Outline*. Translated by G. T. Thomson. London: SCM, 1949.

———. *Evangelical Theology: An Introduction*. New York: Holt, Rinehart and Winston, 1963.

Basil of Caesarea. "De Spiritu Sancto." http://www.documentacatholicaomnia.eu/02g/0330-0379,_Basilius_Magnus,_Liber_de_Spiritu_Sancto,_MGR.pdf.

———. *St. Basil the Great: On the Holy Spirit*. Popular Patristics Series 42. Translated by Stephen Hildebrand. New York: St Vladimir's Press, 2011.

Bauckham, Richard. "The Divinity of Jesus Christ in the Epistle to the Hebrews." In *The Epistle to the Hebrews and Christian Theology*, edited by Richard Bauckham et al., 15–36. Grand Rapids: Eerdmans, 2009.

———. *Moltmann: Messianic Theology in the Making*. Basingstoke: Marshall Pickering, 1987.

———. *The Theology of Jürgen Moltmann*. London: T. & T. Clark, 1995.

Bauckham, Richard, ed. *God Will Be All in All: The Eschatology of Jürgen Moltmann*. Edinburgh: T. & T. Clark, 1999.

Bauckham, Richard et al., eds. *The Epistle to the Hebrews and Christian Theology*. Grand Rapids: Eerdmans, 2009.

Beck, T. David. *The Holy Spirit and the Renewal of All Things: Pneumatology and Jürgen Moltmann*. Princeton Theological Monograph Series 67. Eugene: Pickwick, 2007.
Behr, John. *The Nicene Faith, Part 2: One of the Holy Trinity*. Formation of Christian Theology 2. New York: St. Vladimir's Seminary Press, 2004.
Belleville, Linda L. *2 Corinthians*. IVP New Testament Commentary Series. Downers Grove: INTERVARSITY, 1996.
Berkhof, Hendrikus. *The Doctrine of the Holy Spirit*. Annie Kinkead Warfield Lectures, 1963–64. Richmond: John Knox, 1965.
Bettenson, Henry, ed. *The Later Christian Fathers: A Selection of Writings of the Fathers from St. Cyril of Jerusalem to St. Leo the Great*. London: Oxford University Press, 1970.
Beza, Theodore. *Iesu Christi Domini nostri Novum Testamentum sive Novum Foedus*, 1582. http://www.e-rara.ch/gep_g/content/pageview/4477914.
———. *Novum Domini nostri Iesu Christi Testamentum*, 1559. http://www.e-rara.ch/gep_g/content/pageview/1958733.
Bird, Michael F. *Romans*. Story of God Bible Commentary. Grand Rapids: Zondervan, 2016.
Bloch, Ernst. *The Principle of Hope*. Translated by Neville Plaice et al. Cambridge: MIT, 1986.
Bock, Darrell L. *Acts*. Baker Exegetical Commentary. Grand Rapids: Baker Academic, 2007.
Boethius. "De persona et duabus naturis." In Jacques Paul Migne, *Patrologia Latina*, vol. 64. http://www.archive.org/details/patrologiaecurs12unkngoog.
Bonhoeffer, Dietrich. *Letters and Papers from Prison*. 3rd ed. Edited by Eberhard Bethge. Translated by Reginald Fuller et al. London: SCM, 1971.
Borchert, G. L. "Gnosticism." In *Evangelical Dictionary of Theology*, edited by Walter A. Elwell, 485–88. 2nd ed. Grand Rapids: Baker Academic, 2001.
Bray, Gerald, ed. *Ancient Christian Commentary on Scripture: New Testament VI: Romans*. Downers Grove: InterVarsity Press, 1998.
Brown, Alan. "On the Criticism of *Being as Communion* in Anglophone Orthodox Theology." In *The Theology of John Zizioulas: Personhood and the Church*, edited by Douglas H. Knight, 35–50. Aldershot: Ashgate, 2007.
Brown, Francis, S. R. Driver, and Charles. A. Briggs. *The Brown-Driver-Briggs Hebrew and English Lexicon*. Peabody: Hendrickson, 1906.
Bruce, F. F. *The Book of Acts*. Rev. ed. New International Commentary on the New Testament. Grand Rapids: Eerdmans, 1988.
———. *Commentary on Galatians*. New International Greek Testament Commentary. Exeter: Paternoster, 1982.
———. *The Epistle to the Hebrews*. New International Commentary on the New Testament. Grand Rapids: Eerdmans, 1964.
———. *The Gospel of John*. Grand Rapids: Eerdmans, 1983.
Burgess, Stanley M. *The Holy Spirit: Ancient Christian Traditions*. Peabody: Hendrickson, 1984.
Byrne, Brendan. *Romans*. Sacra Pagina Series, vol. 6. Collegeville: The Liturgical Press, 1996.
Calvin, John. *Commentaries on the Epistle of Paul the Apostle to the Romans*. Translated and edited by John Owen. Grand Rapids: Eerdmans, 1948.

———. *The Epistle of Paul the Apostle to the Hebrews and the First and Second Epistles of St. Peter*. Calvin's Commentaries. Translated by William B. Johnston. Edinburgh: Saint Andrew Press, 1963.

———. *In Epistolam Ad Hebraeos Commentarius*, vol. 2. Translated by August Tholuck. Sumptibus Librariae Gebauriae, 1831. https://books.google.com.au/.

———. *Institutes of the Christian Religion*, vols. 1 and 2. Edited by John T. McNeill. Translated by Ford Lewis Battles. Louisville: Westminster John Knox, 1960.

Campbell, Constantine R. *Paul and Union with Christ: An Exegetical and Theological Study*. Grand Rapids: Zondervan, 2012.

Carson, Donald A. *Showing the Spirit: A Theological Exposition of 1 Corinthians 12–14*. Moore Theological College Lecture Series. Homebush West, NSW: Lancer, 1988.

Cassuto, Umberto. *A Commentary on the Book of Exodus*. Jerusalem: Magnes, 1967.

Chrysostom, John. "Ad Homilias S. Joannis Chrysostomi: In Epistolam Ad Hebraeos." https://books.google.com.au/books?id=aIbHbKSijYQC&pg=PR5&lpg=PR5&dq=Ad+Homilias+S.+Joannis+Chrysostomi:+In+Epistolam+Ad+Hebraeos&source=bl&ots=YqlKy2rUdL&sig=ACfU3U1jku8wK_5UogMwHyTpmjglTEgW-g&hl=en&sa=X&ved=2ahUKEwj657zose-XhAhWIfnoKHRcwD9AQ6AEwB3oECAcQAQ#v=onepage&q=Ad%20Homilias%20S.%20Joannis%20Chrysostomi%3A%20In%20Epistolam%20Ad%20Hebraeos&f=false.

———. "Homilies on the Epistle to the Hebrews." In *A Select Library of the Nicene and Post-Nicene Fathers of the Christian Church*, Series 1, edited by Philip Schaff, translated by Frederic Gardiner, 14.366–522. Edinburgh: T. & T. Clark, 1889.

Ciampa, Roy E., and Brian S. Rosner. *The First Letter to the Corinthians*. Pillar New Testament Commentary. Grand Rapids: Eerdmans, 2010.

Clements, Keith W. "Atonement and the Holy Spirit." In *Expository Times* 95 (1984) 168–171.

Cole, Graham A. *He Who Gives Life: The Doctrine of the Holy Spirit*. Illinois: Crossway, 2007.

Collins, Raymond F. *First Corinthians*. Minnesota: Liturgical Press, 1999.

Congar, Yves. *I Believe in the Holy Spirit*, vols. 1–3. Translated by David Smith. London: Geoffrey Chapman, 1983.

Conzelmann, Hans. *1 Corinthians*. Translated by James W. Leitch. Philadelphia: Fortress, 1975.

Cranfield, Charles E. B. *A Critical and Exegetical Commentary on the Epistle to the Romans*, vol. 1. Edinburgh: T. & T. Clark, 1975.

Cross, Terry L. "A Proposal to Break the Ice: What Can Pentecostal Theology Offer Evangelical Theology?" In *Journal of Pentecostal Theology* 10 (2002) 44–73.

Cyril of Alexandria. *On the Unity of Christ*. Popular Patristics Series 13. Translated by John Anthony McGuckin. New York: St. Vladmir's Seminary Press, 1995.

Dabney, D. Lyle. *Die Kenosis des Geistes: Kontinuität zwischen Schöpfung und Erlösung im Werk des Heiligen Geistes*. Düsseldorf: Neukrchener Verlag, 1997.

———. "Naming the Spirit: Towards a Pneumatology of the Cross." In *Starting with the Spirit*. Task of Theology Today III, edited by Stephen Pickard and Gordon Preece, 28–58. Hindmarsh: Australian Theological Forum, 2001.

———. "Starting with the Spirit: Why the Last Should Now Be First." In *Starting with the Spirit*. Task of Theology Today 3, edited by Stephen Pickard and Gordon Preece, 3–27. Hindmarsh: Australian Theological Forum, 2001.

Danker, Frederick W., et al. *A Greek-English Lexicon of the New Testament and other Early Church Literature.* 3rd ed. Chicago: University of Chicago Press, 2000.

DeSilva, David. *Perseverance in Gratitude: A Social-Rhetorical Commentary on the Epistle "to the Hebrews."* Grand Rapids: Eerdmans, 2000.

Dodd, C. H. *The Epistle of Paul to the Romans.* Moffatt New Testament Commentary. London: Hodder and Stoughton, 1932.

Duggan, Michael. "The Cross and the Holy Spirit in Paul: Implications for Baptism in the Holy Spirit." *Pneuma: The Journal of Pentecostal Studies* 7 (1985) 135–46.

Dunn, James D. G. *Baptism in the Holy Spirit: A Re-examination of the New Testament Teaching on the Gift of the Spirit in Relation to Pentecostalism Today.* Studies in Biblical Theology 2, vol. 15. London: SCM, 1970.

———. *The Christ and the Spirit, vol. 1: Christology.* Grand Rapids: Eerdmans, 1998.

———. *The Christ and the Spirit, vol. 2: Pneumatology.* Grand Rapids: Eerdmans, 1998.

———. *Jesus and the Spirit.* New Testament Library. London: SCM, 1975.

———. *Romans 1–8.* World Biblical Commentary 38. Dallas: Word, 1988.

———. *Romans 9–16.* World Biblical Commentary 38B. Dallas: Word, 1988.

———. *The Theology of Paul the Apostle.* Grand Rapids: Eerdmans, 1998.

———. "Towards the Spirit of Christ." In *The Work of the Spirit: Pneumatology and Pentecostalism*, edited by Michael Welker, 3–26. Grand Rapids: Eerdmans, 2006.

Durham, John I. *Exodus.* Word Biblical Commentary, vol. 3. Waco: Word, 1987.

Ellingworth, Paul. *Commentary on Hebrews.* New International Greek Testament Commentary. Grand Rapids: Eerdmans, 1993.

Elliot, John H. *1 Peter.* Anchor Bible. New York: Doubleday, 2000.

Elowsky, Joel C., ed. *Ancient Christian Doctrines, vol. 4: We Believe in the Holy Spirit.* Downers Grove: IVP Academic, 2009.

Elwell, Walter A., ed. *Evangelical Dictionary of Theology.* 2nd ed. Grand Rapids: Baker Academic, 2001.

Emmrich, Martin. *Pneumatological Concepts in the Epistle to the Hebrews: Amtscharisma, Prophet, and Guide of the Eschatological Exodus.* Lanham: University Press of America, 2003.

Erasmus, Desiderius. *Novum Instrumentum.* 1st ed., 1516. http://images.csntm.org/PublishedWorks/Erasmus_1516/Erasmus1516_0237b.jpg.

Erickson, Millard J. *Christian Theology.* 2nd ed. Grand Rapids: Baker, 1998.

Fee, Gordon D. *The First Epistle to the Corinthians.* Rev. ed. New International Commentary on the New Testament. Grand Rapids: Eerdmans, 2014.

———. *Galatians.* Pentecostal Commentary Series. Dorset: Deo, 2007.

———. *God's Empowering Presence: The Holy Spirit in the Letters of Paul.* Peabody: Hendrickson, 1994.

———. *Paul, the Spirit, and the People of God.* Grand Rapids: Baker Academic, 1996.

Ferguson, Everett. "Neoplatonism." In *Evangelical Dictionary of Theology*, edited by Walter A. Elwell, 821–22. 2nd ed. Grand Rapids: Baker Academic, 2001.

Ferguson, Sinclair B. *The Holy Spirit.* Downers Grove: INTERVARSITY, 1996.

Fitzer, Gottfried. "σφραγίς, σφραγίζω, κατασφραγίζω." In *Theological Dictionary of the New Testament*, edited by Gerhard Kittel and Gerhard Friedrich, translated by Geoffrey W. Bromiley, 939–53. Grand Rapids: Eerdmans, 1964–74.

Fitzmyer, Joseph A. *The Acts of the Apostles.* Anchor Bible, vol. 31. New York: Doubleday, 1998.

———. *First Corinthians: A New Translation with Introduction and Commentary.* Anchor Yale Bible Series 32. Yale: Yale University Press, 2008.

———. *Romans.* Anchor Bible, vol. 33. New York: Doubleday, 1993.

Flannery, Austin. "*Nostra Aetate*: Declaration on the Relation of the Church to Non-Christian Religions (28th October 1965)." In *Vatican Council II: Conciliar and Post-Conciliar Documents*, 738–42. Rev. ed. New York: Costello, 1988. http://www.vatican.va/archive/hist_councils/ii_vatican_council/documents/vat-ii_decl_19651028_nostra-aetate_en.html.

Fox, Patricia A. *God as Communion: John Zizioulas, Elizabeth Johnson and the Retrieval of the Symbol of the Triune God.* Collegeville: Liturgical Press, 2001.

Furnish, Victor Paul. *II Corinthians.* Anchor Bible, vol. 32A. New York: Doubleday, 1984.

Garland, David E. *1 Corinthians.* Baker Exegetical Commentary on the New Testament. Grand Rapids: Baker Academic, 2003.

———. *2 Corinthians.* New American Commentary. Nashville: Broadman & Holman, 1999.

Gloer, W. Hulitt. *An Exegetical and Theological Study of Paul's Understanding of New Creation and Reconciliation in II Corinthians 5:14–21.* Mellen Biblical, vol. 42. Lewiston: Edwin Mellen, 1996.

González, Justo L. *The Story of Christianity, vol. 1: The Early Church to the Dawn of the Reformation.* New York: Harper Collins, 1984.

Gorman, Michael J. *The Death of the Messiah and the Birth of the New Covenant: A (Not So) New Model of the Atonement.* Eugene: Wipf & Stock, 2014.

Gowan, Donald E. *Eschatology in the Old Testament.* Philadelphia: Fortress, 1986.

Grebe, Matthias. *Election, Atonement, and the Holy Spirit.* Princeton Theological Monograph Series. Eugene: Pickwick, 2014.

Green, Joel B. *1 Peter.* Two Horizons New Testament Commentary. Grand Rapids: Eerdmans, 2007.

Green, Joel B., and Mark D. Baker. *Recovering the Scandal of the Cross.* Downers Grove: IVP Academic, 2000.

Green, Michael. *I Believe in the Holy Spirit.* Grand Rapids: Eerdmans, 1975.

Gregory of Nazianzus. "On the Holy Spirit." In *A Select Library of Nicene and Post-Nicene Fathers of the Christian Church, Series 2*, edited by Philip Schaff and Henry Wace, translated by Charles G. Browne and James E. Swallow, 7.318–28. Grand Rapids: Eerdmans, 1893.

Gregory of Nyssa. "On the Making of Man." In *A Select Library of Nicene and Post-Nicene Fathers of the Christian Church, Series 2*, edited by Philip Schaff and Henry Wace, translated by William Moore and Henry Austin Wilson, 5.385–425. Grand Rapids: Eerdmans, 1893.

Grenz, Stanley J., and Roger E. Olson. *20th-Century Theology: God and the World in a Transitional Age.* Downers Grove: InterVarsity, 1992.

Guthrie, George H. *2 Corinthians.* Baker Exegetical Commentary on the New Testament. Grand Rapids: Baker Academic, 2015.

Habets, Myk. *The Anointed Son: A Trinitarian Spirit Christology.* Princeton Monograph Series. Eugene: Pickwick, 2010.

———. *Theology in Transposition: A Constructive Appraisal of T. F. Torrance.* Minneapolis: Fortress, 2013.

Hamilton, Victor P. *The Book of Genesis, Chapters 1–17*. New International Commentary on the Old Testament. Grand Rapids: Eerdmans, 1990.
Hansen, G. Walter. *Galatians*. IVP New Testament Commentary Series. Downers Grove: InterVarsity, 1994.
———. *The Letter to the Philippians*. Pillar New Testament Commentary. Nottingham: Apollos, 2009.
Harris, Murray J. *Prepositions and Theology in the Greek New Testament*. Grand Rapids: Zondervan, 2012.
Hart, Trevor. "Imagination for the Kingdom of God? Hope, Promise, and the Transformative Power of an Imagined Future." In *God Will Be All in All: The Eschatology of Jürgen Moltmann*, edited by Richard Bauckham, 49–76. Edinburgh, T. & T. Clark, 1999.
Hawthorne, Gerald F. *Philippians*. Word Biblical Commentary, vol. 43. Waco: Word, 1983.
Hays, Richard B. "'Here We Have No Lasting City': New Covenantalism in Hebrews." In *The Epistle to the Hebrews and Christian Theology*, edited by Richard Bauckham et al., 151–73. Grand Rapids: Eerdmans, 2009.
Heron, Alasdair I. C. "Filioque." In *The Encyclopedia of Christianity*, edited by Erwin Fahlbusch et al., 2:313–14. Grand Rapids: Eerdmans, 2001.
———. *The Holy Spirit: The Holy Spirit in the Bible, the History of Christian Thought and Recent Theology*. Philadelphia: Westminster Press, 1983.
Hillyer, Norman. *1 and 2 Peter, Jude*. New International Biblical Commentary, vol. 16. Peabody: Hendrickson, 1992.
Hoehner, Harold W. *Ephesians: An Exegetical Commentary*. Grand Rapids: Baker Academic, 2002.
Holland, Tom. *Romans: The Divine Marriage*. Eugene: Pickwick, 2011.
Holmes, Stephen R. "Death in the Afternoon." In *The Epistle to the Hebrews and Christian Theology*, edited by Richard Bauckham et al., 229–52. Grand Rapids: Eerdmans, 2009.
Hooker, Morna D. "Christ, the 'End' of the Cult." In *The Epistle to the Hebrews and Christian Theology*, edited by Richard Bauckham et al., 189–212. Grand Rapids: Eerdmans, 2009.
Hoppin, Ruth. "The Epistle to the Hebrews is Priscilla's Letter." In *A Feminist Companion to the Catholic Epistles and Hebrews*. Feminist Companion to the New Testament and Early Christian Writings, 8.147–71. London: T. & T. Clark, 2004.
Hughes, Graham. *Hebrews and Hermeneutics: The Epistle to the Hebrews as a New Testament Example of Biblical Interpretation*. Society for New Testament Studies Monograph Series, vol. 36. Cambridge: Cambridge University Press, 1979.
Hughes, Philip E. *The Second Epistle to the Corinthians*. New International Commentary on the New Testament. Grand Rapids: Eerdmans, 1962.
Hunsinger, George. "The Crucified God and the Political Theology of Violence." *Heythrop Journal* 14 (1973) 379–95.
———. *Disruptive Grace: Studies in the Theology of Karl Barth*. Grand Rapids: Eerdmans, 2000.
———. "The Mediator of Communion: Karl Barth's Doctrine of the Holy Spirit." In *Cambridge Companion to Karl Barth*, edited by John Webster, 177–94. Cambridge: Cambridge University Press, 2000.
Hur, Ju. *A Dynamic Reading of the Holy Spirit in Luke-Acts*. London: T. & T. Clark, 2004.

Irenaeus. "Against Heresies." In *Ante-Nicene Fathers*, edited by Alexander Roberts and James Donaldson, 1.315–567. Grand Rapids: Eerdmans, 1885.

Jewett, Robert. *Romans: A Commentary*. Hermeneia. Minneapolis: Fortress, 2007.

Jobes, Karen H. *1 Peter*. Baker Exegetical Commentary on the New Testament. Grand Rapids: Baker, 2005.

Johnson, Luke Timothy. *Hebrews: A Commentary*. New Testament Library. Louisville: Westminster John Knox, 2006.

Johnston, Philip S. "Death and Resurrection." In *Dictionary of Biblical Theology*, edited by T. Desmond Alexander et al., 443–47. Downers Grove: InterVarsity, 2000.

———. *Shades of Sheol: Death and Afterlife in the Old Testament*. Downers Grove: InterVarsity, 2002.

Kalaitzidis, Pantelis. "Academic Laudatio for the Most Reverend Metropolitan of Pergamon John Zizioulas". Translated by Fr. Gregory Edwards. http://www.acadimia.gr/content/view/382/111/lang.en/.

Kärkkäinen, Veli-Matti. "'How to Speak of the Spirit among Religions': Trinitarian Prolegomena for a Pneumatological Theology of Religions." In *The Work of the Spirit: Pneumatology and Pentecostalism*, edited by Michael Welker, 47–70. Grand Rapids: Eerdmans, 2006.

———. *An Introduction to the Theology of Religions: Biblical, Historical and Contemporary Perspectives*. Downers Grove: IVP Academic, 2003.

———. *Trinity and Religious Pluralism: The Doctrine of the Trinity in Christian Theology of Religions*. Aldershot: Ashgate, 2004.

Käsemann, Ernst. *Commentary on Romans*. Grand Rapids: Eerdmans, 1980.

Kenyon, Frederick G. *The Chester Beatty Biblical Papyri Descriptions and Texts of Twelve Manuscripts on Papyrus of the Greek Bible: Fasciculus III Supplement—Pauline Epistles*. London: Emery Walker, 1937.

Kings, Graham. "Mission and the Meeting of Faiths: The Theologies of Max Warren and John V. Taylor." In *The Church Mission Society and World Christianity, 1799–1999*, 285–318. Grand Rapids: Eerdmans, 2000.

Kistemaker, Simon J. *1 Corinthians*. New Testament Commentary. Grand Rapids: Baker, 1993.

———. *2 Corinthians*. New Testament Commentary. Grand Rapids: Baker, 1999.

Kittel, Gerhard, and Gerhard Friedrich, eds. *Theological Dictionary of the New Testament*. Translated by Geoffrey W. Bromiley. Grand Rapids: Eerdmans, 1964–74.

Knight, Douglas H. *The Theology of John Zizioulas: Personhood and the Church*, edited by Douglas H. Knight. Aldershot: Ashgate, 2007.

Koehler, Ludwig, et al. *The Hebrew and Aramaic Lexicon of the Old Testament*. Translated by M. E. J. Richardson. Leiden: Brill, 2000.

Koester, Craig R. *Hebrews: A New Translation with Introduction and Commentary*. Anchor Bible, vol. 36. New York: Doubleday, 2001.

Kotsko, Adam. "Gift and *Communio*: The Holy Spirit in Augustine's *De Trinitate*." In *Scottish Journal of Theology* 64 (2010) 1–12.

Kruse, Colin G. *The Letters of John*. The Pillar New Testament Commentary. Nottingham: Apollos, 2000.

———. *Paul's Letter to the Romans*. The Pillar New Testament Commentary. Nottingham: Apollos, 2012.

LaCugna, Catherine Mowry. *God for Us: The Trinity and Christian Life*. San Francisco: Harper, 1991.

Ladd, George Eldon. *A Theology of the New Testament*. Rev. ed. Grand Rapids: Eerdmans, 1993.
Lauber, David. *Barth on the Descent into Hell: God, Atonement and the Christian Life*. Barth Studies. Aldershot: Ashgate, 2004.
Letham, Robert. *Union with Christ in Scripture, History and Theology*. Phillipsburg: P&R, 2011.
Lewis, Alan E. *Between Cross and Resurrection: A Theology of Holy Saturday*. Grand Rapids: Eerdmans, 2001.
Lieu, Judith M. *I, II, & III John*. Louisville: Westminster John Knox, 2008.
Lightfoot, J. B. *Saint Paul's Epistle to the Philippians*. Classic Commentary Library. Grand Rapids: Michigan, 1953.
Lincoln, Andrew T. *Ephesians*. Word Biblical Commentary, vol. 42. Dallas: Word, 1990.
Lindars, Barnabas. *The Theology of the Letter to the Hebrews*. New Testament Theology. Cambridge: Cambridge University Press, 1991.
Longenecker, Richard N. *Galatians*. Word Biblical Commentary, vol. 41. Dallas: Word, 1990.
Lossky, Vladimir. *The Mystical Theology of the Eastern Church*. Cambridge: James Clarke, 1957.
Loudovikos, Nicholas. "Person Instead of Grace and Dictated Otherness: John Zizioulas' Final Theological Position." *Heythrop Journal* 52 (2011) 684–99.
Lünemann, Gottlieb. *Critical and Exegetical Handbook to the Epistle to the Hebrews*. Edinburgh: T. & T. Clark: 1882.
Luther, Martin. *Luther's Works, vol. 29: Lecture on Titus, Philemon, and Hebrews*. Edited and translated by Jaroslav Pelikan (Titus, Philemon) and Walter A. Hansen (Hebrews). Saint Louis: Concordia, 1968.
———. *Table Talk*. Translated by William Hazlitt. London: HarperCollins, 1995.
Macchia, Frank D. *Justified in the Spirit: Creation, Redemption, and the Triune God*. Grand Rapids: Eerdmans, 2010.
Mackie, Scott D. "Early Christian Eschatological Experience in the Warnings and Exhortations of the Epistle to the Hebrews." *Tyndale Bulletin* 63 (2012) 93–114.
Marshall, I. Howard. *Acts*. Tyndale New Testament Commentaries. Leicester: InterVarsity, 1980.
———. *The Epistles of John*. Grand Rapids: Eerdmans, 1978.
———. *1 Peter*. IVP New Testament Commentary Series. Downers Grove: InterVarsity, 1991.
Martin, Ralph P. *Philippians*. Tyndale New Testament Commentaries, vol. 11. Downers Grove: InterVarsity, 1987.
———. *2 Corinthians*. Word Biblical Commentary, vol. 40. Waco: Word, 1986.
Martyn, J. Louis. *Galatians*. Anchor Bible, vol. 33A. New York: Doubleday, 1997.
Maximus the Confessor. "Difficulty 41." In *Maximus the Confessor*. Early Church Fathers, translated by Andrew Louth, 155–62. London and New York: Routledge 1996.
McCormack, Bruce L. "'With Loud Cries and Tears': The Humanity of the Son in the Epistle of the Hebrews." In *The Epistle to the Hebrews and Christian Theology*, edited by Richard Bauckham, et al., 37–68. Grand Rapids: Eerdmans, 2009.
McDougall, Joy Ann. *Pilgrimage of Love: Moltmann on the Trinity and Christian Life*. New York: Oxford University Press, 2005.

McGrath, John J. *"Through the Eternal Spirit": An Historical Study of the Exegesis of Hebrews 9:13-14*. Rome: Pontificia Universitas Gregoriana, 1961.

McIlroy, David H. "Towards a Relational and Trinitarian Theology of Atonement." *Evangelical Quarterly* 80 (2008)13-32.

McKnight, Scot. *1 Peter*. NIV Application Commentary. Grand Rapids: Zondervan, 1996.

Meeks, M. Douglas. *Origins of the Theology of Hope*. Philadelphia: Fortress, 1974.

Metzger, Bruce M. *A Textual Commentary on the Greek New Testament*, 2nd ed. Stuttgart: German Bible Society, 1994.

Metzger, Bruce M., and Bart D. Ehrman. *The Text of the New Testament: Its Transmission, Corruption and Restoration*. Oxford: Oxford University Press, 2005.

Michaels, J. Ramsey. *1 Peter*. Word Biblical Commentary, vol. 49. Dallas: Word, 1988.

Migne, Jacques Paul. *Patrologia Graeca*, 1862. http://patristica.net/graeca/.

Migne, Jacques Paul. *Patrologia Latina*, 1891. http://patristica.net/latina/. http://www.archive.org/details/patrologiaecurs12unkngoog.

Millard, Alan. "מתח." In *New International Dictionary of Old Testament Theology and Exegesis*, edited by Willem A. VanGemeren, 2:324-25. Grand Rapids: Zondervan, 1997.

Moffatt, James. *The Epistle to the Hebrews*. International Critical Commentary. Edinburgh: T. & T. Clark, 1924.

———. *The First Epistle of Paul to the Corinthians*. London: Hodder and Stoughton, 1938.

Moffitt, David M. "'If Another Priest Arises': Jesus' Resurrection and the High Priestly Christology of Hebrews." In *A Cloud of Witnesses: The Theology of Hebrews in its Ancient Contexts*, 68-79. London: T. & T. Clark, 2008.

Moltmann, Jürgen. *A Broad Place: An Autobiography*. Translated by Margaret Kohl. Minneapolis: Fortress, 2008.

———. *The Church in the Power of the Spirit: A Contribution to Messianic Ecclesiology*. Translated by Margaret Kohl. Minneapolis: Fortress, 1993.

——— *The Coming of God: Christian Eschatology*. Translated by Margaret Kohl. Minneapolis: Fortress, 2004.

———. "The Crucified God." *Theology Today* 31 (1974) 6-18.

———. *The Crucified God: The Cross of Christ as the Foundation and Criticism of Christian Theology*. 2nd ed. Translated by R. A. Wilson and John Bowden. London: SCM, 2001.

———. *The Experiment Hope*. Edited and translated by Douglas Meeks. London: SCM, 1975.

———. *Experiences in Theology: Ways and Forms of Christian Theology*. Translated by Margaret Kohl. Minneapolis: Fortress, 2000.

———. "The Final Judgement: Sunrise of Christ's Liberating Justice." *Anglican Review of Theology* 89 (2007) 565-76.

——— *God in Creation: A New Theology of Creation and the Spirit of God. The Gifford Lectures 1984-1985*. Translated by Margaret Kohl. Minneapolis: Fortress, 1993.

———. *History and the Triune God: Contributions to Trinitarian Theology*. Translated by John Bowden. London: SCM, 1991.

———. "Hope and Reality: Contradiction and Correspondence. Response to Trevor Hart." In *God Will Be All in All: The Eschatology of Jürgen Moltmann*, edited by Richard Bauckham, 77-85. Edinburgh, T. & T. Clark, 1999.

———. *How I Have Changed: Reflections on Thirty Years of Theology*. Translated by John Bowden. Harrisburg: Trinity International, 1997.

———. *The Spirit of Life: A Universal Affirmation*. Translated by Margaret Kohl. Minneapolis: Fortress, 2001.

———. *Sun of Righteousness, Arise! God's Future for Humanity and the Earth*. Translated by Margaret Kohl. Minneapolis: Fortress, 2010.

———. *Theology of Hope: On the Ground and the Implications of a Christian Eschatology*. 2nd ed. Translated by J. W. Leitch. London: SCM, 2002.

———. *Theology Today: Two Contributions Towards Making Theology Present*. Translated by John Bowden. London: SCM, 1990.

———. "The Trinitarian Story of Jesus." In Elisabeth Moltmann-Wendel and Jürgen Moltmann, *Humanity in God*, 70–89. London: SCM, 1983.

———. *The Trinity and the Kingdom: The Doctrine of God*. Translated by Margaret Kohl. Minneapolis: Fortress, 1993.

———. *The Way of Jesus Christ: Christology in Messianic Dimensions*. Translated by Margaret Kohl. Minneapolis: Fortress, 1993.

Moo, Douglas. *The Epistle to the Romans*. New International Commentary on the New Testament. Grand Rapids: Eerdmans, 1996.

Morris, Leon. *The Epistle to the Romans*. Pillar New Testament Commentary. Grand Rapids: Eerdmans; Leicester: Apollos, 1988.

Morse, Christopher. *The Logic of Promise in Moltmann's Theology*. Philadelphia: Fortress, 1979.

Motyer, Alex. *The Message of Philippians*. The Bible Speaks Today. Downers Grove: InterVarsity, 1984.

Müller-Fahrenholz, Geiko. *The Kingdom and the Power: The Theology of Jürgen Moltmann*. Translated by John Bowden. London: SCM, 2000.

Murray, John. *The Epistle to the Romans*. Paperback ed. New International Commentary on the New Testament. Grand Rapids: Eerdmans, 1997.

Neder, Adam. *Participation in Christ: An Entry into Karl Barth's Church Dogmatics*. Columbia Series in Reformed Theology. Louisville: Westminster John Knox, 2009.

Nemer, Larry. "A Tribute to Bishop John V. Taylor." Accessed March 21, 2011. http://www.joondalupanglican.com/download/publications/A%20Tribute%20to%20Bishop%20John%20V%20Taylor.pdf.

Nestle, Eberhard, and Erwin Nestle. *Novum Testamentum Graece*. 28th rev. ed. Edited by Barbara Aland et al. Münster: Deutsche Bibelgesellschaft, 2012. http://www.joondalupanglican.com/download/publications/A%20Tribute%20to%20Bishop%20John%20V%20Taylor.pdf.

Nygren, Anders. *Commentary on Romans*. Translated by Carl C. Rasmussen. Philadelphia: Fortress, 1949.

O'Brien, Peter T. *The Letter to the Ephesians*. Pillar New Testament Commentary. Grand Rapids: Eerdmans, 1999.

———. *The Letter to the Hebrews*. Pillar New Testament Commentary. Grand Rapids: Eerdmans, 2010.

Olson, Roger E. *The Story of Christian Theology: Twenty Centuries of Tradition and Reform*. Downers Grove: InterVarsity, 1999.

Osborne, Grant R. "Resurrection I: Gospels." In *IVP Dictionary of the New Testament*, edited by Daniel G. Reid, 896–913. Downers Grove: InterVarsity, 2004.

———. *Romans*. IVP New Testament Commentary Series. Downers Grove: InterVarsity, 2004.

Otto, Rudolph. *The Idea of the Holy: An Inquiry into the Non-Rational Factor in the Idea of the Divine and its Relation to the Rational*. Translated by John W. Harvey. London: Oxford University Press, 1936.

Owen, John. *An Exposition of the Epistle to the Hebrews*. The Works of John Owen, vol. 23, edited by William H. Goold. Edinburgh: Johnstone and Hunter, 1855.

———. *The Death of Death in the Death of Christ*. The Works of John Owen, vol. 10, edited by William H. Goold. London: Johnstone and Hunter, 1852.

———. *The Work of the Holy Spirit*. The Works of John Owen, vol. 4, edited by William H. Goold. 3rd ed. Edinburgh: Banner of Truth Trust, 1979.

Page, Sydney H. T. "Obedience and Blood Sprinkling in 1 Peter 1:2." *Westminster Theological Journal* 72 (2010) 291–98.

Pannenberg, Wolfhart. *Systematic Theology*, vol. 2. Translated by Geoffrey W. Bromiley. Grand Rapids: Eerdmans, 1994.

Papanikolaou, Aristotle. "Is John Zizioulas an Existentialist in Disguise? A Response to Lucian Turcescu." *Modern Theology* 20 (2004) 601–7.

Pásztori-Kupán, István, trans. *Theoderet of Cyrus*. Early Church Fathers. Edited by Carol Harrison. Abingdon: Routledge, 2006.

Peterson, David G. *The Acts of the Apostles*. The Pillar New Testament Commentary. Grand Rapids: Eerdmans, 2009.

———. *Hebrews and Perfection: An Examination of the Concept of Perfection in the Epistle to the Hebrews*. Society for New Testament Studies Monograph Series, vol. 47. Cambridge: Cambridge University Press, 1982.

Pinnock, Clark. *Flame of Love: A Theology of the Holy Spirit*. Downers Grove: INTERVARSITY, 1996.

———. *A Wideness in God's Mercy: The Finality of Jesus Christ in a World of Religions*. Grand Rapids: Zondervan, 1992.

Pugh, Ben. "The Spirit and the Cross: Insights from Barth and Moltmann." *Evangelical Review of Theology* 36 (2012) 292–301.

Rahls, Alfred, ed. *Septuagint*. Stuttgart: Wüttembergische Bibelanstalt/ Deutsche Bibelgesellschaft, 1935.

Roberts, Alexander, and James Donaldson, eds. *The Ante-Nicene Fathers: Translations of the Writings of the Fathers down to A.D. 325*. Buffalo: Christian Literature, 1885–1896.

Robertson, Archibald, and Alfred Plummer. *A Critical and Exegetical Commentary on the First Epistle of St. Paul to the Corinthians*. International Critical Commentary. Edinburgh: T. & T. Clark, 1914.

Rosato, Philip J. *The Spirit as Lord: The Pneumatology of Karl Barth*. Edinburgh: T. & T. Clark, 1981.

Rossé, Gérard. *The Cry of Jesus on the Cross: A Biblical and Theological Study*. New York: Paulist, 1987.

Sanday, William, and Arthur C. Headlam. *A Critical and Exegetical Commentary on Romans*. 5th ed. International Critical Commentary. Edinburgh: T. & T. Clark, 1902.

Sanders, Ed Parish. *Paul and Palestinian Judaism*. London: SCM, 1977.

Sanders, John Oswald. *No Other Name: An Investigation into the Destiny of the Unevangelized*. Grand Rapids: Eerdmans, 1992.

Sarna, Nahum M. *The JPS Torah Commentary: Exodus*. Philadelphia: Jewish Publication Society, 1991.
Schaff, Philip et al., eds. *A Select Library of the Nicene and Post-Nicene Fathers of the Christian Church*. New York: Christian Literature Publishing. Series One, 1887–94. Series Two, 1890–1900.
Schleiermacher, Friedrich. *The Christian Faith*. Edited by H. R. Mackintosh and J. S. Stewart. Translator unnamed. Edinburgh, T. & T. Clark, 1928.
Schnakenberg, Rudolf. *The Epistle to the Ephesians*. Translated by Helen Heron. Edinburgh: T. & T. Clark, 1991.
Schramm, Tim. "σφραγίς." In *Exegetical Dictionary of the New Testament*, edited by Horst Balz and Gerhard Schneider, 3:316. Grand Rapids: Eerdmans, 1993.
Schreiner, Thomas R. *New Testament Theology: Magnifying God in Christ*. Grand Rapids: Baker Academic, 2008.
———. *Romans*. Grand Rapids: Baker Academic, 1998.
———. *1, 2 Peter, Jude*. New American Commentary. Nashville: Broadman & Holman, 2003.
Schweizer, Eduard. *Spirit of God*. Bible Key Words from Kittel's *Theologisches Wörterbuch zum Neuen Testament*, vol. 9. Translated by A. E. Harvey. London: Adam & Charles Black, 1960.
Shepherd, William H., Jr. *The Narrative Function of the Holy Spirit as a Character in Luke-Acts*. SBL Dissertation Series 147. Atlanta: Scholars Press, 1994.
Shults, F. LeRon, and Andrea Hollingsworth. *The Holy Spirit*. Guides to Theology. Grand Rapids: Eerdmans, 2008.
Skaggs, Rebecca. *1 Peter, 2 Peter, Jude*. Pentecostal Commentary Series. London: T. & T. Clark International, 2004.
Smail, Thomas A. *Reflected Glory: The Spirit in Christ and Christians*. London: Hodder and Stoughton, 1975.
Smalley, Stephen S. *1, 2, 3 John*. Word Biblical Commentary, vol. 51. Waco: Word, 1984.
Smith, S. M. "Hope, Theology of." In *Evangelical Dictionary of Theology*, edited by Walter A. Elwell, 575–79. 2nd ed. Grand Rapids: Baker Academic, 2001.
Snaith, Norman. "The Sprinkling of Blood." *Expository Times* 82 (1970) 23–24.
Studebaker, Steven M. "Pentecostal Soteriology and Pneumatology." *Journal of Pentecostal Theology* 11 (2003) 257.
Tan, Carolyn E. L. "Humanity's Devil." *Evangelical Review of Theology* 34 (2010) 136–154.
Tanner, Norman P., ed. *Decrees of the Ecumenical Councils, vol. 1: Nicaea I—Lateran V*. Washington: Georgetown University Press, 1990.
Taylor, John V. *The Christlike God*. 2nd ed. London: SCM, 2004.
———. *Enough is Enough*. London: SCM, 1975.
———. *The Go-Between God: The Holy Spirit and the Christian Mission*. London: SCM, 1972.
———. *A Matter of Life and Death*. London: SCM, 1986.
———. *The Primal Vision: Christian Presence amid African Religion*. London: SCM, 1963.
———. *Weep Not For Me*. Geneva: World Council of Churches, 1986.
Thielman, Frank. *Ephesians*. Baker Exegetical Commentary on the New Testament. Grand Rapids: Baker Academic, 2010.

Thiselton, Anthony C. *The First Epistle to the Corinthians*. New International Greek Testament Commentary. Grand Rapids: Eerdmans, 2000.

Thomas, Rodney. "The Seal of the Spirit in the Religious Climate of Ephesus." *Restoration Quarterly* 43 (2001) 155–66.

Thompson, John. *The Holy Spirit in the Theology of Karl Barth*. Princeton Monograph Series 23. Allison Park: Pickwick, 1991.

Torrance, Alexis. "Personhood and Patristics in Orthodox Theology: Reassessing the Debate." *The Heythrop Journal* 52 (2011) 700–707.

Torrance, Thomas F. *Atonement: The Person and Work of Christ*, edited by Robert T. Walker. Milton Keynes: Paternoster. Downers Grove: IVP Academic, 2009.

———. *Incarnation: The Person and Life of Christ*, edited by Robert T. Walker. Downers Grove: IVP Academic, 2008.

Turcescu, Lucian. "'Person' Versus 'Individual,' and Other Modern Misreadings of Gregory of Nyssa." In *Re-thinking Gregory of Nyssa*, edited by Sarah Coakley, 97–109. Oxford: Blackwell, 2003.

Van Gemeren, Willem A., ed. *New International Dictionary of Old Testament Theology and Exegesis*, vol. 2. Grand Rapids: Zondervan, 1997.

Vanhoye, Albert. *Structure and Message of the Message of the Epistle to the Hebrews*. Subsidia Biblica 12. Translated by James Swetnam. Rome: Editrice Pontificio Istituto Biblico, 1989.

Wallace, Daniel B. *Greek Grammar Beyond the Basics: An Exegetical Syntax of the New Testament*. Grand Rapids: Zondervan, 1996.

Ware, Kallistos (Timothy). *The Orthodox Way*. Rev. ed. New York: St. Vladmir's Press, 1995.

Welker, Michael, ed. *The Work of the Spirit: Pneumatology and Pentecostalism*. Grand Rapids: Eerdmans, 2006.

Wenham, Gordon J. *Genesis 1–15*. Word Biblical Commentary, vol. 1. Nelson Reference & Electronic, 1987.

Westcott, Brooke Foss. *The Epistle to the Hebrews*. London: Macmillan, 1889.

White, Reginald E. O. "Resurrection of the Dead." In *Evangelical Dictionary of Theology*, edited by Walter A. Elwell, 1017–19. 2nd ed. Grand Rapids: Baker Academic, 2001.

Williams, David T. *Vinculum Amoris: A Theology of the Holy Spirit*. Lincoln: iUniverse, 2004.

Witherington III, Ben. *Letters and Homilies for Hellenized Christians, vol. 2: A Socio-Rhetorical Commentary on 1–2 Peter*. Downer Grove: IVP Academic, 2007.

———. *Letters and Homilies for Jewish Christians: A Social-Rhetorical Commentary on Hebrews, James and Jude*. Downers Grove: InterVarsity, 2007.

———. *Paul's Letter to the Romans: A Social-Rhetorical Commentary*. Grand Rapids: Eerdmans, 2004.

Wood, David. "Christian Mission with John V. Taylor." *International Review of Mission*, 92 (2003) 427–33.

———. *Poet, Priest and Prophet: Bishop John V. Taylor*. London: Churches Together in Britain and Ireland, 2003.

Wright, Terry J. "The Seal of Approval: An Interpretation of the Son's Sustaining Action in Hebrews 1:3." In *The Epistle to the Hebrews and Christian Theology*, edited by Richard Bauckham et al., 140–48. Grand Rapids: Eerdmans, 2009.

Yong, Amos. "As the Spirit Gives Utterance: Pentecostal, Intra-Christian Ecumenism and the Wider Oikoumene." *International Review of Mission* 92 (2003) 299–314.

———. *Beyond the Impasse: Toward a Pneumatological Theology of Religions*. Grand Rapids: Baker Academic, 2003.

———. *Hospitality and the Other: Pentecostal Christian Practices and the Neighbour*. Mary Knoll: Orbis, 2008.

———. *The Spirit Poured Out on All Flesh: Pentecostalism and the Possibility of Global Theology*. Grand Rapids, Baker Academic, 2005.

Zahl, Paul F. M. "The Spirit in the Blood." *Anglican Theological Review* 83 (2001) 493–98.

Zizioulas, John D. *Being as Communion: Studies in Personhood and the Church*. Contemporary Greek Theologians 4. New York: St Vladimir's Seminary Press, 1985.

———. *Communion and Otherness: Further Studies in Personhood and the Church*. Edited by Paul McPartlan. London: T. & T. Clark, 2006.

———. *Eucharist, Bishop, Church: The Unity of the Church in the Divine Eucharist and The Bishop During the First Three Centuries*. Translated by Elizabeth Theokritoff. Brookline: Holy Cross Orthodox Press, 2001.

———. *Eucharistic Communion and the World*. Edited by Luke Ben Tallon. London: T. & T. Clark, 2011.

———. "Human Capacity and Human Incapacity: A theological Exploration of Personhood." *Scottish Journal of Theology* 28 (1975) 401–48.

———. *Lectures in Christian Dogmatics*. Edited by Douglas H. Knight. London: T. & T. Clark, 2008.

———. *Lessons on Christian Dogmatics*. http://www.oodegr.com/english/dogmatiki1/perieh.htm.

———. *The One and the Many: Studies on God, Man, the Church, and the World Today*. Edited by Gregory Edwards. Alhambra: Sebastian Press, 2010.

Online sources:

https://books.google.com.au/
http://dhspriory.org.thomas/
http://gallica.bnf.fr/
http://www.acadimia.gr/
http://www.archive.org/details/patrologiaecurs12unkngoog
http://www.ccel.org/
http://www.csntm.org/
http://www.documentacatholicaomnia.eu/
http://www.dukhrana.com/
http://www.e-rara.ch/
http://www.independent.co.uk/news/obituaries/
http://www.joondalupanglican.com/
http://www.thelatinlibrary.com/augustine/
http://www.oodegr.co/english/dogmatiki1/perieh.htm

www.ingramcontent.com/pod-product-compliance
Lightning Source LLC
Chambersburg PA
CBHW050621300426
44112CB00012B/1599